DISCIPL.

Discipline

and the Other Body

✳

Correction, Corporeality, Colonialism

edited by

STEVEN PIERCE & ANUPAMA RAO

Duke University Press   Durham and London   2006

© 2006 Duke University Press

All rights reserved

Printed in the United States of America

on acid-free paper ∞

Designed by C. H. Westmoreland

Typeset in Minion by Keystone Typesetting, Inc.

Library of Congress Cataloging-in-Publication Data

appear on the last printed page of this book.

Contents

Acknowledgments   vii

ANUPAMA RAO AND STEVEN PIERCE
Discipline and the Other Body: Humanitarianism, Violence, and the Colonial Exception   1

KERRY WARD
Defining and Defiling the Criminal Body at the Cape of Good Hope: Punishing the Crime of Suicide under Dutch East India Company Rule, circa 1652–1795   36

SHANNON LEE DAWDY
The Burden of Louis Congo and the Evolution of Savagery in Colonial Louisiana   61

ISAAC LAND
"Sinful Propensities": Piracy, Sodomy, and Empire in the Rhetoric of Naval Reform, 1770–1870   90

DOUGLAS M. PEERS
The Raj's Other Great Game: Policing the Sexual Frontiers of the Indian Army in the First Half of the Nineteenth Century   115

ANUPAMA RAO
Problems of Violence, States of Terror: Torture in Colonial India   151

STEVEN PIERCE
Punishment and the Political Body: Flogging and Colonialism in Northern Nigeria   186

DOROTHY KO
Footbinding and Anti-footbinding in China: The Subject of Pain in the Nineteenth and Early Twentieth Centuries   215

LAURA BEAR
An Economy of Suffering: Addressing the Violence of Discipline in Railway Workers' Petitions to the Agent of the East Indian Railway, 1930–47   243

SUSAN O'BRIEN
Spirit Discipline: Gender, Islam, and Hierarchies of Treatment in Postcolonial Northern Nigeria   273

YVETTE CHRISTIANSE
Selections from *Castaway*   303

Bibliography   317

Contributors   347

Index   349

Acknowledgments

We thank David Scott, a discussant on the panel at the 1998 Annual Meeting of the American Anthropological Association where this volume was first conceived. A special issue of *Interventions: The International Journal of Postcolonial Studies* (vol. 3, no. 2 [July 2001]) featured earlier versions of the essays by Isaac Land, Susan O'Brien, Steven Pierce, and Anupama Rao. We are grateful for permission to include the current versions. We also thank Gyanendra Pandey, whose discussions of our papers at the "Pairing Empires" conference at Johns Hopkins University in 2000 aided our reconceptualization of the current volume. Kerry Ward and Laura Bear commented extensively on an earlier draft of the introduction; we thank them and the anonymous reviewers for Duke University Press for their challenging insights, which have greatly improved the final version.

Anupama Rao thanks the students in her graduate seminar "Native Bodies and Colonial Discipline" at Columbia University for their comments on earlier versions of this project, and more generally for their enthusiasm and intellectual acumen in addressing questions of violence and the body in a comparative frame. She also thanks Tanya Fernando, Arvind Rajagopal, Jared Stark, and Rajeswari Sunder Rajan for their support and guidance. A fellowship from the National Endowment for the Humanities provided crucial leave time for the final preparation of the manuscript.

Steven Pierce thanks students in seminars at Yale, Michigan, and Tulane for their comments on various incarnations of this project, and especially Brooke Fochler, Elizabeth Manley, and Shelene Roumillat for very timely challenges. Linda Pollock and Stephen Vella forced important rethinking at crucial moments. An International and Area Studies Fellowship sponsored by the American Council of Learned Societies, Social Science Research Council, and National Endowment for the Humanities, and a Junior Leave from Tulane University, provided the time necessary to complete the project. Steven Pierce also thanks Donna Denneen and Ali Zaidi for critical logistical help and Siva Sithraputhran for his support and guidance in navigating these treacherous waters.

DISCIPLINE AND THE OTHER BODY

ANUPAMA RAO AND STEVEN PIERCE

※

Discipline and the Other Body

Humanitarianism, Violence, and

the Colonial Exception

During the Mau Mau rebellion of the mid-1950s, the white settler and official populations of Kenya were swept by increasingly lurid rumors about Africans' oaths of resistance to colonial rule. At the height of the hysteria, the oaths were supposed to involve murder, blood-drinking, cannibalism, and necrophiliac bestiality. Worse, experts in the prisons department claimed, oaths once taken caused Africans to revert to savagery. Sixty years of the civilizing mission could be swept away in a night, as formerly docile peasants returned to murderous barbarism. The Kenyan government conceived of oath taking as creating a psychological problem that could be cured through an elaborate set of disciplinary techniques: Mau Mau prisoners were sent to special detention camps and forced to work in a "normal" manner, thereby returning to civilization:

> If any detainee refused to comply with a lawful order to weed, [the] plan was that two warders should be allocated to that detainee and, by holding his hands, physically make him pull weeds from the ground. From [one official's] experience he was convinced that once such token work had been performed by the detainee he would have considered that he had broken his Mau Mau oath which had, by superstitious dread, previously prevented him from cooperating . . . and thus [the detainee would] start on the road to freedom.[1]

Both the rumors and the rehabilitative strategies of the detention camps reveal a curious logic to the Kenyan government's approach to ruling its African subjects. Engaging in a set of highly specific corporeal acts—ritual murder, cannibalism, sex with dead goats—seemed sufficient to destroy utterly the government's ability to rule, which could, however, be restored by forcing prisoners to mimic the motions of disciplined agricultural work. Governmental order could be achieved in relatively minimal ways (though requiring the coercive force of concentration camps), but savagery always lurked under the surface. The illegibility of natives' intentions and their susceptibility to the unreasonable worlds of magic and superstition rendered them the target of consistent and violent disciplining; native unreason could only be addressed by the exercise of unreasonable violence.[2] Colonial discipline was justified as exceptional, a necessary disregard for metropolitan norms of justice and civility. Very often this ethos blurred distinctions between situations of war that engendered sustained campaigns of annihilation and the routine, rationalized forms of discipline through which "natives" were returned to the folds of virtuous labor and accumulation. The exigencies of governing the colonized ultimately produced uncomfortable similarities between the so-called barbarism of native practices and the acts of terror and violence used to contain them.

Only twenty years after this particular instance of colonial counterinsurgency, "human rights" came increasingly into popular discourse. In the United States, for example, President Jimmy Carter's emphasis on human rights opposed the excesses of Henry Kissenger's international realpolitik and was dismissed as ridiculously naïve by Carter's successor, Ronald Reagan.[3] Even so, human-rights discourse has become central to a post–Cold War governmental order, and actors of all political stripes have embraced human rights as a justification for their actions—as with the United States' and its allies' claims for invading Afghanistan and Iraq as humanitarian endeavors.[4] But human-rights discourse coexists uneasily with the exercise of imperial power.

At the time of this writing, the scandals of torture in the American-run prison of Abu Ghraib in Iraq and of prisoners' torture and shadowy legal status in Guantánamo Bay reflect a continuing tension between humanitarianism and the treatment of "other" subjects. This is illustrated by the curious nominalism inherent in the U.S. government's attempts to distinguish between torture, "abuse," and "stress and duress" and to label the tortured "terrorists." As with the moral justification of earlier imperial ventures through ideas of progress and improvement, human rights today have become that which we "cannot not want,"[5] though contemporary events underline that they seem most desirable when manifestly denied. Because human rights are so obviously a good, it is necessary to inquire into the fraught history of the concept, since their commonsensible desirability would seem to preclude deeper investigation or exploration. The sometimes peculiar use of human rights can be located within a longer-term history of humanitarian justifications for political projects: colonizing India to abolish widow burning, for example, or Africa to missionize and abolish slavery. Violence and deprivation enabled by Western technological superiority and legitimated by ideologies of democratic humanitarianism appear to be novel. In fact, they repeat a historical process that has consistently redefined the "human" through political projects of control and governance. Contemporary debates over rights, recognition, and ethical responsibility—whether addressed to domestic issues such as affirmative action and access to birth control or to appropriate international responses to human-rights violations—mark concerted attempts to elaborate and demarcate the limits of worthy humanity. To the extent that the liberal individual has become the presumed subject of contemporary human-rights discourse, it is useful to historicize the process by which histories of the "human" have intersected with and helped to constitute liberal paradigms of rights and responsibility.

The essays collected here are empirical explorations in how the history of control relates to the career of political liberalism and humanitarian intervention. Through an examination of the relationship between the political career of bodily violence and its ideological basis in colonial reason, the volume illuminates the troubled dialectic between violation and protection, between governance and atrocity. United by a basic concern with people defined as "other," as not susceptible to reason in the way "universal" (white, male, European, adult, Christian, heterosexual, middle- or upper-class) subjects were supposed to be, these essays investigate the relationship between histories of the colonial body and repertoires of colonial governance. If colonialism was about the management of difference—the civilized ruling the uncivilized—the allegedly necessary violence of colonial government threatened to undermine the very distinction that justified it. Disciplining "uncivilized" people through the use of force could often seem the only way to correct their behavior, but this was a problem: Violence also appeared to be the antithesis of civilized government. The essays collected here highlight the interdependence of and contradictions between the key terms "corporeal," "violence," "colonial," and "governance," thereby illuminating a crucial characteristic of colonial states, the paradox of colonial discipline.

COLONIAL VIOLENCE AND THE OTHER BODY

This volume traces the emergence of the "other" body. In that process, ideologies of colonial corporeality came to contrast with the rational subject produced by the disciplinary technologies of modern government. The essays collected here follow diverse trajectories of the colonial body across space and time, even while addressing similarities among strategies of punishment and discipline that stigmatized the colonial body, calling it in need of corrective violence even while insisting that violence was a problem. Ideas of rights and protection are entangled with the development of techniques and practices of discipline and punishment; ideas of full personhood and complex interiority are most successfully examined at their limits.

The late nineteenth and early twentieth centuries saw the emergence of ethnographic, taxonomic states, where minute distinctions of race and status were elaborately encoded into forms of rule that ranged from the use of extreme bodily violence to the more overtly benign "rule of law." Objectifications of culture—the most visible end of a more complex process by which culture and biology were conflated and often deployed as justification of the natives' civic disability—served to make the "other" body a natural object for racially discriminatory governance, even while the violence that went along with it promised scandal. Colonial disciplinary correction was understood to be a consequence of native inadequacy, which justified the use of almost any level of force and violence. The visceral, embodied experiences of domination and control—the immediate manifestation of colonial corporeality—were an integral part of governmental practices of codifying, categorizing, and racializing difference. Various corporeal technologies, and most specifically bodily violence, have acted to mark and constitute boundaries of alterity. Over time corporeal violence has increasingly been applied along lines of difference, even as its application has helped to define those very distinctions. The dialectical relationship between violence and difference, governance and atrocity, has been at the center of strategies of modern power and of the human-rights discourses that critique them.[6]

The body of the colonized became a critical locus through which ideologies of racial and cultural difference were enacted. Politicized alterity then moved to inform other relations of difference. As scholars from Michel Foucault to Judith Butler have argued,[7] the body is not a historically static entity. Its political extensions and its social entailments have radically shifted over the past several centuries. Examining the trajectory of claims about racialized embodiment suggests a larger political subtext to universalistic liberal claims about bodily integrity and point to the constitutive role humanitarian concerns have played in the emergence of a global "concerned" public. Corporeal technologies inscribed difference on the body of an emergent other, and thus the racial politics of colonial states meshed with the peculiar modernity of colonial governance. Bridging the gap between institutional histories of the body as a productive, politically worthy, laboring instrument and histories of subjectivity that examine the ways in which the human body is understood as a locus of pain, suffering, and injury, the essays in this volume provide a comparative historical and ethnographic perspective on the emergence of the body as a political entity in colonial and postcolonial contexts. We offer a general trajectory from the early modern period to the present in which official practices of corporeal violence (flogging, torture, spectacular modes of punishment) were increasingly applied to categories of people deemed irrational (non-Europeans, the young, the working classes, religious minorities, women) even as they simultaneously emerged as scandals and targets of humanitarian reform. This history of colonial corporeality not only elucidates the lexicon of colonial control but also addresses the increasing fascination of human rights by locating that discourse within its broader genealogy.[8]

Frantz Fanon's classic work on violence and colonialism, *The Wretched of the Earth*, provides a useful point of departure, eloquently memorializing the tremendous violence of colonial regimes and arguing for the necessity of an answering violence from anticolonial movements, in part because nonviolent transfers of power would not properly eradicate the structures of colonialism. He also suggested that the increasing successes of anticolonial wars—Vietnam, Algeria—were a precondition for greater attention to atrocities perpetrated against the colonized, which would ultimately prove a precondition for revolutionary change. But while Fanon underestimated the attention colonial atrocities sometimes attracted—though nonetheless radically insufficient—he also overestimated the revolutionary potential of postcolonial regimes that came to power through violence. Indeed, the years since *Wretched of the Earth* was written have posed a different set of questions about colonial violence and the possibilities for overcoming it. The Cold War and post–Cold War neocolonial orders have underlined the flexibility *and* the imperfect, incoherent success of metropolitan countries' dominance over their former colonies.[9] The imperial adventures of the United States under the second Bush administration have re-vivified centuries-old colonial paradigms with an extraordinary deafness to the lessons of the twentieth century.[10] Does this represent a series of tragic coincidences that have allowed neoconservative ideology temporarily to replace a neoliberal global consensus, or does it mark a new chapter in a centuries-long history of colonialism? Whatever the answer, contemporary events call into question how and under what circumstances subordinated groups make effective claims on this newer world order.

This history of bodily difference, governmental control, and humanitarian intervention poses thorny questions for historical analysis. The problems examined in this collection demand juxtaposing histories of extreme violence with genealogies of governmental strategy; both present distinct methodological challenges. We propose exploring their connection by bringing the writings of Walter Benjamin on the relationship between violence, law, and state legitimacy into dialogue with Foucault's account of bio-political states and disciplinary regimes. Benjamin famously argued that violence forms and maintains state authority, even though it is consistently disavowed as contaminating and unjustifiable force.[11] Legal regimes are founded through violent practices, and legal practices ultimately depend on the threat of violence and its application under state sanction. This dependence also poses a political problem, as officials who claim the public good as their mandate are implicated in the injury of certain citizens or subjects through a persistent, if unarticulated, belief in a hierarchy of persons of differentiated worth. The dialectic of governing exigency and humanitarian reform has consistently pushed at the boundaries of the human, creating debates over appropriate treatment for categories of people deemed less than rational. As many of the following chapters suggest, the boundaries between discipline and punishment, between the normal and the exceptional, were always blurred and often most notably represented in the public scandals that were channeled through particular colonial and postcolonial public spheres. Even while colonial states labored to disavow phenomenal violence (as nonexistent, as treatment, as education, as necessary), it consistently escaped into metropolitan discourse as scandal, exposing a peculiarly colonial structure of publicity.[12] This volume addresses colonial violence as well as the complex public manifestations of guilt, sympathy, and outrage provoked by its discovery.

CAPITALISM, GLOBAL EXPANSION, AND COLONIAL CORPOREALITY

That this version of bodily alterity emerged as a consequence of European colonization raises the question of what is particular to those forms of imperialism. Imperial projects are nothing new. The forms of colonialism that animate the concerns of this volume, however, are linked to a particular set of empires—ruled by European countries from the sixteenth through the twentieth centuries,[13] involving colonized peoples increasingly understood as racially different from their rulers (and thereby helping to constitute contemporary categories of race),[14] and self-consciously modernizing.[15] The history of colonial corporeality thus encompasses a particular kind of modernizing project caught up in the rise of global capitalism, which comprised a distinctive relationship between the organization and exercise of political power and which enabled changing conceptions of personhood.[16]

As global capitalism developed in tandem with European colonialism, encounters between Europe and other parts of the world produced new human taxonomies and facilitated intimate interactions of great political consequence. Assumptions about people, their innate capacities, and the nature of personhood are inevitably central to the imagination of political power. These changed across time and across the history of colonialism. There were crucial differences between Iberian empires based on trade and plunder, in which merchant capital and missionization acted hand in hand, and the company states promoted by the Dutch and British East India companies during the seventeenth and eighteenth centuries, between the genocidal strategies of conversion and containment practiced in the New World, and the attempts to rule through traditional social forms in South and Southeast Asia and many parts of Africa. These distinctions across time and space reflect the diverse cultural and social worlds to which colonial powers adapted, forcing them to justify colonization against the backdrop of changing political ideologies. The net result was a radical reworking of ideologies of embodied personhood.

Benedict Anderson has argued that early empires were ruled by elites whose links to the metropole were increasingly attenuated, as settlement and the establishment of family ties began to produce racial aristocracies within the colonies whose ways of life and political interests were increasingly marked off from those of the metropole.[17] Anderson argues that for this reason the colonies of the New World—from Haiti to the Americas—emerged as revolutionary societies marked by their struggles for freedom and (national) independence. This argument is certainly borne out by broad shifts in conceptions of identity and personhood that had occurred by the nineteenth century. The elites of early modern empires conjoined social standing, race, and wealth, enacting these through elaborate sumptuary rules for displaying and redistributing wealth. Minute hierarchies of rank and status produced ties of duty and obligation for both rulers and ruled. No absolute distinction separated slaves from those considered free. Rather, people occupied a position somewhere between these two poles, with high status often taking precedence over racial identity. By the end of the eighteenth century, however, the relationship between politics, power, and personhood had been altered.[18] The rise of monopolistic markets in global commodities such as tea, sugar, and spices during the eighteenth century had been enabled by the use of bonded and slave labor and by new methods of work discipline and surplus extraction.[19] Increasingly, however, even as practices of control and enslavement proved to be economically profitable, they became ideologically suspect.[20] The contradictions of imperial expansion are nowhere more visible than in debates about the practice of slavery.

Scholars have tended to view the Atlantic slave system as exceptional because of the vast numbers of people enslaved, the profitability of the trade, the extreme brutality of the slave systems, and the breadth of antislavery sentiment that ended it. There have been extensive debates about whether slavery provided the capital that enabled Western industrialization. Most scholars now agree that modern forms of slavery, which resulted in a near total commodification of people, bear a complex relationship to capitalist logic.[21] Slavery also occasioned an extended reflection on the meaning of individual freedom, a central problem of Enlightenment thought.[22] Abolitionist rhetoric drew inspiration from evangelical conceptions of human equality and free will, as well as growing political concerns about the propriety of owning persons. Political theorists increasingly viewed enslavement as illegitimate, a status that denuded both master and slave of humanity.[23] Added to this, slave rebellion and resistance both challenged slave systems and provided a new set of arguments about the universality of human freedom.[24]

Political liberalism addressed the intrinsic worth of human beings through ideas of human equality and thereby posed a direct challenge to earlier conceptions of servitude and sociality. Antislavery movements distilled such concerns first through a global movement against the slave trade, and then against the system of slavery in toto. Viewed as an early stage in the growth of human-rights discourse, attempts to replace slavery by new systems of "free" labor reveal the contradictions engendered by the gap between ideologies of freedom and practices of colonial disenfranchisement. Claims for individual freedom in the form of slave emancipation coexisted uneasily with projects of collective unfreedom in the form of colonization. The economic and political history of Atlantic slave systems are intimately linked to modern racial categories, for their rise and for the concomitant linkage of "Africans" with the "black race" and then with slavery, links that created forms of racial identification unlike those that had existed before. The shifting contours of racial categories cannot, however, be solely equated with the ideological underpinnings for a particularly brutal system of unfreedom and exploitation. Especially since race emerged as critically important for projects of colonization and liberation, charting the changing logic of its articulation of difference is crucial for understanding modern systems of governance. By the middle of the nineteenth century, colonial states had begun to focus on the individual's identity as a political problem, and "natives" had become subjects of correction and objects of modernization. Even in places that did not experience direct European colonization—for example, China, Japan, Ethiopia—ideologies of European modernity enjoyed increasing currency.[25]

The missionary movements of the eighteenth and nineteenth centuries were another arena in which the figure of the liberal individual was elaborated as a problem of governance.[26] Mission stations not only served as a source of new religious ideologies and systems of symbolic capital; they also proved to be a means of mobility: Individuals disenfranchised in their own societies (slaves and former slaves, women, other people of low status) could find an alternative community and means of social advancement, one that often gained them privileged access to the colonial state and the colonial economy.[27] While both abolitionism and missionization brought to colonial areas new forms of sociality one might call "modern," such changes played out in locally specific, idiosyncratic ways. Even as colonial subjectification assumed the rigid hierarchies between colonizer and colonized, earlier mechanisms of organizing personhood along more fluid axes of rank, status, and gender were sometimes erased, sometimes recast and transformed. Antislavery and colonialism created a governmental contradiction as regimes attempted to rule subjects they considered poised between freedom and irrationality. As the dichotomy between (and the justification for) unfreedom became increasingly somaticized, race became understood as a biological category, and racialized differences in governing technologies had important ramifications as those techniques took on their contemporary forms.

CATEGORIES OF DIFFERENCE

Pointing out that contemporary categories of difference emerged recently and through the demands of colonial governance then raises the question of what is specific to them. One means of addressing the problem is from the perspective of the psychic effects of the colonial encounter, by examining how colonial modes of control addressed their subjects as racially different or as otherwise inadequate. Fanon famously described colonial racial categories as constituting a peculiar and deformed structure of recognition.[28] Fanon suggests that colonial racism operated through ascribing identity to the colonized—"Look, a Negro!"—even while specifically blocking any of the psychic particularities indigenous identities might have. The act of recognizing someone as colonized was not an act of *recognition*, of reflecting what was already there. Rather, because the colonial context was inherently dehumanizing and inegalitarian, it deprived both colonizer and colonized of full humanity and placed the colonized in the category of the other, a position both injurious and inherently unstable. White and black became positions that reflected not biology, not culture, but a position of privilege or disenfranchisement determined by one's relation to "whiteness" as a phantasm. Relations of intimacy and interdependence became impossible to acknowledge even though they constituted the very condition for colonialism's survival.[29] The disavowal of colonial intimacy thus produced disgust, violence, and fear in the colonizer and self-hatred in the colonized:

> "Mama, see the Negro! I'm frightened!" Frightened! Frightened! Now they were beginning to be afraid of me. I made up my mind to laugh myself to tears, but the laughter had become impossible.... My body was given back to me sprawled out, distorted, recolored, clad in mourning that white winter day. The Negro is an animal, the Negro is bad, the Negro is mean, the Negro is ugly.[30]

Ironically, even as categories of self and other, white and black emerged unevenly and were deeply contested, they were veiled by a seemingly static quality to the "naturalness" of colonial difference. Fanon's formulation treats racialization as a psychic wound from which both colonizer and colonized suffered, a wound that locked them together in a dance of terror and violence. Examining the subjection of the colonial body to discipline therefore brings into focus the intimate domain of racialized inadequacy as conjoined with modes of colonial governance.

Fanon addressed the encounter between colonizer and colonized as premised on a deformed and ultimately destructive form of identification. Feminists and historians of gender have also addressed the politics of intimacy and the consequences of gender as embodied difference. In contrast to Fanon's emphasis on the intimate and ambiguous nature of racial domination rather than what had been understood as the somatic truth of racial difference, theorists of gender have moved from understanding gender as an intimate and private question to locating its operation squarely in macro-questions of power. Feminists have connected gendered violation and control to broader structures of state control and domination by drawing on Foucault's arguments about the bio-political states of the nineteenth century, states for which control over a population meant intrusion into private, intimate spaces and regulation of forms of identity and modes of life. Race for Foucault extended beyond its commonsensible associations with skin color and instead incorporated many forms of somatized or biologized difference and embodied distinction. Similarly, sexual identity was a historically contingent mode of being even though it was understood as a biological fact.

As such gender cannot be considered a transhistorical category that functions in the same, predictable ways across time and space.[31] Ann Stoler among others has argued that there was a marked shift from allowable forms of intimacy between merchants, traders, and colonial administrators, and native women of all classes during the seventeenth and eighteenth centuries.[32] These racialized intimate relationships had arisen from forms of slavery and concubinage—as Indrani Chatterjee and Jean Taylor have shown for the British in India and the Dutch in Indonesia—but they had been tolerated and often encouraged for providing sexual services and the comforts of family life.[33] As intimacy was increasingly policed as a result of colonial anxieties about maintaining racial boundaries during the mid– to late nineteenth century, however, racial purity and gendered respectability became more tightly intertwined. Commentators took issue with both legitimate and illegitimate forms of sexual access and mixed-race unions that had been common during the seventeenth and eighteenth centuries.

The racialized transformation of gender is of far-reaching significance because it suggests that changes in the forms of colonial rule cannot be separated from bourgeois conceptions of the family. Increasingly, western European legal systems curtailed women's rights to property and diminished their legal personhood, even as ideologies of the family defined the domestic sphere as a female space where family ties were forged in opposition to the public world of "interests."[34] By the late nineteenth century, gender had become crucial to public debates about respectability, character, and virtue and to labeling particular, especially urban, spaces as being dangerous and disordered.[35] Women were subjected to ever greater forms of surveillance and regulation through medical discourses of female fragility and vulnerability and through pedagogical campaigns to train women to become worthy mothers.[36] These intimate forms of power knowledge, biopolitical strategies, health and well-being of the population justified unprecedented intervention into family life in the interest of the health and well-being of the population.[37] The family was produced as an object of public knowledge even while new forms of privacy and interiority became the hallmarks of bourgeois femininity.

Feminist demands for rights in the West emerged from and took on the forms of Enlightenment reason through a focus on difference and similarity: Women had the same capacity for reason as men; their seeming lack of reason stemmed from unequal opportunity, a misrecognition of the difference between female and male bodies.[38] Even as feminists drew on the logic of "same yet different" to mark the particularities of gendered disenfranchisement, they began to exhort Western women to agitate on behalf of their more helpless and backward sisters.[39] Imperialist feminism was a form of liberalism seeking to redress the cultural disabilities from which non-Western women suffered, rehearsing narratives of colonial scandal as justification for moral and military intervention.[40] Such claims involved an assumption that the only relevant part of other women's identity was their victimization by traditional practices such as veiling, footbinding, genital operations, or *sati*.[41] Gendered susceptibility to violence and violation came to stand in for the other woman's subjectivity, and pain and suffering were its unique expression. Other women's suffering was transformed into a marker of *their* civilizational status, and troubling issues of embodied difference were displaced onto other spaces, other bodies. The constitutive contradictions of gendered embodiment—how women were to be included within, yet marked off from, the generic category of the "human"—is nowhere more evident than at the edges of empire.

The period between the French Revolution and World War I, the "long nineteenth century," was thus a critical period in which strategies of power and ideologies of racialized and gendered embodiment took on their modern forms. The margins of what were in many instances newly acquired empires were critical to these new paradigms and strategies, though they also complicated the metropolitan histories at the center of

Foucault's account. The imperial periphery posed multiple challenges to the distinctions that might seem absolute in western Europe. Spectacular punishment might (haltingly and imperfectly) be giving way to disciplinary correction when imposed on European criminals, but recurrent problems with corporeal chastisement of people outside the center demonstrated a more complicated trajectory. Foucault's work on bio-politics thus offers a way of understanding for addressing the dialectical interplay between race and gender, between two distinct though interconnected forms of embodiment that have critically shaped colonial corporeality over the last two centuries. While acknowledging the qualities of purity, accumulation, and productivity through which bio-power operates in its "modern" manifestations, the essays in this volume by Shannon Lee Dawdy, Douglas Peers, and Kerry Ward address earlier moments, when sumptuary cultures were governed by the dictates of display, virtue, and violence. The essays by Isaac Land, Anupama Rao, Laura Bear, Dorothy Ko, and Steven Pierce then point to later moments at which forms of bio-power were simultaneously extended while being problematized and debated. Finally, the essay by Susan O'Brien points to a moment at which technologies of bio-political regulation have moved beyond the realm of the state while also extending to encompass differences in religion. This trajectory suggests new ways to periodize the evolution of the bio-political state and the forms of modern power.

MODERNITY AND POSTCOLONIALITY

"Modernity" itself is a fraught and contradictory label. It is variously used to describe a set of political projects associated with greater democracy and the rise of a bourgeois public sphere, the socioeconomic changes associated with capitalism, a cultural and philosophical ethos arising with the Enlightenment, new forms of sociality (e.g., the decline of kin-based social organization, unprecedented levels of urbanization), and an attitude emphasizing a sharp disjuncture between contemporary times and the past. People who use the term can imply meanings as minimal as "everything about the present" and as consequential as the inevitability of a universal process of social evolution. "Modernity" can mean almost nothing, or it can be used as a one-size-fits-all explanation for any pattern of recent historical change.[42]

We would avoid either of these extreme positions, instead taking "modernity" as a label for a host of developments and practices. Calling something modern is often an attempt to claim a certain kind of legitimacy for it by incorporating it ideologically into a desirable, inevitable state of affairs. European colonialism claimed modernity as a legitimizing label and as a consequence of imperial endeavors; having colonies was itself a credential of a country's modernity. But colonial modernity had more consequential implications. Foucault has argued that the past several centuries have seen a shift in the ways in which states have exercised power over their subjects. Where in an earlier period power stayed at the center of the state and was exerted through the exercise of visible threats and intimidation, there has more recently been a shift to more dispersed modes of rule, in which power quietly but systematically monitors its subjects, teaching them to behave in the desired manner and ultimately moving to govern subjects through networks of knowledge and systems of incentives—a capillary form of power, as Foucault termed it.[43] While this account could be—and often is—read as one more narrative of unilinear modernization, the essays collected here, especially Land's and Bear's essays on the practices of discipline on ambiguously racialized subjects such as sailors and Anglo-Indians, suggest a more complicated historical trajectory. Rather than seeing particular strategies of power as succeeding one another in a preordained sequence, our contributors chart the uneven, even contradictory emergence and coexistence of particular modes of addressing power's subjects, and they point out the ways in which shifts and transitions must be located within particular debates and political circumstances. This suggests a way to extend Benjamin's formulation of the relationship between violence and state-centered rationalization. To the extent that violent practices were a primary means by which governing strategies were deployed and forced to alter, the halting and troubled career of the bio-political colonial state provides a fascinating window onto the intimacy of law and violence. Indeed, the colonial fascination with law functioned as a mechanism of legitimizing "traditional" forms of violence, as both Rao and Pierce suggest, even as legality became the discursive cover for the more recent experiments in instituting new forms of control and surveillance, as Bear notes. Thus law's violence, whose visible manifestations appear here as scandalous publicity, becomes a moment for addressing disciplinary power as well as its failures.

Frederick Cooper has pointed out that in colonial contexts power was not capillary but arterial; strategies of governance followed well-defined, blatant pathways from governments through various forms of chieftaincy and on down to subjects. While power did not for the most part follow the logic of the spectacle, neither did it take on the dispersed forms common in Europe.[44] These case studies can be used to support Foucault's account, with the caveat that the shift in modes of governance has taken place unevenly. The temporal coexistence of spectacular and disciplinary modes (in colony and metropole, as applied to different categories of person, or as extended at random) is part of what fueled humanitarian criticism of colonial corporeal technologies. Foucault cannot be dismissed because of the long persistence of "earlier" modes of power; instead, he must be read as arguing for a mode of political normalization, one that is unevenly or not always successful. The specific, arterial, and embodied forms that colonial power knowledge took on cannot be separated from ideologies of racial inadequacy that made colonial subjects inherently limited, as Pierce suggests.

To the extent that colonial modernity placed racial or cultural alterity at the heart of governmentality, what is distinctive about the deployment of colonial disciplinary technologies is that it was organized around a dialectic of the subject's inadequacy and the subject's pathos. The colonized were not fit to be independent citizens, but their suffering was nonetheless unacceptable. This dimension of colonial governance provoked many of the paradoxes of colonial discipline discussed earlier. This tension was neither static nor unaffected by independence. As Partha Chatterjee has argued, decolonization is historically significant because of its imagination of power as located in an alternative political community, the "national" state.[45] This allowed a distinct form of political identification to be imagined through the postcolonial state's focus on popular consent and national belonging. At the same time, however, the moment of decolonization both internalized and exemplified the multiple legacies of colonial governance. Thus, while we would agree with Mahmood Mamdani that colonial modes of governance have critical postcolonial implications,[46] we would also suggest that the colonial legacies of the postcolonial state only took form during the late colonial period.[47] In the aftermath of the cold war and the failures of nonalignment in the global South it is increasingly obvious how postcolonial forms of governance have mimicked their colonial predecessors even while discourses of development and national self-determination have often occluded both colonial culpability and the distinctive violence of postcolonial rule.[48]

Decolonization partially masked a longer-term process by which indigenous elites assumed the mantle of agents of development and modernization in the late-colonial sense of those terms. The infrastructure and bureaucracies of most decolonized nations resembled and even imitated the hierarchies of racially bifurcated colonial states, even while marking the end of the explicit racialization of the (post)colonial state's inadequate, non-modern subjects. Thus, while decolonization does not mark an ultimate break in technologies of governance based on alterity, it does indicate an important moment in which such strategies began to move beyond the purview of the state. This observation is not meant to suggest a one-size-fits-all legacy of colonialism: Indonesia's colonial legacies are very different from Nigeria's, India's from South Africa's. Any attempt to consider such trajectories must be grounded in particular histories. Much of the scholarship on the postcolonial transition influential in the U. S. academy and from which we draw inspiration emerges from South Asia, whose history is often taken as simultaneously exceptional and a model for all other colonial experiences. A part of this emerges from the specific historical conditions making South Asia (and primarily India) the most significant Anglophone scholarship with intensive dialogues between scholars based in the global North and global South—a fascinating topic we cannot address here. There are, however, other ways to think about the experiences of colonization and postcoloniality. Critical positions following from pan-Africanism and *negritude* have suggested a distinctive experience emerging from the connections between Africa and the New World, connections that are only incidentally related to the history of nation-states.[49] Considering the persistent legacies of colonization requires the rhetoric of decolonization, its political status as a moment that imagines and inaugurates new futures, even while remaining agnostic about its material outcomes.

VIOLENCE, SCANDAL, AND DISCIPLINE

For these reasons, it should be possible to historicize shifts in colonial governmentality by exploring the changing status of corporeality and the development of techniques to control and contain the colonized body. As Ward, Dawdy, and Land suggest, there was a hardening of racial categories and development of a range of corporeal technologies aimed at dealing with inadequate subjects. Where during the early modern period religion, linguistic competence, and employee status within the great merchant companies determined the ways in which individuals were subjected to state-sanctioned bodily violence, racial categories hardened across the nineteenth century, and corporeal technologies took on resonances within this logic of modernist governance and colonial inadequacy. This racializing shift took place in consonance with the emergence of humanitarian concerns about the well-being of those subject to discipline. The pathos of the disciplined contrasted with claims about the difference in particular groups' susceptibility to discipline. This dynamic has driven a dialectical process through which categories of racial (and other) difference have been used to justify forms of violence that are otherwise unacceptable. Scandals and debates that resulted from specific incidents then acted to transform the categories themselves, emphasizing the "other" as female, as sick, as non-Muslim, as deviant rather than as "native." This move "into" and then "out of" race was simultaneously a move into and out of the state as responsibility for violence shifted from entities concerned with achieving sovereign authority to internationally recognized states and then to individual, "private" practitioners of arguably justifiable violence, as the essays by Bear, Ko, and O'Brien demonstrate.

Comparative approaches raise thorny questions about the legitimacy of comparison. We do not claim that the trajectories we describe represent a universal process. While the history of embodiment is necessarily local, there *are* uncanny parallels around the world in political technologies of the body. These must be acknowledged but not fetishized. Colonial regimes communicated with one another. They sometimes found similar situations on the ground, and they confronted problems of governance with a common intellectual apparatus, one that serves sometimes to homogenize disparate phenomena. They also depended on approaches to government that moved very roughly in tandem. The net result of these facts is to suggest both the utility and the limits of a comparative approach. One can therefore discern an implicit trajectory in these essays: Beginning with an early modern fluidity of racial categories, the ambivalences of humanitarian concern within global liberalism and strategies of recognizing alterity within the "facts" of the body or of culture have resulted in the dialectical development of colonial corporeality around the world and been a precondition for objectification, subjectification, and resistance. This trajectory reorients narratives of colonial expansion by highlighting the broad spectrum of practices that tie the most intimate domains to logics of state.

The scandals that regularly emerged from colonial attempts to rule through the other body point ultimately to the difficulty of describing violence, both within governmental inquiry and within historical analysis. Some years ago, historians working within particular nationalist historiographies focused on violence in the context of colonized people's resistance to the projects of imperial rule, seeming to imply that resistance was the ideal form of action for all oppressed peoples.[50] Studies of resistance addressed the topic of subaltern violence largely as a critique of the excesses of colonial rule, as evidence of the structural deformations of colonial societies, or as a redemptive force, purifying colonial humiliation.[51] Violence as such was not an important analytic category at the center of colonial encounters traversing a spectrum from intimate sexual relations between colonizer and colonized to the structural violence of the colonial state.[52] Rather, in these works violence was understood either as the excesses of colonial surplus extraction or as collective projects of rebellion and counterinsurgency.

We approach violence differently. Colonial corporeality was a self-fulfilling prophecy but a troubled one: Colonial subjects were ruled through violence; violated bodies were by definition colonial. Violence constituted colonial difference, but the brutality of violating native bodies continually threatened scandal. Corporeal practices that governed the colonized en masse conflicted with liberal claims to universal equality. Equal (if separate) bodies implied a right to bodily integrity, but this norm emerged only through its scandalous violation, a pattern repeated from India to King Leopold's Congo, everywhere the Royal Navy sailed. Stories of colonial brutality conveyed pain as a universal experience and quantifiable datum, implying that corporal punishment was an unworthy technique for civilized government. This moment coincides with the humanitarian critique of violence, one that demarcated violence from the legitimate force of law. If colonialism's repetition of violence implicated it in the reproduction of native conceptions of force and political authority, there was the even greater danger that colonial discipline inaugurated new forms of brutal violence that could not be named as such but recognized only through their approximation of that which had preceded them.

Corporeal techniques (torture, flogging, bodily violence) indexed, enforced, and helped to constitute categories of difference in colonial and postcolonial contexts. Their very corporeality helped to constitute socially recognized categories of difference as *bodily* difference, as the essays by Ward, Dawdy, and Land in this volume suggest. Modern categories of alterity (race, gender, ethnicity, sexuality, religion) emerged in this context. From early on this process was spectacular and exceptional, and was often regarded as a species of violation. The scandal of practices was almost inevitable, since universal conceptions of rights and justice existed alongside domination and unfreedom. Debates about violence—whether fueled by lurid descriptions of slavery and the sexual misdemeanors of colonial officials or by reformist movements advocating subjectification through work discipline and carceral regimes—produced theories of native bodies that in turn enabled material practices of governance. The body of the colonized was a critical site both for maintaining alterity and for enacting governance. Thus, the development of human rights was produced and bedeviled by the tolerance of spectacular forms of violent discipline for those considered beyond the pale of rationality, producing contradictory discourses of suffering and of corrective punishment. The emergence of the human as a political subject was intimately tied to its emergence as an *injured* subject.

Indeed, phenomenal pain, as the essays by Ko, Pierce, and Rao suggest, produced debates over the distinction between corporeal violence as a violation or exception to universal liberal mores and as a grim necessity in dealing with a reified other. This principle can be extended further, suggesting that colonialism itself was an exception, a space whose realities reveal a logic usually euphemized in liberal states.[53] One can follow this through the sustained impact of discourses of violence and violation as they connected metropolitan and colonial publics through periods of colonial expansion, from the seventeenth century to their postcolonial legacies. And tragically today, the same discursive logic, the same structure of publicity, is at play in discussions of atrocities in the war against terror and of counterinsurgency in Iraq. Recent work in the anthropology of violence and of embodiment provides further clues to how one might address the problems of colonial corporeality, suggesting possible methods of addressing pain and suffering or of representing violence and violation. Many scholars have considered the ethical dilemmas of representing violence.[54] How can one examine the experience of phenomenal violence without giving in to explanatory categories that mitigate it, fetishize it, or turn it into pornography? When are human beings merely victims, and when can they be addressed as people who have rights, as moral subjects susceptible to bodily violation who must therefore be protected from it? Historicizing colonial violence, however conceived at the time, can enhance the theoretical and methodological yield of studies of the production of bodily alterity, of ethnographic studies of different conceptions of human vulnerability. Physical vulnerability and specific conceptions of harm and injury must be simultaneously addressed; phenomenal violence must ultimately be considered in relation to its meaning and significance for both victims and perpetrators. Historians and anthropologists have argued that cultural understandings of the body (and to a certain extent the very experience of being embodied) are historically contingent. The emergence of contemporary racial categories and of sexuality as a discrete domain represents historical novelties in the guise of universal history.[55] The processes by which these have come into being are not just contingent but are subtended by a complex of sexual, national, and international politics[56] and by the multiple legacies of colonialism.[57]

Our genealogy of colonial violence and embodiment begins in the early modern period with a pair of essays examining penal practices in the Cape Colony of the Dutch East India Company (VOC) and in French Louisiana. In "Defining and Defiling the Criminal Body at the Cape of Good Hope: Punishing the Crime of Suicide under Dutch East India Company Rule, circa 1652–1795," Kerry Ward describes the challenges suicide posed to authorities. Especially in the early years of the colony, in the late seventeenth and early eighteenth centuries, the corpses of suicides were subjected to various forms of judicial defilement and then buried in unconsecrated ground. Suicide represented a direct challenge to the VOC's claim to control the bodies of its employees and subjects, and while its punishments for suicide were in consonance with practices in western Europe, they persisted in the Cape rather longer than they did in the metropole. The basic principle was challenged by cultural difference and by slave status: Was a non-Christian's suicide the same kind of crime as a Christian's, and how did an owned body differ from a free one? Ward describes the long persistence of these dilemmas and notes that they suddenly ended when the British took control of the colony at the turn of the century, abolishing judicial torture and other practices of judicial defilement. Shannon Lee Dawdy's essay, "The Burden of Louis Congo and the Evolution of Savagery in Colonial Louisiana," explores Louisiana's innovations, in 1725, to the metropole's Code Noir, which supposedly ruled the ways in which whites and blacks, slave and free were to interact in the French colonies. The authorities freed an African slave named Louis Congo and appointed him public executioner. For at least twelve years, Louis Congo was the only man in the colony invested with the power to whip, brand, amputate, break, and hang subjects—white, Indian, or African. For Congo to whip or hang a Frenchman symbolized the near equivalence of black slaves and poor whites before absolutist law. But as the local elites became more involved with slavery, they worried about the fraternizing of slaves and poor Frenchmen, and such equivalence presented a danger. Creole rulers altered their strategy in the 1740s to one in which state punishments began to exaggerate the differences between black and white bodies. They attempted to make the former appear more "savage" by barbaric dismemberment. This essay traces Louisiana's deepening involvement in slavery, marked by the trend toward gruesome spectacle that escalated, until in 1795 the road from Pointe Coupée to New Orleans was lined with posts topped with the severed heads of Bambara rebels.

Ward's and Dawdy's cases can be used to suggest that the eighteenth century saw a hardening of racial categories that took place in tandem with an increasing squeamishness within governments to punish people with the savagery of earlier periods. These dilemmas of treating different categories of subject are expanded on in Isaac Land's essay, "'Sinful Propensities': Piracy, Sodomy, and Empire in the Rhetoric of Naval Reform, 1770–1870," which discusses debates in England in the 1780s about the appropriateness of flogging and torturing sailors, marking the importance of discourses of race and masculinity in the formation of "reasonable" Englishmen. The realities of corporeal violence stood in for subjectification, given the need for maintaining discipline aboard ship. Images of the sailor, paradoxically both very English and unreasonably un-English, provide a powerful model of the ambivalence of difference that quickly emerged across the empire. Reformist societies both of and for sailors championed white sailors, arguing that as Englishmen they could not be expected to endure the harsh treatment the Navy was inclined to impose.

Douglas Peers provides another military example in "The Raj's Other Great Game: Policing the Sexual Frontiers of the Indian Army in the First Half of the Nineteenth Century." In looking at how the military addressed marriage, pseudo-marriage, and casual sex in the late eighteenth and early nineteenth centuries, Peers reveals how sexuality and matrimony were then understood. As time went on, the gap grew between rhetoric and reality. Unmistakable signs arose of growing opposition to interracial sexual and matrimonial relations; in practice, however, such relations continued, and in some cases were even encouraged. No blanket injunction existed against interracial sexual activity; nor was sexual discourse hegemonic. This sexual counterpoint to the judicial and disciplinary practices discussed in the earlier essays provides an important point of reference: Here one sees state attempts to regulate racial categories through affective ties and to deal with illicit forms, and consequences, of sexuality (venereal disease, sodomy, interracial sexuality) in ways that proved contradictory and almost equally problematic. In this way, therefore, we can see a hardening of the gendered forms of racial colonial identity.

Anupama Rao's "Problems of Violence, States of Terror: Torture in Colonial India" is concerned with the secret life of torture in British India. Torture was used extensively to extract confessions from natives, who were viewed as being accustomed to such practices under precolonial regimes but abhorred as a sign of the irrational use of force by local police. Rao focuses on an 1855 case of police torture that led to intense debate among colonial administrators about what such incidents revealed about the extent to which torture was used in extracting confessions from people accused of crimes. Her discussion points to the dual problem colonial administrators perceived themselves as facing: that of dealing with the recalcitrance of "native" criminals and of "native" judicial institutions. Where in earlier periods problems of judicial administration or discipline were the subject of criticism and reform, Rao's case represents a new departure in that it highlights a sense of official culpability as well.

This set of dilemmas is mirrored in Steven Pierce's essay, "Punishment and the Political Body: Flogging and Colonialism in Northern Nigeria," which focuses on the political dilemmas posed by flogging at the turn of the twentieth century. As a form of punishment, flogging was considered necessary to mark and maintain the boundaries of difference among Africans as proper colonial subjects. Different ethnic and religious affiliations, the British believed, corresponded to different degrees of social evolution: "Advanced" people were more susceptible to pain and more responsive to non-corporeal punishment. Pierce examines the vexed administrative history of flogging in Northern Nigeria's native courts, considering it in relation to the insights it offers into the culture of colonialism and the ways in which colonized peoples were incorporated theoretically as citizens of the colonial state. It suggests that questions of punishment are vital in understanding the targets and consequences of a colonial regime of governmentality.

Dorothy Ko addresses efforts to abolish footbinding at the turn of the twentieth century as crucial to an emergent discourse of Chinese masculinity and nationalism. Her essay, "Footbinding and Anti-footbinding in China: The Subject of Pain in the Nineteenth and Early Twentieth Centuries," examines the troubled relationship between violence and visibility through an exploration of discourses of female and national pain that contributed to the popularity of the anti-footbinding movement in the late Qing and early Republican periods. Footbinding was doubly significant. It functioned as a sign of Chinese men's brutality and thereby threatened to remove them from the circle of liberal reason. It also could be used to mobilize a capacity for sympathetic identification with the powerless and vulnerable (female) victims of the practice. Women's liberation from tradition came to rest on their capacity to articulate the horrors of footbinding as the condition of possibility for their own transformation into agentive subjects. National identity was premised on the modernization of masculinity and the liberation of women. Focusing on literary testimonies, as well as the evidentiary regimes that were made available by new medical technologies such as the x-ray, Ko explores how new forms of visualizing and narrating pain produced cultural discourses regarding women's suffering as well as gendered embodiment.

Laura Bear's essay, "An Economy of Suffering: Addressing the Violence of Discipline in Railway Workers' Petitions to the Agent of the East Indian Railway, 1930–47," draws on petitions preserved in the agent's record room at Eastern Railway headquarters in Calcutta, which seem not to belong in this atmosphere of routinized discipline at all. Speaking in a supernatural, royal, and moral language of violence, tyranny, suffering, and despair, these petitions tell of secret conspiracies, physical disfigurement, and brutal beatings; they predict riots and forecast impending disasters. The petitions represent a continuing struggle on the part of railway employees to be ruled as "adequate" subjects, and the polyvocality of their arguments demonstrates just how contested this terrain remained. Bear argues that the significance of these documents rests not only on the idea that they reveal the scandalous truth of the violent discipline of the railway bureaucracy, but also in the fact that they are revealing, as most petitions are, because they are material artifacts that chart a particular moment in the legitimation of a bureaucracy. Thus, we perceive ways in which arguments about identity continue and have moved out from the state into parastatal entities.

In "Spirit Discipline: Gender, Islam, and Hierarchies of Treatment in Postcolonial Northern Nigeria," Susan O'Brien takes the argument a step further, demonstrating that bodily violence understood as an Islamic healing practice serves a similar purpose in maintaining potentially contested sexual and religious hierarchies in postcolonial northern Nigeria. Spirit possession in Kano, as is the case through much of the region, has long been treated by a group of specialists called *'yan bori*, whose practices are considered antithetical to Islam. Since about 1996, a group of Quranic scholars has been treating people possessed by the *bori* spirits. O'Brien highlights the corporeal technologies that designate young girls as subject to medical discourses of cure and healing and that simultaneously discipline the unruly spirits possessing them. At the same time, these practices subject the spirits to the dictates of religious orthodoxy.

Both discourses are enacted outside the domain of direct state intervention, and this complicates seeing the state as the place from which classificatory projects are elaborated.

Finally, through her poetry, Yvette Christianse addresses issues of history, colonization, and violence by conjuring the ghosts of the past and memories of violation both remembered and forgotten. The island of St. Helena was a site of slavery and racial violence; it was also a place of exile. Christianse explores the possibilities of poetic language to evoke the related yet divergent histories of personal loss and founding violence through the figure of the remarkable Fernão Lopez, a Portugese convert to Islam, whose act of "betrayal" was met by disfigurement and the removal of his ears, his nose, and most significant, his tongue. Exiled in St. Helena, Lopez's disability and disfigurement become the occasion for acts of perceptual remembrance and the imagination and longing for sensual, embodied pleasure. Christianse's imaginative reconstruction of Lopez's diaries is an allusion to the ways in which autobiographical narratives such as personal diaries and travelogues have typically functioned as both archival fetish and testaments to violence. And yet, as an allegory for the power and force of poetic and literary language to resist both representation and recognition, Christianse's Lopez becomes a sign of the very possibilities of finding a different language for writing the histories of loss and violation and thinking outside normative forms of embodiment—issues with which this volume is centrally concerned.

The trajectory outlined by this collection has taken on a terrible timeliness during the past several years. The problematic, scandalous emergence of the "other" body, the move of corporeal technologies into and then out of the bio-political state, and ongoing shifts in strategies of government are all at play in the unconscionable acts perpetrated by the United States and its allies in Iraq and elsewhere as part of the "War on Terror." The simple use of the term "detainee" speaks volumes about the laws of exception that characterize governance in Iraq. The American government claims that detainees lack the status of prisoners and therefore are not entitled legal representation or to habeas corpus. Detainees can be forgotten and subjected to torture or intense violence, yet it is claimed no rights are infringed or laws broken. Because their legal status is both ambiguous and exceptional, the prisoners are outside the domain of representation. There is an uncanny resemblance between the legal status of detainees and those currently being held at Guantánamo Bay, defined as "unlawful combatants" and denied the rights due prisoners of war. As U.S. Secretary of Defense Donald Rumsfeld argued in January 2002, "Technically they do not have any rights under the Geneva Convention." In a press conference regarding the allegations of abuse in Abu Ghraib, Rumsfeld noted that he was unable to bring himself to use the "T word" and argued instead, "My impression is that what has been charged thus far is abuse, which I believe is technically different from torture." Such definitional niceties are perverse readings of the 1984 Convention against Torture and Other Cruel, Inhuman or Degrading Treatment or Punishment, which prohibits the use or justification of torture on any grounds. The right not to be tortured is the one absolute human right that is not susceptible to the laws of sovereign states, though Rao's essay in this volume suggests an alternative genealogy of the troubling ubiquity of torture. In any case, the actions of the American government crudely violate governmental compromises that have evolved over centuries.

This very crudity raises questions too large to address in this introduction or this collection. Does the breakdown in the neoliberal world order that the actions of the Bush administration represent point to a permanent shift in technologies of power and governance, or is this an exception that ultimately will be contained? To no small extent, the bizarre actions of U.S. government officials underline the contingent and ideological nature of the state. Although for analytic purposes in this introduction we have treated state actors as if they represent a consistent and coherent entity, we also recognize that this is a heuristic move only. Ultimately, the trajectories of the bio-political state must be considered in relation to the ideological project of labeling a host of actors and entities the "state."[58] This becomes particularly pressing at a moment in which the U.S. Secretary of Defense has canceled a planned trip to Germany, apparently because of a lawsuit pending there that charges him with war crimes.[59] When government actors are simultaneously limited in their actions because of their reception as criminal, the artificiality of state conceits becomes increasingly apparent. We cannot predict the future trajectory of colonial corporeality. These efforts to historicize discourses of human rights and the colonial body offer an indication, however, of the enormous challenges involved in crafting an ethical response to our troubled present.

NOTES

1 "Report of the Committee" set up under Colonial Regulation 60 to inquire into disciplinary charges against Superintendent Michael Gerard Sullivan and Assistant Superintendent Alexander von Coutts of the Kenya Prison Service, as cited in Rosberg and Nottingham, *The Myth of "Mau Mau,"* 344.

2 For an important argument about the logic of subaltern resistance see Guha, *Elementary Aspects of Peasant Insurgency in Colonial India.*

3 For a recent look at U.S. approaches to Islam during this period, see Mamdani, *Good Muslim, Bad Muslim.*

4 For recent examinations of this history and suggestions for new approaches to thinking about human rights, see Balfour and Cadava, "And Justice for All?"; Cmiel, "The Recent History of Human Rights."

5 We borrow this phrase from Gayatri Spivak's many justly famous descriptions of deconstructive practice.

6 Darius Rejali suggests that in Iran under the shah, torture itself became inflected with "modern" strategies of power: Rejali, *Torture and Modernity.* Within the history of European modernity, National Socialism illustrates this point admirably: see Aly, *Architects of Annihilation*; Mazower, "Violence and the State in the Twentieth Century."

7 Butler, *Bodies That Matter*; idem, *Gender Trouble*; Foucault, *The History of Sexuality, Volume 1*; idem, *The History of Sexuality, Volume 2*; idem, *The History of Sexuality, Volume 3.*

8 Asad, "On Torture, or Cruel, Inhuman, and Degrading Treatment"; Rejali, "Torture as a Civic Marker."

9 Michael Hardt and Antonio Negri have made a very influential argument

that a new "empire" has emerged based not on extending the limits of European territorial sovereignty over the rest of the world, but, rather, on incorporating the world into a unified global system in which sovereignty is decentered and deterritorialized: see Hardt and Negri, *Empire*. A difficulty of their argument is that almost any development fits into this paradigm of emerging empire, with little scope for understanding the limitations, frustrations, and contingencies of the process, an appreciation that is necessary for creating an adequate historical account of the dominance of neoliberalism. Even so, Hardt and Negri do describe an important historical moment, though now it appears that their description has been bypassed by contemporary events. Current American imperialism does not look very much like their account of the new form of empire.

10   See, for example, the apologetics for American and British imperialism in Ferguson, *Colossus*; idem, *Empire*.

11   Benjamin, "Critique of Violence." See also Derrida, "Force of Law."

12   Nicholas Dirks discusses the recurrent scandals of imperial culpability and its relationship to empire and state formation in Britain and India in Dirks, *The Scandal of Empire*. For an earlier argument about the staging of colonial guilt in the context of the trial of Warren Hastings, see Suleri, *The Rhetoric of English India*.

13   On these colonialisms, see Cain and Hopkins, *British Imperialism: Crisis and Deconstruction*; idem, *British Imperialism: Innovation and Expansion*; Canny and Pagden, *Colonial Identity in the Atlantic World, 1500–1800*; Greenblatt, *Marvelous Possessions*; Pagden, *Lords of All the World*.

14   On race, see Appiah, *In My Father's House*; Goldberg, *Anatomy of Racism*; idem, *The Racial State*; Gould, *The Mismeasure of Man*; Holt, *The Problem of Race in the Twenty-First Century*; Stoler, *Race and the Education of Desire*.

15   Scott, "Colonial Governmentality."

16   Chakrabarty, *Provincializing Europe*.

17   Anderson, *Imagined Communities*.

18   See Bennett, *Africans in Colonial Mexico*; Seed, *Ceremonies of Possession in Europe's Conquest of the New World, 1492–1640*.

19   Mintz, *Sweetness and Power*; Roseberry et al., *Coffee, Society, and Power in Latin America*.

20   See Davis, *The Problem of Slavery in the Age of Revolution, 1770–1823*; idem, *The Problem of Slavery in Western Culture*.

21 Drescher, *Capitalism and Antislavery*; Eltis, *Economic Growth and the Ending of the Transatlantic Slave Trade*; Solow and Engerman, *British Capitalism and Caribbean Slavery*; Williams, *Capitalism and Slavery*.

22 Buck-Morss, "Hegel and Haiti"; Davis, *The Problem of Slavery in the Age of Revolution, 1770–1823*; idem, *The Problem of Slavery in Western Culture*; Holt, *The Problem of Freedom*.

23 Hegel, *Phenomenology of Spirit*.

24 Blackburn, *The Overthrow of Colonial Slavery, 1776–1848*; Dubois, *A Colony of Citizens*; idem, *Les esclaves de la République*; Karl, *Staging the World*; Linebaugh and Rediker, *The Many-Headed Hydra*.

25 Duara, *Rescuing History from the Nation*; Harootunian, *Overcome by Modernity*; Karl, *Staging the World*.

26 On the role of Protestantism in creating societal and cultural preconditions for capitalism, the classic text is, of course, Max Weber's *The Protestant Ethic and the Spirit of Capitalism*. There is an extremely large literature on missionization in colonial contexts. For particularly notable examples, see Ballhatchet, *Caste, Class and Catholicism in India, 1789–1914*; Beidelman, *Colonial Evangelism*; Jean Comaroff and John L. Comaroff, *Of Revelation and Revolution*; John L. Comaroff and Jean Comaroff, *Of Revelation and Revolution*; Dube, *Untouchable Pasts*; Hunt, *A Colonial Lexicon*; Kooiman, *Conversion and Social Equality in India*; Landau, *The Realm of the Word*; Oddie, *Social Protest in India*; O'Hanlon, *Caste, Conflict, and Ideology*; Sanneh, *West African Christianity*.

27 On the intricate politics of religious conversion and its politico-cultural implications, see Comaroff, *Body of Power, Spirit of Resistance*; Jean Comaroff and John L. Comaroff, *Of Revelation and Revolution*; John L. Comaroff and Jean Comaroff, *Of Revelation and Revolution*.

28 Fanon, *Black Skin, White Masks*.

29 Bhabha, *The Location of Culture*; Sanders, *Complicities*; Young, *Colonial Desire*; idem, *White Mythologies*.

30 Fanon, *Black Skin, White Masks*. See Bhabha, *Location of Culture*; Suleri, *The Rhetoric of English India*.

31 Riley, "*Am I That Name?*"; Scott, *Gender and the Politics of History*.

32 Stoler, "Making Empire Respectable."

33 Chatterjee, *Gender, Slavery and Law in Colonial India*; Taylor, *The Social World of Batavia*. See also Ballhatchet, *Race, Sex, and Class under the Raj*; McClintock, *Imperial Leather*.

34 Davidoff and Hall, *Family Fortunes*.

35 Walkowitz, *City of Dreadful Delight*.

36 Davin, "Imperialism and Motherhood"; Poovey, *Uneven Developments*.

37 Foucault, *The History of Sexuality, Volume 1*.

38 Burton, *At the Heart of the Empire*; idem, *Burdens of History*; idem, *Dwelling in the Archive*; Davin, "Imperialism and Motherhood"; Poovey, *Uneven Developments*; Scott, *Only Paradoxes to Offer*.

39 Burton, *At the Heart of the Empire*.

40 The classic text is Gayatri Chakravorty Spivak's essay on *sati*, or widow burning, in colonial India. In that essay she offers the memorable phrase, "White men saving brown women from brown men," to highlight an earlier moment in such intervention on behalf of other women: Spivak, *A Critique of Postcolonial Reason*, 284–92.

41 See Mani, *Contentious Traditions*; Thomas, *Politics of the Womb*; Walley, "Searching for 'Voices.'"

42 Frederick Cooper suggests that the current cachet of the term "modernity" arises directly from older discourses of progress and improvement popularized as modernization theory and that most commentators use "modernity" descriptively as 1) an indigenous category (describing what people in a particular place call modern); 2) a vacuous category; or 3) an incorrect and misleading category: see Cooper, *Colonialism in Question*.

43 Foucault, *Discipline and Punish*; idem, "Governmentality"; idem, *History of Sexuality, Volume 1*.

44 Cooper, "Conflict and Connection." But see Apter, "On Imperial Spectacle"; Pemberton, *On the Subject of "Java."*

45 Chatterjee, *The Nation and Its Fragments*.

46 Mamdani, *Citizen and Subject*; idem, *When Victims Become Killers*.

47 Cooper, "Review." See also Atieno Odhiambo, "Woza Lugard?"; Murray, "Configuring the Trajectory of African Political History"; Youe, "Mamdani's History."

48 Chatterjee, *Wages of Freedom*; Comaroff and Comaroff, "Occult Economies and the Violence of Abstraction"; idem, *Civil Society and the Political Imagination in Africa*; Cooper and Packard, *International Development and the Social Sciences*; Escobar, *Encountering Development*; Gupta, *Postcolonial Developments*.

49 Appiah, *In My Father's House*; Moses, *Afrotopia*; Mudimbe, *The Invention of Africa*.

50 For example, Guha, *Elementary Aspects of Peasant Insurgency in Colonial India*; Ranger, *The African Voice in Southern Rhodesia, 1898–1930*; idem, *Revolt in Southern Rhodesia, 1896–7*.

51 For critical discussions, see Ortner, "Resistance and the Problem of Ethnographic Refusal"; Scott, *Weapons of the Weak*.

52 This is not to say that violent practices under colonialism have not been the subject of extensive examination. For examples from a vast literature, see Chakrabarty, "Domestic Cruelty and the Birth of the Subject"; Crowder, *The Flogging of Phinehas Mcintosh*; Dirks, "The Policing of Tradition"; Guha, "Chandra's Death"; Mani, *Contentious Traditions*; Nigam, "Disciplining and Policing the 'Criminals by Birth,' Part 1"; idem, "Disciplining and Policing the 'Criminals by Birth,' Part 2"; Pandey, *Remembering Partition*; Singha, *A Despotism of Law*; Van Onselen, *Chibaro*; Worger, *South Africa's City of Diamonds*.

53 In this suggestion we are inspired by Giorgio Agamben, who argues that the concentration camp is the place where politics encounters its own limits, where acts in the name of the preservation of life becomes indistinguishable from barbaric violence. The singularity of the camp, its status as an exception, is conflated with the exercise of legitimate rule. Agamben argues that this is an extension and refinement of Foucault's arguments, in *The History of Sexuality*, about institutions such as prisons and hospitals that further the modern biopolitical state's investment in forms of racial exclusion: Agamben, *Homo Sacer*.

54 Comaroff and Comaroff, "Occult Economies"; Daniel, *Charred Lullabies*; Das, *Mirrors of Violence*; idem, *Violence and Subjectivity*; Feldman, *Formations of Violence*; Malkki, *Purity and Exile*; Scheper-Hughes, *Death without Weeping*; Taussig, *Shamanism, Colonialism, and the Wild Man*.

55 Goldberg, *Anatomy of Racism*; idem, *The Racial State*; Laqueur, *Making Sex*; Martin, *The Woman in the Body*.

56 Brown, *States of Injury*; Butler, *Bodies That Matter*; Crenshaw, ed., *Critical Race Theory*; Grosz, *Space, Time, and Perversion*; idem, *Volatile Bodies*.

57 Burke, *Lifebuoy Men, Lux Women*; Hendrickson, *Clothing and Difference*; Hunt, *A Colonial Lexicon*; Povinelli, *The Cunning of Recognition*.

58 This is a theme we have explored elsewhere. See Pierce, *Farmers and the State in Colonial Kano*; Rao, *The Caste Question*. In general, we would endorse the claims made in Abrams, "Notes on the Difficulty of Studying the State (1977)." For other useful approaches, see Coronil, *The Magical State*; Corrigan and Sayer, *The Great Arch*; Das and Poole, *Anthropology at the Margins of the State*; Ferguson, *The Anti-Politics Machine*; Fuller and Benei, "Introduction"; Gupta, "Blurred Boundaries"; Hansen and Stepputat, *States of Imagination*; Mitchell, *Rule of Experts*. There is a large and rapidly growing literature on the U. S. administration's War on Terror. Publications on the administration of justice and the treatment of prisoners include Butler, *Precarious Life*; Danner, *Torture and Truth*; Gardener and Young, *The New American Empire*; Hersh, *Chain of Command*; Khalidi, *Resurrecting Empire*.

59 "Rumsfeld to Bypass Munich Conference," *Deutsche Welle*, Internet ed., www.dw-world.de/dw/article/0,1564,1465263,00.html (accessed 21 January 2005).

KERRY WARD

※

Defining and Defiling the Criminal Body at the Cape of Good Hope

Punishing the Crime of Suicide under Dutch East India Company Rule, circa 1652–1795

In Château-Gontier in 1718 Marie Janguelin, a poor girl six months pregnant, poisoned herself out of shame. The unfortunate girl did not realize that only the nobility could kill themselves with impunity. Her cadaver was disinterred, brought to trial, sentenced, then dragged on a hurdle face down. When the group reached the town square, the executioner slit her womb and extracted what remained of the foetus, which was buried in the section of the cemetery reserved to the unbaptized. Marie's lacerated body was hanged by the feet and left, ignominiously exposed to the public gaze, until it rotted. It was eventually burned, and the ashes were thrown to the wind.

—GEORGE MINOIS[1]

Suicide is a crime that does not properly appear to admit of punishment, which in this case must fall either upon the innocent or upon a body already lifeless and cold. In the latter case it will make no more impression on the living than would be made by hogging a statue, in the former it will be unjust and tyrannical, inasmuch as a man's political freedom necessarily presupposes that punishment should not be other than personal.

—CESARE BECCARIA[2]

Suicide remains one of the most controversial and culturally complex human acts, one to which no society has been indifferent.[3] The criminalization of suicide in Europe coalesced as both a judicial and a theological issue in late antiquity. But the punishment of individuals remained ambivalent throughout the Renaissance and the early modern period. Although in Dante's *The Inferno* most people who did injury to themselves or their own property were condemned in the second ring of the seventh (and lowest) circle, only one ring above murderers, not all suffered this fate. Dante's vivid depiction of suicides wandering the horrid forest of hell was attenuated. At the heart of the issue was who owned the body: God, the state, or the individual? Suicide directly challenged competing claims over control of the individual in European cultures and societies, and the ambivalence about suicide already apparent in *The Inferno* continued through the early modern period. The issue was even further complicated in the early modern multicultural global encounters of Europeans as traders, rulers, and colonists. Dante's connection between suicide and property was therefore even more complex outside Europe. The first wave of European colonialism was often predicated on the use of slave labor. Slave suicide became both a form of resistance and a crime against property. This chapter explores the overlapping circles in the early modern world and argues that suicide provides a lens through which one can bring into focus the varied relationship between the individual body and the body politic in state, colonial, and imperial contexts.

The crime of suicide was central to debates about secular and sacred meaning of the body and criminality in the early modern state. It also complicated the transition to the secularization of criminality. Murder was unequivocally a criminal act, but attitudes toward suicide, or self-murder, were changeable and sometimes ambiguous. The epigraphs that opened this chapter contrast the most extreme form of state spectacle condemning the suicide's body with that of the proposed secularization and decriminalization of suicide fifty years later.[4] But a focus on suicide during the early modern period reveals how this transition was uneven and contradictory both within Europe and beyond.[5] Europeans themselves struggled with the multiplicity of religious and folk beliefs and the state's assertion of its exclusive right to impose justice in the construction of sovereign legal realms. These ambiguities were multiplied when European involvement in the rest of the world intensified, particularly with the first wave of European colonialism. Suicide was fundamentally about whether or not individuals, their bodies, and their souls should be condemned by the state for the finite human act of self-destruction. Rather than claiming a strict chronological progression of changing practices and attitudes on the nature of suicide as a crime, suicide was a focal point in a complex discourse around the meaning of the individual's place in society.

Scholars of colonialism have complicated the historical canvass of crime and punishment in Europe by showing that the transition of penal practices was different in the colonies and that colonial practices affected what happened in the metropole. The issue of suicide can therefore be used to examine this complex circulation of ideas and practices between Europe and its colonies and European attitudes toward other cultures that were not within its direct colonial or legal orbit.[6] It is probable that communication between the colonies and Europe about suicide, particularly in colonies where slavery was practiced, also helped generate the debate about the legal and philosophical meaning of the act in both sites during the early modern era.[7] During this period, Europeans came into intimate contact with other literate and nonliterate cultures that had completely different perspectives on the meaning of life and death, including suicide, particularly the Hindu and Buddhist cultures of Asia. The new genre of travel literature brought these foreign cultural practices to the attention of the educated classes of Europe, who were not necessarily professional theologians or intellectuals. The dialogue that ensued as a result of this expanding knowledge about the world involved negotiations within Europe and the colonies that engaged notions of status, race, and gender. An examination of suicide in the Dutch East India Company's colony of the Cape of Good Hope from the mid–seventeenth century to the end of the eighteenth century demonstrates that the punishment of suicide existed within the disciplinary regime of the company for the entire period as part of a broad spectrum of corporal punishment that was applied differentially according to status, ethnicity, and gender. But suicide in a colonial society could not be defined in simplistic "black-and-white" terms. The deliberations over individual cases of suicide at the Cape reveal the tensions in the categorization and control of individuals in the company's colonial realm, particularly over the cultural meaning of people as property that existed in a slave society.

SUICIDE IN DUTCH COLONIES AND IN EUROPE DURING THE EARLY MODERN PERIOD

Seventeenth-century colonial society as it emerged under the rule of the Dutch East India Company at the Cape created a complex hierarchy of status, race, freedom, and gender. At the pinnacle of colonial society, the European male elites of the company embodied the ruling class. However, their wives and children were not necessarily European, although they became categorized as such through their husbands and fathers. Not all free people were European, but all slaves were non-European, whether locally born or from the littoral societies of the Indian Ocean. Although indigenous Khoekhoe could not legally be enslaved, they often became bonded laborers with little differentiation from slaves. Exiled Muslim princes from Asia who were prisoners of state were sometimes treated as the social equals of the governor and sat at his table, while Christian European convicts, particularly company servants, were condemned to lives very similar to those of slaves.[8] In a colonial society with such subtle hues of status, religion, race, and culture, the negotiation of crime and punishment was equally complex. Although the company firmly held the monopoly on the power to define crime and to punish it, the colonial state was not insensitive to the mélange of people in its midst and the various interpretations that could be applied to committing a crime.[9] Suicide was a crime during the company period, but it was not interpreted as the same crime with the same significance for all people. As such, suicide engages with notions of personal and state power and with the religious and cultural interpretation of this social struggle between the individual and the categorization of difference imposed by the state.

The Castle of Good Hope was the symbolic center of Dutch East India Company power at the Cape. Its imposing fortifications were designed to deter invasion and to impress locals with the company's overwhelming size and strength. It was the seat of government, law, and the military. The spectacle of the company's court was enacted at the castle. The condemned listened as their sentences were read out at the castle and were accompanied through the gates by soldiers to the nearby scaffold for the performance of their punishment. A European soldier who had the effrontery to commit suicide inside the castle was buried beneath the scaffold as a warning to his fellow company servants. As a Christian, the soldier was thereby denied a proper burial, and his soul was condemned to hell. As a lesson to his comrades, this form of burial would remind them of his punishment every time they stood guard at the place of execution.[10] The symbolism of the soldier's burial outlasted the spectacle that would have accompanied the defilement of his body on the gibbet, for the impact of exposure was determined by the rate of decomposition of human flesh and bones. His burial under the scaffold was a perpetual punishment and constant warning. This was one of the few cases in which a European was condemned for committing suicide at the Cape. Because the soldier defiled the castle and thereby defied the company, the authorities brought the full force of the law to bear in his punishment.

European servants of the Dutch East India Company often rationalized their motives for committing crimes by claiming that they had been under diabolical influence that goaded them into acts of evil. During interrogation, these men would declare, "I am the devil's own."[11] Company servants, particularly soldiers and sailors, were subjected to almost the same degree of surveillance and the imposition of punishment as slaves. Whereas the Dutch Calvinist church, although weak in the colonies, often dealt with infractions of behavioral norms among civilians (sometimes even those who could be defined as criminal), this was not the case for most company servants and slaves. They were the most heavily disciplined sectors of the population and were the most likely to be brought before the courts for crimes and misdemeanors. Penal transportation of European company servants resulted in a sector of the Cape

European population living under conditions of sentences to "public labor in chains" that were often more onerous than the lives led by many slaves.[12] Soldiers, sailors, slaves (and those who formerly had this status) made up the vast majority of the working population of the Cape. The social boundaries, both of enmity and camaraderie, between the colonial underclasses were fluid and complex. Many of the laws governing company servants were based on military and naval discipline, which was severe in Europe and abroad.[13] It was therefore not surprising that company officials at the Cape sought to control these groups through judicial processes and, in particular, through the infliction of physical punishment for transgressions against law and order.

SHIFTING ATTITUDES TOWARD SUICIDE IN EUROPE AND THE CAPE

But suicide in Europe and at the Cape was even more complex than this social milieu suggests. The fact that so few upper-level company officials or burghers were convicted of suicide at any of the company settlements is somewhat suspicious. Were there no people of privilege driven by desperation to end their lives in the almost 150 years of the company's rule at the Cape and elsewhere? That is unlikely to have been the case. However, as the opening epigraph suggests, state officials and members of the ruling classes sometimes colluded to hide the fact of suicide within their own social ranks from judicial punishment. This was not surprising, considering that the state was able to confiscate all of the suicide's property. For middle- and upper-class families, the suicide of the head of the household could mean ruin and destitution if the state imposed its right to confiscate the estate.[14] Under Dutch laws of inheritance, this desperate situation would not necessarily have been the case, as inheritance was partial among spouses and children within the family. Nevertheless, suicide of a patriarch would severely erode the inheritance of the surviving family members. The punishment of suicide in Europe and in the colonies could therefore be determined by status. The double standard of punishment of suicide for rich and poor was commonly recognized throughout the period. As the gravedigger in Shakespeare's *Hamlet* commented about Ophelia's suicide, "If this had not been a gentlewoman, she should have been buried out o' Christian burial."[15] Mitigating circumstances were sometimes negotiated before these cases were brought before the law in societies where suicide had to be condemned as a crime.

In general there was consensus among Protestants, particularly those preaching from the pulpits, that, following St. Augustine, suicide was by nature an expression of despair brought on by diabolical influence and manifesting the absolute opposite of Christian hope.[16] Richard Gilpin's 1677 treatise on the devil's wiles included the invocation that "Satan seeks the ruin of our Bodies, as well as of our Souls, and tempts Men often to Self-Murther."[17] MacDonald and Murphy argue that there was an increasing secularization of suicide in Europe between the sixteenth century and the end of the eighteenth century. This shift took place particularly through the influence of humanism and the Enlightenment on the secularization of intellectuals. The social and cultural transformations that took place in this period were far more uneven but were affected by these changing moral and intellectual attitudes toward the individual in society.[18]

Changes in attitudes toward suicide were not linear; nor were they the same across the social spectrum. While intellectuals like Thomas More, in his 1515 publication *Utopia*, could sanction suicide under certain social conditions for the good of the polity, this was not the position taken within the church.[19] The secular theories of classical scholars about suicide entered into intellectual discourse in early modern Europe, including the Roman philosopher of Stoicism, Seneca (4 b.c.e.–c.e. 65), who was forced by the emperor Nero to practice what he preached about voluntary suicide.[20] Of course, the most famous early modern secular contemplation of suicide in English literature was that of Shakespeare's Hamlet, whose soliloquy on the question "To be, or not to be" cut to the very heart of secular and sacred definitions of suicidal motivation battling with self-preservation.[21] Other scholars of the sixteenth century contemplated suicide, intellectually if not literally. John Donne's *Biathanatos*, subtitled "A Declaration of that Paradoxe, or Thesis, that Selfe-homicide is not so naturally Sinne, that it may never be Otherwise" (written in 1610 and published posthumously 1647), was recognized as a theological innovation in the analysis of suicide, but the work did not have popular circulation or influence. It was only in 1700 that John Adams wrote the first purely philosophical treatise on suicide, "An Essay Concerning Self-Murther," which removed theological considerations from the debate and treated suicide as a social issue. Minois claims that this was a turning point in the relaxation of punishment—or, at least, the condemnation—of suicide. David Hume's philosophical defense of suicide, his essay "Of Suicide" (written and prepared for publication in 1757), was only published posthumously in 1783 because of pressure on Hume by politically powerful orthodox Anglicans in London not to include it in an edited collection of philosophical essays. The debate on suicide raged among the philosophes and other Enlightenment intellectuals, with no consensus on the issue. Immanuel Kant remained firmly opposed to suicide, unlike Montesquieu, Rousseau, and Diderot who argued both for and against without revealing their beliefs on the issue.[22]

In general, the Protestant and Catholic churches maintained the belief that suicides should be denied Christian burial. The treatment of cadavers of suicides was similar to that of the Cape, as described earlier. Dutch practice tended to follow that of the rest of western Europe. In the case of suicide in Europe, a report was written about the circumstances of death, and the body was examined by a surgeon. If suicide was suspected, a trial was organized:

> During all this time the body was preserved in sand or salt or was sprinkled with quicklime to prevent it from decomposing too much before the sentence could be carried out. Once a guilty verdict had been reached, the cadaver was fetched, then dragged through the streets on a hurdle, face down, with the sergeant-at-arms in the lead proclaiming the reason for the sentence. The body was then hanged by the feet from a gibbet, and after being exposed, was thrown onto the communal dump along with rotting horse carcasses.[23]

In the Dutch East India Company empire, the official faith was that of the Calvinist Dutch Reformed church. But church officials were also company employees. They were therefore subject to contracts imposed by the company, and the church was often in an ambiguous position of power vis-à-vis the state. The church controlled the ceremonies of Christian life and death, but the state defined who could enjoy these privileges in relation to those on whom it rendered criminal punishment.[24]

The most significant difference in attitudes toward suicide between Europe and the Cape was the development during the seventeenth century in western Europe of the recognition of suicide by reason of insanity being exempt from judicial or church punishment. "For the theologians, jurists, and casuists, the soul remained untouched by insanity, and the madman bore no moral responsibility, no matter what act he committed."[25] Once this avenue was opened, it gave a loophole to the upper classes in particular to protect their wealth and reputation from being sullied by stain of suicide in the family. The church did not fail to grasp at the opportunity provided by this logic. All suicides by priests were determined to be as a result of madness, for it would otherwise be impossible to contemplate such an act by one of God's servants, and therefore priest suicides were not denied a Christian burial. As far as can be determined by the judicial records, there was no case of upper-class or ecclesiastical suicide masquerading as insanity at the Cape during the company period. Insanity was itself difficult to determine in a racially and culturally complex colonial society. Whether or not there are cases that simply did not enter the archival record is a matter for speculation. The class differences in the punishment of suicide mirrored those in the evolution of imprisonment: Social status counted in the treatment meted out by the state, and this situation was recognized throughout society, for better or worse.

It was during the eighteenth century, in the midst of the Enlightenment, that the word "suicide" came into common usage in English. I have hitherto been using the term somewhat anachronistically for the sake of consistency; the most common term in English was "self-murder," and it retained this form as *zelfmoord* in Dutch.[26] It seems that by the late eighteenth century, at least, suicide had become a matter of public debate instead of the preserve of intellectuals and theologians. Minois points out that "in London in the 1780s public debates were organized on the subject. *The Times* . . . declared that suicide was 'at present a general subject of conversation among all ranks of people.' "[27] But the state attempted to squash the predilection for suicide among its subjects, and sometimes to conceal the crime, because it was fundamentally a threat to its own authority, whether manifested in crown or republic, through the individual's rejection of further participation in society on the terms of its rulers.

SUICIDE IN A COLONIAL SLAVE SOCIETY

The Cape of Good Hope was situated in the middle of the most strategically important shipping route between Europe and Asia in the early modern period. But as a colony of the Dutch East India Company, the Cape also lay at the intersection of several orbits that constituted the legal realm of empire. The first was the legal relationship between the Dutch East India Company and the United Provinces of the Netherlands. The issuing of the charter that brought the company into being also devolved certain sovereign rights that enabled the company to establish its own legal system, although it was a system based on configurations of Dutch law, particularly the laws of Holland. Company law, based on the articles of naval discipline and defined in its statutes and resolutions, took precedence over the legal codes of the United Provinces. The second legal orbit centered on Batavia as the imperial capital of the company. Batavia was built on the conquered ruins of the Javanese port town Jayakarta in 1619. The Dutch East India Company assumed sovereignty over the city, which soon became the center of its imperial nexus in the Indian Ocean. It was both an imperial capital where trade and diplomacy were conducted and a vibrant, multiethnic entrepôt that operated along many of the same patterns as other indigenous port cities in Southeast Asia. The third legal orbit was that between Batavia and the other company colonies and factories. Batavia officially ruled the "outer stations," as they were known, including the Cape of Good Hope. Laws passed in Batavia were valid at the Cape insofar as they were locally applicable. Batavia was also the Court of Appeal for the whole company empire. Finally, the local legal orbit of the colonies had its own dynamic, as the Statutes of Batavia, the official law codes of the empire, contained a provision for the passing of local laws and for the modification of laws issued in Batavia for local use. Furthermore, it is doubtful whether many of the company's high-ranking officials who governed the colonies were actually familiar with the Statutes of Batavia in any detail. Very few had formal legal training and were more conversant with the Bible than with legal texts. Nevertheless, Cape criminal law does not seem to have differed greatly from that of Batavia.[28]

The legal orbits of the company empire did not operate as systematically as my schema might suggest. They were more like legal tangled webs. Company law was often contested by indigenous peoples who did not recognize its legitimacy (except through the application of force) and continued their own moral and legal practices.[29] The company could not operate without the cooperation of free indigenes, especially in Batavia, where the colonists depended heavily on Asian—particularly Chinese—immigrant labor. The company therefore set in place a complex system of deciding what laws applied to whom under particular circumstances.[30] This was especially the case with civil law, which for non-Christian residents was more or less left in control of their communities, with community leaders being answerable to the company in areas claimed under Dutch East India Company jurisdiction. For Dutch citizens living in company territories, civil law also raised the possibility of appeals to the courts in the Netherlands. But for criminal law, the situation was more straightforward. The company's charter included the sovereign right to determine its own laws and to impose punishments of its choice, including the death penalty. The company imposed the right to apply its laws in cases that took place within its territories, or when cases outside its official jurisdiction involved company personnel or burghers. These powers of jurisdiction were negotiated with indigenous polities and differed between colonies. However, there was an overall tendency by the end of the seventeenth century in the Dutch East India Company outposts to attempt the consolidation of sovereign rule and extend jurisdiction over all people within these territories. The Cape was no exception, although it differed to the extent that indigenous Khoekhoe law was at first recognized within the evolution of local legal practices, including the practices regulating suicide.[31] Moreover, the slaves who made up most of the laboring classes, particularly those in the towns, were imported from around the Indian Ocean, and it was not until the 1760s that Cape-born slaves equaled in number those brought from other societies.[32] Given that the Cape was such a complex cultural and ethnic milieux, it cannot be presumed that there was a common understanding of suicide and the appropriateness of punishment for the act by the state.

In the context of the Dutch East India Company empire, the language of the judicial process, including the full confession of the defendant, preceded punishment. As Susan Newton-King has observed, "Criminal cases at the Cape were tried under the extraordinary process which was inquisitorial rather than accusatorial in nature."[33] The threat of torture to induce confession was predicated on the ability of the court to record and translate the testimony of defendants and translating the testimony of witnesses to assist in extracting a confession. Elaborate notations of language and translation are included in the written record of the courts, which are all in Dutch for the purposes of official transcription. The criminal records give a sense of the presumed translatability of the whole process, the sense that everyone understood what was happening in the rituals of justice. The enactment of judicial processes was derived exclusively from European—and, more specifically—Dutch culture. The language of the court was preceded by, and defined, the logic of acting on the body. The ceremony of witnessing guilty parties as they listened to their sentences being read in public was part of the spectacle of the scaffold. But what happened in the case of suicide? The defendant was already dead and by definition unable to hear his or her condemnation, admit guilt, and plead for mercy or forgiveness (or, alternatively, defy these strictures of the court). In the case of suicide, issues of cultural or literal translation were ignored in favor of European cultural norms for the punishment of this crime. It was assumed by the Dutch that self-murder was universally considered a crime against humanity and was therefore worthy of punishment under all civilized law. Suicide was a crime, the colonial state declared, that must be discouraged among the underclass population, no matter what its level of civilization, race, status, or gender. The element of spectacle in the punishment of a suicide was therefore double-edged and aimed at the victim as well as the audience who bore witness to the silent defilement of the corpse.

SUICIDE AND SLAVERY AT THE CAPE

In a slave society, suicide by a slave was a crime not only against humanity but also against property. By committing suicide, a slave literally stole his or her master's property by refusing to live and labor under the master's ownership. Slave suicide was therefore a more complicated social and legal issue than the suicide of a free person. The laws of slavery that governed the Cape, based on Roman law, did not give slaveowners the right of life and death over their slaves. In other words, masters were not legally allowed to kill their slaves with impunity. Practically, when slaveowners did take legal corporal punishment (or "domestic correction," as it was known) too far, an act not uncommon at the Cape, the company imposed a fine for accidental death rather than for murder on the slaveowner. Although the brutality of some slaveowners was widely known, and some sadistically brutal masters even had their slaves confiscated by the state for the safety of the community, it was thought that few slaveowners would purposefully destroy their own property. Therefore, killing a slave was determined an accidental extension of "severe domestic correction," even in cases in which torture was obvious. Only the state had the right to take life, and the company employed officials to examine every death, including slave deaths, to determine their cause.[34] It was a crime not to report a death to Company officials and thereby allow examination of the corpse by the company surgeon. Court records pronouncing slave suicide quoted the formula "from the slave's own hand without the least cause" to differentiate between suicide and possible manslaughter or murder.[35] But even these inspections were not applied consistently. The difference in governance and in the application of company law between town, countryside, and remote rural areas was immense during the whole company period. The frontier areas had a well-earned reputation for being beyond the reach of colonial law, and crimes in these remote areas were often difficult to identify and investigate without the cooperation of colonists who were themselves living at the margins of company legality.

Historians of slavery at the Cape have noted that there were very few incidents of slave rebellion. But as in other slave societies, suicide was "the most tragic form of slave response, reflecting the desperation of the slave condition."[36] As Nigel Worden notes, the motives for slaves' committing suicide varied. Some did so out of fear of further corporal punishment from their masters; others did so to avoid inevitable punishment by the state for crimes they had already committed; and still others did so out of despair for the interminability of their enslavement or because they labored so ceaselessly that their will to live ebbed away.

However, there is another cultural dimension to consider. Slaves taken from Indian Ocean societies found themselves inserted into a slave system that was foreign to their own cultural understandings of slavery. This made their adaptation to life at the Cape all the harder because Dutch colonial chattel slavery was usually so different from slavery within their own societies. Moreover, it cannot be assumed that their notions of suicide were the same as European ideas, and especially those declared in company law. It is therefore not sufficient to attach these "social" motives purely to a form of slave resistance. One must also consider, despite the lack of archival evidence in the form of testimony, that some slaves did not consider suicide criminal, morally abominable, or religiously heretical. These variations in the cultural meaning of attitudes toward suicide were most likely to be manifested in foreign-born slaves rather than creolized slaves who were born at the Cape; the latter were more acculturated into Dutch colonial society.

This cultural difference is confirmed by the fact that most of the slaves who committed suicide were foreign males.[37] However, gender was also a significant indicator for patterns of suicide among slaves at the Cape. Female slaves often combined suicide with infanticide or the murder of their children, particularly when they lost the protection of their partners or did not want their children to be raised as slaves. Slave women were the most vulnerable members of Cape society, where the gender ratio was overwhelmingly in favor of men. Slave women in particular were subjected to rape and abuse from their masters and from other men, including slaves, with little recourse to self-protection. The cultural and legal complexities of suicide and infanticide were profoundly disturbing for the colonial state. In December 1669, a slave woman owned by the company was lying in the Slave Lodge, dying of smallpox. She was found to have "strangled her infant, a half-caste girl. . . . The Council . . . ordered that the murderous pig should be placed in confinement in order to be punished according to her deserts." The woman was tied into a sack and thrown into Table Bay to drown.[38] Although this case was not technically suicide, the implications to the company were clear: The dying woman knew that her act would be discovered and that she would be executed for infanticide.[39]

She had thereby robbed the company of a valuable asset in killing her infant child, all the while knowing that the value of her own life for the company was rapidly diminishing with her failing health. This kind of case continued throughout the slave era at the Cape. In 1792, Anna, a pregnant slave woman in Stellenbosch, drank brandy mixed with soot and ate a snakeskin, trying to kill herself and her unborn child.[40] Suicide combined with abortion, infanticide, or child murder was obviously overwhelmingly the dilemma of slave women. One of the most tragic cases of slave suicide occurred in 1786 when a woman named Sarah living near the country town of Swellendam murdered her four children by throwing them into a river before jumping in after them to drown. Her motive was that her partner (slaves were not legally entitled to marry at the Cape), a male slave on a neighboring farm, had recently died by accidental drowning. Sarah did not want her children or herself to live without the protection of her partner and in her grief chose the same death as her lover. Her body was taken from the river and, in the absence of trees in the vicinity, placed by company officials on a plank for exposure so that the spectacle would be a disincentive to other slaves considering such desperate acts.[41] The dead children in this case were not subjected to the same punishment. This is extremely significant, as the company realized that slave women used suicide and various forms of child murder to escape not only their own enslavement, but also that of future generations. Because slave reproduction at the Cape was very low, these acts attacked the very heart of slavery and property at the Cape.[42]

There do not seem to have been the same discussions about diabolical intent in slave suicides as there was in the case of Sara, the Khoekhoe woman. The question of diabolical intent was not ultimately related to postmortem punishment in the case of suicide. The defiling of criminals' bodies was meant to be an obvious lesson to all who bore witness to this form of judicial punishment. Worden estimates that there were about fifteen to twenty attempted or successful slave suicides every year at the Cape. These peaked at certain periods, such as in the 1730s and 1740s and again in the 1780s, when labor demands on slaves increased significantly. Male slaves who bore the brunt of the heaviest work were more likely to commit suicide to end their lives in these periods. Jan, the slave of the Stellenbosch farmer David Heufke, said outright before he inflicted a fatal stab wound to his own head: "I wish to die or be sold, because I cannot keep working."[43] There are multiple cases in the Cape archival records of slave men so exhausted that suicide appeared to be their only hope for rest. There are also several cases where male slaves murdered their lovers in jealousy and then killed themselves. This was again a feature of Cape society, where women were in such a minority that competition over partners often boiled over into violence against rivals or, more commonly, against the women themselves. In one such case in Stellenbosch, a slave who attacked his lover ran into the fields to kill himself. The officers of justice had to drag his body by the feet and leave it exposed on the ground because of the lack of trees on which to hang his corpse.[44]

The self-awareness of the state of enslavement among slaves as a motive for suicide could be further complicated by the wish to damage one's master without actually inflicting physical injury on him or her. In the most extreme case of this motive, a male slave in Cape Town murdered a friend who was enslaved in the same household. He was brought to trial for murder but, when interrogated, confessed that he had committed the crime as an alternative to attacking his master, because in this way he could deprive his master of two slaves. The slave claimed that his master was so avaricious that purposefully inflicting such a huge financial loss on the man would cause greater pain than physical injury and would endure for the term of his natural life. The slave was duly executed for murder, but it is clear that he actually used the legal system to his own advantage and, in a sense, had committed suicide and robbed his master. Robert Shell calls slave suicide and the recognition by slaves of their status as property a form of "exquisite revenge." The slaves "were secure in their knowledge that the owner, bereft of slave property, would in all probability sink economically and certainly sink in status. In the Cape slave society, with its well-defined code of honor, itself a derivative of slavery, no revenge could be more exquisite."[45]

Slaves also committed suicide in detention while awaiting trial, thereby thwarting the intentions of company law in terms of judicial procedures designed to extract a confession before sentencing. In 1746, September and Sibella, who appear to have been a slave couple, hanged themselves in their cells before the court could convict them of escape and the murder of another slave.[46] The court officials were incensed by this presumptuous act. Because they cheated the company out of the imposition of justice, their bodies were dragged through the streets by the feet and hung upside down in the gallows.[47] Graham Botha claims this was a direct application of Roman law, which decreed that the body of a suicide be "placed on a hurdle and dragged by an ass through the streets to the place of execution and hung upon a gibbet as carrion."[48] This punishment was common for suicides throughout Europe. But at the Cape, the exposure of bodies as judicial punishment was often carried out at the spot where the crime had been committed or where the spectacle of the defiled body would have had the most impact, like at the crossroads entering the town itself.

CULTURAL DIFFERENCE AND SUICIDE IN COMPANY LAW

The cultural relativity of suicide was not a primary part of the debate on suicide within Europe. However, it was recognized that there were other forms of suicide that did not conform to any social equivalent in Europe. Such was the case with "amok" (commonly incorporated into English as "running amuck or amok"), which first entered into English in the early sixteenth century to mean a form of murderous frenzy committed by Malays: "That all those which were able to bear arms should make themselves Amoucos, that is to say, men resolved either to dye, or vanquish."[49] Amok does not appear to have been incorporated into the philosophical or theological treatises on self-murder, but it was acknowledged as a culturally specific form of murder. Amok was known during this period as being defined by both ethnicity and gender. Only Malay or Javanese men committed amok, and when they did so, it was an act of murderous rage that could be stopped only by the death of the perpetrator through suicide or the infliction of death by another. In that sense, amok was recognized as a murderous suicidal rage.

This crime was defined under Malay legal codes in Southeast Asia and included the exemption from judicial punishment of anyone who killed an amok. It was incorporated into the Dutch East India Company's legal codes in the edicts or proclamations that applied throughout the empire.[50] In that sense, it was one of the only indigenous crimes recognized under company law but was still defined by gender and ethnicity. Although amok was a rare event, its reputation was widespread, and the fear of amok was ever present in the company settlements that contained Malay free populations or Malay slaves. At the Cape, with its reputation for brutality, amok was a constant fear among Europeans. By the late eighteenth century, this had led the Cape Company authorities to try to ban the importing of Malay male slaves into the colony as a form of public protection. "Without any apparent cause, on these occasions, they would rush into the streets armed with short-handled krisses or knives, crying out 'Amok! amok!' and slashing, hacking, cutting at every person they met until they themselves were overpowered or killed. . . . To these Malays, amok-running was the national and honourable way of committing suicide."[51]

This appeal for a ban on the importing of Malay men by the Cape was precipitated by a case of amok that shocked the entire town. The company relied on Asian exiles and convicts to form the ranks of the executioner's assistants and the night patrol that constituted the Cape's nascent police force. In an inversion of colonial authority, these men, known as caffers, were the ones who inflicted minor corporal punishment and assisted the executioner with more rigorous forms of torture and execution. They also assisted in arrests and could chastise Europeans in public for breaking minor rules (like smoking in the streets), a matter of great annoyance on the part of the colonists who resented the imposition of authority by these Asian convicts and exiles under the command of the company. It is possible that convicts and exiles accepted being assigned as caffers to improve their chances of being pardoned and sent back home; they were therefore mostly compliant in their duties for the company. The denial of pardon and repatriation appears to have been the motive behind the case of amok at the Cape by the convict Soera Brotto, probably a Javanese man of moderate social rank, who was sentenced to indeterminate banishment from Batavia in 1772.[52]

Edna Bradlow has analyzed the case of amok by Soera Brotto within the dichotomy of "mental illness or a form of resistance."[53] Soera Brotto began his sentence at the Cape in 1781 as a general laborer but was promoted to the ranks of the caffers in 1786. When the Cape's governor refused Soera Brotto's request to be repatriated to Batavia for services rendered, the incensed man felt he had nothing to live for and soon after armed himself with several knives. He attacked his European superior officer and ran amok in town, killing seven men and wounding another ten. Significantly, Soera Brotto did not attack a single woman; his anger was targeted at men. A day later, having terrorized the whole town, he was eventually arrested by a group of soldiers and was taken to court already dying of a severe head wound. Soera Brotto, who was too incoherent to confess or answer charges, was immediately convicted and taken to the place of execution where he was broken on the wheel; while he was still alive, his right hand was cut off and his heart was cut out of his body, whereupon he was hit in the face with both hand and heart. He was then decapitated and quartered; his body parts were dragged through town and then displayed on poles at prominent street corners.[54] The Council of Justice at the Cape wielded its full force in the punishment of this crime as a lesson to other Malays and in retribution for the damage he had inflicted on the community.

Soera Brotto was recognized as having run amok, but what had triggered his outrage was probably a cultural misinterpretation by the caffer of his terms of bondage. He believed that his debt had been sufficiently repaid and demanded his freedom, as would have been the case under Malay law, where he probably would not have been subject to perpetual bondage. When he was denied his freedom, he invoked a cultural response that declared his rejection of company law and society. From the moment he chose amok, Soera Brotto knew he was doomed to die.

CONCLUSION

Judicial torture and the punishment of suicide in Europe vacillated from the sixteenth century to the end of the eighteenth century. The spectacle of public corporal punishment was becoming rarer in Europe, as was the public punishment of suicide. This was not the case at the Cape. The criminalization of suicide, the infliction of judicial torture and public execution, and the bodily defilement of suicides remained in operation at the Cape for the entire Dutch period. This form of state control, however, was mitigated through status, race, and gender. But like the early Tudor state, the company was notorious for profiting monetarily by the imposition of its own legal system in the form of fines, withheld wages, and the awarding of various court costs. The executioner, a company servant, was paid at "piece work" rates according to the act performed. When the Cape was conquered by the British at the end of the eighteenth century, the leading colonists were consulted about reforms to the justice system.

They replied that judicial torture and public execution were necessary to instill a proper degree of terror among the lower classes, particularly slaves. However, the British chose to abolish judicial torture and the most spectacular forms of public execution. John Barrow states in his travel account of the Cape that

> the fate of the other hangman was singular enough: On hearing that the abolition of the rack and torture was likely to take place, he waited upon the chief magistrate to know from him whether it was the fashion among the English to break on the wheel. A few days after this he was found hanging in his room. It was thought that the fear of starving, for want of employment, on account of his having held such an odious office, had operated powerfully on his mind as to have led him to the perpetration of self-murder.[55]

The suicide of the executioner marks the symbolic end of a disciplinary regime based on judicial torture and spectacular forms of public corporal punishment, execution, and the defilement of dead bodies (including suicides) at the Cape of Good Hope. The end of Dutch East India Company rule brought the Cape into the orbit of the emerging British Empire, where debates were emerging in the metropole over the morality of slavery and the slave trade by the end of the eighteenth century. Nevertheless, this transition did not mean the end of judicial execution, slavery, or suicide at the Cape. Slave suicide remained a major form of resistance at the Cape until emancipation. Surprisingly, over the course of the nineteenth century, amok became a much less ethnically specific act and shaded into a form of temporary insanity with which individuals of different ethnicities could be inflicted. This complex cultural configuration of attitudes toward suicide was particularly apparent in colonial situations. In the region of the world that became known as "the West" in this period, suicide emerged as a distinct field of scientific study. Foucault identifies this transition of the social significance of suicide in terms of the power of the state over the bodies of its subjects:

> It is not surprising that suicide—once a crime, since it was a way to usurp the power of death which the sovereign alone, whether the one here below or the Lord above, had the right to exercise—became, in the course of the

nineteenth century, one of the first conducts to enter into the sphere of sociological analysis; it testified to the individual and private right to die, at the borders and interstices of power that was exercised over life. This determination to die, strange and yet so persistent and constant in its manifestations, and consequently so difficult to explain as being due to particular circumstances or individual accidents, was one of the first astonishments of a society in which political power had assigned itself the task of administering life.[56]

Foucault and other scholars who have examined suicide have done so with more or less of a Eurocentric perspective. However, the debates over suicide during the early modern period coincided with the first period of European imperialism and colonization, as well as with the rapid expansion of European-driven slave trading and slavery in the colonies. While debates over suicide raged as a theological, moral, and ethical issue in early modern Europe, in the slave colonies or in encounters with other cultural attitudes toward suicide, different considerations about motive and meaning of the act had to take place. Nevertheless, at the Cape of Good Hope, the Dutch East India Company officials punished suicide in a way that was consistent with the most conservative practices in Europe. In doing so, they were not only acting on theological arguments but also demonstrating to others, particularly in the case of slave suicides, that this course of action would not end the state's ability to control the fate of their bodies. They were not able, however, to control either suicide or amok among their unfree subjects. Although company officials at the Cape did not discuss the cultural translatability of their actions, they relied on the horrific spectacle of defiling dead bodies as being an obvious warning and an ultimate show of power of the state.

NOTES

1   Minois, *History of Suicide*, 202.
2   Beccaria, *Of Crimes and Punishments*, 96.
3   Thanks to Pamela Scully for insightful comments on this chapter. Thanks

also to Gerald Groenewald and Nigel Worden for assistance and archival references to suicides at the Cape, and to Eva Haverkamp, Michael Maas, Laura Mitchell, Steven Pierce, Carol Quillen, Anu Rao, Allison Sneider, Martin Wiener, and the participants of the April 2003 "Complexity" workshop at the University of Michigan, Ann Arbor, for advice and readings. Any mistakes are, of course, my responsibility.

4 In what is arguably his most famous narrative passage, Foucault opens *Discipline and Punish* with an excruciating three-page description of the execution of the regicide Damiens on 2 March 1757, startlingly juxtaposed with Léon Faucher's precisely regimented daily routine for the "House of young prisoners in Paris" from the 1830s. This dramatic use of contrasting cases summarizes his argument about the shift in disciplinary regimes "from being an art of unbearable sensations punishment has become an economy of suspended rights": Foucault, *Discipline and Punish*, 3–11.

5 Foucault has been criticized for this sleight of hand with the historical evidence on execution practices from the early modern era. Pieter Spierenberg argues that the transition between disciplinary systems was much less clear-cut and that older practices persevered alongside the evolution of new theories of crime and punishment: Spierenburg, *The Spectacle of Suffering*, viii.

6 Foucault, *Discipline and Punish*, 7. Rao and Pierce, "Discipline and the Other Body," 159–68.

7 Stoler and Cooper, "Between Metropole and Colony," 28–30.

8 Elphick and Giliomee, *The Shaping of South African Society, 1652–1840*; Keegan, *Colonial South Africa and the Origins of the Racial Order*; Newton-King, *Masters and Servants on the Cape Eastern Frontier*; Penn, "The Northern Cape Frontier Zone, 1700–1815"; Ross, *Cape of Torments*; Shell, *Children of Bondage*; Ward, "The Bounds of Bondage"; Worden, *Slavery in Dutch South Africa*.

9 Ross, *Cape of Torments*, 2.

10 De Kock, *Those in Bondage*, 184.

11 McVay, "I Am the Devil's Own."

12 Ward, "The Bounds of Bondage," 224–74.

13 Van Deursen, *Plain Lives in a Golden Age*, 25.

14 The prosecution of suicide among the nobility was apparently crown policy during the early Tudor period in England. With a system of inheritance based

on primogeniture, the male head of household owned all of the property, and his suicide could plunge his entire family into poverty: MacDonald and Murphy, *Sleepless Souls*, 24.

15   *Hamlet*, act 5, scene 1, as quoted in Minois, *History of Suicide*, 146.

16   MacDonald and Murphy, *Sleepless Souls*, 32.

17   Ibid., 34.

18   Ibid., 109.

19   Minois, *History of Suicide*, 67.

20   MacDonald and Murphy, *Sleepless Souls*, 17.

21   *Hamlet*, act 3, scene 1, line 1. G. R. Hibbard, ed. Oxford World Classics. *The Oxford Shakespeare* (Oxford: Oxford University Press, 1998), 322.

22   MacDonald and Murphy, *Sleepless Souls*, 160.

23   Minois, *History of Suicide*, 137.

24   Biewenga, *De Kaap de Goede Hoop*, 211–66.

25   Minois, *History of Suicide*, 140.

26   *Oxford English Dictionary*, 2d ed. (1989), s.v. "suicide." The word "suicide" entered the English language in the mid–seventeenth century but did not come into common usage until a century later.

27   Minois, *History of Suicide*, 210.

28   Ward, "Imperial Discipline," 1.

29   Raben, "Batavia and Colombo."

30   Blussé, *Strange Company*.

31   For an extended discussion of gender, suicide, and the Khoekhoe at the Cape, see Kerry Ward, "Sara's Suicide: Gender and Ethnicity at the Cape," Rice University, work in progress, November 2005.

32   Shell, *Children of Bondage*, 46–48.

33   Newton-King, *Masters and Servants on the Cape Eastern Frontier*, 5.

34   Worden, *Slavery in Dutch South Africa*, 112–13.

35   Ibid., 136.

36   Ibid., 134–35.

37   Ibid., 136.

38   Whiting-Spilhaus, *The First South Africans and the Laws Which Governed Them*, 129.

39   Pamela Scully's research on infanticide at the Cape at the end of the slave

era speaks to the dilemmas of child rearing for slave and former slave women: see Scully, *Liberating the Family?* esp. 134–52.

40 Worden, *Slavery in Dutch South Africa*, 59.

41 Raad van Justitie, Inkoomende Brieven, 1785–86, State Archives: Cape Town, South Africa, CJ [Court of Justice] 1489 Deel [Volume] 5, 59–61. I thank Nigel Worden and Gerald Groenewald for archival extracts on slave suicides.

42 Shell, *Children of Bondage*, 442.

43 Notarieele Verklaringen 1706–14, Cape Archives 1/STB 18/155.

44 De Kock, *Those in Bondage*, 184.

45 Shell, *Children of Bondage*, 397.

46 Heese, *Reg en Onreg*, 256, 258.

47 Botha, *General History and Social life of the Cape of Good Hope*, 289.

48 Ibid., 289.

49 *Oxford English Dictionay*, 2d ed. (1989), s.v. "amok." The entry defines "amok" as "a name for a frenzied Malay, . . . a murderous frenzy, the act of running amok." The first reference comes from a circa 1516 translation of *Barbosa*, in which "amuco" is used as a noun or an adjective.

50 Van der Chijs, *Nederlandsch-Indisch Plakaatboek, 1602–1811*.

51 De Kock, *Those in Bondage*, p. 195.

52 Ward, "The Bounds of Bondage," 254.

53 Bradlow, "Mental Illness or a Form of Resistance?"

54 NA, Dutch East India Company (VOC) 10805, 24–27 September 1786. Bradlow, "Mental Illness or a Form of Resistance?" 8–12.

55 Barrow, *An Account of Travels into the Interior of Southern Africa in the Years 1797 and 1798*, 44–45.

56 Michel Foucault, "Right of Death and Power over Life," in idem, *The History of Sexuality, Volume 1*, 138–39. Foucault is referring to Durkheim, *Suicide*. Originally published in French 1897, *Suicide* was the first sociological study of suicide, and it remains a seminal text that is still a major focus of analysis: See, for example, Pickering and Walford, *Durkheim's* Suicide. The modern study of suicide has metamorphosed into its own field of study—suicidology—which is a recognized interdisciplinary field incorporating the disciplines of sociology, criminology, psychology, psychiatry, medicine, philosophy, religion, and literature, to name but a few. See Leenaars, *Suicidology*, 4–5.

SHANNON LEE DAWDY

※

The Burden of Louis Congo and the Evolution of Savagery in Colonial Louisiana

In 1725, Louisiana officials freed an African slave named Louis Congo and appointed him public executioner. For at least twelve years, Louis Congo was the only man in the colony invested with the power to whip, brand, amputate, break, and hang subjects, be they white, Indian, or fellow Africans. His appointment to this position was a local innovation to the metropole's Code Noir that supposedly ruled the ways in which whites and blacks, slave and free, were to interact in the French colonies. The rationale behind Congo's selection is unknown, but the power he held to whip or hang Frenchmen seems to symbolize the near equivalence of black slaves and poor whites before absolutist law. This symbolic equation served a colonial state that at first worried more about mutinous whites (many of whom arrived as convicted laborers) than about unruly slaves. During the early period of French colonial rule in Louisiana, the punishments meted out to white and black offenders for similar crimes were comparable. Subsequently, Louisiana witnessed two major shifts in the balance of colonial power—the first from loyal French and Canadian administrators to a set of self-interested Creole merchant-planters in the 1740s and the second from the Creole slaveowners to a corps of lawabiding Spanish officials in the 1770s. Each shift in colonial power in Louisiana was accompanied by a different pattern in race and punishment exemplifying the conflicts and constituencies that fractured colonial rule.[1]

Louis Congo appears numerous times in Louisiana's surviving civil and criminal records. It is clear that he was well known in the local community and well connected with the colonial administrators on the governing Superior Council. Following Louis Congo's unrecorded death or retirement in the late 1730s or early 1740s, his duties fell to a shifting set of anonymous white functionaries who appear not to have had the same prominent role in the community. Paralleling this change in the role of the executioner was a significant shift in the pattern of punishment in the 1740s to one in which public punishments for black and white offenders began to differentiate and to exaggerate the differences between black and white bodies. This occurred during a period when contemporaries complained that the metropole had "abandoned" Louisiana. As a result, the Superior Council became stacked with native-born (or Creole) slaveowners who often acted in violation of metropolitan directives. The increasingly brutal exemplary punishments they meted out to slaves in New Orleans's public square seemed designed to make black bodies appear more "savage" by barbaric dismemberment. Under Spanish rule (1769–1803), the colonial state once again intervened between slaveowners and slaves, reserving the right to administer corporal punishment and meting it out with relative restraint. But when an interracial conspiracy in 1795 threatened to topple both slaveowner and imperial power, "justice" once again swung toward gruesome spectacle. In that year, the road from Pointe Coupée to New Orleans was lined with posts topped with the severed heads of African and Afro-Creole rebels.[2]

The strategies employed under Louisiana's French (1699–1731), Creole (1732–68), and Spanish (1769–1803) regimes reveal the tensions between two major powers in the colonial scene: imperial governments committed to maintaining territorial gains at minimal cost and major slaveowners committed to maintaining their hold over slaves and maximizing their investment. In Louisiana, first the French and later the Spanish colonial governments used the law to insert themselves as mediators between slaveowner and enslaved in the disciplinary regime. By law, corporal punishment of slaves such as torture, severe flogging, branding, mutilation, or execution could be meted out only by the state, which also intervened when owners abused their slaves. The specter of slave revolt and colonial rebellion haunted colonial policy long before the Haitian Revolution, and many strategies were aimed at checking the excesses of slaveowners that might provoke a coordinated reaction. In 1731, France virtually abandoned Louisiana and allowed Creole slaveowners to take the reins of power through the Louisiana Superior Council.[3] As a result, from that period until 1768 (when the Spanish once again imposed a degree of imperial control over the colony), slaveowner justice and state justice were essentially the same.

Locally, this paper builds on two questions: What was the significance of having a black executioner in a colonial slaveholding society? and, How do we understand the development toward increasingly "savage" forms of corporal punishment inflicted on black bodies over time in colonial Louisiana? Globally, the story of colonial justice and race in Louisiana helps underscore a common tension of empire. In many cases, the colonial state was neither the sole arbiter of racial categories nor even the party most interested in creating these divisions. In answer to the first question, I believe the example of Louis Congo demonstrates that in some situations an exaggerated racial hierarchy could be considered by some strategists as counterproductive to the colony's efforts to control unruly European immigrants. Louisiana provides a complicated example that reminds us not to assume any simple alignment of colonial power along the lines of race or to automatically equate corporal punishment with the interests of the state. Political imperialism and economic imperialism are often at odds, and it is not always clear in whose interest the categories of race are being deployed. As a result, the categories themselves are not always clearly articulated. In answer to the second question, the two moments that seemed to propel colonial justice in the direction of exemplary brutality toward black subjects in both cases were moments in which the interests of the state and the interests of the labor regime clearly intersected. In the 1740s, slaveowners *were* the government. In the 1790s, an interracial conspiracy threatened to topple both the system of slavery and the sovereignty of Spain over the colony.

In what follows, I break down the local story of law and discipline in colonial Louisiana into four sections: the legal backdrop of the Code

Noir; the early French period of Louis Congo; the interregnum of Creole slaveowner rule; and the Spanish regime.

A CODE NOIR

Laws, policing, and punishment were among the bluntest instruments of metropolitan control over the colonies. In the early period, much of Louisiana's civil code and criminal procedure arrived as a direct import from France. However, Louisiana law and order departed from French models in at least four important ways. Two changes were intentional; one seems to have resulted from a planning oversight; and the fourth appears to have been a local innovation. The first contrast arose from the most dramatic demographic and legal difference between France and Louisiana: the presence of slaves. In writing the Code Noir, crown advisers tried to anticipate new categories of crimes and problems arising from the quasi-subjecthood of slavery.[4] Learning from experiences in Saint Domingue, they made significant changes in the Louisiana version of the law. The second intentional modification made by metropolitan planners was to legislate lawyers out of the colony. In doing so, they hoped to curtail civil suits and challenges to royal authority. A third important difference between France and Louisiana may have been unintentional. Louisiana's social engineers failed to provide for an institutional police system. In France during the eighteenth century, police forces and policing technologies were rapidly expanding, but in New Orleans, law enforcement was ad hoc and understaffed.

The fourth deviation involved using black men to administer state discipline against offenders of all colors. This appears to have been a local innovation. It is this improvised strategy of rule that I am interested in understanding, as well as its abandonment during the Creole regime. What does the selection of a black executioner say about race and status in early Louisiana? What does it say about the local administration of power? In the Creole generation, local slaveholders took the experiment further into their own hands, selectively enforcing the Code Noir according to common practice and writing new amendments.

Comparing Louisiana's Code Noir of 1724 with its predecessor written for Saint Domingue forty years earlier illustrates how French ministers built up knowledge of their colonies and adjusted their tactics with each new venture.[5] It specifically shows that the state was simultaneously moving toward a greater consideration of slaveowners' interests and a more sharply defined color line. The authors of Louisiana's slave law based it on the 1685 Code Noir of Saint Domingue, but they made several changes in the content and language of the code. Seven out of the sixty original articles were dropped or recombined; four articles were substantially modified; and two new articles were added.[6] Three new or revised articles addressed forms of punishment. One made the status of free people of color much less secure by adding a new punishment: Freed slaves or freeborn people of color who gave refuge to runaways could be returned to slavery.[7] Another new article gave permission to owners of fugitive slaves to search for them wherever they might be and to take whatever actions they deemed appropriate to regain them, granting slaveowners a significant new police power.[8] Finally, one new article prescribed specific punishments for transgressing slaves and who would mete them out. "*Juges ordinaires*" of the local jurisdiction could administer whippings, brandings, and ear cutting as a last resort, while only the Superior Council in New Orleans could order executions or hamstringing. Masters were prohibited from directly administering any of the more severe corporal punishments.[9]

With the Louisiana Code Noir of 1724, ministers attempted to design an "improved" slave society that did three things: made slavery more permanent by narrowing the chances for manumission; drew a starker color line between white and black by delegitimizing any kind of *métissage*; and intervened in the master–slave relationship in the area of corporal discipline. A major purpose of the first two changes appears to have been to prevent rapid growth in the free colored population, which in Saint Domingue threatened the slavery regime in various ways, most concretely by aiding and abetting maroons.[10] The limits on corporal punishment expressed the worries of Saint Domingue officials that an escalation in violence and abuse perpetuated by individual owners and managers threatened to unleash a slave revolt that would topple the entire colonial endeavor. But the attempt to control racial slavery and its social consequences through legal instruments was a clumsy science.

Metropolitan planners had intended the Code Noir to serve the colony as a legal code that would preserve the volatile balance of power in a slave society. On the ground, the code was selectively enforced, at best, and often rewritten by local ordinances or ignored altogether in judicial proceedings. The crown had never granted the local colonial governing body (the Louisiana Superior Council) legislative powers, yet it began issuing ordinances in the mid-1730s. As a result, the government of Louisiana became less representative of France's interests and more representative of local interests: "The king's will did not prevail. . . . The Superior Council had never functioned in the manner prescribed by royal law, and in its mature stage it differed radically from the institution designed by the French Crown."[11] A returning colonial secretary reported to the court in 1758: "The marked independence of the inhabitants has always been their greatest vice, and the group which should be the instrument for the maintenance of the king's authority [the Superior Council] acts in truth just like the others. From this spirit of independence in all the classes, there come cabals, intrigues, and muttering."[12] These independent-minded and bickering colonials, most of whom were also major slaveowners, enforced the Code Noir selectively and improvised new strategies of rule.

LOUIS CONGO

In the area of corporal punishment, Louisiana officials acting for the crown made an innovation in the administration of colonial justice through an inversion of the perhaps expected relation of white and black bodies. Their tactics underscore how in eighteenth-century New Orleans the tools of power were experimental. Although the Code Noir specified a few specific punishments to be meted out to slaves for particular offenses, neither France nor its colonies yet possessed a universal criminal code that provided a predictable calculus between crime and punishment. Sentencing was at the discretion of the attorney general (the King's representative) and the judges on the Superior Council. Property crimes were typically punished by fines, jail time, flogging, or beating (*battre de verges*), or by a sentence to galley servitude, depending on the severity of the crime and the status of the offender. Assaults were often treated as a civil offense, not a criminal offense (being a form of insult), and so were rarely punished corporally. Desertion, marooning, and mutiny were treated with severity in the colony, as, of course, was murder. French thieves, smugglers, and deserters were often branded with a fleur-de-lys or the appropriate letter of the alphabet—a punishment extended to slaves and expanded to include hamstringing and amputation. Offenders receiving capital punishment in the early days were either hung on the scaffold or keelhauled, but over time, breaking on the wheel seemed to gain favor. Torture was still an accepted form of judicial examination in the eighteenth century. As in France, authorities in Louisiana rarely applied corporal punishment and torture to the noble and bourgeois elite, whatever the offense, although several served long prison sentences in the New Orleans jail.[13]

What did it mean that, in Louisiana's early years, a freed African slave named Louis Congo administered these punishments to European as well as to Indian and African offenders? I see three possibilities for the intentions behind Congo's selection: (1) he could be used to demean unruly white subjects symbolically, demoting their status below that of a black man and creating a deliberate ambiguity as to who was "enslaved" within the absolutist state; (2) he was selected because only a man of the lowliest station wishing to escape forced servitude would perform the function willingly and effectively; and (3) his selection was part of a "divide-and-rule" strategy that would promote resentment within the slave community and antagonism between Afro-Louisianans, Native Americans, and Euro-Louisianans. The evidence suggests that all of these rationales were at work.

The first instance of interracial corporal punishment in 1720 preceded both Congo and the large-scale importation of Africans to Louisiana by several years.[14] In 1720, the court-martial sentence of a soldier convicted of robbery specified that he was "to be whipped by a negro for three days" before beginning his term in the galleys.[15] The vagueness of the sentence suggests that just about any "negro (*nègre*)" would do, and the fact of his color was intended to add racial insult to injury on white subjects.

In November 1725, this form of black-on-white justice was formalized when Louisiana officials reported back to the Ministry of the Marine that they had appointed a "nègre" named Louis Congo "*exécuteur des hautes oeuvres*."[16] They freed Congo and his wife from slavery in return for his public service and granted him a small land concession on the outskirts of New Orleans.[17] Louis Congo acted as the colony's public executioner for at least twelve years, from 1725 to 1737. He was the only man in the colony invested with the power to whip, brand, amputate, and torture subjects in the name of the king. His job required breaking men and women on the wheel and hanging them on the scaffold, be they white, Indian, or fellow Africans.

At the time he was "hired" as *l'executeur de haute oeuvres* in 1725, officials were looking for someone to break a man named Coussot on the wheel while another prisoner waited on "death row." The lack of reference to their status suggests that these were free Frenchmen. Later in his career, Louis Congo whipped "at the crossings of this town" a man named Meslun (nicknamed "Bourguignon" because he hailed from Burgundy), a Frenchman who had stabbed a man who had caught him stealing bacon. The whipping proceeded despite the pleading of Meslun's wife, who said her husband was mentally ill and addicted to strong drink. Meslun's sentence states that he was convicted of "faire de violences voyes de fait et coups de couteau." His punishment: "Condamné a etre battu de verges dans les carfours de cette ville par lexecuteur de justice et banny de cette ville a perpetuité" (condemned to be beaten at the crossroads of this town by the executioner of justice and banished from this town forever).[18]

We have detailed records of two executions performed by Louis Congo, although many more were performed during his tenure.[19] In 1728, he hanged an Indian slave named Bontemps for the crimes of "aggravated desertion" and robbery. In 1729, he hanged a European immigrant named Joseph Graff, who had fatally stabbed his business partner.[20] It is also likely that Congo was the executioner who placed eight Bambara slaves on the wheel and an enslaved woman on the scaffold in 1731 for an alleged conspiracy to kill the French and take over the colony.[21] In sum, Congo served as the executioner for the full range of *petits gens* (roughly, common folk) who, from the perspective of local administrators, posed a serious threat to the colonial order.

The fact that Louis Congo was African and a former slave seems to us now imbued with symbolism and irony, but it is much more difficult to read in eighteenth-century terms. Although he embodied the ultimate power of the state over its subjects, his job title did not elevate him to the ranks of the powerful. Probably few Louisianans envied his position. In France, such men were often convicts themselves who had been spared execution or a life sentence in the galleys. In exchange, they became feared pariahs. To call someone a *bourreau*, or executioner, was one of the strongest insults that could be hurled in eighteenth-century French.[22]

Worse than insults, the anger directed at the individual responsible for meting out the state's punishment could be immediate and physical. In 1726, Louis Congo appears in the Superior Council records as a victim of a vicious attack in his home by three runaway Indian slaves. Eleven years later, he was jumped and severely beaten again, this time by two "negro slaves" (one a runaway) near the King's Plantation. Officials took these attacks on their agent of justice seriously. In the first case, the attorney general said that "for a long time now a large troop of Indian slaves have banded together and deserted. Well-armed, they run and thieve around the city and it is feared they plan to do worse. . . . [L]et us punish the deserters with a swift blow, acting with impunity."[23] He then went on to cite Louisiana's newly minted Code Noir, specifying Articles 12, 13, and 32, which he interpreted to mean that the death penalty would be allowed in this case of aggravated desertion. Of course, Louis Congo would be the one to impose this capital punishment on his own attackers.[24] In the 1737 case, Congo and the attorney general appealed jointly to the council, requesting an investigation and punishment to the full extent of the law, as "the life of said Congo would not be secure if such murderous thugs (*assassins*) were tolerated."[25] This attack was probably in retribution for a sentence he had carried out two weeks earlier on a baptized slave named Guala, who had had his ears cut off and a fleur-de-lys branded on his right shoulder. The plantation manager had requested Guala's punishment for the crime of chronic marooning.[26] Congo was a target of Native American and Afro-Louisiana slaves who had witnessed his administration of French justice. Perhaps they viewed him as a key instrument in the enforcement of slavery itself, and as a traitor. We have no record of vengeful attacks on Congo from the French majority of New Orleans, although they were also the subject of his ministrations. The attorney general's interested patronage of Louis Congo may have given pause.

In many of the documents concerning Louis Congo, the writers make a point of identifying his race and status. As this type of identification of free people of color was not habitual in Louisiana's civil records—even in its population censuses—the fact of Congo's color seems to have carried significant meaning for the observers and administrators of justice. Administrators may have advocated this practice as a variation of a general divide-and-rule tactic they deployed to drive a wedge of animosity between the diverse segments of Louisiana's population. Governor Bienville used Native American bounty hunters against black maroons. Governor Périer sent black mercenaries after the Natchez, Chaouchas, and marooning Indian slaves. He wrote explicitly about the "great misfortune which could befall the colony" by a "union between the Indian nations and the black slaves, but happily there has always been a great aversion between them which . . . we take great care to maintain."[27] Using a black executioner against French free subjects suggests that administrators also feared co-conspiracies between poor whites and people of color.

But perhaps more important, this penal strategy in a way "leveled" the colony's petit gens, obscuring the differences between slave and free, black and white. The work of Louis Congo demonstrated to the unruly colonial subject that the government, not biology or even religion, determined who was to be free and who was to be enslaved. This message served absolutism better than statements of indivisible white superiority. Colonial administrators did not hesitate to use the threat of slavery to make subjects submissive. In fact, French *forçats*, or convict laborers, arrived with a legal status somewhat similar to that of black and Indian slaves and were themselves known by the same term, "*esclave*." Many had originally been exiled to the colony as a cheap alternative to Africans.[28] The fact that being the executioner was the lowliest (and perhaps loneliest) position a free man could occupy meant that Louis Congo did not enjoy an elevated status among law-abiding free people. However, those that violated the colonial order would be debased below him. Not only would their bodies receive the castigation of the state; their social being would receive the lash of denigration.

SLAVEOWNER JUSTICE

Louisiana's experiment in interracial punishment worked only to a certain point. After 1737, we find no further mention of a "negro executioner." In fact, patterns in capital punishment applied to white and black bodies begin to diverge around this time, simultaneous with moves by local Creole slaveholders to take the reins of the Superior Council in the 1740s. At the same time that slaveowners were becoming more economically powerful and politically influential, the differences between white and black, and free and enslaved, subjects became better articulated through the actions of the Superior Council, including its administration of justice.

We have detailed court records for nine executions that took place between 1740 and 1752, although the documents fail to mention who carried them out. Two executions were of soldiers: One was by firing squad for the instigator of the famed "Bread Mutiny" (discussed later); the other was a hanging for attempted murder. This soldier had attacked two enslaved women with a bayonet while they were washing clothes in the river. In a separate civilian case, a hanging was performed in effigy for a fugitive innkeeper named Gauvain who had killed an unruly patron in a brawl (if he was caught, the sentence would be repeated on his person).[29]

Enslaved men received the remaining six death sentences for crimes of burglary, murder, and assault. Before his hanging, Jupiter dit Camelle underwent torture to name his accomplices in a burglary spree.[30] François dit Baraca, a baptized man of the "Poulav" nation, was hanged in 1748 for beating his wife to death. After his hanging, the judges ordered his body put on view in New Orleans's public square for twenty-four hours as "an example to others."[31]

By the 1740s, exemplary forms of corporal punishment for slaves and maroons were becoming more dramatic and distinct from penalties imposed on freemen for similar crimes. This trend seems to be related to a movement toward a greater articulation of racial categories among Creoles representing the second generation of settlement. As an example, a 1742 case marks one of the first instances that "*blanc* (white)" was used in a local document to describe a French Louisianan, all the more important in a case that hinged on differential treatment of black-on-white crime. Pierrot dit Jasmin was a runaway who battered a French soldier at the Natchez post so severely that the attorney general considered charging him with attempted murder. Purportedly known as "a bad subject (*un mauvais*)," Jasmin was asked under torture whether he knew that "when a slave raises a hand to a white man it deserved death." He responded that he did. After building a heavy-handed case, the attorney general asked for death by hanging. The Superior Council commuted his sentence to ear amputation, branding, flogging, and a permanent chain around his leg. Perhaps the council thought Jasmin's scars would make a more lasting spectacle than execution.[32] In contrast, the Superior Council treated several white-on-white assault cases in the same period as civil suits or limited the penalties to fines and prison terms.[33]

Charlot Kakaracou, an unbaptized slave of the "Coneda" nation, was condemned for allegedly killing a white soldier who had been poaching in his hunting territory. Kakaracou's 1744 sentencing reads as follows:

> [He is] found guilty of murder, condemned to have his arms and legs broken, and to be broken on the wheel on the public square of this City, on a scaffold erected to that effect, and afterwards placed on a wheel, his face turned towards the sky, to end his life, where his body shall remain for

twenty-four hours. He shall ask pardon before the main entrance of the parochial church of this City where, with a torch in hand, he shall declare that he wickedly murdered the said Pierre Olivy, for which he begs pardon of God, the King and justice.[34]

Even though the council added a marginal note to its official record that "said Charlot dit Cacaracou, after having received all the blows living shall secretly be strangled," Kakaracou's method of execution was among the most horrific applied during the French period. Prior to Kakaracou, executions for individual crimes had been death by hanging.[35] A slave's killing of a white man, even a thieving soldier, represented more than an act of murder; it was an act of sedition.

One caveat to the differential treatment of slaves and free people during this period is the forms of punishment employed against French soldiers, who subsisted at the lowest rungs of free colonial society—in fact, whose status might only generously be termed "free." In 1757, four soldiers mutinied and killed their commanding officer. One committed suicide to escape his sentence; two were broken on the wheel; and a Swiss soldier was placed alive in a coffin and sawed in half. His head and hands were cut off and "his body exposed for a week on the gallows." This exemplary form of justice was even more dramatic than that employed against Kakaracou, perhaps because the social distance between perpetrator and victim was greater in their case than in that of Kakaracou and the poaching soldier, but also because the state feared the crime of mutiny more than the crime of unpremeditated murder.[36]

Around the same time, the Superior Council began to deal with violence *against* slaves more as a private, civil matter and to pull back from the state's role in serving as the disciplinary mediator between slaveowner and slave.[37] In 1747, for example, when a settler with a prior criminal record was convicted of shooting and critically wounding a slave named Touta, the court did not take punitive measures, which had earlier been the practice. It merely ordered the offender to give Touta's owner a replacement slave.[38] Owners who turned over their slaves to public justice were also compensated for their cooperation and the loss of the slave. The Creole government simultaneously stepped back from punishing slaves for lesser crimes, returning slaves to their masters "to have administered such correction as the Master shall judge proper," as was decided in the case of the maroons Mamourou and Bayou in 1748.[39] Instead of the state intervening in the relationship between slave and master, as intended in many parts of the Code Noir, under the Creole regime the colonial government switched to doing what it could to help slaveowners enforce stricter discipline.

Officials also began to implement a new form of punishment for free people of color. The accused could be returned to or reduced to slavery for relatively minor offenses. Whereas in 1722 the free negro La Roze was sentenced to flogging and six years in the galleys for stealing from the company stores (probably the same punishment a white man would have received), in 1743 Jean Baptiste, a twenty-year-old manumitted black man, was returned to slavery for stealing a few items of clothing from his employer. The most interesting case, however, is that of the "*negresse libre*" Jeannette. In September 1746, the council summoned her to appear for the crime of assembling domestic slaves at her house in the city for evening supper parties. The slaveowner-controlled council reprimanded her and warned her not to repeat the offense. A few months later, she appeared in court on vague charges of theft and unpaid debts. The council condemned her to become a slave once more. One suspects that the councilors were alarmed more by the assemblies of slaves and servants at her house than by any irregularities in her accounting.[40] Besides whatever social organizing she was engaged in, she was probably suspected of harboring runaways. In fact, in imposing these re-enslavement sentences on Jean Baptiste and Jeannette, the councilors went far beyond the letter of the Code Noir, which stipulated this form of punishment only for free blacks who abetted runaways, not for those who committed minor property crimes.

Other legal changes under the Creole regime show a growing interest in tightening the controls of slavery. Beginning in 1738, the Superior Council required slaveowners to register a report whenever a slave died or ran away.[41] This death register was designed in part to curb disciplinary excesses by masters and overseers. In these reports, owners carefully justified the "natural" or "accidental" causes of their slaves' deaths.[42] On the other side, a new mandatory register of runaways represented an attempt to gain control over a growing maroon problem along the outskirts of New Orleans. The Superior Council began requiring owners to register runaways so they could be apprehended and punished by the government's agents or other members of the community.[43] The council was attempting to mend a growing rift between large slaveholders, to whom most maroons technically belonged, and smallholders in both town and country whose livelihoods were threatened by maroon thefts and predations. Although the new crackdown seems to have led to a few more captures in 1738 and 1739, Councilor Fazende complained in 1745 that many "Negres Marrons" were still habitually entering the city at night.[44]

The destination of runaways depended on their origin. City slaves ran to the country or to other settlements. Some plantation slaves ran to New Orleans. As early as 1728, the governor complained that runaways were flocking to the city.[45] By that time, the town seems to have reached a size and a diversity that made it possible to blend into the hustle and bustle. Many runaway reports state that a missing slave was suspected to be "somewhere in the city."[46] The runaway Guala (or Guela) had been taken to the city by a "negro belonging to Bienville," where he lived for some time before being recognized and caught.[47] Interrogators of several slaves suspected of a rash of burglaries in the city were particularly interested in ascertaining how well they knew the city. One man could circle the houses of major officials on a map; another disclaimed any regular familiarity with the drinking houses, saying he only went there for the Sunday market.[48] In another case, a mulatto woman named Charlotte ran to the city, where she was eventually caught hiding, half-dressed, in the bed of a ship captain. She offered her captors the large sum of 100 piastres for her release, but they apprehended her anyway. Her owner sued the ship captain for harboring a runaway. For her part, Charlotte requested the opportunity to plead for leniency with the governor's wife on the grounds of her master's abuse and the unfairness of a flogging in such a case. Charlotte was a resourceful person who not only knew the town well, but also knew the discretionary gaps in its system of justice.[49]

Both slaves and slaveowners could use provisions of the Code Noir to their advantage, but they invoked the law selectively. Creole Louisianans declined to enforce many of the code's articles, such as the ban on slaves' carrying guns or weapons, or the ban on concubinage.[50] In his assessment of slave regulation in French Louisiana, Carl Brasseaux writes: "As slave ownership passed into the second generation of native-born Louisianans, slaveholders demanded not only greater personal control over their human property, but a greater degree of submission from their workers, as well. This quiet revolution was waged through the legislative arm of the Superior Council and culminated with the appointment of a Creole slaveholder as attorney general in 1763."[51]

I would only add one caveat. In the streets and fields, the revolution was not so quiet. Rather, it was fought with fists, whips, and words.

THE SPANISH REGIME

When the Spanish empire took over Louisiana in 1768, its representatives attempted to impose a new legal order on the colony, as well as a new and more rigid form of racial classification. Many of the provisions regarding slaves in Spain's colonial laws, like the original Code Noir of the French, were intended to limit the abuses of slaveowners which could provoke a revolt the lightly garrisoned colony would be hard-pressed to suppress. The Spanish seemed bent on re-establishing authority over the slaveholder elite who had taken over the Superior Council during the previous generation. One key way in which they intervened was to introduce new protections for slaves who could now travel to New Orleans to plead a case of abuse against their masters and be juridically resold. They also provided for new and easier paths to manumission and encouraged the growth of a newly identified class of free people of color, complete with their own militia.[52]

Despite the lingering effects of the "Black Legend" of Spanish colonial brutality, both on the minds of eighteenth-century Louisianans and within contemporary historiography, Spanish Louisiana's system of justice appears to have operated in general with greater fairness, regularity, and policing than under the French.[53] Although torture and capital punishment were still employed, authorities practiced relative restraint. Historians have long debated the "Tannenbaum" thesis regarding the perception of better conditions for slaves under late Spanish colonialism in comparison with the French and British systems due to Spain's greater commitment to Catholicism. While there are good reasons to be skeptical about such sweeping evaluations, it is true that, legally, the codes that governed slavery and race relations under the Spanish allowed for greater protection of enslaved subjects, greater concern for their religious status, and more opportunities to escape slavery through manumission. Spanish colonial law was also much more precise about defining race—to the extent of breaking race down into a multiplicity of categories such as griffe, octoroon, quadroon, mulatto, etc. Enforcement, of course, was not automatic, but Spanish authorities in Louisiana did seem prepared to defend slaves against slaveowners.[54]

As the Spanish administrators took over the reins of power in the colony, they attempted to impose a more moderate and predictable justice system, particularly in regard to matching punishment to the crime. The first example of Spanish justice introduced to Louisiana was the case of the Creole conspirators and rebels who ousted the first Spanish governor sent to take over Louisiana. The conspirators were either imprisoned or politely executed by firing squad in 1768. Governor Alejandro O'Reilly decreed that there be no public spectacle of hanging, dismemberment, or breaking on the wheel for the planters, merchants, lawyers, and officials who had committed the high crime of treason. While the status of these men and the delicate diplomatic balance between France and Spain no doubt influenced Spanish prudence, the governor nevertheless became known as "Bloody O'Reilly" among Louisiana locals.

Capital punishments for slaves in the Spanish period seems to have declined for crimes such as theft or aggravated marooning. Death sentences were meted out only in cases in which slaves had raised a hand to, or even murdered, their owners or members of the same class. The trend toward gruesome forms of exemplary punishment that had occurred under the Creole slaveowners' rule circa 1731–68 subsided until near the end of the Spanish period. Even the trial for a slave conspiracy by "Mina" slaves resulted in most of the accused simply languishing in jail while the case twisted around legal and linguistic confusion.[55]

The reaction of Spanish authorities to another conspiracy in 1795, however, represented a near about-face. The justice administered to those accused of involvement in the "Pointe Coupée Conspiracy" was swift and graphic. After nearly half of the fifty-seven slaves accused were hanged, their heads were cut off and placed on poles that lined 100 heavily trafficked miles of the Mississippi from the post of Pointe Coupée to New Orleans. Three white conspirators were flogged and exiled. Many more suspected of Jacobin leanings were forced out of New Orleans.[56]

What had changed? Perhaps the most important context was that the conspiracy occurred shortly after the outbreak of the Haitian Revolution, when convulsions of fear seized slaveowners throughout the Americas. But the Spanish authorities feared something more: a cross-racial alliance among Jacobin freemen and slaves. The conspirators purportedly uttered cries for freedom not only from slavery, but also from Spanish despotism. Although neither the 1790 Mina conspiracy nor the 1768 French Creole rebellion had been a cause for spectacular punishment, the coming together of these malcontent forces in the 1795 conspiracy gripped both imperial strategists and slaveowners. In the face of this joint threat, the state did not hesitate to employ methods of savagery. While the severed heads were clearly meant to warn all who might have considered similar actions, the differential treatment of blacks and whites in the outcome of the trial seems intended to cut a division that had been bridged with revolutionary fervor. There is a way in which the "uncivilized" mutilation of those of African descent reinscribes their supposed savagery in death, as in life. A sort of equation pertains that those who live as savages die as savages. In contrast, the Spanish once again exercised extreme and "civilized" restraint against the white conspirators.

Metropolitan ministers had revised the Code Noir for Louisiana with the intent of creating a more rigid slave society than that of Saint Domingue and to make sure that the practice of slavery did not threaten

France's greater geopolitical ambitions. The outcome of the Louisiana experiment was ambivalent, at best. In 1720, local administrators introduced an innovation in the form of a "negro executioner," who symbolized the near equivalence of black slaves and poor whites before the king's law but also served as a divisive wedge between several elements of Louisiana's enslaved and free peoples. When Creole slaveholders took over the Superior Council in the 1740s, the sentences they handed down began to exaggerate rather than obscure the differences between black and white bodies. They even attempted to make the former appear more "savage" through barbaric dismemberment. The increasingly Creole-dominated Superior Council also introduced new legislation to reinvigorate and amend the Code Noir. In doing so, it stepped outside the powers granted it by the king.

Loyal administrators in early Louisiana manipulated the thin lines between free and enslaved, white and black, to control the colony's unruly petits gens in the interest of the king. By the 1740s, however, local interests overruled those of the king. And local interests—or, at least, those represented on the Superior Council—hinged more on the effective control of slaves than of poor white subjects. Councilors deeply invested in slaveholding took it upon themselves to promulgate laws and reshape legal practices, a privilege usually reserved for the king. They began to draw a deeper line between black and white justice. After the 1740s, punishments for serious crimes by whites such as murder shifted away from exemplary forms such as branding and breaking on the wheel to imprisonment and banishment.[57] For slaves, however, petty theft could be serious enough to merit the public spectacle of capital punishment. The scene shifted again in the 1760s with the arrival of the new Spanish administration. Even more than the original French administrators, Spanish officials attempted to mediate between slaves and slaveholders. Exemplary forms of punishment declined during the peaceful years of Spanish rule. But under the shadow of the Haitian Revolution in the 1790s, Louisiana's colonial authorities abandoned all restraint. The Spanish state resorted to terrorist tactics against Louisiana slaves when some of the former threatened to unite with white Louisiana Jacobins to create a doubly free and independent state.

Louisiana's complexity is not merely a case of the particular. The colony's shifting strategies of racial rule and criminal justice illustrate quivering fluctuations in the "tension of empire" between metropolitan and local interests, between those with political will and those with economic power. The peculiar logic of having a "black executioner," or pretending to torture a man already secretly strangled, cannot be understood outside the colonial tensions that complicate power. Louis Congo was used simultaneously to erase the privilege of race for transgressing whites and to help divide and rule the colony's multiethnic population. Subsequently, gruesome forms of exemplary punishment were used against slaves to reinforce the shared interests of slaveholders and the colonial government—particularly the shared interest in preventing mass rebellion. The Louisiana example suggests that corporal punishment of colonial bodies may evolve into a form of institutionalized savagery especially under conditions in which the labor regime and the imperial regime are ominously in sync.

NOTES

1 The primary context for my thinking about the complications of colonial rule and race is Cooper and Stoler, "Between Metropole and Colony"; Stoler, *Carnal Knowledge and Imperial Power*; idem, "Tense and Tender Ties."

2 For a justification of this periodization and more detail on the "Creole" transition, see Dawdy, "La Ville Sauvage," esp. chaps. 3–4. For other periodizations and accounts of the Spanish period, including some detailed discussions of the Pointe Coupée conspiracy, see Hall, *Africans in Colonial Louisiana*; Ingersoll, *Mammon and Manon in Early New Orleans*; Spear, "They Need Wives"; Usner, *Indians, Settlers, and Slaves in a Frontier Exchange Economy*.

3 For an account of this takeover, see Micelle, "From Law Court to Local Government."

4 Legally, slaves were referred to as property, but they were also considered subjects of the king owed specific protection under the law, such as the right of parents not to be separated from young children and the right to what was

considered a decent minimum of working and living conditions. Under French and Spanish law, it was also considered the responsibility of slaveowners to baptize their slaves and to permit them to observe the Sabbath on Sunday. For discussions of the Louisiana Code Noir, see Brasseaux, "Slave Regulations in French Louisiana"; Spear, "Colonial Intimacies"; Watson, *Slave Law in the Americas*.

5   The influential finance minister, Jean Baptiste Colbert, was one of the principal authors of the 1685 law. Who was behind the Louisiana rewrite is less certain. Overall, the contrasts between Saint Domingue and Louisiana nearly outweigh their similarities, although they coexisted under the same French regime for seventy years. Saint Domingue, established forty years earlier than Louisiana, quickly became a very profitable colony that was fully invested in African slavery and plantation agriculture. Although a group of lower-status European workers (primarily artisans and overseers) were important to the founding of Saint Domingue, the white population was soon dwarfed by the black population by a ratio of 9 to 1. In Louisiana, African slavery did not become significant until almost thirty years after the colony's founding, and the demographic ratio throughout the French and Spanish colonial periods hovered close to 50–50 between enslaved and free people. This colonial population was significantly outnumbered by Native Americans in all except the New Orleans region. The colonial population of the huge territory of Louisiana, at about 15,000, was minuscule compared with that of the tiny island colony of Saint Domingue, which numbered 500,000 in 1788. Finally, Louisiana's economy often struggled and soon diversified into deerskin trading, modest plantation agriculture, smuggling, and subsistence agriculture. Although it was no peaceable kingdom, Louisiana's slave regime did not seem as marked by habitual cruelty as was the case in the tinderbox of Saint Domingue. What all these contrasts mean is that historical actors had difficulty applying any "modal" rules of colonial rule and that historians should similarly be cautioned.

6   Articles 5, 7, 8, 18, 25, and 52 of the 1685 code, "Édit du roi sur les esclaves des îles de l'Amérique, Mars 1685, à Versailles" (hereafter, Saint Domingue), were dropped in the Louisiana version, "Le Code Noir pour les îles de France et de Bourbon, Édit Royal de décembre 1723 [promulgated 1724]" (hereafter, Louisiana). The original Articles 22 and 23 were combined into Louisiana Article 18. The articles that were substantially modified were Articles 9, 22, 39, and 55 (corre-

sponding to Louisiana Articles 6, 18, 34, and 50). Louisiana Articles 33 and 35 were new additions. These royal edicts were published in Duboys, *Recueils de Reglements*, 135–56, and reproduced more accessibly in Sala-Molins, *Le Code noir*. Some articles no longer seemed relevant, such as two that severely restricted the civil life of Protestants. Other omissions or modifications were responses to emerging conditions in the slave societies of the French Caribbean. Two changes marked a move toward self-provisioning of slaves by lifting a ban on Sunday marketing and converting a list of minimum rations owners had to provide to "whatever the Superior Council advises." More dramatic changes had to do with regulating relations between blacks and whites and controlling the free colored population. In the Saint Domingue code, only concubinage between whites and blacks was specifically prohibited; Catholic interracial marriages were tacitly permitted. Further, a free man of any color could marry a slave woman and thereby free her. In contrast, the corresponding Louisiana article forbade marriage between whites and blacks of any station and specified that manumission could result from marriage only in the case of a free black man marrying a slave woman. French ministers modified another article to restrict other routes to freedom. In the original code, masters had the express right to free their slaves without giving a reason ("*sans qu'ils soient tenus de rendre raison de l'affranchissement*"). The Louisiana version, however, dictated not only that masters had to justify manumission, but that they had to obtain the permission of the Superior Council, without which the manumission could be considered null and void. The stated reason was to prevent slaves from committing thefts to raise funds for self-purchase.

7 Saint Domingue, Article 39; Louisiana, Article 34. In the 1685 code, they were simply levied a fine.

8 Louisiana, Article 35: "Permettons à nos sujets dudit pays qui auront des esclaves fugitifs, en quelque lieu que ce soit, d'en faire faire la recherche par telles personnes & à telles conditions qu'ils jugeront à propos, ou de la faire euxmêmes ainsi que bon leur semblera."

9 Ibid., Article 33. Additional articles retained from the Saint Domingue code prohibited the killing or torture of slaves by owners (rights reserved for judicial authorities). These provisions offer a contrast to the practices of slave law in the United States: see Morris, *Southern Slavery and the Law, 1619–1860*.

10   This legal proscription against a population of free people of color may have been one of the reasons Louisianans seemed reluctant to identify free blacks on the census returns.

11   Micelle, "From Law Court to Local Government," 419–20.

12   "Thiton de Silègue au minstre," 12 December 1761, Archives Nationales de France, Archives Coloniale (hereafter ADF-AC) C13A 42, fol. 249; translation from Villiers du Terrage, *The Last Years of French Louisiana*, 102.

13   For further background and discussion, see Dawdy, "La Ville Sauvage," chap. 4.

14   In 1720, only two slave ships had arrived in Louisiana, and Africans were still far outnumbered by Europeans. Most slave ships arrived between 1726 and 1731: Hall, *Africans in Colonial Louisiana*, 59–60.

15   "Court Martial Sentence," 23 February 1720, in "Abstracts of the Louisiana Superior Council Records," *Louisiana Historical Quarterly* (hereafter, SCRA-LHQ) 1, no. 1: 106. He is described only as a "négre" wielding a whip but was probably a predecessor of Louis Congo.

16   "*Exécuteur des hautes oeuvres*" is a hangman, according to Baker, *Cassell's French–English, English–French Dictionary*, 322.

17   "Diary Entries [probably by Delachaise]," 21 November 1725, ANF-AC, C14A9, fols. 267–75. The 1727 census recorded Louis Congo as living on his plot of land along with an associate named M. de Shautes (Des Hautes?) and their wives. They are listed as "negros" and "workmen": Maduell, *The Census Tables for the French Colony of Louisiana from 1699 through 1732*, 95. Gwendolyn Hall notes that Congo had the relatively unusual ability to sign his name to documents: Hall, *Africans in Colonial Louisiana*, 132.

18   For the early case, see Hall, *Africans in Colonial Louisiana*, 131–32, n. 17. Meslun was probably a discharged soldier. He had two nicknames, "Loranger" and "Bourguignon": "Proces criminal," 29 May 1728, Louisiana Superior Council Records (hereafter SCR). See also "Motion for Trial," 22 May 1728, and "Petition of Mercy," 24 May 1728, SCRA-LHQ 4, no. 4: 484.

19   Dozens of additional executions are briefly mentioned in colonial correspondence, many of them court-martial sentences.

20   "Capital Sentence on Indian Slave," 14 June 1728, SCRA-LHQ 4, no. 4: 489; "Petition for Voiding of Will," 20 July 1729, SCRA-LHQ 4, no. 2: 339. Another man,

"*l'executeur dit la Lanceur* (the Launcher, or the Quick One)," performed the first recorded public execution in New Orleans's Place d'Armes. In 1723, a slave named Napi was condemned to hang for killing his wife. The sentence provided that he first be offered baptism. He received a brief stay in the execution because the gallows were still being built: "Condamnation d'un Nègre appartenant à Sieur Delery," 1 October 1723, SCR.

21 Unfortunately, the trial records for this dramatic event in New Orleans are missing from the fragmentary criminal casebooks, although they are mentioned in letters by officials: "Chronologie des mouvements . . . ," 21 and 28 July 1731, ANF-AC, C13A13, fols. 85–93; "Beauchamp to Maurepas," 5 November 1731, ANF-AC, fols. 197–201.

22 Moogk, " 'Thieving Buggers' and 'Stupid Sluts.' "

23 "Il y a longtemps qu'une grande bande desclaves sauvages [lest] attroupes et a desertes courant et volant autour de la ville bien armes et il est a craindre quils ne foment de mauvais coups . . . prié de faire chatier les deserteurs assienant [avec] limpunitié": "Report of Procureur General," 17 August 1726, SCR.

24 Two of them may have been the esclaves sauvages Jean Guillory and Bontemps, remanded to l'executeur de haute justice. He assisted Bontemps to the scaffold, while Guillory received "*battre de verges* (flogging or beating)" in prison: "Condamnation," 14 June 1728, SCR.

25 "La vie de dit Congo ne serait pas en sureté sy pareil assassins etaient tollerés": "François et Louis Déclaration," 24 January 1737, SCR. "Assassin" could mean both killer and ruffian.

26 In response to the question of whether he knew that marooning was punishable, Guala responded: "Quil scait bien mais que son maitre battit beaucoup luy et ne luy donne pas assez a manger": "Interrogatoire de nègre Guala," 10 January 1737, SCR. See also "Procureur General à Conseil," 4 January 1737, SCR; "Condamnation du nègre Gaula," 12 January 1737, SCR.

27 "Mouvements des Sauvages . . . par M. de Périer," January 1731, ANF-AC, C13A13, fol. 87; translation suggested in Hall, *Africans in Colonial Louisiana*, 103. Hall discusses this policy in more detail in ibid., 89–106.

28 Like black and Indian slaves, the labor of *forçats* serving life terms could be bought and sold, and they were subject to the physical discipline of their assigned overseers (the crown being their "owner"). They were also branded with a fleur-

de-lys to mark the permanence of their status. The key difference was that their children did not inherit slavery. During this time in France, the association of skin color with slave status was neither fixed nor exclusive. Sue Peabody's study shows that slavery was not even a stable legal status: Under a customary doctrine that said slavery was illegal in France, black slaves from the colonies who traveled to the metropole successfully sued for emancipation. Only in the late eighteenth century did French law begin to distinguish clearly the status of subjects by race alone. Instead of prohibiting the immigration of slaves, a new law in 1777 prohibited the immigration of *noirs*, thereby stemming the growth of a domestic free black population while preserving the liberty principle: Peabody, *"There Are No Slaves in France."*

29 The documents are complete with autopsy. Justice moved slowly. When the sheriff (*huissier*) went to serve notice on the suspect, his wife reported that he had left the house six or seven days earlier. His sentence was announced several months later, reading, "Pour reparation de quoy pendu et etranglé a une potence qui plantee en la place de cette ville . . . sera executé paré a un tableau qui sera attaché de la ditte potence": "Jugement a Gauvain," 19 April 1741; "Exposé de Cendret," 5 November 1740; "Fleuriau a Conseil," 5 November 1740; "Interrogatoires," 7 November, 1740, all in SCR.

30 "The Bad Bread Mutiny," 12–14 July 1745, SCRA-*LHQ* 14, no. 2: 263–67; "Criminal Trial," 8 June 1752, SCRA-*LHQ* 21, no. 2: 567–73; "Des Essarts," 5–11 November 1740, SCRA-*LHQ* 10, no. 3: 434–35; "Confrontation" 8 February 1741, SCRA-*LHQ* 10, no. 4: 569; "Procureur General's Conclusions," 19 April 1741, SCRA- *LHQ* 10, no. 4: 580; "Criminal Prosecution," 15 February–14 March 1744, SCRA-*LHQ* 12, no. 4: 663–74; "Interrogation," 21 March 1744, SCRA-*LHQ* 13, no. 1: 122–23.

31 "Murder Case," 9 February–4 May 1748, SCRA-*LHQ* 19, no. 2: 471–78.

32 "Interrogé sil ne scait pas que quand un esclave met la main sur un blanc il merite la mort, a repondu qu'il le scait": "Interrogatoire du nommé Pierrot dit Jasmin," 9 January 1742, SCR, fol. 3. The soldier had his jaw broken and eye detached. In his indictment, the attorney general contradicted complaints that black prisoners like Jasmin were starving in the city's jail. One document in the record is clearly a list of questions the attorney general jotted down for Jasmin's interrogation; it includes what has been done to feed him (*travailles·pour sa*

nouriture). Jasmin generally answered a simple yes to most of Fleuriau's questions. Interrogations that did not seem to involve torture generally invited the prisoner to provide a more complete narrative explanation: see "Fleuriau à Conseil," 9 January 1742; "Prise de corps," 9 January 1742; "pour quoy il est prisonnier . . ." 9 January 1742; "Déclaration contre Pierre [*sic*] dit Jasmin," 13 January 1742; "Recollement des temoins contre Pierre dit Jasmin,"16 January 1742; "Confrontations du nommé Pierre dit Jasmin," 16 January 1742; "Information contre Pierre dit Jasmin," 16 January 1742; "Interrogatoire de Pierre dit Jasmin," 16, 20 January 1742; "Requeste de Fleuriau," 20 January 1742; "Condamnation du nommé Pierre dit Jasmin," 20 January 1742, all in SCR.

33 See, for example, documents pertaining to "*Jahan v. Carrière*," 2, 26, and 29 November 1743, SCRA-*LHQ* 12, no. 3: 474–77, and "*Bardon v. Beaupre*," 16 September 1743, SCRA-*LHQ* 12, no. 1: 149; "Judgment," 29 November 1743, SCRA- *LHQ* 12, no. 3: 485.

34 This trial occupied the Superior Council from 15 February to 28 March 1744. The original documents of this case are in poor condition. The translation is a slightly corrected version of what appears in "Criminal Trial of Jupiter," SCRA-*LHQ* 12, no. 4: 662–741; ibid. 13, no. 1: 120–24.

35 The one exception was a sailor keelhauled in the early years for theft. I am here speaking of individual crimes rather than of group rebellions or mutinies, which seemed to demand gruesome spectacle throughout the period, whether the instigators were slaves, Indians, or European soldiers. But even in this area, the punishments meted out to slaves continued to escalate. In 1795, the heads of twenty-three slaves accused of conspiracy to revolt were cut off and placed on posts along the river between New Orleans and Point Coupée. For an account of this conspiracy and the reaction, see Hall, *Africans in Colonial Louisiana*, 343–80.

36 A letter from Kerlérec describing the 1757 mutiny (from a private collection) is quoted in Villiers du Terrage, *The Last Years of French Louisiana*, 86.

37 Brasseaux, "Slave Regulations in French Louisiana." A similar pattern is seen in the British colonies, although they were also in the process of fine-tuning an entirely separate legal code and court process for enslaved criminals, a step that Louisiana did not take until the American antebellum period: Schwarz, *Slave Laws in Virginia*; Spindel, *Crime and Society in North Carolina, 1663–1776*; Watson, "North Carolina Slave Courts, 1715–1785."

38 "*Sens v. Malborough*," 16 December 1747, SCRA-LHQ 18, no. 4: 995; ibid., 1 March 1748, SCRA-LHQ 19, no. 2: 485. The accused, Estienne Daigle *dit* Malborough, had assaulted a roofer and his wife in New Orleans in 1736: "Report in Registry," 19 June 1736, SCRA-LHQ 8, no. 2: 296.

39 "Criminal Session," 24 June 1748, SCRA-LHQ 19, no. 4: 1095–96.

40 Jean-Baptiste and Jeannette probably knew one another well, if they were not family. They had been owned by the same man named Coustilhas, who freed them both in his will. Some outstanding creditors of the estate, however, contested the Coustilhas manumissions, suggesting that Jean-Baptiste's and Jeannette's unusual punishment was actually a shady legal maneuver to settle the estate. Jeanette's original summons is damaged but reads: "que la nommé Jeanette Negresse Libre [unreadable] . . . des assemblies en donnant a souper à plusieurs de Negres esclaves domestiques de cette ville attroupés pendant la nuit": "Jeanette Negresse Libre," 3 September 1746, "Fleurieau à Conseil," 8 April 1747, SCR. On the Coustilhas manumissions, see SCRA-LHQ 19 and 22 August 1743, 10–14 September 1743, 3 September 1746, 8–11 April 1747.

41 These registries were obviously begun in response to a local ordinance now missing from the record, though a similar one for the runaway registry was reissued in 1763.

42 For examples of these, see reports on Jeanneton, "aged about hundred years, a savagess . . . , she died of a lingering illness, having always been infirm," and Marianne, a fifty-year-old Afro-Louisiana woman who "had been ailing with a chronic infirmity": 17 October 1739, SCRA-LHQ 19, no. 3: 753; 25 February 1739, SCRA-LHQ 6, no. 2: 301. One wonders how Jeanneton could have "always been infirm" yet live to be one hundred under the conditions of slavery.

43 Examples of these include Famussa, who ran away from Madame Dalcour "for no cause but the runaway habit," and Fabou, who ran away supposedly out of embarrassment because of a love triangle: ibid., 18 May 1740, SCRA-LHQ 10, no. 3: 414; 25 August 1740, SCRA-LHQ 10, no. 3: 426. Anecdotal evidence supports a rise in marronage during the Creole generation. Bienville sent Native American mercenaries after maroons in the neighboring woods in the late 1730s; one caught was La Fleur, "etoit maron de puis tres longtemps" who preyed on the livestock from plantations below the city. He was interrogated about his "bande," of which Papa Congo, Pierrot, Jeanet, and Québra were members: "Fleuriau à Conseil," 11 April

1738, SCR; "Interrogatoire de la Fleur," 11 April 1738. In 1739, the maroons Antoine and Vulcaine were accused of grand marronage and theft: "Chaperon declaration," 7 November 1739, SCR.

44 "Letter of Fazende," 17 February 1745, SCR. In 1744, there had also been complaints of cattle killing by "les nègres du Roi": "Delisle Dupart Déclaration," 18 May 1744, SCR. So many of the slaves in New Orleans were publicly owned, first by the company of the Indies and later by the king, that this less personal ownership seems to have given slaves an opportunity not only for marronage but also for a degree of autonomy in the city and elsewhere. Many of the "king's slaves" lived on their own, working in various trades. For additional examples of marronage in this period, see Hall, *Africans in Colonial Louisiana*, 143–48.

45 "Périer and Delachaise," 30 March 1728, ANF-AC, C13A 11, fols. 97–100.

46 See, for example, "Cantrelle Déclaration," 15 March 1745, SCRA-*LHQ* 14, no. 1: 96.

47 "Motion, Examination and Sentence of Runaway Slave," 4, 10, 13 January 1737, SCA-*LHQ* 5, no. 3: 386–88.

48 "Interrogations," 9 June 1748–24 June 1748, SCA-*LHQ* 19, no. 4: 1090–96.

49 "Testimonies and Inquiries," 15–24 June 1751, SCA-*LHQ* 20, no. 4: 1122–31.

50 Documents indicate that many slaves had guns for hunting and sometimes for tracking down Indians and maroons. A rare complaint about gun possession involved a slave boy who shot another, but the concern was that the boys were too young for the responsibility: "D'Auseville Declaration," 14 December 1739, SCR.

51 Brasseaux, "Slave Regulations in French Louisiana," 220.

52 Under the French, people of mixed descent lived in Louisiana largely as racially unmarked "habitants" with the rights as people of non-African ancestry. For more on Spain's impact on race and law in Louisiana, see Hall, *Africans in Colonial Louisiana*, 25–260, 304–305; Dawdy, "La Ville Sauvage," 216–21.

53 Kerr, *Petty Felony, Slave Defiance, and Frontier Villainy*.

54 On the Tannenbaum thesis and Spanish approaches to race, see especially Hall, *Africans in Colonial Louisiana*; Hanger, *Bounded Lives, Bounded Places*; Ingersoll, *Mammon and Manon in Early New Orleans*; Spear, "They Need Wives."

55 Although the name probably derives from the slave port of Elmina, Hall says that the "Mina" were a distinct linguistic and cultural group, probably of Ewe

origin. For a more detailed description of the Mina conspiracy and trial, see Hall, *Africans in Colonial Louisiana*, 317–42.

56 I do not here intend to add to Hall's work on unfolding the details of the conspiracy; I intend simply to put the sentencing of the accused into a comparative perspective. For a full account of the conspiracy and the documents associated with it, see ibid., 343–74.

57 For example, René Meslier was convicted of assault and revolt in 1747 and sentenced to the galleys. St. François and his wife were suspected of murder, along with other "scandalous behavior," and were banished to Saint Domingue. Similar crimes by whites committed in the first generation were punished more severely: "Petition and Inquiry," 19–22 April 1747, SCA-*LHQ* 18, no. 1: 183–85; "Petition from Procureur General," 21 September 1763, SCA-*LHQ* 25, no. 4: 1148–49.

ISAAC LAND

"Sinful Propensities"

Piracy, Sodomy, and Empire in the Rhetoric of Naval Reform, 1770–1870

William Meacham Murrell's 1840 memoir relates how, as a common seaman on the U.S. Navy's *Columbia*, he participated in a mission to attack Malay towns in reprisal for pirate attacks on U.S. shipping in Asia. Murrell's eagerness to chastise the Malays was not dampened by their complete lack of resistance. "We met with no obstacle, whatever, to impede us in the work of destruction," he remarks, "which was carried on to its fullest extent; the town being burnt to the ground, leaving nought but a mass of ruins." Targeting a town rather than a pirate vessel did not disturb him, because piratical qualities were inherent in the Malay race as a whole: "This act of vengeance on our part would remind the natives of that retaliation which ever would be taken upon them by all civilized nations" as long as the Malays indulged in that "sinful propensity which they have possessed from the earliest periods." Murrell identified the actions of American seamen with the larger cause of civilization itself, although he noted without irony that the U.S. sailors and marines proceeded to loot the settlements on the shore for personal gain—engaging in a form of piracy of their own.[1]

Murrell's account of the punitive expedition against the Malays forms an important, but relatively short, portion of his book. Much more space is taken up with his critique of the U.S. Navy, which humiliates sensitive and worthy men such as himself with the arbitrary use of the lash. Murrell's patriotism (mindfulness of George Washington's birthday, for example) is juxtaposed against the tyrannical officers (such as the "most properly named" Mr. Turk) who victimize him for insignificant failings such as spilling ink.[2] Murrell insists that this "oriental" despotism is unjust when applied to U.S. citizens. The sensitive sailors of the *Columbia*, who regret that there is so little time aboard ship to gaze at sunsets and contemplate the mysteries of nature, are flogged for moving too slowly. They are hurt and offended by the commodore's abusive language: He "plainly told them that the greater part of them were a set of skulking sons of b——s, and he only wished he could take them back again to Toonkoo bay, where they might die and be d——d."[3] The defenders of civilization, Murrell insists, deserve better than this.

Murrell's complaints about shipboard conditions are ironic, since the U.S. Navy had presented itself in many ways as the dignified and humane alternative to Britain's Royal Navy. The fact that the United States did not practice impressment (violent conscription) was trumpeted as proof that the U.S. Navy was a virtuous republican institution, in contrast to its despotic and arbitrary British counterpart. "Sailors' rights" had been a popular American slogan in the War of 1812 and as such figured in the construction of a national identity. This public image does not square with the record of the U.S. Navy in other areas, such as the issue that particularly incensed Murrell: flogging. The new language of rights and revolution promised a more egalitarian social order, but the bodies of common seamen "before the mast" remained subject to flogging, more or less at the whim of their officers, who inhabited the privileged space of the quarterdeck. For Murrell and other advocates of naval reform, this was institutionalized degradation—the antithesis of republican equality.

Murrell's rhetoric of injured or insulted manhood was certainly not unique. Historians such as Anna Clark, Stephanie McCurry, and Catherine Hall have documented many examples of similar language deployed in populist campaigns against elite privilege throughout the nineteenth century.[4] There is one crucial difference: The embattled masculinities of Chartist agitators or South Carolina yeomen could invoke the patriarchal rights of a head of household. If all *men* were created equal, however, the sailor was a culturally and politically ambiguous figure; he lived in a homosocial community of shipmates that constituted, and reproduced, itself in a way that violated the family metaphor that underlay the modern concept of "nation." By living away from women, he cast doubt on the inevitability of the heterosexual order; if he compensated by having "a woman in every port," this fickle conduct suggested foreign allegiances. Loyalty to his shipmates could result in disloyalty to established authority: He might turn mutineer or pirate. Cannibalism was a common consequence of shipwreck; such sailors made a mockery of European claims to moral superiority by becoming "man-eaters." How could a sailor be a patriot, deserving of a patriot's rights and dignity, when he was triply suspect as a sodomite, pirate, and traitor? In the patriarchal language of the eighteenth-century revolutions, rights pertained to "fathers" in the "fatherland," not to rootless and suspect people.[5]

The first section of this essay outlines how, in the eighteenth century, the ship was construed as a special "wooden world" whose sailor inhabitants enjoyed none of the guarantees associated with metropolitan space. Instead, sailors were to be governed according to the "custom of the sea." This was usually expressed as a desire to protect sailors from themselves (drunken childlike beings in need of strict supervision), but should be considered an effort to protect the integrity of metropolitan culture from seaborne vectors of infection from the periphery. Defenders of flogging argued, in effect, that sailors could transgress in unique ways at sea (piracy) or be especially liable to "uncommon" transgressions (sodomy, cannibalism); these corporal possibilities could be held in check only by forms of corporal discipline that would be considered intolerable in the metropolis. Despite the critiques of tradition in general, and of flogging in particular, that emanated from reformist Enlightenment rhetoric, both Britain's Royal Navy and the new U.S. Navy continued to defend and adhere to the "custom of the sea" well into the nineteenth century.

The second section of this essay examines the efforts of common seamen in Britain and United States to advance the cause of naval reform by reforming their tainted, suspect image. Rather than rejecting the metropole–periphery model, these sailors chose to become complicit in it. The objective of their reformist rhetoric was to reposition themselves as metropolitan subjects. Their case against flogging rested on their "white" identity, which they claimed made them think and feel in an exquisite manner. In songs, petitions, and autobiographies, these sailors identified themselves with the cause of imperial expansion and cast themselves as defenders of white honor on a dangerous frontier. Their enemy was the "mongrel" sailor, the pirate/sodomite, whose outrages on white bodies paralleled other atrocity myths. White sailors proclaimed themselves immune—by virtue of their whiteness—to the corrupting influences of the periphery. Flogging a white sailor was not prudent governance on the imperial periphery but was itself an atrocity against whiteness that cried out for restitution, like the Black Hole of Calcutta or the Alamo massacre. Inevitably, some sailors fell outside the charmed and exclusive circle of whiteness. The third and concluding section of this essay discusses how the sexual, cultural, and political threat represented by the pirate/sodomite was now projected on the bodies of these sailors alone, and efforts to exclude them from metropolitan space and segregate them from white sailors increased accordingly. I discuss the role of flogging in two controversies involving non-white seamen: the administration of the East India Company's Lascar barracks in London, where sailors were beaten for misbehavior without recourse to legal remedies and the Negro Seamen Acts in the southern United States, which banned free black sailors from ports in half a dozen states and subjected them to incarceration and whipping if they defied the law. These incidents demonstrate how the triumph of the reformist rhetoric of "white" sailors led very directly to increasing concern with disciplining the body of the Other sailor.

Despite the republican pretensions of the United States, the sexual politics of naval reform were remarkably similar in the U.S. and Royal navies. Winston Churchill's notorious remark that he could summarize naval tradition as "rum, sodomy, and the lash" spoke very directly to the dilemma facing reform-minded sailors in the eighteenth century and early nineteenth century. For men, rights talk was couched in the language of heterosexual privilege, but such language was not taken seriously if it came from the mouths of sailors. The lash implied sodomy, and vice versa. To escape from this trap, individuals like Murrell chose to make race perform the work of gender in constructing manhood. "Whiteness" was intended to shield sailors from suspicions of sodomy and enable claims to rights that other subordinated males had made based on their head-of-household status. In this essentialist logic, sodomy, piracy, and other "sinful propensities" were actually racial traits. The lash, which had been the symbol of subordination, would now serve to index a hierarchy of privilege.

PERIPHERAL SPACE AND "CUSTOMS OF THE SEA"

> Like some poor ever-roaming horde of pirates,
> That, crowded in the rank and narrow ship,
> House on the wild sea with wild usages.
> —SAMUEL TAYLOR COLERIDGE,
> *The Piccolomini*, act 1, scene 4

Traditional military "justice" in Europe relied heavily on the lash, following the ancient Roman maxim that the soldier should fear his commanding officer even more than he feared the enemy. Most historians attribute the decline of flogging to the French Revolution. Once the French had created the first citizen army—resorting to mass conscription to do so—conservative monarchies such as Britain and Prussia felt that they had no choice but to imitate the populist appeals of the revolutionaries in an effort to raise a force of comparable size. Over the course of the Napoleonic Wars it became increasingly common to refer to soldiers as "the nation in arms." As many historians have observed, this newly inclusive and nationalist rhetoric created the expectation that military service would be dignified and rewarding. In the new era of the citizen soldier, who was represented as a "salt of the earth" character embodying the best qualities of the nation, corporal discipline became far more difficult to justify. The draconian disciplinary practices of the eighteenth century appeared less like a necessity than like an atrocity. There was a general trend toward "investigating," restricting, or actually abolishing flogging in European armies beginning in the 1789–1815 period, and it is striking that the conspicuous laggard, Russia, is the country that adopted mass conscription last of all. The U.S. Army followed a similar path: George Washington was an enthusiastic advocate of extensive flogging in the Army, but in 1812 Congress abolished the practice, reinstating it in 1833 exclusively as a penalty for deserters and terminating even that in 1861.

The language of nineteenth-century nationalism referred obsessively to soil and rootedness; soldiers could, perhaps, be seen as an expression of national landscape (like farms, forests, and mountains), but the metaphor faltered when applied to sailors. The ocean was a subversive landscape, if it qualified at all. Naval officers further slowed the pace of reform by arguing that the unique circumstances of a ship at sea demanded instant obedience from the crew and offered few opportunities for judicial niceties. Imprisoning miscreants would leave the ship dangerously short-handed, and waiting for a court-martial at the voyage's end was not a practical option, either. Traditional European methods of shipboard discipline included starting (smacking with a rope's end), gagging, running the gantlet, and, for severe offenses, lengthy floggings before the assembled crew. Warships routinely carried contingents of armed marines to enforce the captain's will and prevent mutiny. In Britain's Royal Navy, the Articles of War left a great deal of discretion to naval officers regarding what penalties to impose, expecting that they would do what was appropriate according to the (unwritten) "custom of the sea." The U.S. Navy was, from its inception, an Anglophile institution, also relying on marines and the lash to maintain order. Federalist lawyer and future President John Adams noted that draconian military discipline had "carried two empires [Roman and British] to the head of mankind"; his Articles of War did prescribe a limit of twelve lashes per offense but otherwise relied on British precedents. This code governed the U.S. Navy until the mid–nineteenth century.[6]

Unstated, but always implicit, in these codes of military justice was a deep fear about other "customs of the sea." In 1816, when accusations of homosexual acts surfaced on the *Africaine*, a vessel in the Royal Navy, four sailors were hanged and two more received hundreds of lashes. One hundred lashes was generally considered a de facto death sentence.[7] Despite the Admiralty's efforts to brush off the *Africaine* as an aberrant case (a "man-fucking ship"), it was only the most publicized case of sodomy or "unclean" acts leading to ferocious retribution from British naval officers. The U.S. Navy had more success in keeping sodomy cases quiet, but John Adams's meticulous enumeration of crimes and punishments began (Article I) with a sweeping mandate: Commanders were to "guard against, and suppress, all dissolute and immoral practices, and to correct all such as are guilty of them, according to the usage of the sea service."[8] The twelve-lash maximum did not apply to these unspecified crimes. Like Coleridge, Adams tells us that isolation on the "wild sea" leads to "wild usages," but as a lawyer Adams takes this a step further and prescribes a solution: Unmentionable transgressions will be met with indescribable torments, at the captain's whim.[9]

Cannibalism was also commonly acknowledged as a "custom of the sea." Coleridge called the ship "crowded," a wickedly double-edged term that could suggest the homoerotic friction of male bodies at permanent close quarters but, in the event of disaster at sea, could imply anthropophagic cravings and ruthless survivalism. The notorious shipwreck of the French frigate *Méduse*, in which 149 people squeezed onto an improvised raft but only 15 survived, keeping a pile of corpses on board as a food supply, was only one of many heavily publicized cases of "wild usages" at sea. It was difficult for sailors to escape the stigma associated with these stories, not because every vessel was seen as a "man-eating" (or "man-fucking") ship, but because the ship was construed as a "wild" or peripheral space in which such things might happen.[10]

Imperialism sought to justify itself by trumpeting the sinful nature of the conquered (devil worship, sodomy, cannibalism), but Europeans who inhabited the exotic, corrupting "periphery" for any prolonged period could be suborned by it. This helps to explain the long European tradition of labeling piracy the *supreme* criminal act, tantamount to an alliance with the devil. Piracy is, quite simply, theft at sea (or seaborne theft), but it was rarely represented as just a crime against property. The pirate was a traitor to his land of birth—thus rejecting both family and nation in one stroke—and by constituting a new community around the pirate ship's motley crew, jurists maintained that pirates became "enemies of humanity." This diverse body of renegades mocked race-based hierarchies, as well as nationalist myths of blood, soil, and allegiance. Pirates, then, were construed not as mere seagoing bandits but as a community of super-villains united by their intent to systematically break *all* of the laws of God and man.[11]

Piracy and sodomy were construed as closely related transgressions from the early modern period onward. Both were seen as particularly infectious forms of behavior. Accounts of "white slavery" at the hands of the Barbary pirates of the North African coast spun out a trajectory: homosexual rape, conversion to Islam, and, ultimately, a career of piracy against Christian Europe. Like piracy, sodomy was seen as more than a personal failing; it was a transgression against national character. The Royal Navy sought to blame Spaniards for the *Africaine* incident because the alternative was even more disturbing. Yet the suspicion that sailors were all "at it" persisted. The custom of *matelotage*, a formally recognized marriage between two men, was characteristic of some Caribbean pirate communities; the sly commentary contained in this French word, which also meant the art of seamanship (tying knots, knowing the ropes) reminds us that anyone who had learned "the sailor's way" was sexually suspect.[12]

This stigma could just as easily have attached to naval officers themselves, who were always already suspect by virtue of their seafaring vocation. By pinning these crimes on their "brutish" subordinates and placing themselves in the role of civilization's embattled guardians, the defenders of the lash sought to keep their own reputations clean. Early efforts to curb corporal discipline (such as the Napoleonic-era prohibition on "starting" in the Royal Navy) were largely ignored in practice. Poor record keeping made flogging difficult to monitor, let alone to regulate. The eventual victory of the naval reformers, then, was no small achievement. In 1850, Congress abolished flogging in the U.S. Navy, although in the short term some officers relied on the "usage of the sea" clause to improvise grotesque substitute punishments such as stringing men up by their thumbs. The Grimes Bill eliminated this loophole in 1862. In the Royal Navy, all forms of flogging had been entirely phased out by 1880.[13] The trinity of rum, sodomy, and the lash had not been dissociated; instead, it was displaced onto a newly invented category of non-white, or "mongrel," seamen. The next section explains what made this possible: a discourse of naval reform that foregrounded a new trinity of heterosexuality, masculinity, and whiteness.

ATROCITY NARRATIVES AND THE WHITE MALE BODY

And as they bound him with thongs, Paul said unto the centurion that-stood by, Is it lawful for you to scourge a man that is a Roman, and uncondemned?—ACTS 22:25 (King James Version)

Certain sailors played a prominent role in making reform possible. Their strategy was to change the question from "*Where* is the sailor?" to "*Who* is the sailor?" Repudiating the notion that the wild sea necessarily carried with it wild usages, self-described "white" sailors sought to displace the stigma of piracy/sodomy (and the disciplinary apparatus that went with it) onto seamen of color. By demonizing this Other sailor, they sought full metropolitan rights for themselves as a legitimate part of the "nation in arms." The work performed by racial difference in these autobiographies and reform texts is to enable sailors who felt stigmatized or feared for their own sexual propensities to articulate a heterosexual, if imperiled, masculine identity. By representing themselves as white bodies in danger of rape or violation on the imperial frontier that they simultaneously claimed they defended, the rhetoric of naval reform still left sailors in an ambiguous gender position, leaving race alone as the "proof" for their original claim to privileged status. This helps to explain their frantic reversion to the race theme as the nineteenth century progressed.

In his autobiography, first published in the 1830s, Charles Pemberton described the humiliating effects of flogging on his fellow sailors in the Royal Navy. John Adams had argued that empires were built on draconian disciplinary practices, but Pemberton drew the opposite conclusion, insisting that the lash endangered British manhood:

> But "will an Englishman submit to a blow?" Ay, will he: I have seen him do so a thousand times. "Take a blow submissively?" Ay, though his fist were hard and heavy enough to fell an ox. . . . This is the effect of discipline. . . . Education had obliterated their true manliness; it had bowed their souls to abject servility; it had bowed down their more beautiful and lofty nature to the degradation of mere hounds of the game. Ay, ay, these bold and boasted British bull-dogs were so bowed down.[14]

Although Pemberton voiced strong antiwar sentiments in his writings, his language in this passage evoked fears that reducing these stalwart "bull-dogs" to a submissive role would compromise the masculinity and martial spirit of the British Empire.

Like St. Paul, who appealed to his Roman citizenship to save himself from flogging, many sailors sought an imperial identity that would grant them similar protection.[15] However, the traditional associations of sailors with piracy, sodomy, and cannibalism cast them in the role of *threats* to metropolitan manhood and liberty. This helps to explain the novelty, and rhetorical potency, of memoirs such as William Meacham Murrell's. By casting himself as the pirate's adversary, Murrell represented the common seaman as empire's protagonist. Writing in the wake of the Texan War for Independence, Murrell equated the East Asian pirates with Mexicans, remarking that his shipmates were eager for "a *bit of a brush* with these Malayan desperados."[16] The popular literature of empire in the nineteenth century was replete with lurid narratives of captivity and atrocity in which victimization was displaced from the conquered onto the "defenseless" bodies of the colonial vanguard; rape, massacre, and "barbarous" confinements were, in turn, evoked as justification for further conquests. Murrell could expect to sell more copies of his book by imitating bestselling yarns about heroic Texas Rangers or depraved Comanche abductors, but he also made naval reform more palatable for his empire-minded readership. In this section, I will show how common seamen not only made the war on pirates their own, but also constructed comparisons between pirate atrocities and the way that flogging violated the white male body.

Navies in search of a purpose after the peace of 1815 went after pirates with unprecedented vigor and global comprehensiveness, seeking to "clear" the Caribbean, the Mediterranean, and the South China Sea and concurrently opening up new territories for European control. For example, the occupation of Algiers by the French in 1830 initiated a process of expansion that would culminate in French rule over a third of the African continent.[17] *The Pirates Own Book*, a popular penny-dreadful publication that chronicled diverse episodes in the war on pirates in the language of Victorian melodrama, represented piracy as a crime of the untrustworthy native against his imperial masters. The Malays would effeminately bow and cringe before Europeans in Singapore and Batavia, but "every part of their behaviour is a tissue of falsehood and deception"—they would unleash spear-waving crews "infuriated [sic] with opium" to butcher those same Europeans on the open seas.[18] The sinister ambiguity of pirates was often emphasized at least as much as their acts of theft and violence, a pattern evident in *Pirates Own* as well as in James Fenimore Cooper's bestselling novel *The Red Rover* (1827). Pirates disguised their bodies, their ships, and their intentions—until it was too late. Accounts of piracy were filled with references to seduction, infection, and addiction; as with the *Africaine*, "where one is guilty of such a crime, it is clear that the associates cannot be free from suspicion."[19] Knowing remarks about the (carefully unspecified) "temperament," "habits," and "uncommon vices" of pirates infused criminality with sexual danger.[20]

The advocates of naval reform eagerly promoted the binary opposition between good sailors and sinful Others. When John Bechervaise lauded the virtues of his fellow sailors—"the plain blue jacket . . . covers a heart largely endowed with the warmest and best affections of our nature"—he confined his endorsement to "a true British seaman (not a mongrel)."[21] References to wicked mongrels were even more common in the United States, where "amalgamation" was a dirty word. Mexicans, for example, were condemned as "a mongrel race of degenerate Spaniards and Indians more depraved than they."[22] The newly inaugurated President of the Republic of Texas, Sam Houston, contrasted the "base" conduct of Mexican troops with the "Anglo-Saxon chivalry" of his own army.[23] In this context, Murrell's claim that piracy was a "sinful propensity" intrinsic to all Malays performed much the same work as Bechervaise's selective praise for the "true British seaman." However, sailors did not find it easy to portray themselves as chivalrous warriors against mongrel hordes, because their own sea experience suggested that they might have been amalgamated by the periphery and, in a sense, mongrelized themselves.

Traditionally, the peripheral location of the seagoing vessel had been used to justify extreme corporal discipline, but Richard Henry Dana Jr.'s famous memoir *Two Years before the Mast* (1840) inverted this logic and dramatized the vulnerable position of the common seaman "in the remote parts of the earth . . . in a country where there is neither law nor gospel, and where sailors are at their captain's mercy."[24] Dana's sadistic captain, Frank Thompson, flew into a rage at an "insolent" sailor who said, "I'm no Negro slave." Thompson replied, "Then I'll make you one," and proceeded to flog the man "like a beast," along with another sailor who questioned Thompson's actions. Dana's patrician Boston upbringing (he dropped out of Harvard and signed on as a common seaman in hopes of improving his poor health) accentuated the horror of this scene for many readers, who could imagine their own status and pretensions shorn away at the whim of a sea captain who called himself a "nigger-driver."[25] Dana's voyage took him to (Mexican-controlled) California, and his book is filled with confident remarks about the future of this "empty" land once it was in the hands of industrious Anglos. Dana retained his Yankee identity on the periphery despite his dealings with Spaniards, Native Americans, and Hawaiians. The gravest threat came from neither Catholics nor cannibals but from Captain Thompson, whose atrocities stripped bodies of their white skin. Contrasting an "exquisite" sensibility with the supposedly inferior bodies and spirits of others implied a double standard. Those within the charmed circle (variously labeled "English," "British," "American," "Anglo-Saxon," or simply "white") were entitled to bodies free from insult. Others, indexed by the stripes of the lash, were marked out for submission.[26]

A tidy linguistic, ethnic, or racial division into "good" and "bad" maritime workers carried with it certain risks for the sailor anxious to improve his status. An Irish seaman in the early nineteenth century, for instance, might fall outside every privileged category: too Celtic to be Anglo-Saxon, too Catholic to be British, too foreign to be American, and, as Noel Ignatiev has reminded us, too black to be white. Precisely for this reason, however, the loudest proclamations of privilege came from members of marginalized groups. Charles Pemberton, defender of "English" honor and "British bull-dog" masculinity, was Welsh; John Bechervaise, staunch foe of "mongrel" seamen, was a native of the Channel island of Jersey and actually spoke French better than English. Individuals like these, in both the British Empire and the American Republic, sought to invent ever larger umbrellas of privilege that would be wide enough to shelter them. From the United States, for instance, came the unlikely neologism "Anglo-Saxon-Celtic," which would have been a hard sell in Britain and even in the eastern United States but served a function on the western frontier, where European bodies were scarce. The extreme arbitrariness of these categories only intensified the self-described "white" sailor's obsession with the lash. Exemption from flogging would be an indisputable badge of status. It would define a white masculinity that evaded the nuances of ethnicity, language, and religion. Moreover, aligning the defense of the white male sailor's body with the defense of empire would provide a secure political foundation for a lasting claim to privilege.[27]

By hitching their reform agenda to the war against pirates and the greater cause of imperial expansion, sailor autobiographers like Murrell, Pemberton, Bechervaise, and Dana turned conventional wisdom about seamen inside out. According to these authors, the white sailor carried the virtues of his race and his native soil with him, even to the farthest seas. They were the agents, not the enemies, of empire. By equating flogging with atrocity narratives of confinement, rape, and torture, the advocates of naval reform dismissed the "customs of the sea," insisting that an insult to white bodies in one place was an insult to white bodies everywhere. Sinful propensities and the "need" for corporal discipline pertained to the body of the Other sailor.

PERIPHERAL BODIES IN METROPOLITAN SPACE

> South Carolina has the right to interdict the entrance of such persons into her ports, whose organization of mind, habits, and associations, render them peculiarly calculated to disturb the peace and tranquility of the State, in the same manner as she can prohibit those afflicted with infectious diseases, to touch her shores.—JOHN L. WILSON, Governor of South Carolina[28]

In 1810, Wentworth Boisseau, kinsman of the famous South Carolinian John C. Calhoun, shocked the family by committing an unspecified sexual crime. Calhoun called it "the first instance of that crime ever heard of in this part of the world" and said that Boisseau was "blasted forever in this country." He added, "I cannot conceive how he contracted the odious habit, except, while a sailor to the West Indies."[29] Calhoun's panic demonstrates both an inclination to erect boundaries of dichotomy (metropole–periphery, inside–outside, homo–hetero, white–black) and an awareness of their flimsiness and extreme artificiality. Empire and capitalism throve on hierarchy but initiated processes of creative destruction that placed all forms of hierarchy in question. How could South Carolina, for instance, survive as an exporter without admitting thousands of potentially subversive seamen into Charleston? The South Carolina governor who endorsed the exclusionist Negro Seamen Acts as a way to shut out forbidden Caribbean influences referred, inevitably, to the much feared Saint Domingue contagion of slave rebellion, but Governor Wilson's vague remark about "habits, and associations" points to the numerous ways that sailors might have transgressed in Caribbean waters. The Negro Seamen Acts served to police sexuality as well as to sustain white supremacy. South Carolina's legislation also illustrates an important consequence of the new sexual politics of naval reform: The stigma of piracy and sodomy rested solely with non-white sailors, who were increasingly hired as cheap labor but simultaneously singled out as dangerous and unwelcome in "metropolitan" port cities.

An all-white fleet was never an option. Steamships shrank the planet; commercial shipping lines craved cheap labor; liberal politicians legislated against restrictions on the movement of goods and people; navies continued to suffer from perennial shortages of willing recruits. The conjunction of these powerful forces created ideal conditions for a further increase in the employment of seamen of color. However, the nineteenth century was also marked by increasing segregation at sea and in port, creating a variety of separate and unequal arrangements. Legislation and informal practice continued to discourage a truly open global marketplace for maritime labor. In many metropolitan destinations, non-white seafarers were placed in a kind of quarantine; captains who brought them were expected to take responsibility for their good behavior and prompt departure. Municipal authorities felt the need to control and discipline these Other bodies. The rhetoric of the naval reformers about "whiteness" and the lash contributed to this trend. Any discussion of corporal discipline was now infused with a racial and sexual subtext. In this section I analyze two instances in which the Other sailor was marked out for flogging and incarceration in metropolitan space, the first in Britain and the second in the United States.

Under the Navigation Act of 1660, which sought to protect the kingdom's "nursery of seamen," the East India Company (EIC) was permitted to use all-Asian crews east of the Cape of Good Hope, but three quarters of the crews in the Atlantic were supposed to hail from the British Isles. In practice, the Atlantic provision was not consistently enforced. As early as 1783, the practice of "dumping" unwanted Asian servants and sailors in British port cities was common enough that the EIC was trying to force anyone bringing such people into metropolitan space to post bond against their abandonment. As an emergency measure during the wars with Napoleon, Lascars were allowed to serve without restrictions, resulting in new responsibilities for the EIC. The apparently simple task of maintaining the Lascars in boarding houses for a few months pending their return to India turned out to be fraught with difficulties and culminated, in 1814, in a scandal and Parliamentary hearings.[30]

Hilton Docker, the physician employed by the EIC to oversee the boarding houses, faced the paradoxical situation of hosting colonial subjects in the heart of London. His response was to attempt to reproduce in the metropolis the geographical divisions of the imperial periphery, segregating different groups of sailors according to their nationality or religion: Chinese, Malays, and the Hindu and Muslim subgroups of Lascars each had to have their own barracks. Furthermore, Docker wished to segregate all of the EIC sailors from the inhabitants of the East End neighborhoods where they were housed; he was particularly concerned about their mixing with white women. Long before the East End became associated with feared and stigmatized Jewish immigrants, it was execrated for hosting "foreign sailors, Lascars, Chinese, Greeks and other filthy dirty people of that description." Despite these anxieties, however, the EIC was unwilling to turn its boarding houses into prisons. No guards were posted, and in practice the seamen came and went freely.[31]

This only intensified Docker's desire to impose order. His attempts to communicate with the sailors often failed because he could not speak the appropriate languages, so Docker increasingly turned to the *serangs*—the equivalent of boatswains or sergeants—who had been in charge of the Lascars on the voyage to Britain and were prepared to assume command again. Turning over day-to-day control of the boarding houses to the serangs meant that they would impose their own form of discipline on sailors who stole or otherwise misbehaved. Docker saw this as completely appropriate; the "customary" punishments dealt out by the serangs would fit the expectations of the Lascars. Just as he strove to provide each group of sailors with culturally specific food, Docker assumed that providing culturally specific forms of corporal discipline was a sensible course of action.

In 1814, a local magistrate—who did not share Docker's enthusiasm for reproducing Asian "custom" in the metropolis—was informed that the serang of the ship *Winchelsea* had flogged a sailor. He had the serang arrested for assault. There was no support or precedent for Docker's allegation that the customs of the sea applied to sailors on shore. His idea that Indians should be disciplined according to Indian custom, even in London, was also a policy innovation with potentially wide-ranging implications for the future. Docker's argument that the Magna Carta and the Common Law did not apply because "the discipline thus recognized by the men, was, in its nature, similar to what they are subjected to on board ship" offended those who believed that British soil was a privileged space.

Rather than defending the claims of colonial seafarers to metropolitan rights, Britain's rulers attempted to evade the questions raised by the Lascar scandal by further restricting the right of Asians, and later Africans, to inhabit metropolitan space. This would permit both metropolitan freedom and imperial disciplinary practices to continue, each in its separate realm. The laws resulting from the Parliamentary investigation of the boarding houses subjected colonial seafarers in Britain to strict regulation and surveillance. In July 1814, Parliament ordered that ships arriving in British ports with "Asiatic sailors" on board must post bond for each man as a guarantee that all would be returned to Asia. The Merchant Shipping Act of 1823 ended bonding but tightened the enforcement of repatriation, stipulating that Lascars who declined to stay in EIC boarding houses or refused to take the next ship home could be arrested for vagrancy and deported at the shipowner's expense. Less than a decade later, merchants trading with Africa were also regulated: If they brought any African seamen to Britain, they had to post a bond of one hundred pounds each.[32]

In this same period, individual states within the United States enacted legislation restricting the entrance and movement of free sailors of color. As early as 1796, the U.S. Congress contemplated a requirement that "every master of a vessel [would] have a certificate of the number and situation [i.e., free or slave] of any negroes or mullatoes he may have on board"; this surveillance proposal was not enacted, but the gradual termination of slavery in the Northern states and the successful slave rebellion on Saint Domingue fed Southern paranoia about free black mariners walking the streets of their port cities and inspiring slaves to resist white authority. South Carolina's Negro Seamen Act of 1822 began this trend, stipulating that "free negroes or persons of color" employed on any vessel entering the state would be "seized" and kept in jail—at the captain's expense—until that vessel was ready to leave. Captains who failed to cooperate could be fined and even jailed themselves. Under the original law, the sailors would be sold as slaves if they dared to return; flogging was later substituted for this controversial provision. The nearby states of Georgia, North Carolina, and Florida passed similar legislation, to be joined eventually—in response to the emancipation of slaves in the British Caribbean—by Alabama, Louisiana, and the slaveowning Spanish colonies of Cuba and Puerto Rico. The best estimate is that at least 10,000 men were jailed because of these laws, which were enforced over a period of decades.[33]

Ironically, in light of its own nearly simultaneous initiatives against Lascar seamen, Parliament strenuously protested when subjects of the British Empire were locked in a jail cell with common felons for no crime other than the color of their skin. They met with little cooperation from the United States. When Henry Elkison, a Jamaican-born seaman jailed in Charleston after arriving there on a British-owned vessel from Liverpool, appealed his conviction under the Negro Seamen Act, the case reached William Johnson, an associate justice of the U.S. Supreme Court then sitting in circuit. Johnson challenged the law on several constitutional grounds, but his 1823 ruling elicited only defiance from South Carolina. In the interests of preserving the federal Union, a series of antebellum U.S. presidents, attorneys general, and members of Congress pronounced that such state laws might be impolite, but they were not unconstitutional. The British government responded equivocally: In heavily publicized cases, such as the South Carolina law, it undertook a cautious but persistent program of lobbying the individual state governments to change either the letter of the law or its enforcement. However, some British consuls were instructed to do nothing (in the case of a Texas law of 1856), and at least one British consul, stationed in Savannah, openly endorsed Georgia's law and refused to help jailed British subjects.[34]

The British government's readiness to jail and deport certain imperial subjects (Lascars) while seeking to defend the rights of other imperial subjects (Caribbean blacks) against eerily similar measures in the United States underscores the fact that the boundaries of "whiteness" (as well as categories like "British seaman") remained uncertain in this period. In 1823, Amos Daley, a sailor from Rhode Island who ran afoul of the Negro Seamen Act for the second time, tried to exploit such uncertainties by informing a South Carolina magistrate that he was exempt from the law because, as the son of a "straight-haired" Narragansett Indian woman, he was not a Negro. The court debated his status, noted that the prisoner's hair was curly, and sentenced him to twelve lashes on his bare back. The law's wording looked different to Supreme Court Justice Johnson when he reviewed the South Carolina law in the same year. He lamented that Nantucket Indians, "known to be among the best seamen in our service"—and included, in Johnson's view, as "persons of color"—could be arrested under the Negro Seamen Act. Johnson's respect for seamen of color was out of step with the 1820s. Britain's Merchant Shipping Act, also dated 1823, stated that "Lascars and other Natives of the East are not deemed to be equal in Strength and Use to European or other Seamen," expressing geographical difference in racialized language, devaluing the labor of a whole category of men, and writing into law a two-tiered system of bodies belonging to superior and inferior maritime workers with distinct, unequal rights and privileges.[35]

Legal distinctions on land were followed, ultimately, by segregation at sea. This topic awaits its historian, but the broad outlines are clear. The African American cook or steward was a familiar stereotype by the end of the nineteenth century. Lascars were relegated to the boiler room as coal heavers ("firemen") on steamships. In situations where jobs could still be shared by whites and non-whites, captains increasingly chose to ship an all-white or an all-black crew to prevent mixing. There were even "checkerboard" ships in which distinct areas of the deck were marked out for each color. The devaluation of non-white seafarers was particularly noticeable in the realm of corporal punishment. An 1856 report describes a ship that arrived in Havre, France, with its crew of twenty black seamen reduced to seventeen, "eight of those so terribly bruised and mangled, as to be sent at once to the hospital." They claimed that the white master of the vessel had beaten the other three sailors to death and then thrown their bodies into the sea "like so many dead dogs." In another incident, an entire crew of Lascars deserted on arrival in London, alleging that sailors had been flogged, "hung up with weights tied to their feet," and force-fed pork in violation of their Muslim faith.[36]

Non-white sailors were also assigned a racial identity inflected by gender and a masculinity that was considered an expression of inborn ethnic traits. The 1823 Merchant Shipping Act had labeled Lascars weak men. This became a badge of exploitability, which was used to justify inferior food, clothing, and allowance of living space, which in turn produced weak, sickly workers who "confirmed" the original premise that these men lacked stamina. Ironically, the belief that Asian sailors were unmanly facilitated their growing prominence in the maritime workforce. Chinese and Filipino "servants" had become a mainstay of U.S. Navy vessels by the early twentieth century; they were preferred to African American sailors, who were now considered incapable of high-status tasks but too insubordinate for servile ones.[37] In Britain, shipowners turned the rhetoric of whiteness against white sailors: "It was the Lascar's low level of skills, greatly inferior to the highly skilled British sailor, which were sought after in the era of steam. . . . According to this argument the British sailor's superior skills, brain-power, initiative and self-reliance had priced him out of the market."[38] A Lascar crew member would work for a fraction of a white sailor's wages, so once the Navigation Acts were repealed (in 1849), many British firms dealing with Asia quickly switched to all-Lascar crews on passenger and cargo ships. Legislation and the restrictive wording of contracts continued to limit Lascars' right to stay in Britain, but their absolute numbers at sea continued to increase. The Lascar presence would attract further attention in the twentieth century, when a new series of global wars drew a sizeable number into British urban space.[39]

Meanwhile, white sailors enjoyed increasing respectability. John Ruskin, in his inaugural Slade Lecture at Oxford (1870), described the British Empire using an elaborate analogy to ships and sailors. He urged his country to "found colonies as fast and as far as she is able, formed of her most energetic and worthiest men. . . . Though they [may] live on a distant plot of ground, they are no more to consider themselves therefore disfranchised from their native land, than the sailors of her fleets do, because they float on distant waves." Ruskin found the sailor analogy so appealing that he stretched it to the point of absurdity: The colonies must be "literally . . . fastened fleets" or "motionless navies" where the empire could "*expect every man to do his duty*."[40] The sailor obeying Nelson's command at Trafalgar was, by the Victorian era, the classic example of a patriotic British subject; the metropolis could expect no more of a colony than that it follow the example of a ship. In the United States, Theodore Roosevelt's suggestively named "Great White Fleet" undertook a world tour. The lengthy, much publicized cruise of these modern warships was represented not as a flirtation with foreignness, but as an expression of American identity.

As I have shown, white sailors themselves played an important role in recasting themselves as affirmations of orthodox, metropolitan masculinity. The key to this process lay in a reconfiguration of the sexual politics surrounding the seafaring life. One convenient marker of this transformation is the new fashion for dressing up small boys as common seamen. The famous 1846 portrait of Queen Victoria's five-year-old son, the future Edward VII, in a sailor suit inaugurated a widespread nursery custom.[41] Sailor suits for small boys implied that sailors were a suitable and safe role model. Displacing the sodomite/pirate label onto non-white sailors had opened up new possibilities for white sailors, who were construed as—not exactly family men—but as a kind of spouse for a (gendered-female) nation. Once white sailors had achieved their goal of representing themselves as unproblematic allies of the imperial cause, "undegenerate" men partaking of the "best northern blood," they distanced themselves enough from the sodomy stigma that certain kinds of naval reform became possible.[42]

In conclusion, the debate over corporal discipline contributed to the construction of new categories of gender and racial difference. In the eighteenth century, crews were diverse and integrated, but subject to the lash; revolutionary rhetoric suggested the possibility of extending metropolitan liberty to the peripheral space of the seagoing vessel. The adoption of a "white" identity by certain sailors as an expedient political tactic in the nineteenth century, however, helped to impose a new grid of race and gender categories on the maritime workforce. This process was neither easy nor simple. Anxiety about who would actually make it into the privileged "white" category only intensified the obsession of sailor reformers with the lash. Those who were exempt from flogging would be certain of their superior status. The victory of the notion that rights belonged to bodies, not spaces, inaugurated a serious and essentially unprecedented effort to restrict the movements and behavior of non-white (therefore "peripheral") sailors in metropolitan space—using, of course, the lash to discipline their unruly bodies. The obvious corollary of the reformers' race-based rhetoric was that non-white seamen could, and perhaps must, be subjected to the lash because of *their* unrefined sensibility and sinful propensities, qualities that by the late nineteenth century were considered the "natural" expression of their inferior niche in an explicitly defined race and gender hierarchy at sea. It is clear that the outcome of the naval-reform movement had not been to demolish the idea that certain groups of people required, or deserved, the lash. Instead, the reformers extended and promoted an ideology of corporal discipline that presumed inequality.

NOTES

I thank the editors for their thoughtful comments on this essay over the various stages of its development. Celeste Land and family provided hospitality while I worked at the Library of Congress in the summer of 2001. A one-course release from the College of Arts and Sciences at Texas A&M University, Commerce, helped me create the essay in its present form, as did a panel at the Association of Asian Studies involving Ian Duffield, Michael Fisher, and Satadru Sen. An earlier version of this article appeared in *Interventions: The International Journal of Postcolonial Studies* 3, no. 2 (July 2001), and I am grateful for permission to publish the current version.

1 Murrell, *Cruise of the Frigate Columbia*, 111–15.

2 Ibid., 131, 137–39.

3 Ibid., 175–77.

4 Clark, *The Struggle for the Breeches*; McCurry, *Masters of Small Worlds*; Hall et al., *Defining the Victorian Nation*.

5 The literature on this topic is vast. For an overview that is broader than most (although it is specific to the United States), see Kerber, "The Meanings of Citizenship."

6 Byrn, *Crime and Punishment in the Royal Navy*; Lavery, *Nelson's Navy* (on the role of Royal Marines); Millett, *Semper Fidelis*; Valle, *Rocks and Shoals*. Valle quotes John Adams on p. 40.

7 For the physical effects of one hundred lashes, see Valle, *Rocks and Shoals*, 9, 141.

8 "Rules and Regulations for the Government of the United States Navy," reprinted in ibid., 285. See also Article 32 of the same document.

9 Gilbert, "The *Africaine* Courts-Martial"; idem, "Buggery and the British Navy, 1700–1861"; Hitchcock, *English Sexualities, 1700–1800*; Langley, *Social Reform in the United States Navy, 1798–1862*, 172–74; Sedgwick, *Between Men*; Trumbach, *Sex and the Gender Revolution, Volume 1*; Valle, *Rocks and Shoals*, 166–75.

10 Arens, *The Man-Eating Myth*; Crain, "Lovers of Human Flesh"; Goldberg, *Sodometries*; Obeyesekere, "Cannibal Feasts in Nineteenth-Century Fiji"; Philbrick, *In the Heart of the Sea*; Wilson, *The Island Race*.

11 Linebaugh and Rediker, *The Many-Headed Hydra*; Rediker, *Between the Devil and the Deep Blue Sea*; Rubin, *The Law of Piracy*.

12 Baepler, *White Slaves, African Masters*; Burg, *Sodomy and the Perception of Evil*; Colley, *Captives*; Turley, *Rum, Sodomy, and the Lash*.

13 Langley, *Social Reform in the United States Navy, 1798–1862*, 131–208; Rasor, *Reform in the Royal Navy*, 34–35; Valle, *Rocks and Shoals*, 80–81, 83–84.

14 Pemberton, *The Autobiography of Pel. Verjuice*, 146–47.

15 *Sailor's Magazine*, an American evangelical publication, invoked Paul's words on this subject in its August 1831 issue: as quoted in Langley, *Social Reform in the United States Navy, 1798–1862*, 147. For a seventeenth-century reference along strikingly similar lines, see Linebaugh and Rediker, *The Many-Headed Hydra*, 134.

"Sinful Propensities" 113

16 Murrell, *Cruise of the Frigate Columbia*, 92, emphasis original.

17 Kennedy, *The Rise and Fall of British Naval Mastery*, 164; Labaree et al., *America and the Sea*, 324.

18 Ellms, *The Pirates Own Book*, 221, 226. The original publication date is 1837.

19 Cooper, *The Red Rover*, 359.

20 Cooper, *The Red Rover*, 313, 372, 375; Ellms, *The Pirates Own Book*, 97, 149–50.

21 Bechervaise, *A Farewell to My Old Shipmates and Messmates*, 6.

22 Roberts and Olson, *A Line in the Sand*, 47–48, 143–44.

23 Horsman, *Race and Manifest Destiny*, 213–14.

24 Dana, *Two Years Before the Mast*, 71.

25 Ibid., 78–80.

26 This kind of thinking was not confined to naval reformers: Sánchez-Eppler, *Touching Liberty*, 18.

27 Anderson, "Race, Caste, and Hierarchy"; Colley, *Britons*; Horsman, *Race and Manifest Destiny*; Morrison and Stewart, *Race and the Early Republic*; Roediger, *The Wages of Whiteness*.

28 As quoted in Hamer, "Great Britain, the United States, and the Negro Seamen Acts, 1822–1848," 11. Governor Wilson's statement appeared in the *Southern Patriot* (Charleston) on 7 December 1824.

29 Meriwether, *Papers of John C. Calhoun*, 1:53.

30 The best comprehensive source for information on Lascar labor in this period is Visram, *Asians in Britain*. See also Fisher, *Counterflows to Colonialism*.

31 This and the following paragraphs are based on British Library, Oriental and India Office Collection, L/MAR/C/902. The quotation is from a London magistrate in Visram, *Asians in Britain*, 32.

32 54 Geo. III c.134; 4 Geo. IV c. 80; 2 & 3 Will. IV c. 84; see also Walvin, *Black and White*, 194, 198.

33 The quotations are from Smith, "Black Seamen and the Federal Courts, 1789–1860," 323, 326. My discussion of the laws and their operation relies primarily on Bolster, *Black Jacks*, 190–214.

34 Freehling, *Prelude to Civil War*; Hamer, "British Consuls and the Negro Seamen Acts, 1850–1860," 167; idem, "Great Britain, the United States, and the

Negro Seamen Acts, 1822–1848" 13; Smith, "Black Seamen and the Federal Courts, 1789–1860," 326.

35   Bolster, *Black Jacks* 196; Smith, "Black Seamen and the Federal Courts, 1789–1860," 326–27; 4 Geo. IV c. 80.

36   Bolster, *Black Jacks*, 180, 218; Visram, *Asians in Britain*, 54, 56.

37   Bolster, *Black Jacks*, 215–32; Harrold, "Jim Crow in the Navy, 1798–1941," 50–51.

38   Lahiri, "Patterns of Resistance," 159.

39   Tabili, *"We Ask for British Justice"*; Visram, *Asians in Britain*, 54.

40   Ruskin, *Complete Works*, 21.

41   Prentice, *A Celebration of the Sea*, 58–59.

42   Ruskin, *Complete Works*, 20.

DOUGLAS M. PEERS

※

The Raj's Other Great Game

Policing the Sexual Frontiers of the Indian Army in the First Half of the Nineteenth Century

A man should, whatever happens, keep to his own caste, race, and breed. Let the White go to the White and the Black to the Black.
—RUDYARD KIPLING[1]

Kipling's maxim is for many the paradigmatic statement of imperial views on interracial marriage and sexuality. Questions of race came to occupy a prominent place in Victorian writings about empire. For Anglo-Indian (meaning Britons domiciled in India) writers like Kipling, racial frontiers were as much part of the Great Game as was shadowboxing in the Hindu Kush.[2] In another of his short stories, "Without Benefit of Clergy" (1891), an English official marries a Muslim woman, and together they are forced to live a secret life—one that ends tragically as disease takes his wife and their child. While Kipling is certainly sympathetic to their plight, his writings betray his opinion that tragedy was inevitable, thereby reminding readers that the empire operates according to certain inescapable rules. If we move from the fictional to the autobiographical, we find further evidence of the extent to which interracial marriages had become stigmatized. By 1835, according to Emma Roberts, "To be seen in public with, or to be known to be intimate in the houses of Indo-Britons, was fatal to a new arrival in Calcutta; there was no possibility of emerging from the shade, or of making friends or connection in a higher sphere."[3] She goes on to warn her readers, "The prejudices against 'dark beauties' (the phrase usually employed to designate those who are the inheritors of the native complexion) are daily gaining ground, and in the present state of female intellectuality their uncultivated minds form a decided objection."[4]

Statements such as these have been taken as proof that racial prejudices had become so normalized that they became a defining characteristic of the mature colonial state. There is certainly evidence in the archival record to conclude that, by the third decade of the nineteenth century, marriages between officers and Indian or Eurasian women had become proscribed—if not necessarily officially, then at least by force of social convention. But if we look at the European rank and file in India, we find a number of important qualifications to what would otherwise appear to be an inexorable shift toward racial exclusivity. Marriages between soldiers and women of either Indian or mixed Indian and European background, common in the eighteenth century, persisted well into the nineteenth century, often with the deliberate encouragement of the military establishment, which viewed such liaisons as beneficial to the discipline and morale of its troops in India.

Thus, while official rhetoric and public discourse would seem to confirm that the nineteenth-century Raj was indeed very different from that which preceded it, the transformation was less dramatic and more ambivalent at the local level, where convention and military necessity helped perpetuate selected aspects of the more fluid and open relationships of the eighteenth century. Through a close reading of contemporary policies and debates, we can begin to unravel the tangled interplay of the army's practical objectives with the various discourses of race, class, gender, and sexuality that informed, and in turn were informed by, colonial rule. By doing so we will be better placed to chart the limits as well as the potentialities of colonial authority over the bodies of its subjects.

CHANGE VERSUS CONTINUITY
IN COLONIAL INDIA

The eighteenth century has historically, if somewhat naively, been viewed as a time of cultural tolerance. British rule, according to this view, was relatively colorblind, at least insofar as sexuality was concerned.[5] It was said, for example, that "between the years 1778 and 1785 . . . the prime sets of dancing girls quitted the cities and repaired to the several cantonments, where they met the most liberal encouragement."[6] But by the early nineteenth century, Anglo-Indians (used here to refer to persons of European ancestry domiciled in India) in major centers like Calcutta were consciously keeping their distance from their Indian neighbors by creating a largely self-contained community known as the "White Town."[7] The ability of Anglo-Indians to seal themselves off did differ according to occupation and by their place in society. Generally, as Durba Ghosh and P. J. Marshall have shown, the higher ranks of Anglo-Indian society could do so with greater ease and in many ways had already begun to do so in the eighteenth century.[8] Nevertheless, whatever prohibitions were in force could be and were evaded, as shown in Garnet Wolseley's confession in 1858 that, while stationed at Lucknow, he managed "to console [himself] with an Eastern Princess and find she answers all the purposes of a wife without giving any of the bother."[9] Transgressions like that of Wolseley notwithstanding (and even then Wolseley's actions hardly signaled any appreciation of or interest in Indian society), a vast gulf existed between Anglo-Indian and Indian society.

Thus, it would appear that by the end of the first quarter of the nineteenth century, interracial sexuality had come to be condemned and, consequently, interracial marriages were proscribed—if not in law, then at least in practice. The institution of marriage, as well as the possibility that marriages could cross racial barriers, had become a subject of intense debate as military imperatives clashed with cultural and political preferences for clearer racial boundaries. At issue were not so much sexual relations between Europeans and Indians but, rather, the product of such relations. By 1800, persons of mixed ancestry, whom we shall refer to as Eurasians, had become increasingly marginalized in colonial society. They were barred in 1791 from serving as combatants in the army as well as from employment in the covenanted civil service. By the mid-nineteenth century, an essayist in the most respectable of Calcutta's magazines had opined of Eurasians that "great talent (I will not mention genius), and sterling abilities seem very scarce amongst them."[10] Race was gaining ground as a means of classifying and ranking communities, and the presence of Eurasians threatened to subvert such efforts.[11] Eurasian women in particular were singled out as being particularly portentous on account of their sexual allure as well as their lack of sexual morality.[12] The profound ambivalence with which officials viewed Eurasians can also be glimpsed in the rules governing the asylums that the company had established for the mentally ill: They did not know where Eurasians were to be placed, for they were neither Indian nor European.[13]

This begs the question of whether Anglo-Indians were inclined toward a blanket injunction against all forms of interracial sexual activity, and whether this in turn encouraged colonial authorities to attempt to stamp out such activity, officially or unofficially. Certainly this is the impression gleaned from a number of recent works that stress colonial preoccupations with racial boundaries. Of late there has been a surge of interest in the closing of the sexual frontier, with most authors fastening on race as the overarching concern.[14] This racializing of sexual relations was by no means confined to India; it was widespread throughout the British Empire in the nineteenth century, and the French were also preoccupied with the "metis problem."[15] Yet India became an especially important stage upon which the politics of racial and sexual identities could be rehearsed, for it was one of the first colonies to which the British dispatched a large number of unmarried men. Close scrutiny of the army's policies on marriage and sexuality in the first half of the nineteenth century reveals a more complex and contested situation than has hitherto been appreciated, thereby calling into question the prevailing wisdom that by the early decades of the nineteenth century a firm consensus had been achieved in India against interracial sexuality. This in turn suggests that the transition to a more regulated form of state authority in the nineteenth century—one that sought to inscribe its authority on the bodies of its subjects—was far from complete.

MILITARY SOCIETY IN COLONIAL INDIA

To make sense of these contradictions and ambiguities, in official actions as well as in popular sentiments, we need to locate them within the context of the military in India, for not only were military personnel chiefly responsible for sexual behavior becoming such an issue—it was, after all, British soldiers who most often took Indian or Eurasian wives—but it was through the rules and conventions of the army that colonial rule sought to deal with the consequences. In theory, the army offered a site where colonial authority could be most firmly imposed, for no other colonial institution enjoyed such sweeping disciplinary authority over the bodies of its subjects, Indian or European. In treating the history of corporeality under colonial rule, attention has customarily been directed at Europe's "others"—those colonial subjects defined by racial difference.[16] But in the army, the state enjoyed as much authority over the bodies of its European soldiers as it did over its Indian sepoys, and consequently we find that class and status played key roles in shaping policy and informing attitudes, sometimes in association with notions of race and sometimes in contradistinction to them. The colonial regime distinguished between what it would not tolerate from its officers and what it permitted to its rank and file. Its ability to enforce its will, however, was tempered by its tradition of not bearing down too heavily on the private lives of its Indian and European recruits.

The sexual politics of the colonial state consisted of more than simply closing racial boundaries. Class, as well as the imperatives—real or imagined—of the army, has to be taken into account. Moreover, Anglo-Indian society rarely spoke with one voice, and even individuals we take to be broadly representative contradicted themselves. Kipling, for example, failed to maintain a consistent position. In "Lispeth," a short story that interestingly appeared in the same collection as "Beyond the Pale," he offers a damning critique of the racial exclusivity of Anglo-Indian society when confronted with the devoted love shown by a Eurasian woman to an Englishman. While officers were certainly not immune to contemporary constructions of race and sexuality, they were often in the first instance concerned with efficiency and discipline, and this prompted them to adopt positions that do not necessarily reflect, at least directly, prevailing prejudices and anxieties. Consequently, the military in India, despite the fact that it had the potential to do so, never fully proscribed interracial sexuality but chose instead to try and contain it within manageable parameters, even if this led it to advocate on more than one occasion that racial boundaries be temporarily opened to allow soldiers to seek Eurasian or Indian wives.

We will consider these issues from two perspectives: the army's policies with respect to soldiers' marrying or cohabiting with Eurasian or Indian women, and the provisions it made for the offspring of such relationships. The focus will be on the other ranks—the soldiers and the noncommissioned officers of the various British forces garrisoning India. Such troops were distributed into a number of discrete military formations. By the end of the eighteenth century, at least 20,000 troops and officers from Britain's regular army were stationed in India, leased to the East India Company by the British government. In addition, the East India Company raised its own European troops and officers. They formed the basis of European regiments that were to be found in each of the three presidency armies that the East India Company established, in Bengal, Madras, and Bombay. The company's European troops also provided the officers and noncommissioned officers of the more numerous sepoy regiments that made up the bulk of the forces available in each of the presidencies. While the differences between company and Crown forces, and between the three presidencies, were largely organizational in nature, there were some important cultural variations. The company's Europeans, for example, were not subject to rotation out of India and hence were expected to spend the rest of their lives in India. Regular British regiments were sent to India for twenty-year tours of duty. Those soldiers who did not die of disease or wounds sustained in combat were therefore viewed as temporary additions to Anglo-Indian society. Moreover, recent research has demonstrated that the company's Europeans were often more skilled and better educated than their counterparts in the regular army, and a good number looked to service in India as a means of improving their fortunes.[17]

THE LANGUAGE OF RACE AND THE POLITICS OF IDENTITY

Before we can begin to look more closely at the military and its position on marriage in India, we need first to address the confusion generated by the terms employed by contemporaries. This confusion not only hampers analysis today; it also speaks to the unstable nature of nineteenth-century identities. Through the course of the nineteenth century, people of mixed ancestry were assigned a number of labels, including East Indians, Eurasians, Indo-Britons, Indo-Portuguese, country-born, half-castes, and so on. But most commonly they were termed "Eurasian." Anglo-Indian, by which they are often known today, was then reserved for people born in Europe but temporarily domiciled in India. As a further refinement, people of European ancestry but born in India were labeled "country-born"; this title normally excluded anyone with any Indian ancestry. These distinctions are neither pedantic nor merely semantic.[18] How one was classified would have an immediate impact on one's legal rights, entitlements, and social status. Pedigree informed employment opportunities and determined pension entitlements.

Moreover, Eurasian was not a monolithic or homogenous category. It contained a wide spectrum of individuals who varied considerably in their complexion as well as the degree to which they emulated European ways. Some, as one commentator complained, "bear the Christian name, but are distinguished from the surrounding heathen by little except their indiscriminate diet."[19] There were some interesting slippages between class and race when it came to discussions about the Eurasians. Such views persisted, as illustrated in a minute by the adjutant general of the army in 1875 in which he noted, "As a class or rather a race, neither their habits nor their physique are suited to service in our army."[20]

There was one particularly illuminating method of differentiating between Eurasians to which many commentators turned: to distinguish between those who had British roots and those with Portuguese ancestry. One statistician claimed that of the Eurasians, the "Indo-Portuguese are thought to be the most numerous." He goes on to argue that there are very few pure Portuguese in India.[21] I draw attention to this fact because contemporary writers were almost unanimous in their condemnation of the Portuguese; hence, the derision that was showered on Eurasians was in many cases as much about their Portuguese ancestry (and with it, their Catholicism) as it was about their Indian roots. People of Indo-Portuguese background were in practice doubly damned. In the words of one anonymous essayist, "The progeny is physically inferior to both father and mother, has the vices of both without their redeeming qualities."[22] In Anglo-Indian eyes, the Portuguese in India were mongrels and consequently symbolized all the evils associated with interbreeding. Roberts was very scathing in her comments on the Portuguese.[23] Another commentator proclaimed, "The whole history of India shows us that no mingling of the white and black man has tended to the advantage of either. The Portuguese were in great strength in Bombay; but they married largely amongst the native women and at this day hardly one pure family of them is in existence."[24] Richard Burton wrote of the people at Goa that the "mental and bodily development of this class are remarkable only as being a strange mélange of European and Asiatic peculiarities, of antiquated civilization and modern barbarism."[25] To British observers, the consequence of such intermixing was all too obvious: The Portuguese had long ceased to be a major force in Asia.

MARRIAGE AND THE IMPERATIVES OF MILITARY DISCIPLINE

Nineteenth-century armies did not generally look favorably on marriage—at least for Europeans, as the practice of allowing sepoys to marry and in some cases to have their families live with them was widespread in India at this time. But military officials were equally convinced that its European soldiers could not be expected to remain celibate. The army's opposition to marriage rested on the calculation that married soldiers could be less easily deployed (because their families would be an encumbrance) as well as the widespread suspicion that marriage would enfeeble their soldiers. Yet the army could not overlook the sexuality of its soldiers. And given that sexuality was encoded in class as well as gendered and racial terms, decision makers concluded that soldiers, unlike their officers, were incapable of suppressing their desires, and therefore a release must be found. Appropriate heterosexual behavior was essential to maintaining military discipline and honor; consequently, outlets were needed.

The army could not therefore escape questions of sexual activity. However, it also had to cope with a restricted list of acceptable options. The alternatives to sexual gratification with women were clearly unacceptable.[26] There were fears that homosexual relations might flourish, for it was assumed that the soldiers, being drawn from the lower classes, were all too often incapable of controlling their sexual desires. It is revealing that while sodomy was viewed as a very serious military crime, the army went to great lengths to deny its very existence.[27] Soldiers accused of sodomy were tried in closed courts-martial, and their sentences were never published in general orders. Little evidence has survived of such trials, but that which has been passed down demonstrates that when soldiers were prosecuted, the kinds of proof that were required to establish homosexuality were very disquieting. Therefore, it is not surprising that many army officers preferred not to know about such activities.[28] It was commonly accepted by officers that they should not enter their soldiers' barracks at night. While fear of confronting homosexuality was one of the reasons for this avoidance, it should also be noted that, given the amount of alcohol consumed by soldiers, barracks were often dangerous places and officers placed themselves at personal risk if they entered at night.

In practice this meant that the army must condone, or at least tolerate, either prostitution or marriage (or something approaching marriage) or some combination of the two. Many military authorities preferred prostitution as an appropriate outlet, as it did not encumber their soldiers. But it came at a cost: The Indian army was beset by an alarmingly high incidence of venereal disease.[29] With rates of infection in the Bengal Army reaching as high as 35 percent in the mid-1830s (although it must be noted that diagnostic abilities were still in their infancy), it should come as no surprise that those who urged the army to permit more soldiers to marry used the prevalence of venereal disease to buttress their arguments.

Military regulations on marriage were drawn up within this context of ambivalence. But there were important differences between the regulations in force in the regular army and those enacted by the East India Company. The latter generally showed a greater tolerance for—or, at least, less resistance to—marriage, which is not surprising given that the company's European recruits were normally expected to pass the rest of their lives in India. In the 1860s, 93 percent of the Queen's troops were unmarried (though regulations would have allowed more to marry), compared with 70 percent of the company's Europeans.[30] There was considerable variation between presidencies. Statistics from the early 1850s show that of soldiers in Royal Regiments posted to Bengal, only 8.75 percent were married; among the company's Europeans, 10.6 percent were married. Yet in Bombay, 11.25 percent of the Royal troops were married and 8.25 percent of the company's Europeans; in Madras, 10.75 percent of the Royal troops and 21 percent of the company Europeans were married.[31] The reasons for the discrepancies between presidencies are not immediately obvious, for there was little difference between the regulations in force. In the case of Madras, the greater number of married soldiers might be accounted for by the fact that its troops did not tend to see as much active service and because of this they might have been in a better position to settle down. There is also evidence to suggest that the Madras army had always been more tolerant of marriage—witness its practice of allowing sepoys to have their families join them in cantonments—and this no doubt spilled over into its European units. An officer with that army declared that "no surer method can be devised of reclaiming a thoughtless soldier than by tying a wife around his neck."[32] Such views were well entrenched. As early as 1810, the observation was made in the military consultations of that presidency that "to the offices commanding [His Majesty's] regiments, who have been any considerable length of time in India, it is well known how much more efficient those corps are, which have native women attached to them, than those are, which have not been provided."[33]

Regulations governing marriage were most strictly laid down and enforced for soldiers in the regular army. The army could hardly take a more enlightened or positive attitude toward marriage when it deliberately sought recruits from men fleeing domestic obligations.[34] Until 1873, soldiers were under no legal obligation to care for their families. In fact, the army offered a refuge from such responsibilities.[35] Yet a token female presence in the army was tolerated, though largely for utilitarian reasons. Soldiers' wives provided essential services such as washing, sewing, cooking, and nursing. Hence, regulations allowed twelve women for every 100 soldiers destined for India and six per 100 for other destinations.[36] Women listed on the strength of the regiment were allowed to live in the barracks (literally in most cases); they were given army rations, sent their children to regimental schools, and received a small allowance. In return, they were subjected to military law and discipline. Some contemporaries estimated that the actual number of women with a regiment was larger, with perhaps as many women again as those who were officially on the strength.[37] When Sergeant Pearman sailed with his regiment for India in 1845, four wives were smuggled aboard.[38]

The East India Company took a more relaxed view of marriage, in part because it had little choice. Its troops, unlike their colleagues in regular service, were not liable to be moved around the globe, and in signing up for long-term service, they were, to all intents and purposes, moving to India permanently.[39] But there was also a more paternalistic attitude at work, and on occasion the company actively tried to persuade its soldiers to marry. Such was the case in the seventeenth century when the company briefly encouraged its employees to seek local wives and raise families, largely because they felt beleaguered by the growing Catholic Indo-Portuguese community.[40] For most of the years of company rule, their European recruits could marry Indian women or Eurasian women as young as thirteen, provided that they had the permission of their commanding officer.[41] The company did not set firm limits on the number of troops who could marry—at least, until the mid–nineteenth century, when it was decided that only twelve wives per 100 soldiers were to be considered eligible for housing in barracks, as well as for other government allowances. The principal reason for this shift in policy was to try to harmonize the company's regulations with those of the regular army. But it was also informed by growing prejudices against Eurasians, for in practice the supply of potential wives was limited to Eurasian or Indian women. It should be noted that marriage had a rather looser definition than it did in civilian society, for in addition to soldiers who married according to religious convention and practice, there were also soldiers who were often in long-term and stable relations with women that counted as marriage to many of their colleagues, though perhaps not to their officers. As we shall see, this would in turn raise questions about the legitimacy of any offspring.

THE MILITARY AND THE DEBATE OVER MARRIAGE IN THE NINETEENTH CENTURY

By the mid–nineteenth century, a number of army officers had begun to expound on the benefits of marriage. This softening of attitudes was brought about in part by a shift in public perceptions about British soldiers. Public sympathy for British soldiers who had fought in the

Crimea and the Indian Mutiny bolstered the demands of those who had been pressing the army to improve conditions for its soldiers.[42] Soldiers and their families came to be seen as members of the deserving poor—though this must be set against persistent stereotypes of soldiers' wives as drunks and prostitutes. But as has been noted elsewhere, reforms in the British Army, be they to its discipline, tactics, or organization, were not all post–Crimea developments.[43] During the course of the Napoleonic Wars, for example, the British government was forced to pay closer attention to soldiers' families.[44] While it would be an exaggeration to talk of these developments as foreshadowing the rise of the modern welfare state in the twentieth century, they are nevertheless proof of the growing commitment by and ability of the state to intervene in areas hitherto excluded from its purview. Wives and children could no longer be ignored, in part because more troops were needed and some allowance had to be made to married soldiers. Consequently, the army began to explore methods by which soldiers could direct monies to their families, a government-funded school for the children of its soldiers was established (the Royal Military Asylum), and funds were earmarked to secure passage home for wives and family members from embarkation ports when their husbands had been dispatched overseas. The Navy was even more proactive, having introduced a scheme under which sailors could remit monies to their families as early as 1757.

The British Army's adoption of a more interventionist role, however haltingly, was partly inspired by practices current in India. The East India Company had for a number of reasons already taken on a much more paternalistic role.[45] This can be glimpsed in the founding of a pension plan in the mid–eighteenth century (Lord Clive's fund), as well as orphanages dating back to 1783, pensions for sepoys and their families, provisions to house sepoy families in the cantonment, and opportunities for sepoys' sons to follow their fathers into service. Schools and libraries were also introduced in the early nineteenth century. The East India Company had to become more engaged in the lives of its employees, for unlike in Britain, there was no parish system that would take care of soldiers' dependents. But these developments also speak to the emergence of a distinctive East India Company military culture, one that had infused into itself elements of precolonial military culture, or what it perceived to be its traditions, including acknowledging the wives and families of its soldiers and sepoys, as well as an emerging commitment to social engineering. The civilizing mission, about which much has been written, was by no means exclusively entrusted to missionary groups. Nor was it aimed exclusively at recently conquered peoples. Governments like the East India Company, albeit hesitantly and somewhat reluctantly, also sought to civilize their own employees (whites as well as non-whites) and, in so doing, began to expand their mandate. In taking on wider responsibilities by moving into the realm of what we might today define as social engineering, the East India Company played a critical role in the growth of a particularly colonial variant of governmentality. The expanding responsibilities of the state, while determined in the first instance by military needs, helped to energize contemporary debates about the nature of society and its relations with political authority within a colonial context.

There can be no denying that there were pressures to improve the conditions of soldiers, and out of these came arguments in favor of allowing them to marry and to have their wives and families with them. Yet it would be an exaggeration to interpret these voices in exclusively Whiggish terms—in other words, to conclude that reform slowly, inexorably, and inevitably took root in the British army. No clear consensus emerged; in fact, it arguably became less and less clear, for while a number of voices could be heard extolling the benefits of letting soldiers marry, there were at least as many voices declaring against it. Those who can be fairly termed traditionalists viewed any efforts to tame the soldier as not only doomed to failure but potentially corrosive to military efficiency. Their ideal soldier was a devil-may-care, hard-drinking, hard-living womanizer. Given those criteria, it is not difficult to see why marriage was anathema to many officers, as were libraries, savings banks, and temperance societies.[46] Such sentiments crystallized in statements like this one:

> Although by no means a Malthusian, I am of the opinion of Marshal Saxe, qu'une femme n'est pas un meuble pour un soldat, and the fewer women there are in a regiment the better, more particularly in our service, where we cannot move from home without a ship.[47]

Ranged against the forces of conservatism and tradition were officers and civilians who pressed for a more humane regime in the army, one that would reengineer the army to improve the mental, moral, and physical well-being of its rank and file, particularly the British soldiers who were commonly viewed as intellectually and morally inferior to the sepoys. While contemporaries were unanimous in their view that British soldiers were superior fighters to Indian sepoys, most officers acknowledged that sepoys were much more socially and culturally refined than British soldiers and were drawn from a more respectable strata of society. Consequently, the disciplinary techniques used on sepoys were less brutal.[48] The irony of this situation, with European troops being treated more roughly than Indian troops, was not lost on contemporaries and helped to fuel demands for military reform.

One of the more outspoken of these reformers in India was Henry Lawrence, who wrote a number of articles and pamphlets on the subject of military reform. In one of these he declared,

> Marriage is thought by some to incapacitate a man for the duty of a soldier, and to deteriorate him for all active business. My own experience contradicts the opinion: an active man will be active and a sluggard slothful, be he either benedict or bachelor; nor would any woman, worthy of the name of wife, think of interfering with what she regards to the credit of her husband, unless to urge him onward, to cheer him by her counsel on departure and in absence, and to brighten his home to him on his return[49]

Joining Lawrence were a number of medical officers who favored increased opportunities for marriage as a way to improve the soldiers' health. This comes as no surprise given the ways in which physical health had moral overtones. One surgeon declared, "The Anglo-Saxon is essentially a domestic animal, and although soldiers are not, as a class, celebrated for the practice of household virtues, no men are more easily weaned from vicious courses by judicious management."[50] Other surgeons, such as Kenneth Mackinnon, chimed in and pleaded for marriages to be allowed so as to improve the soldiers' health.[51]

THE MILITARY AND THE MATRIMONIAL MARKET IN COLONIAL INDIA

Arguments in favor of allowing soldiers to marry were entangled with questions of whom should soldiers marry: European, Eurasian, or Indian women. Finding potential European wives for soldiers raised a number of problems. The first was that of supply. In 1810, for example, it was estimated that there were only 250 European women in all of Bengal; at the time, there were over 10,000 European troops in that province.[52] Yet demographics do not account completely for a greater willingness to consider marriages between soldiers and Eurasian or Indian women. Indian or Eurasian wives were preferred for two principal reasons: They were thought to be better suited to the climate, and they were believed to be more malleable and useful than European wives. One officer declared that these "girls make grateful and agreeable wives, were it too that soldiers in general make such bad husbands."[53] Soldiers who managed to establish long-term relations with Indian wives were "not only kept free from venereal infection, but [had] more attention paid to the providing and dressing of their victuals, and to other comforts, conducive to their health, than can be given in this climate by European women."[54] European women were thought to deteriorate rapidly in the Indian climate. They also stood accused of being more troublesome. The kinds of class characterizations that had informed stereotypes of the rank and file were projected onto European women of the laboring classes. European wives of soldiers stationed in India were suspected of undermining discipline by trading in liquor, gambling, flirting, and generally causing troubles in the barracks. In contrast, by drawing on Orientalized stereotypes of Asian women, Indian and Eurasian wives were presented as being much more tractable.⁵⁵ Just as European soldiers were thought to be much more disorderly than sepoys, European women were viewed as much rowdier than their Indian counterparts. While such disorderliness might have had its value on the battlefield, it was not wanted in the barracks.

That the company did try to broker marriages between its soldiers and local women, albeit sporadically and sometimes halfheartedly, has hitherto escaped the attention of most historians. One notable exception is Indrani Chatterjee, who has argued that such efforts were really attempts to impose a form of state-sponsored concubinage that bore little resemblance to the ideals or even practices of marriage as understood in domestic Britain.⁵⁶ Her analysis concludes that the East India Company's objective was to exploit the slave-like status of such women to gain control over their reproductive capabilities with the intention of ultimately producing a community of servile workers. As she puts it, "This encouragement to the marriage of the European soldier in India was an inducement to biologically reproduce servile labour, while socially reproducing its marginality."⁵⁷ Examining the colonial state's views on marriage in terms of its labor imperatives is an important and innovative perspective—one that usefully reveals much about the structures of domination under which Indian and Eurasian women existed as well as the ideologies that informed such structures. But an instrumentalist explanation such as this has its limits. If the East India Company's policies on soldiers' marriages were primarily motivated by the desire to breed workers, we would expect that they would have acted much more forcefully and systematically in trying to bring about junctions between their soldiers and local women. Marriage was tolerated, not necessarily encouraged. And while the female offspring of European–Indian or European–Eurasian couples could be easily placed, it was initially much more difficult to find employment for male children, and this situation would persist throughout much of the nineteenth century. As one commentator put it, "While in India matrimony is almost the be-all and end-all of female orphans, in England trained labour is in great demand, and marriage does not enter into the calculation of the Guardian."⁵⁸ We need also to bear in mind that the one rationale for keeping even a limited number of women on the strength of a regiment—that they provided valuable labor—was not that relevant in India. Soldiers' wives filled a number of valuable roles in Britain, but in India servants satisfied most of those needs, thereby stripping soldiers' wives of much of their immediate value.

We need also to ask whether there was much demand for a racially engineered labor force. In fact, through much of the early nineteenth century, colonial officials were at a loss in trying to identify suitable occupations for the growing Eurasian community. As one writer noted, the seemingly endless supply of cheap labor meant that there was little demand for the Eurasians.[59] There was some call for Eurasians in technical employment, where their education gave them an edge: The surveying department preferred them to Indians, though the numbers involved were not that great, and later the railway and telegraph departments would hire them in greater numbers. But prior to the great expansion in railways (which was largely a post–1857 development and therefore after the demise of the company), British officials were hard pressed to find employment for Eurasians.[60] Moreover, the belief that Eurasians were intrinsically well suited to technical employment does not explain their use as bandsmen in the army, which was the only real niche they enjoyed in any great numbers before they were recruited to serve on the railways. They became bandsmen primarily because the army refused to allow them employment as soldiers. The argument used against their being employed more generally in the army was that Indian sepoys, who the British had convinced themselves were acutely sensitive to issues of status and race, would never agree to serve with, much less under, persons of mixed ancestry.[61] This is an important and interesting example of how colonial rule came to depend on the projection by the colonizer of their prejudices on the colonized. Roberts declared that Indians would never submit to the authority of "persons springing from outcaste females."[62] An added objection to Eurasians was that many were Christian, at least nominally, and British officers were always concerned lest their sepoys think that their religion was under threat.

From that perspective, it is easier to understand why the argument against recruiting Eurasians was very similar to that employed to frustrate efforts to secure recruits from the lower castes. The axiom that Eurasians should not be entertained as recruits was deeply entrenched in the colonial psyche. Efforts made by Eurasians later in the nineteenth century to persuade the British government to relent and allow Eurasians to join as combatants consequently made little headway.[63] Race was an obvious barrier to their employment, as indicated in the terms that determined who the army would accept as recruits—namely, "men whose fathers and maternal grandfathers, or whose mothers and paternal grandfathers are of pure European origin."[64] Formulae such as these were obviously intended to ensure that as far as possible the army remained the preserve of Europeans and Indians, thereby preventing racial boundaries from becoming too blurred.

Thus, while finding suitable employment for Eurasian males was difficult (at least until mid-century), it was relatively easy to deal with Eurasian women by marrying them off to soldiers and noncommissioned officers. The army had to contend with a shortage of possible wives—at least, wives of European extraction. A common theme running through most contemporary accounts of cantonment life in India is just how few eligible European women there were. The situation is summed up in one fictional account of a sergeant's quest for a wife at a cantonment where two regiments of Europeans were stationed. He fails in four attempts—either beaten by a competitor or considered simply too old at thirty-three by some women as young as thirteen.[65] Contrary to reports of so-called fishing fleets of eligible European women arriving in Indian ports,[66] comparatively few single European women emigrated to India, especially before the second half of the nineteenth century, when the introduction of steam shipping and the opening of the Red Sea made the voyage to India quicker and easier than it had once been. The single women who did come to India, often accompanying brothers or fathers, could choose their husbands from a wide field of prospective suitors: Poorly paid and poorly housed soldiers and noncommissioned officers would not have fared well in such circumstances.[67]

One option for those soldiers eager to marry was to seek out the widows of fellow soldiers as well as the women left behind when regiments were posted out of India. The mortality rates of European soldiers in India ensured that there was a steady supply of widows. In the first half of the nineteenth century, statisticians calculated that European regiments in India experienced on average an annual loss of 10 percent of their strength.[68] One soldier in India remarked, "I knew one woman personally who was the wife of three husbands in six months, and another who had married the fifth husband, having children by every one of them."[69] Widows in India often had little choice but to find a new husband. If a widow's deceased husband had been in the regular British Army, and she was not officially listed on the strength of the regiment, there was no provision for her repatriation back to the United Kingdom. As William Bentinck complained in 1834, it is "revolting to humanity and morality, that the greater part [of the Indian wives and their children] are left behind without any provision, and are in general turned over en masse to the relieving regiment."[70] Attempts by the East India Company to force the British government to provide some relief for such women came to naught.

The issue climaxed in 1819 when the East India Company was confronted with a large number of women who had been abandoned when the 66th Regiment was rotated out of India. The commander of the 66th Regiment had allowed his men to bring a number of women with them when they came to India from a tour of duty in Sri Lanka.[71] The company's Court of Directors argued unsuccessfully that, as the women had come to India from territories outside their control, the company was under no obligation to care for them and that they were therefore the responsibility of the British government. The commander-in-chief of the British army did not agree, insisting that this was an extraordinary charge owing to "local habits incident to the Country," and resulting costs were the responsibility of the company. And as far as the twenty-seven children that had been left behind, "His Royal Highness can only say, that unless any of them shall be the children born of European women in wedlock, there is no possible mode of providing for them."[72]

But even in instances where return to Britain was possible, some widows appeared to be quite happy to stay on in India. It had become home to them; they could look forward to having servants (something unavailable to most of them back in Britain), and there were opportunities to earn between 50 and 100 rupees a month as domestic servants and wet nurses (by way of comparison, sepoys received 10 rupees a month, and many Indian laborers would have been lucky to receive 5 rupees a month).[73] Even Bentinck, who had spoken out forcefully against the practice of leaving women and children behind, conceded that the situation might not be much better if such women were allowed to accompany their husbands to Europe. Indian or Eurasian women "are ill able to support the severity of a Northern Climate, while the restrictive means of the soldiers in Europe do not enable him to afford the same comforts to his family as in India."[74] In the end, Bentinck saw little future for such women. They were destined to lives of misery and exploitation.

Another source of potential wives was the daughters of European servicemen in India. It was said that, in India, "he is a fortunate man who has two or three tolerable looking daughters on the eve of womanhood; he requires no fortunes to get them off his hands; but, on the contrary, propitiatory presents shower in upon him from a dozen individuals, all ready to pay handsomely in that way or any other for being permitted to marry into his family."[75] Occasionally, wives and concubines were acquired as spoils of war. Such acquisitions are hard to track, as, not surprisingly, the imperial archive is rather reticent on such subjects. But occasionally out of the silence emerges some evidence of women who were forcibly abducted or purchased. For example, troops who participated in the seizure of Ganjam and Cuttack in 1815 seized many women, while their officers divvied up the wives left behind when the raja took flight.[76] Other Europeans purchased concubines, rendering them in practice little more than slaves—thus confirming, at least in part, some of what Chatterjee has argued elsewhere.[77] But purchasing a concubine was not something that the majority of the rank and file are likely to have considered. Concubines cost something in the range of 20 to 40 rupees a month, an amount that was within the range of an officer but well beyond that of a private.[78]

The remaining supply of potential brides was to be found among the orphans of European soldiers serving in India (the term "orphan" in India included those children who had lost their parents as well as children of parents that colonial authorities had declared to be unfit for the task of raising their children). By the early eighteenth century, orphanages had been established in the Madras presidency. Most were small and run by private charities. The expansion of British military activity in India led to an increased numbers of soldiers' children for whom care needed to be arranged. The Lord Clive Fund was established in the aftermath of the conquest of Bengal. Under its terms, widows and orphans of soldiers who had served in India would be entitled to a pension. However, this pension was initially denied to widows or orphans residing in India. Only those dependents who had returned to Britain were eligible. As Eurasian and Indian wives and children were not entitled to repatriation, Eurasians were effectively ineligible for any assistance. Moreover, an affidavit of parentage was required. When several Eurasian wives applied for pensions, they were refused.[79] The government only relented in the 1820s, when the fund was opened to beneficiaries in India as well as in Europe.[80]

Not long after the foundation of the Lord Clive Fund came the establishment of orphanages expressly designed for the children of soldiers and officers. The first of these was erected in Bengal in 1783. Its intention was to provide an environment where orphans could be raised and educated to become useful members of society.[81] Education focused on helping students acquire a useful trade or, in the case of girls, domestic skills to make them marriageable. But it was first and foremost an institution intended to meet the demands of the army. As the author of a handbook intended for recent arrivals in India put it: "This orphan institution is now intimately blended with the military establishments throughout India; the Company making it a part of their regulations, for all persons admitted into their military service, to become, ipso facto, subscribers to the fund."[82] It was eventually partitioned into a Lower Orphan Asylum in Alipore and an Upper Orphan School near Kidderpore. There again, the "objects of the institution are, to educate, and settle out in life, Children of both sexes, begotten by Officers and Soldiers on the Bengal Establishment."[83]

But there were several crucial differences between these institutions. The Upper Orphan School was intended for children of officers who had died, and eligibility was not tied to legitimacy. Its purpose was to settle these children back into Britain, and that was only available to those children for whom it could be established that both parents were European. Its rules insisted, "Children born in wedlock only are sent home by the Society, and alone participate in the benefits of an English education."[84] It goes on to declare, "Illegitimate orphans will be taken care of in India—girls will be sent to Kidderpore House and the boys placed in an appropriate school." The Upper Orphan School was funded by direct subscription from all officers. This in effect released fathers from fiscal and legal obligation for their children, but at little cost to the company.

The qualification noted earlier—that of "illegitimate orphans"—illustrates an important point with respect to orphans in India. Many of these so-called orphans would not be considered orphans today, as a number of them still had living parents. Being an orphan in colonial India did not mean that one's parents were dead. Instead, it meant that the child had no legitimate living parents. Legitimacy in nineteenth-century India was coded in gendered and racial language. As Chatterjee has pointed out, to be declared an orphan in India only required proof that the father was dead; the mother, who would most often be either Eurasian or Indian, was irrelevant in the eyes of the law.[85] Illegitimacy was therefore assigned to children born of an Indian or Eurasian mother and a European soldier. The company clearly intended that children born to a European officer and an Indian mother would remain in India and it was not obliged to care for them. However, it was assumed that these children were entitled to more respect than those born to a European soldier and Indian mother. Race, therefore, was not the sole factor at work. Class also came into play, for children of European officers and Indian mothers secured better treatment than those children born to a European soldier and an Indian woman. As noted earlier, the regular army also refused to recognize as legitimate children born to a British soldier and either an Indian or a Eurasian wife. Race was obviously a critical factor, but here again we find some glaring inconsistencies. British soldiers arriving in India with black wives from the West Indies found that their wives were deemed to be exempt from the regulation that "wives of non commissioned officers and privates not born of European parents are excluded from receiving the allowance of 8 sonaut rupees per mensem."[86] In this instance, the exemption was justified on the basis that the purpose of the original regulation was to discourage local marriages, and in these cases, the wives, though not of European background, had been brought to India.

The Lower Orphan Asylum was intended for the children of privates and noncommissioned officers:

> Children . . . of parents belonging to regiments leaving the country, who may not be allowed to accompany them, and who are left without natural protectors, the orphans of deceased fathers, who were attached during their life to Queen's corps serving in India—and finally children of men belonging to HM service, who are destitute of guardians or means of support, are occasionally ordered into the school, by the charitable consideration of the Government, as special cases[87]

The Lower Orphan Asylum was funded directly by the company, for few soldiers had much pay remaining after all the stoppages had been made for clothing, equipment, and food. What little was left was usually spent on liquor, a practice that the army only belatedly and halfheartedly sought to discourage.[88] Money for the asylum came through a combination of grants, donations, legacies, and the income from a nearby bazaar, known as "Orphan Gunge."[89] Some income was also generated from the sale of needlework that was undertaken on commission by the girls and by the printing press that the older boys had been taught to operate.[90] Children were given a rudimentary education to outfit them for the limited career openings available to them. Girls were taught household economy and domestic duties, as they were expected to marry European soldiers and noncommissioned officers stationed in India. An exception was made for girls raised in the Upper Orphan School: They were given an education intended to make them more marriageable among the middle and upper classes in Britain and, hence, "accomplishments" were stressed.[91]

The intention of the Lower Orphan Asylum, according to its own mandate, was to "encourage the European soldier to enter a marriage state; to relieve him from the heavy burden of rearing a large offspring with scanty means."[92] Fathers were paid 3 rupees per month per child but only until each child turned three. At that point, the company would only continue to pay for the children's upbringing if they were placed in one of the orphanages that had been established for them. Later this was amended to allow children to stay with their parents, but only if proof was regularly provided that the children were being educated in the regimental schools.[93] The Royal army officially recognized only children who had been born to wives on the strength of the regiment. All others were in theory left to fend for themselves, though often such orphans would be placed in company or charity-run orphanages—or, in some cases, the father's regiment would make unofficial arrangements for them.[94] On occasion, Masonic Lodges, which had sprung up in many regiments, also contributed to the care of widows and orphans.[95]

It is important to bear in mind that, while the Lower Orphan Asylum and the Upper Orphan School were directed at different classes of orphans, and the former was funded directly by the government and the latter through subscription, they were both administered by committees of army officers, and their proceedings reveal just how much these institutions were guided by military values and imperatives as well as the growing authority of racialized discourses. A case in point is the series of decisions taken in the nineteenth century, on the basis of contemporary fixations on the perceived relationship between climate, health, and race, to relocate a number of orphanages to the hill stations.[96] Attention had turned to the more salubrious climate of the Himalayan foothills, and by the mid–nineteenth century, European children were being sent to asylums and schools in the hill stations. The Lawrence Military Asylums, the first of which was established near Simla in 1847, showed a clear preference for what Lawrence called "pure European parentage," for they were the children most likely to suffer from the heat of the plains.[97] The Lawrence Asylum was initially set up by subscription to provide a healthy place to educate the children of European soldiers.[98] Exclusion of Eurasian children was justified on the basis that their having Indian mothers made them more resistant to the climate and diseases of the plains. Catholics were also made to feel unwelcome.[99] Implicit, however, was an anxiety that racially ambiguous children threatened to undermine an increasingly race-conscious regime.

It is clear that a principal function of these orphanages was to provide wives for suitable soldiers: "Suitable" normally meant noncommissioned officers and long-serving soldiers who had managed to convince their officers that they merited permission to marry. Between 1800 and 1818, 380 women left the Orphan School in Bengal through marriage. Of these women, 274 married noncommissioned officers and privates of the East India Company, 65 married noncommissioned officers and privates in Royal regiments, and the remaining 41 found husbands in civil or private employ.[100] At the beginning, partnering orphans and soldiers was done rather haphazardly, often involving dances.[101] Over time, elaborate systems evolved to match soldiers with prospective wives, all of which were firmly controlled by the directors of the orphanages. The matron then made a match, and if both parties were agreeable, the marriage was arranged. But it is not clear just how much freedom of choice these young women enjoyed. While most sources seem to suggest that they had some voice, it is clear that pressure was brought on them to marry men who were acceptable to the asylum's matron, which would thereby relieve the asylum and ultimately the government of the costs of caring for them.[102] Roberts spelled the process out more clearly:

> Some of its regulations, though judicious, are rather singular. Should the non-commissioned officers or privates of European regiments desire to take a wife out of this asylum; they are, if men of character, permitted to do so, but they must choose by eye alone at a single interview. They are not allowed to pay their addresses to the object which has attracted them, or to transfer their affections to another after their selection has been made: no previous acquaintance can be granted, and the bride has only the privilege of rejection.[103]

Throughout the "courting ritual," the authority of the matron was maintained. Regulations from 1850 are explicit on this point. The asylum is required to record "the name of every person applying for a wife, together with his rank and corps," and "if he applies for any particular girl, her name is also to be entered: the Testimonials which every person brings with the order, are to be kept by the Head Mistress, with the order itself as a voucher." Moreover, prospective suitors are warned: "No Girl is, on any account, to be permitted to be receive money, trinkets, or presents of any kind, from any man by whom she may be addressed, until the marriage is concluded upon and sanctioned by the Deputy Governor."[104] A similar practice was followed in Bombay. One soldier recollected that a number of his colleagues "had very pretty half-caste wives, whom they had got out of the Byculla orphan school at Bombay, where any soldier of good character and possessed of capital to commence house-keeping, may obtain a helpmate."[105] There the routine was that a soldier would "take tea three times at the school during which he [could] observe all the girls"[106]

But there were always limits to what the company would tolerate with respect to interracial marriages. As already noted, the practice of officers taking Indian wives or mistresses fell out of fashion first. While guidebooks at the turn of the century were quite candid about the practice, later authors were silent on the subject.[107] This growing intolerance can also be glimpsed in the government's response to a proposal it received to send female orphans and children of the Lower Orphan Asylum to New South Wales. The government questioned "whether the transplanting of females of pure European extraction would not tend to the more rapid propagation of the mixed breed in India."[108] They were also worried about sending away any Eurasians. Put another way, if European and Eurasian children were sent to New South Wales, it would leave only Indian women as possible wives for the soldiers. To this the managers of the Lower Orphan Asylum responded, "Any diminution of this supply would infallibly multiply the instances of illicit cohabitation with native women of the lowest description."[109] For the officers of the Bengal army, Eurasians might not have been suitable for their level of society, but they were ultimately preferable to any of the alternatives for the rank and file.

What is perhaps most difficult to fathom is how soldiers viewed these orphanages and, especially, the rules that placed their children in them.

Chatterjee's work on wills found an intriguing difference: Officers often made provisions for their children, legitimate or illegitimate. She found few soldiers' wills that made allowance for their offspring. Several explanations occurred to her to explain this: low birthrate, homosexuality, low fertility, or loss of rights over the children.[110] She leans toward the last explanation. However, to these can be added further possibilities. One is that soldiers never really accepted these children as their own; that, in fact, soldiers might have eschewed any responsibility whatsoever. Unfortunately, few soldiers' accounts survive, and those that I have surveyed make little reference to wives and families. In a few instances, one can detect obvious signs of paternal affection and responsibility. But more often all one finds is silence. And rather than supposing that this is the consequence of the system working to frustrate fathers, it might be that the military culture in which the soldiers themselves participated did not encourage them to assume a paternal role. A number of officers certainly thought this to be the case: "The soldier, at present, neither educates nor provides for his offspring in India. . . . Therefore the soldier is at present relieved from all care and trouble in rearing his own children."[111]

CONCLUSION

The army in India's position on soldiers, marriage, and families—an ever shifting one—highlights the many anomalies that existed there with respect to the articulation and maintenance of racial, gender, and class hierarchies. Colonial authorities were always beset by questions of security. Yet security itself cannot be isolated from questions of sexuality for the soldiers (not to mention the officers) on whom that security rested were themselves sexual beings. Thus, the bodies of the soldiers, as well as of those with whom they were in contact, became sites of contestation. Moreover, given the symbolic weight attached to soldiers as manifest signs of colonial authority, there was a growing commitment to ensuring that soldiers received the care and attention that had hitherto eluded them. The idealization of domestic life which was such a powerful feature of

Victorian Britain, when combined with the increasing acknowledgement of the role played by soldiers in defending Britain's empire, led to heightened demands for improvements to the conditions in which they served. Not surprisingly, marriage was fastened on to by many as the means by which the soldier could be reclaimed and used as a symbol of what the empire could bestow on its subjects. But marriages could not be easily arranged, given the nature of Anglo-Indian society and growing apprehensions over metissage. As one officer put it in his advice to those soon to depart for India, "This is the Scylla of European life in India; the Charybdis is left-handed alliances with native females, and the 'medio tutissimusibis' is either through the Straits of Continence or of Matrimony."[112]

If as the nineteenth century progressed there were signs that the army was becoming more inclined to take the Straits of Matrimony (if for no other reason than few had any faith in the Straits of Continence), an equal number of indicators demonstrated that by mid-century it was becoming less tolerant of interracial marriages. While it is certainly true that there was a growing swell of opinion that was decidedly against encouraging marriage or sexual relations between Indians and Europeans, it is equally evident that the army not only condoned such acts within certain parameters, but went so far as to facilitate them. This highlights a point raised by Robert Young—namely, that while racial discourse was always informed by the potential of interracial sexuality, it was done in fragmentary and unstable ways.[113] Commentators might rail against the growing Eurasian community and demand, "We must root up the weeds of idleness and effeminacy which spontaneously spring from the soil of their nature, and implant the sturdy virtues, the enterprise, the perseverance, the masculine vigour of British heart and soul."[114] But even a jeremiad such as this one was qualified, however grudgingly, with the caveat that until the lives of soldiers were considerably improved, and the supply of marriageable European women increased, there would be little change.

By the 1830s, race had gained considerable purchase on Anglo-Indian culture.[115] Prior to that period, those who stressed cultural rather than biological differences could still be heard, arguing that racial differences were environmental in nature and as such could be overcome through time, education, and acclimatization. As race came to be seen as a foundational difference, colonial policy making came to reflect many of its assumptions, though the impact of race was itself qualified by the twin pressures of military imperatives and the customs and traditions of the East India Company army. This placed colonial officials in a dilemma, for they had to cope with a rising chorus of demands that they allow their soldiers to marry while simultaneously seeking to demarcate sharper racial boundaries. The result was that the military never gained the kind of total control over the bodies of its subjects that its public discourse might otherwise suggest.

NOTES

I thank several friends and colleagues for their critical insights and comments in preparing this paper. I have shared elements of it with Antoinette Burton, Durba Ghosh, Mark Harrison, Philippa Levine, and Javed Majeed. The end product benefited from their wise counsel, although they are in no way responsible for its conclusions.

1   Rudyard Kipling, "Beyond the Pale," in *Plain Tales from the Hills* (London: Penguin, 1994 [1888]), 171.

2   This was true in the later stages of empire, as well. See Levine, *Prostitution, Race and Politics*.

3   Roberts, *Scenes and Characteristics of Hindos*, 3:95.

4   Ibid., 1:43.

5   This is evocatively, if somewhat romantically, captured in Dalrymple, *White Mughals*.

6   Williamson, *The East India Vade-Mecum*, 1:452.

7   Marshall, "The White Town of Calcutta under the Rule of the East India Company."

8   Ibid. See also Ghosh, "Making and Un-Making Loyal Subjects."

9   Kochanski, *Sir Garnet Wolseley*, 24. The shifting sexual landscape of Lucknow in the immediate post–1857 period is addressed in detail in Oldenburg, *The Making of Colonial Lucknow, 1856–1871*.

10 Hobbes, "Calcutta," 366.

11 Caplan, "Iconographies of Anglo-Indian Women," 865–67. See also the pioneering work done on this topic by Ann Laura Stoler, especially her "Rethinking Colonial Categories."

12 The manner in which the Eurasian body—how it was clothed and presented—factored into these prejudices is addressed in Collingham, *Imperial Bodies*, 65–66. Collingham's focus, however, is primarily on the civil service, for she argues that "it was their bodies which formed the main focus of official and medical discourses about how the British should rule in India": ibid., 6. Yet as I have shown here and elsewhere, the health—physical, mental, and moral—of troops in India was a major issue for colonial policy making.

13 Ernst, "Colonial Policies, Racial Politics and the Development of Psychiatric Institutions in Early Nineteenth-Century India," 83. See also idem, "Colonial Lunacy Policies and the Madras Lunatic Asylum in the Early Nineteenth Century."

14 For a discussion of the unease generated by the presence of mixed races, see Malchow, *Gothic Images of Race in Nineteenth-Century Britain*. For a sampling of recent works that deal more specifically with the intersection of sexual and racial boundaries in India, see Ballhatchet, *Race, Sex and Class under the Raj*; Hall, *White, Male and Middle Class*; Levine, "Rereading the 1890s"; Peers, "Privates Off Parade"; Stoler, *Race and the Education of Desire*; Whitehead, "Bodies Clean and Unclean." See also, most notoriously, Hyam, *Empire and Sexuality*. With respect to the Hyam, see Berger, "Imperialism and Sexual Exploitation."

15 White, *Children of the French Empire*. This work suggests the value of more comparative studies of this phenomenon.

16 Pioneering works in this respect include Arnold, *Colonizing the Body*; Vaughan, *Curing Their Ills*. On India, see also Collingham, *Imperial Bodies*.

17 On the social and cultural life of the company's European soldiers, see Stanley, *White Mutiny*.

18 As Elizabeth Buettner has shown for the late nineteenth century and early twentieth century, the modes and terms of classification became even more contested with the growth of a poor white community, a group, often locally born, that threatened to undermine the already precarious distinction between Anglo-Indian and Eurasian: Buettner, "Problematic Spaces, Problematic Races."

19 "English Women in Hindustan," 124.

20 Eurasians and Native Christian Company of Artillery, 1875, Oriental and India Office Collections (British Library) (hereafter OIOC) L/Mil/5/673.

21 Tait, "On the Mortality of Eurasians," 326.

22 "The Portuguese in North India," 289.

23 Roberts, *Scenes and Characteristics of Hindos*, 1:72–73.

24 "The Colonization Mania," 346.

25 Burton, *Goa, and the Blue Mountains*, 100.

26 This is a point which I briefly allude to in Peers, "Privates Off Parade."

27 Ibid.

28 Hough, *Military Law Authorities*, 74–75, 130, 165.

29 Peers, "Imperial Vice," 30.

30 Martin, *The Sanitary History of the British Army in India, Past and Present*, 31.

31 Military letter to India, 17 March 1852, OIOC E/4/814.

32 "The Madras Native Army." I am grateful to Carina Montgomery for bringing this article to my attention.

33 Madras Military Consultations, 20 March 1810, OIOC P/256/63.

34 See Spiers, *The Army and Society, 1815–1914*; Trustram, *Women of the Regiment*.

35 Trustram, *Women of the Regiment*, 54–55.

36 Ibid., 86.

37 Senior, *British Regulars in Montreal*, 31.

38 Trustram, *Women of the Regiment*, 85.

39 Stanley, *White Mutiny*.

40 Ernst, "Colonial Policies, Racial Politics and the Development of Psychiatric Institutions in Early Nineteenth-Century India.

41 Hough, *Military Law Authorities*, 206.

42 See, for example, "From Camp to Quarters," 84–94, 244–54, 376–85, 546–56, 401–12; Morley and Wills, "The Soldier's Wife." The reformist agenda has also been explored by several recent historians, including Hendrickson, *Making Saints*; Hichberger, *Images of the Army*. But there is a danger in exaggerating the impact of the Crimean War and the Indian Rebellion, for reforms were already under way: see Strachan, *Wellington's Legacy*.

43 The popular reception of the British soldier as Christian hero is addressed in Hichberger, *Images of the Army*. With respect to reforms more generally in the British army, see Strachan, *Wellington's Legacy*.

44 Cockerill, "The Royal Military Asylum (1803–1815)."

45 Some discussion of this can be found in Alavi, *The Sepoys and the Company*; Peers, *Between Mars and Mammon*; Stanley, *White Mutiny*. Carina Montgomery's forthcoming Oxford University D.Phil thesis on the Madras Army of the late eighteenth century and early nineteenth century also has much to say about the army's role in the domestic lives of its soldiers and their families.

46 Peers, "Imperial Vice."

47 Firebrace, "On the Errors and Faults in our Military System," 544.

48 Peers, "Sepoys, Soldiers and the Lash."

49 Lawrence, *Adventures of an Officer in the Service of Runjeet Singh*, 1:269.

50 Mouat, *The British Soldier in India* (London: R. C. Lepage, 1859), 73.

51 MacKinnon, *A Treatise on the Public Health, Climate, Hygiene, and Prevailing Diseases of Bengal and the North-West Provinces*.

52 Williamson, *The East India Vade-Mecum*, 1:453.

53 MacMullen, *Camp and Barrack Room*, 164.

54 Madras Military Consultations, 20 March 1810, OIOC P/256/63.

55 Sherwood and Sherwood, *The Life of Mrs. Sherwood*, 485–86.

56 Chatterjee, "Colouring Subalternity."

57 Ibid., 88.

58 Lawson, *At Home on Furlough*, 257.

59 Gilchrist, *The General East India Guide and Vade Mecum*, 210.

60 The relationship between Eurasians and Indian railway colonies, see Bear, "Miscegenations of Modernity."

61 Williamson, *The East India Vade-Mecum*, 1:468. The logic and assumptions that informed British officers' readings of the sepoys under their authority has been examined for the early nineteenth century in Peers, "The Habitual Nobility of Being." On the period after 1857, see Omissi, *The Sepoy and the Raj*.

62 Roberts, *Scenes and Characteristics of Hindos*, 3:97–98.

63 Military Department to Salisbury, 1876, OIOC L/Mil/7/12778, no. 68.

64 Ibid.

65 Crowquill. "Barrack Sketches."

66 Victor Jacquemont was partially responsible for this myth: see Jacquemont, *Letters from India*, 169.

67 The matrimonial market of India features prominently in Anglo-Indian light literature. See, for example, the writings of J. W. Kaye, an army officer, historian, and government official: Kaye, *Doveton*; idem, *Peregrine Pulteney* (first published in India in serial form circa 1840–41); idem, *The Story of Basil Bouverie*. The non-official Anglo-Indian community in India is the subject of Renford, *The Non-Official British in India to 1920*.

68 Peers, *Between Mars and Mammon*, 83.

69 MacMullen, *Camp and Barrack Room*, 165.

70 William Bentinck, minute, 5 July 1834, Bentinck Papers, OIOC MSS Eur E424/9.

71 Court of Directors to Board of Control, 26 August 1819, OIOC L/Mil/5/376.

72 Horse Guards to Board of Control, August 1819, OIOC L/Mil/5/376.

73 Roberts, *Scenes and Characteristics of Hindos*, 3:47.

74 Bentinck, minute.

75 MacMullen, *Camp and Barrack Room*, 164.

76 Chatterjee, "Colouring Subalternity," 61.

77 For an example of such a purchase, see Peers, "Privates Off Parade," 845. For further examples, see Chatterjee, "Colouring Subalternity"; Collingham, *Imperial Bodies*, 74.

78 Williamson, *The East India Vade-Mecum*, 1:451–52.

79 Military letter to Madras, 7 September 1808, OIOC F/4/360.

80 Military letter from India, 17 June 1828, OIOC F/4/1115.

81 David Arnold, "European Orphans and Vagrants in India in the Nineteenth Century," *Journal of Imperial and Commonwealth History* 7 (1979): 104–27.

82 Gilchrist, *The General East India Guide and Vade Mecum*.

83 Military Orphan Society, *Rules and Regulations of the Lower Branch of the Military Orphan Society*, 1.

84 Samuel Brown, *Report on the Bengal Military Orphan Society and Valuation*, 128.

85 Chatterjee, "Colouring Subalternity," 69–70.

86 Military letter from Bengal, 23 December 1814, OIOC F/4/485, no. 11644.

87 Military Orphan Society, *Rules and Regulations of the Lower Branch of the Military Orphan Society*, 32.

88 Trustram, *Women of the Regiment*, 54–55.

89 R. G. Hobbes, "Scenes in the Cities and Wilds of Hindostan," n.d. (ca.1830), OIOC MSS Eur B260, fol. 113.

90 Military Orphan Society, *Rules and Regulations of the Lower Branch of the Military Orphan Society*, 39.

91 Hobbes, "Scenes in the Cities and Wilds of Hindostan," fol. 113.

92 Military Orphan Society, *Rules and Regulations of the Lower Branch of the Military Orphan Society*, 2.

93 Ibid., 11–12.

94 Hawes, *Poor Relations*, 25.

95 Gould, *Military Lodges*. Jessica Harland-Jacobs's forthcoming work on freemasonry and empire has much more to say on the welfare function fulfilled by Masonic Lodges throughout the empire.

96 For a discussion of the pervasive influence of climatic theories on colonial rule, see Harrison, *Climates and Constitutions*, 140–50.

97 Kennedy, *The Magic Mountains*, 136.

98 "Lawrence Asylum," *Mofussilite*, 10 March 1848, 157; see also "Upper Orphan Asylum; Kidderpore," *East India United Service Journal* 21 (1836): 214-20.

99 "Lawrence Asylum," 157.

100 Chatterjee, "Colouring Subalternity," 91.

101 Roberts, *Scenes and Characteristics of Hindos*, 2: 42–43.

102 Hobbes, "Scenes in the Cities and Wilds of Hindostan," fol. 113.

103 Roberts, *Scenes and Characteristics of Hindos*, 2:108–109.

104 Military Orphan Society, *Rules and Regulations of the Lower Branch of the Military Orphan Society*, 39.

105 MacMullen, *Camp and Barrack Room*, 164.

106 Paget, *Camp and Cantonment*, 105.

107 Collingham, *Imperial Bodies*, 73–74.

108 Military letter from Bengal, 27 November 1829, OIOC F/4/1240, no. 40737.

109 Enclosure to Military letter from Bengal, 27 November 1829, OIOC F/4/1240, no. 40737.

110 Chatterjee, "Colouring Subalternity," 90.
111 "Military Colonization in India," 540.
112 McCosh, *Advice to Officers in India*, 175.
113 Young, *Colonial Desire*.
114 Hobbes, "Scenes in the Cities and Wilds of Hindostan" fol. 109.
115 This is the thesis underpinning Harrison, *Climates and Constitutions*.

ANUPAMA RAO

Problems of Violence, States of Terror

Torture in Colonial India

On 17 October 1855, 1,989 inhabitants of the town of Nasik sent a petition to Governor-General Monstuart Elphinstone seeking the reinstatement of one Mohammed Sheikh, joint police officer, or *foujdar*. The petitioners noted:

> We at present learn from the newspaper that the Government has dismissed [the Foujdar] from his situation, and on inquiry found that last year a Coonbee had murdered his niece for her ornaments, and was apprehended by the Police peons, who put a stick up his anus for extorting confession, and that the Government has decided that the Foujdar had ordered to do this to the above Coonbee who died while in custody—but we feel certain that the Foujdar could not have ordered to the above effect because in the deceased prisoner's deposition which was taken down before the Government authorities, no mention is made about the Foujdar's orders, nor did the Police peons who were tried and punished say anything in their depositions concerning the Foujdar's orders for putting a stick up the prisoner's anus or for doing such other evil action.[1]

Although the petitioners seek the foujdar's reinstatement, the excess of detail that they provide in this petition further implicates the foujdar rather than exonerates him. In the absence of any positive proof of the foujdar's innocence, the petitioners are ironically forced to rely on his alleged victim's dying declaration. The petition capitalizes on the obvious fact that the dying declaration could not be verified, because it was precisely that: a dead man's last words. Reading this petition today, one is tempted to accuse the petitioners of distorting the significance of the victim's last words. They take an omission as a positive indicator and thus fabricate a version of events that seems to suppress the truth of torture.

The story at stake cannot be so easily judged, however. The truth of torture lies not simply in its opposition to the torturer's version of events but rather, in a more complex matrix that situates the foujdar and his defenders themselves within a regime of violence. To unravel the relationship between the tortured body and the silences that surround the practice and perpetration of torture, it is necessary to inquire into how colonial law participated in a regime of torture while simultaneously erasing its own complicity in the reproduction of that regime.

How did these contradictions come to the fore in the violent death of a young man, a Coonbee, who was convicted for theft? A young man of about nineteen named Gunnoo is mentioned in the petition only by his caste label, Coonbee, or *kunbi*, which identifies a broad and inclusive category of agriculturalists.[2] The chain of events began when Gunnoo was accused of taking the ornaments of his five-year-old niece Syee and then drowning her in a well. Gunnoo was suspected as the perpetrator of the young girl's murder after witnesses, including his relatives, suggested that he was of doubtful character. Archival records of intimate violence from this period are plentiful. Accounts of husbands murdering wives, women attempting to poison husbands or lovers, widows committing infanticide, and violent claims to property and inheritance all attest to the contested and volatile nature of an extended domain of domesticity where family ties and relationships enabled acts of physical violence.[3] Though an uncle's murder of his young niece was a horrific crime, it would not have been considered outside the realm of possibility.

Once the police fixed on Gunnoo as the likely murderer, they interrogated him in public. Though Gunnoo denied knowing about Syee's whereabouts, when police peons "gave him a slap on the turban . . . a silver Suklee [chain] fell out—on searching him other ornaments were found." According to the witness, when asked about the girl again, Gunnoo pleaded that the ornaments must have been planted on him and repeated that he did not know Syee's whereabouts. At this point in the public interrogation, the foujdar is supposed to have said, "[Gunnoo] is frightened in this crowd; take him to one side and *Sumjao* him [make him understand, teach him]."[4] Gunnoo was then taken into the cowshed of a prostitute named Lateeb, where he was tortured. Soon thereafter, Gunnoo led the police to a well outside the town from which the young girl's body was dredged up. He also confessed to his crime at the well. Gunoo died in custody four days later, on 13 August 1854.

LAW'S VIOLENCE

Nasik was the name of both a district and its main town in western India. Western India, also known as the Deccan, was the last region of the subcontinent to come under direct East India Company control in 1818 with the defeat of Peshwa Bajirao II. By then, British techniques of governance had acquired some maturity with Britain's experience in Bengal and Madras. In the Deccan, the British encountered a settled sociopolitical formation with an intricately developed administrative history that compelled respect. The peshwai of the eighteenth-century has been characterized as a "brahminical state," invested in the caste morality of its subjects. The peshwa came from the powerful Chitpavan brahmin community, who had usurped political control from the Marathas, a community of peasant soldiers who, by the seventeenth century, had managed to break free of the direct control of the Mughal Empire. The peshwas were deeply committed to the ritual superiority of brahmins and used their temporal power to regulate caste hierarchies as a matter of state policy.

Though the peshwas claimed to be following the *dandaniti*, or penal law prescribed by Sanskrit texts, the kinds of punishment administered for crime more often than not bore little resemblance to the methods prescribed by them. Colonial administrators in the Deccan had noted that caste and village communities had the right to discipline their members.[5] Punishment appears to have been thoroughly political and decentralized, and the sovereign was not the only person who had the capacity to punish or inflict harm. This was reflected by the extent to which punishment remained context-specific and therefore open to bargaining and negotiation. V. T. Gune's important work on this period has noted that

> the individual lived in several penal jurisdictions apart from that of the king and his ministers; he or she might be subject to punishment in various degrees by the caste, the village community, the chief of the merchants, the preceptor (*dharmadikari*) and the head of the family.[6]

An elaborate penal regime was the most significant effect of this brahminical state, where the practice of extending fines for the commutation of physical harm existed alongside the use of practices such as scarring, beatings, mutilation, and disfigurement. The last practice appears to have been an especially popular form of disciplining women accused of adultery or otherwise breaching caste and sexual etiquette.[7]

The British experienced these diverse and competing legal pronouncements and bureaucratic regulations as the abundance, rather than the absence, of law, though these practices were degraded as lacking the precision and rigor of law as such. Although colonial officials tried to ground sovereignty on a moral and ethical foundation that elided the company's history of conquest, political exigencies made it imperative that new legal structures resemble or mimic earlier forms. Drawing on custom also offered scope for plausible deniability. Practices of discipline that appeared to exceed civilizational norms could always be rationalized as the natives' proclivity for barbarism and cruelty. As colonial officials tried to transform extant conceptions of personhood—based on highly differentiated caste and community-specific notions of honor and status—into those governed by the principles of possessive individualism, they found themselves forced, they argued, to counter the traditional despotisms of Oriental societies with the despotism of law.

Colonial law was a hybrid entity from the very start. The company state's claims to sovereignty came to rest on the twin pillars of settling (and taxing) land and establishing a law to govern the people so settled.[8] As the initial conquest of Bengal gave way to the efforts to establish permanent territorial control over large sections of the subcontinent, the settlement of mobile, peripatetic communities became especially acute.

Peasant soldiers, nomadic communities engaged in pretty trade, and so-called Criminal Tribes with a hereditary proclivity for violent crime all came under intense surveillance. The challenges that British colonial officials encountered in their efforts to govern natives were articulated in the way that exception was folded into the very structures of colonial law: *sati* was shorn of its ritual sanction and translated into murder; communities understood to be habituated or addicted to crime were prosecuted collectively as though they were driven by the singular intent of a "caste mind"; and informal practices of surveillance through spies and paid informants gained legal recognition in the figure of the approver.[9] We must locate our Nasik torture case in the context of such experiments with lawmaking and not merely of legal codification.[10]

Gunnoo's torture occurred at a critical conjuncture, just before two crucial events dramatically altered the landscape of colonial government in India. In the aftermath of the Sepoy Mutiny of 1857, a fundamental reorganization of the relationship between metropole and colony occurred. Queen Victoria's Proclamation of 1858 brought India under the direct control of the crown, thereby recognizing it as an integral part of the British Empire. In 1857, the violent rebellion against colonial rule had yoked together the disaffections of displaced peasantry, *zamindars* (landlords), and petty kings stripped of their political authority, and growing tensions among native soldiers, or sepoys, over the disrespect of customary distinctions of caste and religion within the British Army. In the aftermath of the mutiny, the colonial state maintained a strict policy of noninterference in matters concerning religion, since missionization and other forms of social intervention during the early nineteenth century were understood to have been one of the main causes of native disaffection. The post-mutiny order was based on the strict racial separation of rulers and ruled, and a colonial "ethnographic state" increasingly came to focus on caste and religion as governing all manner of social organization and intercourse.[11]

These transformations of the social and political landscape were visible and highly contested. A silent yet extensive restructuring of the colonial bureaucracy complemented them. The period between 1837, when a draft

Penal Code was proposed for British India, and 1861, when the Indian Penal Code came into existence, was a period of intense debate about the structure and organization of the colonial bureaucracy, with far-reaching implications for the exercise and organization of political power. Policing and revenue-gathering functions were particular targets of reorganization in the attempts to reduce corruption and ensure greater efficiency. Debates occurred at a presidency-wide level, and there was some variation in the Bengal, Madras, and Bombay models, with greater affinity between the latter two presidencies. The Bombay Regulation of 1827, or the Elphinstone Code, regulated criminal proceedings in Bombay until the Indian Penal Code of 1861 unified the administration of criminal law across the three presidencies. Efforts to address the juridical bases of sovereign power saw the extension of disciplinary power deep into native society.

This broader political context illuminates the conditions under which colonial officials "discovered" the pervasiveness of torture as a form of discipline and abuse of political authority. Instead of implicating colonial excess, revelations of the ubiquity of torture were converted into a persistent struggle against the remnants of a traditional and barbaric penal regime. Excessive violence was displaced onto "native" practices of policing and staged as an example of the spectacular brutality that was "law" in precolonial contexts. Reciting a litany of tortures—intimate, excessive, and cruel—was not an end in itself, however. Sciences of detection such as forensic medicine, which were assuming significance during this period, addressed physical vulnerability, the body's capacity to experience pain and suffering, as an integral aspect of human embodiment.[12] The scandalous publicity accorded to acts and instruments of torture and to images of physical mutilation and suffering were meant to illustrate the incomplete humanity of natives as well as the necessity of colonial intervention. As a limit condition both for the practices of policing and representations of colonial legality, debates about torture illuminate the peculiar ways in which "traditional" practices of violent punishment were reproduced due to the political exigencies of colonial governance. In this, the debates about torture can be distinguished from those other native practices such as sati, hook swinging, or human sacrifice that were so profoundly marked as performances of native religiosity and barbarism that they stood—and stand today—as eternal reminders of native backwardness and difference. Torture's distinctiveness lies in the fact that, although it was coded as the perpetuation of native disciplinary practices, it came to be incorporated into an emerging medical-penal complex as both problem and possibility at a transitional point in the colonization of Indian society. As a technology of violence, the commission of torture came to be associated with practices of physical mutilation and disfigurement understood to have been prevalent in Old Regime polities even while new evidentiary regimes and mechanisms of identification were mobilized to confirm their surreptitious prevalence. A close analysis of a single case of torture as it moved through the circuits of colonial law illustrates emerging structures of juridical verification as well as of colonial publicity.

COLONIAL SOVEREIGNTY AND NATIVE POLICE

Gunnoo's death in custody prompted a judicial inquiry that set colonial administrators against the native police. Colonial officials attempted to distance themselves from any culpability for this unfortunate incident of death in custody. The intensive inquiry that the Bombay government launched in the aftermath of Gunnoo's death was a ritual enactment of colonial justice that allowed officials to condemn the torture as an aberrant event. However, Gunnoo's death in custody and allegations of police torture put the Bombay government in a difficult position. The discovery of torture and the simultaneous efforts to contain it produced a political contradiction. Even as they investigated the charge of torture by the police, colonial administrators were anxious about the extent to which the practice was used to produce evidence, and they were therefore reluctant to bring the incident to public notice. Colonial administrators could punish the guilty policemen while preserving the aura of colonial justice only if torture could be distinguished from legitimate punishment.

This tension was evident in the legal documents that circulated after the Sessions Court sentenced the six police peons who were accused of torturing Gunnoo.[13] The court described the acts of these six men as "atrocious" and truly outside the bounds of law. The crimes were therefore treated as renegade acts committed without the authority of a superior. For this reason, the foujdar himself was not named as a defendant in the case. Indeed, in arguments later made in defense of the foujdar, it was maintained that such an act, committed "in great haste," this "desperate measure of cruelty" performed in a "clumsy manner," could not have been a premeditated act that took place with the connivance of a government official.[14] Supporting statements came from eyewitness testimony of the European officer, Alexander Bell, assistant superintendent of police, who testified that Gunnoo had appeared in perfect health when he had seen him at the well immediately after the alleged torture.

Further inquiry by the High Court, however, called the foujdar's innocence into question. A resolution from the governor-in-council to the registrar of the Sudder Adalut on 30 August 1855 noted that the native police had been let off too lightly; that "the punishment is far too light to operate as a warning to the Police subordinates in Nassick and throughout the Presidency." Furthermore, this letter held that the Sessions Judge was remiss in his duties. After all, the Sessions Court had noted that "when the Foujdar ordered the unfortunate prisoner to be taken aside he intended that a confession should be retracted from him by threats and ill-usages" but had not implicated him in Gunnoo's death. Due to pressure from the Bombay government, the Sudder Foujdari Adalat (Supreme Criminal Court) initiated a case against the foujdar, arguing, "It is not fitting [that] the subject and active agents in this crime should be punished while their superior is held blameless because he took care to keep out of sight himself of the outrage perpetrated."[15] Where, indeed, did culpability lie, and with whom did the responsibility for the murder ultimately rest?

The possibility that Gunnoo's torture was not simply the act of renegade police peons but, perhaps, an official act ordered by the foujdar moved this case onto a larger stage. For if Gunnoo's torture could be generalized as a practice of policing, rather than as an aberration, it would be necessary to conduct an inquiry into this practice at the highest levels. Thus, in response to a letter dated 20 July 1855 from Elphinstone, the governor-general of the Bombay Presidency, inquiring into the measures for preventing police abuse, the Supreme Criminal Court replied that it thought the law to be sufficient in handling cases of police abuse as well as extraction in the pursuit of revenue collection.[16] But colonial officials repeatedly gave vent to their mistrust of native police and considered them a necessary evil. As British officials attempted to scapegoat the perpetrators of police torture—the native police, who themselves appeared to require surveillance—a bifurcation within the institution of police was revealed. Even though the police were regarded as state servants and functionaries of the law, as native subjects they were compromised by their primitivism, which absolved the colonial state of any direct responsibility for their actions, even when it was performed in an *official* capacity. If legal reform was at all a possibility, the native police force had to be drastically reformed and modernized.

TORTURE AS A (COLONIAL) TECHNOLOGY OF TRUTH

As early as 1832, the *Select Committee on East India Affairs* (Judicial) had discussed the prevalence of torture and suggested that the police force had to be reformed and modernized to curtail the use of corporal violence.[17] In response to a query from the committee—"Are you aware whether the practice of torture by the native officers, for the purpose of extorting confessions or obtaining evidence, has been frequently resorted to?"—Alexander Campbell, former registrar of the Sudder Diwani (Supreme Civil Court) and Supreme Criminal Court in Madras replied:

> Under the native governments which preceded us at Madras, the universal object of every police officer was to obtain a confession from the prisoner with a view to his conviction of any offence; and notwithstanding every endeavor of our European tribunals to put an end to this system, frequent instances have come before all our criminal tribunals of its use.[18]

Campbell went on to note that policemen above the rank of common peon often functioned as witnesses to crimes, which literally allowed the police to take the law into their own hands. In 1857, a member of the House of Commons noted the popular conviction that "dacoity is bad enough, but that the subsequent police inquiry is worse."[19] This had much to do with the fact that confessions in the presence of the police were seen to be adequate for a judicial indictment. Magistrates with a poor command of native languages were often unfamiliar with the customary or religious codes that regulated people and communities. They found themselves relying on confessions taken by the police rather than conducting their own inquiries. The police often acted in a de facto judicial capacity, taking confessions, deciding guilt, and punishing wrongdoers. Were the police merely law's functionaries, or were they in fact *producing* the evidence that law courts relied on in the dispensation of justice?[20]

Corporal violence might have been an accepted feature of "traditional" repertoires of policing. The exercise of excessive violence by a colonial government that justified its distinctive moral mission to be the civilization and improvement of the natives, however, suggested that there was very little difference between the terrors exercised by Oriental despots and their imperial successors, between the rule of law and brutality. In 1857, officials were still arguing that "there was a deficiency in the police and in the administration of justice in India."[21] Interestingly, police reform and attempts to discontinue the use of excessive corporal violence were situated on a continuum with the abolition of other "horrible practices," such as hook swinging, infanticide, and Meriah (human) sacrifice, all "cruelties which disgraced society in India."[22] The problems of judicial administration could therefore be linked to native intransigence rather than the failures of colonial governance. Placing police torture alongside a stream of indistinguishable acts of barbarity and violence of varying motivations was a self-fulfilling prophecy. It confirmed, to British officials, that the native police were inured to the use of corporal violence in extracting confessions. Compromised by the fact of being "native"—hence, fundamentally irrational and prone to excess—the police were represented as a *cultural* institution. Repeatedly, native policemen rather than the colonial conditions of policing became the targets of criticism.

The publication of the two-volume *Report of the Commissioners for the Investigation of the Alleged Cases of Torture in the Madras Presidency Submitted to the Right Honourable Governor-in-Council of Fort Saint-George on the 16th April 1855* marked the culmination of internal debates about the problematic institution of police.[23] Responding to publicity generated by Parliamentary debates and newspaper reports regarding the pervasiveness of torture among police and revenue officials, the East India Company's Court of Directors ordered an inquiry into the matter even as it acknowledged that torture had long been a matter of private concern among colonial officials.[24] The commission was established on 9 September 1854, and the report was released on 16 April 1855, marking a crucial moment in the anxieties regarding colonial governance.[25] The report was initially meant to explore complaints about torture in the extraction of revenue in the Madras Presidency, but the government of India extended the scope of the report to address the relationship between torture and policing.[26] It could be argued that the exponential rise of demands for revenue with the inauguration of company rule had provided fertile ground for the abuse of authority and the perpetration of physical violence, but the report's mandate to explore the practice of policing quickly allowed the commissioners to address torture as a practice endemic to the native officials, including the police.[27] At the broadest level, the report was a self-incriminating document, a record of colonial culpability. However, in distinguishing the perpetrators of the practice, native functionaries, from the conditions of possibility for the performance of torture—namely, the extractive demands of the company state—the report addressed torture as a problem of personnel management, not as a symptom of the founding violence of colonial rule. The metropolitan public was thus spared the effort of imagining that an extractive revenue policy and the administration of justice on the cheap, via native authority, might have anything to do with this fascination with Indians' propensity for violence. A brief exploration of the structure and organization of the report further elucidates how colonial culpability came to be represented as colonial benevolence.[28]

The report addressed the difficulties of governing the country given the small number of colonial administrators and the enormity of their tasks in administering vast areas populated by natives who were habituated to violence.[29] The commission acknowledged "personal violence practised by the native revenue and police officials generally prevails throughout this presidency, both in the collection of revenue and in police cases."[30] The commission also recognized that "the collection of the Land Revenue was entrusted [by the colonial government] to the very class who had from time immemorial been accustomed to practise the most cruel and violent tortures upon the persons of the prisoners."[31] Under the Bombay and Madras tenurial systems of *ryotwari*, revenue gathering and policing were combined in the same person. The same person engaged in acts of bribery and extortion and acts of physical humiliation and cruelty. The definition of bribery and extortion as forms of corruption was itself new, and reflected a reconception (and curtailment) of political authority. In Old Regime polities, political authority and status derived from the distribution and dispersion of honor, status, and money. As local officials who had been integral to this system of power and prestige were transformed into public officials under the oversight of colonial administrators, their local power was curtailed and redefined as an abuse of public authority even while their native knowledge and skills were sought in governing a foreign population.

Having created the conditions for corruption and abuse of authority, especially when the demand for revenue was unconscionably high, the commission disregarded suggestions that there might be structural conditions that enabled the commission of violence. Instead, the report argued that the tolerance of corporal violence stemmed from the fact that "torture [had been] a recognised method of obtaining both revenue and confessions" since pre–British times.[32] The exercise of violence in the collection of the public revenue, the original rationale for the establishment of the commission, was quickly displaced onto broader concerns with the institution of police, then confined to a focus on the native police. Even Thomas Munro, the governor of the Madras Presidency, acknowledged that

> many irregularities are used in obtaining confessions, and . . . in some instances, atrocious acts are committed; but when we consider the great number of prisoners apprehended, and the habits of the people themselves, always accustomed to compulsion where there is suspicion, how difficult it is to eradicate such habits, and how small the proportion of cases in which violence has been used is to the whole mass, the number of these acts is hardly greater than was to be expected, and is every day diminishing.[33]

According to Munro, the interventions of the colonial government had managed to alleviate what was otherwise an almost daily occurrence of excessive violence. Natives had a propensity to indulge in despotic acts of violence and cruelty. These habits were deeply rooted and characterized the "cruelty and oppression" that marked the exercise of political power. The perpetrators of violence and their victims were united in regarding torture as a mark of submission to penal authority, making it almost impossible to abolish torture completely. Even if the natives could not refrain from the practice of barbaric acts of cruelty when left to their own devices, colonial officials acted as a crucial mediating force, making it clear that they did not countenance the use of violence and that they held such practices in "abhorrence."[34]

According to the report, colonial officials were a source of redress. The commission noted that the natives desired colonial intervention in the form of investigations against guilty officers. In fact, they actively invited such intervention. "The whole cry of the people, which has come before us, is to save them from the cruelties of their fellow natives, not from the effects of unkindness or indifference on the part of the European officers of Government."[35] Thus, colonial settlement came to be framed as an inaugural moment in the administration of justice, as an opportunity to instill more civilized rules and regulations regarding the practices of discipline. The investigative force of the Torture Commission thus came to be framed as an inquiry into "whether there has arisen anything in the civil administration of the last few years, which has exercised a special influence, or had any preventive operation upon the continuance of the practice, [of torture] or any particular tendency towards its extinguishments."[36] Torture was simultaneously acknowledged and disavowed by the report.

In 1826, the Court of Directors issued a "Judicial Despatch" regarding the prevalence of torture in the presidency,[37] and the Supreme Criminal Court Faujdari Adalat had issued over ten circulars regarding the rules governing the extraction of confessions by native police.[38] However, "little regard [was] paid by the head Police Officers to the orders passed from time to time for their guidance by the Court of the Faujdaree Udawlut," and police peons continued to be used as attesting witnesses to prosecute alleged criminals.[39]

> The practice which the Court finds still universally prevalent, of detaining persons in custody *for weeks and even months* before their transmission to the criminal Court offers opportunity which might not otherwise be found of resorting to the atrocious abuse of authority here referred to: and the Court of the Faujdaree Udawlut do not see an amelioration of the conduct of the police officers in these respects, unless the exertions of Magistrates are more strenuously directed to the enforcement of the provisions of the law, and abuses of authority when discovered are invariably visited with adequate punishment.[40]

The report mentioned the negligible conviction of police officials guilty of practicing torture as well as the mild punishment meted out to those so convicted.[41] The recommendations for overhauling the colonial bureaucracy competed with another set of interests, however.

How could the allegations of torture be believed at all when natives were typically mendacious, and given to untruth, when they were "litigious and revengeful"?[42] It was also clear that it was improbable that such acts would be "committed under the eyes of Europeans" and must depend on "hearsay evidence," which was difficult to "substantiate."[43]

The commissioners noticed that medical men had also not mentioned any familiarity with evidence of torture, leading them to argue that

> the effect of the medical testimony is a cogent argument in favor of the secrecy, and comparative lightness of the violence ordinarily inflicted. . . . Cases in which death or wounds, or injury to the limbs such as are found in the Calendars [annual register of cases tabulated by the Civil and Criminal Courts] and mentioned in some of the reports, must be looked upon as highly exceptional; ordinarily the violence is of a petty kind, although causing acute momentary pain, and even many of the severe kinds invented by native ingenuity leave no mark behind them.[44]

However, reports from district-level officials and officials "intimately acquainted with the country, its administration, its people, and their character" convinced the commissioners of the extent to which torture was prevalent in the presidency.

The report is filled with descriptions of torture and the instruments used to administer pain. Testimonials from complainants reproduced the terrorizing spectacles of violation, supporting British officials in their contention that Indian society was suffused by acts of violence and cruelty from which natives sought protection. The report suggests that under colonial protection, the natives could indeed feel safe enough to give vent to their pain and suffering. Examples of such testimony included Reverend C. F. Muzzy from Madura, who mentioned an instrument of torture used by a headman of a village "composed of four or five thongs of leather, three or four feet long, used as a scourge or a whip."[45] Reverend H. A Kaundiya from Mangalore noted that, when confessions were to be extracted from women, "a disgusting application of red chili pepper is sometimes employed."[46] And Mr. Simeon, an agent of Messrs. Hart and Simpson, mentioned that his wife had once seen a man whose turban was passed over his neck and under his knees, with a heavy stone placed on his head for many hours.[47] T. D. Lushington, collector of Masulipatnam, noted the use of an instrument called a "kittee" or "cheerata" that compressed the fingers.[48] Reverend E. Webb from Bellary also mentioned "fastening the body to a limb of a tree under which a fire has been kindled for the purpose of suffocating with the smoke, plucking at flesh with large iron pincers, and pulling out the hair of the face."[49] J. J. Minchin, acting joint magistrate of Nellore mentioned the case of Subbee, who was accused of having stolen a sepoy's knapsack and subsequently tied up by one arm to the branch of a tree, suspended above the ground, and "whipt with tamarind switches on her private parts."[50] Such retributive acts were on a continuum with the practice of intimate violence. As the report noted, "We have instances of torture being freely practiced in every relation of domestic life. Servants are thus treated by their masters and fellow servants, children by their parents and school masters, for the most trifling offences."[51] C. F Chamier, acting sub-judge of Mangalore, mentioned parental discipline. He noted the case of a native who had "tied his child's hands together, and then put some pepper in his eyes, as a mode of punishment after castigation failed."[52]

Natives who testified before the commission addressed the demands of excessive revenue as well as of bribes by native officials. Narraina Pillay of Casbah Seyaulee, Tanjore district, spoke of his young, unmarried niece Streerungum, age seventeen, who was alleged by the village Kurnom (*karnam*, or scribe) to have died due to the administration of medication to induce an abortion. The karnam used this allegation as the occasion to demand a bribe from Pillay for not filing a criminal complaint. When Pillay refused to pay the bribe, Streerungam's body had undergone an "indecent" examination before the members of the village. Pillay and his sister, Streerungum's mother, were also interned by the Police Amin.[53] Baulambal, a widow from the village of Vyathesware Covil, in Combaconum (Kumbakonam) district, testified to sexual violence. She gave evidence that she had been asked to visit the village munsiff's home for "bed purpose." On refusing, she was accused of theft, taken to the Covil (*koil*, or temple) where the munsiff, Wooleganauda Tamberan, along with twelve or thirteen people, had assembled. When Balaumbal proclaimed her innocence, she was dragged by her hair into a large room and abused "most indecently." Then she was suspended above the ground by a rope, with a cloth stuffed in her mouth. Two kitties, "one to each breast," had been applied, and she had fainted of the pain. Baluambal had filed a case and had been examined by a "native dresser" as well as an

"English doctor," but without physical proof of torture, the munsiff had been acquitted.[54]

Particularly revealing testimony came from a former revenue officer of North Arcot district, who gave evidence that he had practiced torture in the collection of revenue. When asked if there were particular periods of the agrarian calendar when torture was particularly prevalent, he noted, "From April, Tahsildar directs much attention to the collection, and when he sees the Balance is large in the comparative statement of collections, and centage of collections are low, the ill-treatment will be forcible." When asked where such violence was practiced, the officer replied, "Both in Talook Cutcherry [sub-district courts] and in villages." He noted that no instruments of torture were kept in the courthouse in his district, because "the Torture of former time [was] more cruel than that of the present one," even though he alleged the use of the kittee (or kitteecole) and other instruments by officers in other districts of the presidency. When asked whether he had authorized acts of violence, he said, "I have authorized such acts many times, openly; many of those who are subjected to such acts had no intention of complaining against the persons who authorized, or against those who do it."[55] Torture was practiced in the extraction of revenue, but the commissioners asserted that "the evil lies even deeper than the level of the public Revenue." Bribes and extortion for private pecuniary gain were rampant, they argued, when "Revenue demands and Police Authority" were combined in the same person.[56]

Testimony of violation, minor and severe, repeatedly portrayed natives' bodies as responsive to violence as a form of correction and the administration of pain as a form of subjectification. Brutal acts committed by native officials in utter secrecy, unknown to their European superiors, were publicized in all their spectacular detail. Descriptions of barbaric instruments of torture, repertoires of physical violation, and the horribly quotidian prevalence of corporal violence succeeded in convincing the public back home of the routinization of torture in native society. A visual pornography of acts and images was both a sign of the commission's successful investigation of native allegations and a symptom of the visceral brutality of native life. In a revealing instance of the politics of publicity, the humanitarian concerns of a metropolitan public were channeled toward addressing the incomplete humanity of natives. Yet the repeated "discovery" of torture suggested the fundamental instability of the rule of law, its reliance on excessive force. The colonial state fundamentally misrecognized its role in both producing and disavowing scandalous practices in recognizing the extent to which a "new" relationship between the state and its subjects, as well as among subjects, themselves had come to be represented as a form of violence, as physical violation. Attempts to distinguish between moderate and excessive violence become doubly significant in this context. Was it impossible to maintain legitimate practices of punishment that did not run the risk of transmogrifying into the exercise of excessive force and violence in a colonial situation? Was colonial law, then, haunted by a violence of its own making?

In the aftermath of the report's publication, a broad and far-reaching reform of the police force was undertaken with the understanding that the native police were ignorant, even abusive, of legal norms. The report had focused on the police because the police represented law yet appeared consistently to exceed the bounds of legality.[57] This produced the paradoxical need to "police the police."[58] The report had noted that "the whole police is underpaid, notoriously corrupt" and argued that "the character of the native when in power displays itself in the form of rapacity, cruelty, and tyranny, at least as much as its main features are subservience, timidity, and trickery, when the Hindoo is a mere private individual."[59] The construction of the native police as fundamentally unreliable (because racially inferior) thus produced a problem of surveillance and control *within* the police force. The discovery of torture represented this split in spectacular fashion by displacing the question of colonial culpability onto precolonial or traditional practices of policing. When read alongside demands for institutional reform, such as the Select Committee Report or the 1837 draft penal code, it is easy to focus on this aspect of the report. Yet, the report in fact articulated a more far-reaching concern—the relationship of law to truth.

THINGS SEEN AND UNSEEN: SECRECY, SUFFERING, AND THE ADMINISTRATION OF PAIN

The report indicted the native police, but it also addressed popular conceptions of justice that sanctioned torturing the alleged perpetrators of crimes. "Notwithstanding that confession may have been wrung out of the accused or suspected by bodily anguish, [there is abundance of testimony before us] to induce our belief that torture is ordinarily applied only when there are very good grounds for believing that the really guilty party is the sufferer."[60] Punishing violence with counter-violence was to be expected when justice was retributive. "Indeed it seems to be the universal opinion amongst natives themselves that in Criminal cases the practice is not only necessary but it is right."[61] The report's discussion of the conditions under which confessions were gathered troubled the credibility of evidence produced by the police. Torture implicated police excess, but it also produced "false" truth—false because it was contaminated by its relationship to fear and corporal violence. How worthwhile was a confession produced by the threat of force or even death? Could one be certain that confessions had been extracted through legitimate means when torture often left no marks on the body?

Torture was an open secret. Beatings and threats of torture were common in extracting confessions, and typically the physical violence did not lead to death, according to colonial officials. Medical testimony was a crucial form of evidence that drew on the experiential dimensions of pain and suffering—discourses of physical vulnerability—to verify the perpetration, even though bodily signs, physical marks, were difficult to detect even if one was willing to believe the claims of torture.

> It is obvious that much cruelty may be practiced, such as that by means of scratching insects, dipping in wells, starvation, prevention of sleep, and the like, without any mark being left on the person. . . . The criminal procedure is so slow that marks even of severe torture would be obliterated or very indistinct at the time of the trial.[62]

Assumptions that natives were habituated to violence in the most intimate and the most public domains of social interaction made it difficult to detect the administration of pain. When faced with a death in custody, however, medical testimony became a contentious site of debate. I now turn to the uses to which medical technologies of identification were put in verifying allegations of torture.[63]

Sessions Judge J. W. Woodstock presided over the Nasick torture case and acquitted the six policemen accused of torture on 26 December 1854.[64] The decision was appealed on the grounds that the medical evidence provided before the court was faulty: The judge had relied on the questionable claim that Gunnoo had died due to the exacerbation of a prior condition—that is, piles.[65] The claims of torture were credible only if Gunnoo's body bore the marks of intentional physical violation, but that was not enough. Physical evidence was to be corroborated by expert testimony and possibly by the victim's declaration.

Initially, Gunnoo had been unwilling to recount his experience in the cowshed because of shame and humiliation or because he feared further violence in police custody. Bala Bhow, the first hospital assistant, said that Gunnoo had complained of pain in his stomach, and "in his stools passed two ounces of pure blood unmixed with feces—blood dark and thickened." When Bhow "asked [Gunnoo] if he had been beaten—[he] replied he had not—each day deceased complained of greater pain in his stomach." Finally, Gunnoo admitted that he had been tortured by the six policemen. Dr. Pelly, the civil surgeon, deposed that

> the deceased was brought to the Hospital on the 12th of August and was when he saw him suffering from great pain in the abdomen which increased by the touch of the hand and from other symptoms of acute enteritis that *Gunnoo complained to him of having been kicked and beaten by the police but mentioned no names*—Had no recollection of Gunnoo's saying anything that day about a stick having been thrust up his anus.[66]

Eyewitness accounts had noted that

> [after] the lapse of 10 minutes according to one witness and half an hour as deposed to by another, the whole party emerged from the premises, the

accused Gunnoo resting his head on a policeman's shoulder and his hands clasped on his stomach, the seat as he said of the pain he was enduring. In that condition he was conveyed to the well; in that condition he made his confession, and he was then removed to the chowkee, still in a state of suffering.[67]

Given the allegations of Gunnoo's violent murder of his niece, the crowd appears to have supported his torture as an act of retribution. Gunnoo's dying declaration before Joint Acting Magistrate Turquand and Dr. Pelly, the civil surgeon, indicted the police for having shoved a stick up his anus in a cowshed.[68] But this indictment occurred when it was too late. Gunnoo's dying declaration was paraphrased for the court:

> [Gunnoo] said that on the day of his apprehension the first six prisoners [the police] had taken him to a cowshed belonging to a prostitute by the name of Lateeb—shut the door forced him down with his face to the ground which prevented him from being heard and then thrust the handle of a paper or China umbrella 1½ span up his anus twice or thrice *but that he could not see who did it*—That he found his Anus bloody and that the cloth he had on was also stained with blood—and was washed the following day by a Bhungy [an untouchable who "traditionally" removes nightsoil]—That on his way from the cowshed to the Foujdar's Cutchery he was beaten by the Police as well as by the Villagers who had assembled none of whom however could he recognize.[69]

In his declaration, Gunnoo had testified that he was unable to name his aggressors because he could not see them while he was lying face down in the cowshed. The deposition of witnesses and Gunnoo's dying declaration that he had not seen the faces of his aggressors affirmed secrecy as a precondition of torture's performance, even though everyone knew why Gunnoo had been taken to Lateeb's cowshed. Though it was performed in secret, torture apparently could not remain invisible for long.[70] The possibility of being tortured circulated as an unspoken threat and promise and produced fear among the public. Torture was a terrorizing possibility and a traumatic experience, but, ironically, it was also a communicative act. Physical violation and the assault of bodily integrity were forms of persuasion, perverse and thwarted forms of recognition that established a social relationship between the torturer and his victim.[71] Governed by the dialectic of intimate contact, repulsion, and depersonalization, acts of torture were premised on the incomplete humanity of the victim.

For their part, the medical practitioners focused on the visible, external signs of internal damage. Medical jurisprudence as an expert knowledge that had access to deeper, hidden layers of the body was itself a form of objectification that addressed the experiential dimensions of the body only insofar as they could be calibrated or measured by adjectives of intensity, depth, and duration. On the morning of 11 August, the native doctor, Bala Bhow, had gone to the *cutcherry*, having been called on the night of 10 August to inspect the prisoner. On 11 August, Bhow administered a purgative. The prison sweeper had cleaned the earthen pan containing Gunnoo's stools. The prison sweeper's testimony mentioned the presence of blood in Gunnoo's stools. Imam Wallud Gottee, a sweeper, deposed to having washed the *dhotur* (the long cloth used to wrap the lower half of the body), which had stains of dried blood on it.[72] Ahmed Wallud Dawood remembered "having cleaned a pan of a prisoner confined in the Foujdar's Cutcherry [courthouse] on a charge of murder. [He said he] saw about a handful of blood in it. There was no excrement."[73] Bhow applied leeches to Gunnoo's stomach that night, and at 7 p.m., Gunnoo had confessed to Bhow that the police had "mishandled" him. The foujdar had been informed of this, and Bhow claimed that the foujdar went to see Gunnoo that very night—that is, 11 August. Gunnoo was taken to hospital to be examined by Dr. Pelly the next morning.[74]

Dr. Pelly testified that Gunnoo had first been brought to him between 7 and 8 A.M. on 12 August, when Gunnoo had told him that he had been kicked and beaten by the police. Pelly had ordered him leeched and fomented, and ironically, the foujdar accused of ordering Gunnoo to be tortured, Muhammed Sheikh, was called in to record Gunnoo's deposition.[75] The next morning, Gunnoo was worse, and Pelly suspected that his patient might not live long. He went to get Mr. Turquand and Assistant Superintendent of Police Alexander Bell, who were in the presence of the prisoner when he gave his dying declaration.

Gunnoo's death on 13 August prompted an inquest. Gangaram Bhoojaree, a member of the inquest who had seen the body at about 5 P.M. on 13 August and again at 7 P.M. stated that he had not seen any marks of violence on the body but that Gunnoo's anus was enlarged and his abdomen swollen. He had also seen "3 pieces of intestines which the doctor said were those of the deceased. These were black and in a decomposed state having marks of coagulated blood on them."[76] Bhoojaree thought that a stick thrust up the anus might have penetrated Gunnoo's abdomen.

Debates about medical evidence had become critical to the indictment of the police, and medical testimony attempted to *quantify* ineffable qualities such as pain and suffering through a focus on the body's physical signs.[77] Medical discourses addressed the victim's body as the primary evidence regarding police torture, especially when the victim's silence sprang from the fear of further violence if he complained against the authorities who had incarcerated him. Unlike the police, who appeared to assume that physical violence produced a more trustworthy confession than verbal interrogation, for the judiciary, torture was problematic because it produced a questionable truth that was tied too closely to pain as an embodied experience.

Senior officers of the judiciary in Bombay suggested that part of the problem with this case was the insufficient medical knowledge available to the medical officer when he had first met Gunnoo in prison, as well as the failure of the postmortem to reveal torture or the excessive use of force with any certainty. The medical evidence was adduced to be of a "defective character," according to a letter submitted to the Medical Board by the governor-in-council on 30 August 1855, after the decision by the Sudder Foujdari Adalat.[78] When the Puisne Judges of the Sudder Foujdari Adalat reconsidered the evidence gathered by the Sessions Court, they argued that the lower court had been unclear about whether Gunnoo's injuries were "new" or manifestations of an older complaint of piles. Though Puisne Judge M. Larken believed the police to be culpable, unlike his colleague, A. Remington, Larken also recognized that the medical evidence was unclear about Gunnoo's injuries and its location. There was a contradiction in the medical testimony: Dr. Pelly, the medical officer, had deposed that Gunnoo's rectum was found unlacerated during the postmortem, while Bala Bhow had given evidence that the anus was "not usual but extended."[79] Were the injuries located in the rectum, the intestine, or the peritoneum, and how old were the injuries? Medical experts had argued that a prior condition such as piles might mimic Gunnoo's symptoms, making it difficult to have suspected torture when he was first treated by doctors. As Judge Remington noted, however, the evidence of violence in the manner in which Gunnoo's anus was torn, had been ignored, and Pelly's deposition that he felt that the top of the umbrella had been cut off, causing Gunnoo's injury, was also cast aside.[80] Medical testimony, a form of expert knowledge that objectified the body as a site of evidence, had come up against its own limits. Ironically, the state's reliance on medico-legal evidentiary structures to produce a more precise and embodied truth was not always successful. However, Acting Puisne Judge W. H. Harrison commented that "this case should be laid before Government with the object of drawing their attention to the conduct of the Nassick Native Police of all grades who are concerned with this inquiry."[81] The Bombay government's indictment of the foujdar, Muhammed Sheikh, with which this paper begins must be understood as an effort to manage and contain the scandalous discovery of torture by displacing culpability from the structures of colonial policing onto the racially inferior native police who would then be subject to the state's discipline. Harrison noted, "It is not fitting the subject and active agents in such a crime should be punished while their superior is held blameless because he took care to keep out of the sight of the outrage perpetrated."[82]

CONCLUSION

The dialectic of secrecy and publicity is torture's scandalous mode of existence. Torture is enabled by the anonymity of bureaucratic authority and the adjacency of excessive violence to sovereign or legitimate power: The latter becomes an enabling condition for the exercise of the former. It is especially useful if torture can also be racialized as a native inclination—as with colonial India, so with revelations of torture in Iraq today. Brutal violence among natives, the suggestion that violence saturates all aspects of daily life, becomes the occasion to bring in the rule of law and civilized government. Yet once colonization is justified as legitimate government, one always runs the risk that the colonizer's law-preserving violence looks uncannily like its Manichean other, despotic or retributive violence.

Torture became a problem at a moment of germination of new forms of subjectivation and embodiment nominally categorized as "modern" in the context of a significant transformation of ideologies of personhood and physical vulnerability.[83] Colonial ideologies of civilizational sufficiency addressed natives as individuals who ought to have achieved full selfhood voluntarily, in their own interest. Yet native proclivities for fearful despotism—their misrecognition of violence as law—prevented the colonized from undertaking the journey toward full humanity on their own. Correction, according to colonial officials, performed a violently civilizing function under exceptional conditions. It was a violence that became problematic only when it became public. Colonial publicity produced a peculiar form of visibility that revealed, implicated, and stigmatized native excess even while it evaded culpability for its own founding violence. Colonial publicity was propaganda for empire as a humanizing process, and its violence was unfortunate but necessary. If natives mistook violence for law, colonial officials equally misjudged the violent correction of minds and bodies as a "better" justice. Thus, we are led to ask: Did the scandal of torture lie in its commission by natives who confused public office with private gain or in the forms of visibility, the material conditions of *colonial* governance, that rendered torture a public secret?

NOTES

An earlier version of this paper appeared in *Interventions: The International Journal of Postcolonial Studies* 3, no. 2 (July 2001). I am grateful for permission to reprint this version. Research for this paper was supported by grants from the American Council of Learned Societies, a Junior Research Fellowship from the American Institute of Indian Studies, the Rackham School of Graduate Studies at the University of Michigan, and the Social Science Research Council. Previous versions of this paper were presented at the 1998 American Anthropological Association meetings; "Investigating and Combating Torture," University of Chicago, 4–7 March 1999; "The Middle East and South Asia: Exploring Comparisons," New York University, 6 April 2000; and "Pairing Empires," Johns Hopkins University, Baltimore, 10 November 2000. I am grateful to Talal Asad, Gyan Pandey, and David Scott for their comments at these venues. I thank Steven Pierce, Jared Stark, and Rajeswari Sunder Rajan for their invaluable suggestions.

1   Maharashtra State Archives, Judicial Department, Volume 123, 1855. Unless noted otherwise, all archival citations are from the material contained in this volume.

2   The term "Maratha" was the name given to the landed gentry who identified as a caste community during the late seventeenth century. During the second half of the nineteenth century, ordinary peasant cultivators, or *kunbis*, claimed Maratha status as a means of upward mobility. By 1870, a majority of kunbis had begun to identify themselves as Marathas: O'Hanlon, *Caste, Conflict, and Ideology*.

3   I will mention one representative case from my research. Khundoo bin Sidhojee Jadhav paid Hurree Jadhav to rid his first wife, Bhagoo, of devils. Hurree strangled Bhagoo and threw her corpse into a tank with Khundoo's help. The case file begins with a petition from Khundoo's second wife pleading against the imposition of capital punishment for Khundoo's crime: Criminal Calendar, Sudder Faujdari Adalat, 1860, Case Number XIV, Judicial Department, Volume 37. See also Anagol, "The Emergence of the Female Criminal in India"; Waters, "Family Disputes, Family Violence."

4   Deposition, Luximan Sukrajee Chowan. "Analyses of the proceedings of the Nassick Torture Case held before J. W. Wood, Esquire, Sessions Judge of Ahmednagar," n.d., Volume 123, Maharashtra State Archive.

5   See Gune, *The Judicial System of the Marathas*; Steele, *The Hindu Castes*.

6   Gune, *The Judicial System of the Marathas*, 110.

7   Prisoners, including women, were transported or incarcerated in forts

where they performed manual labor. Precolonial regimes rarely resorted to penal incarceration, however: Fukazawa, *The Medieval Deccan*; Guha, "An Indian Penal Regime"; Kadam, "The Institution of Marriage and the Position of Women in Eighteenth Century Maharashtra." On colonial prisons, see Martha Kaplan, "Panopticon in Poona," and Anand Yang, "Disciplining 'Natives.'"

8   See Cohn, *An Anthropologist among the Historians and Other Essays*; Guha, *A Rule of Property for Bengal*; Stokes, *The English Utilitarians and India*; Washbrook, "Law, State and Agrarian Society in Colonial India." On western India. see Ballhatchet, *Social Policy and Social Change in Western India*; Choksey, *The Aftermath 1818–1826*; idem, *Montstuart Elphinstone*; Kumar, *Western India in the Nineteenth Century*.

9   See Amin, *Event, Metaphor, Memory*; Mani, *Contentious Traditions*; Nigam, "Disciplining and Policing the 'Criminals by Birth,' Part 1"; idem, "Disciplining and Policing the 'Criminals by Birth,' Part 2."

10   The codification of criminal law in the Indian Penal Code in 1861 was preceded by the draft penal code of 1837, but attempts at codification were interrupted by the mutiny of 1857. In her important work, Radhika Singha addresses this process of codification through a consideration of precisely those exceptional sites that reveal the constitutive contradictions of colonial legality: Singha, *A Despotism of Law*. See also Fisch, *Cheap Lines, Dear Limbs* and Yang, *Crime and Criminality in British India*.

11   For histories of the mutiny that locate that event in the context of the sociopolitical changes inaugurated by early colonial rule, see Alavi, *The Sepoys and the Company*; Metcalf, *The Aftermath of Revolt*. For an argument about the ethnographic state, see Dirks, *Castes of Mind*, esp. sec. 3. An argument about race as "the rule of colonial difference" can be found in Chatterjee, *The Nation and Its Fragments*.

The mutiny became a watershed in British histories of imperial conquest, demarcating the predatory company state from its more civilizing successor, the British Crown. As an almost successful rebellion against colonial rule, the mutiny was represented as India's first War of Independence and spawned extensive commentary by Indians of varying political commitments during the late nineteenth century and early twentieth century. For example, the Hindu nationalist V. D Savarkar wrote *The First War of Independence* (1909), and the Muslim modernist Sir Syed Ahmed Khan wrote *Asbab-I-Baghawat-I-Hind* (first published in Urdu in 1858). Among international commentaries that addressed the mutiny as an anti-imperialist struggle led by a peasant-soldier combine, the most famous is Karl Marx and Friedrich Engels, *The First Indian War of Independence, 1857–1859* (Moscow: Foreign Languages Publishing House, 1959).

12 Medical technology, like other technologies of identification, was central to the detection of crime. For the history of medical jurisprudence in Britain, see Crawford, "Legalizing Medicine"; White, "Training Medical Policemen." On India, see Chevers, *A Manual of Medical Jurisprudence in India*. Chevers argued that medical jurisprudence could expose the "lies" of native truth telling. See also Baynes, *Hints on Medical Jurisprudence*.

13 The police peons were sentenced to four years of hard labor and four months in solitary confinement, with the first and last weeks of each month to be spent on a *conjee* (rice water or gruel) diet. Two of the police peons were related to Gunnoo, and they were described as "enraged" by Syee's murder. One villager was found guilty of aiding and assisting the police peons in their crime. He was sentenced to two years of hard labor and two months of solitary confinement.

14 Letter No. 727 of 1855, A. R. Grant, Acting Joint Magistrate, to H. L. Anderson, Secretary to Government, Judicial Department, September 14, 1855.

15 Minute recorded by W. H. Harrison, Acting Poison Judge, Sudder Foujdari Adalat. The foujdar was dismissed from service by an order dated September 6, 1855 and petitioned that he had been wrongly accused.

16 Letter No. 219 of 1855, H. L Anderson to Secretary, Government, Judicial Department. Interestingly, I. G. Lumsden's minute of September 17, 1855 noted that caste was the reason torture and other barbarous practices were tolerated.

17 I should note here that the use of the term "torture" by colonial officials seems to attach itself generically to forms of corporeal discipline, to any method of inflicting excessive pain as a form of punishment. See *Police Torture and Murder in Bengal* and V. D. Rao, "Note on the Police of the City of Poona."

18 *Select Committee Report* (Judicial), 114.

19 *Parliamentary Debates*, 11 June 1857, col. 1602.

20 Benjamin, "Critique of Violence," suggests that it is precisely this uncertain, liminal character of the police (understood as both form and function) that implicates law in the moment of founding or originary violence. In his lectures

on governmentality and elsewhere, Foucault, "Governmentality," suggests that the modern, Western bio-political state is characterized by the transformation of politics into police.

21 Parliamentary Debates, House of Commons, 11 June 1857, col. 1607.

22 Ibid., col. 1610.

23 The term "torture" was capacious, and it was used to describe all kinds of violation, from public humiliation to death in custody. A lurid term suggesting all manner of evil and excess that was thought to suffuse native society, "torture" was commonly used to describe any act of excessive violence. It is precisely through the definitional parameters established by the report that "torture" was more precisely defined as the illegitimate exercise of corporal violence—the administration of pain—by state officials, especially police, to extract money or confession: *Report of the Commissioners for the Investigation of Alleged Cases of Torture in the Madras Presidency*, 1:45.

24 For details regarding press coverage regarding these allegations and the racism that underwrote descriptions of native acts of barbarism, see Peers, "Torture, the Police and the Colonial State in Madras Presidency, 1816–1855." On 28 August 1857, Karl Marx wrote, in the *New York Daily Tribune*, that the "British rules of India are by no means such mild and spotless benefactors of the Indian people as they would have the world believe." To substantiate his charge of colonial guilt, Marx cited from the Blue Books, *East India (Torture) 1855–1857*, that were laid before the House of Commons during the 1856–57 session. Ironically, Lord Dalhousie, whose policies of outright annexation as well as indirect destabilization of princely states in northern India were largely responsible for creating the social and political conditions for the mutiny, testified to the prevalence of acts that spanned the spectrum from "gross injustice, to arbitrary imprisonment and cruel torture." The spectacular nature of these revelations, as well as the supposedly effective response to such widespread allegations, enabled the British to disregard the deeper political issue of the legitimacy of their rule in India.

25 The trial of Warren Hastings, then governor-general of Bengal, attests to the anxieties that surrounded colonial acquisitions. Edmund Burke's impeachment of Hastings and Hastings's subsequent trial before the House of Commons between 1786 and 1795 brought the misdeeds of the East India Company servants

before a metropolitan public in spectacular fashion. In his indictment of Hastings, Burke drew attention to the unspeakable acts of looting and plundering and the many abuses of political authority that marred the company's record in Bengal stemming from the East India Company's exercise of a dual authority as merchant and sovereign. Hastings was the apotheosis of imperial corruption. The highly theatrical and personalized nature of the trial was a performance of colonial guilt and culpability that individualized blame. Yet the trial had also succeeded, as Nicholas Dirks argues, in making empire "an affair of state answerable to the nation": see Dirks, *The Scandal of Empire*, esp. chap. 2.

26 A three-member commission was appointed to inquire into the "use of Instruments of Torture by the Native Subordinate Servants of the State for the purpose of Realizing the Government revenue." However, the scope of the inquiry was soon expanded by a government order issued 19 September 1854 to include "the alleged use of torture in extracting confessions in Police cases." The commission drew up a notification to inform the public of its existence, and advertisements ran in all of the vernacular newspapers of the presidency for a month, with the exception of Malayalam, for which types could not be procured. The government also published 150 copies of the notifications in English; 10,000 copies each in Tamil, Telugu, and Canarese (Kannada); and 5,000 copies each in Malayalam and Hindustani (Hindi). By 1 February 1855, when the commissioners held their last inquiry, 1,440 written complaints had also been received, and almost 519 complainants had appeared in person before the commission, with some traveling distances as large as 300–400 miles. "In an act of supreme consideration of its central location in town, the committee had planned to hold the inquiry in the General Police Office (*sic*) and shifted to a new venue, the Polytechnic Institution, after the commission's scope was expanded": *Report of the Commissioners for the Investigation of Alleged Cases of Torture in the Madras Presidency*, 1:3–5. The three commissioners were E. F Elliot, superintendent of police and magistrate of Madras City, 1834–53; H. Stokes; and J. B. Norton, former advocate general.

27 Singha argues that the report solidified racial distinctions between British and native; that the "primary address was to the British public, to reassure them that the natives could not possibly believe that the European functionaries condoned torture": Singha, *A Despotism of Law*, 305.

28 Although there was no comparable investigation in the Bombay Presidency, the report had sensitized the colonial bureaucracy to the power of categories: The practice of torture had the potential to indict the colonial state. Hence, the anxiety about controlling allegations of torture traveled across the presidencies and is reflected, for instance, in the fact that the three judicial files labeled "Torture" available in the Maharashtra State Archives in Bombay are confined to the period 1855–57, coeval with the period in which the report was released.

The Bombay government mooted the idea of a similar report for Bombay, maintaining that Regulations XII and XIII, Chapter 1, Sections 8–10, of the 1827 Elphinstone Code covered cases of bribery, extortion, and other abuse of police authority. However, the Bombay government appointed a special Torture Commissioner for a short period.

29 *Report of the Commissioners for the Investigation of Alleged Cases of Torture in the Madras Presidency*, 1:54, 58.

30 Ibid., 1:45.

31 Ibid., 1:58–59.

32 Ibid., 1:5.

33 Ibid., 1:9.

34 Ibid., 1:50.

35 Ibid., 1:52.

36 Ibid., 1:4.

37 "Judicial Despatch," Court of Directors, 11 April 1826, in ibid., 1:5.

38 Ibid., 1:9.

39 Ibid., 1:8.

40 "Judicial Despatch," Court of Directors, 11 April 11 1826, which cites undated reports from the Faujdari Adalat, in ibid., 1:6.

41 Ibid., 1:7, 41–44.

42 Ibid., 1:16.

43 Ibid., 1:15.

44 Ibid., 1:14–15.

45 Ibid., 1:18.

46 Ibid., 1:19.

47 Ibid., 1:20.

48 Ibid., 1:app., lix.

49 Ibid., 1:app., cv.

50 Ibid., 1:app., lxxxiv.

51 Ibid., 1:49–50.

52 Ibid., 1:app., cxv.

53 Ibid., 2:app, E, no. 50, lxiv–lxv.

54 Ibid., 2:app, E, no. 24, xxix–xxxx.

55 Ibid., 2:app. G, no. 1, cxxxiii–cxxxvii.

56 Ibid., 1:47.

57 Foucault refers to the police as a critical component in the elaboration and control of population. He argues that through the idea of "security," disciplinary power—dispersed, anonymous, and impersonal—creates the conditions for permanent surveillance: Burchell et al., *The Foucault Effect*. See also B. Chatterjee, "Cornwallis and the Emergence of Colonial Police"; Edmund Cox, *Police and Crime in India*; Anandswarup Gupta, *Crime and Police in India up to 1861*.

58 The commission recommended greater discretionary control of native police by their European superiors and suggested the introduction of superintendents of police, a system that was introduced in Bombay in 1853. The idea that a "separation of powers" would remedy the abuse of authority—the substitution of policy for politics—was the great discovery of Utilitarian thought. For an exploration of the racialized colonial-military models—for example, the Irish Constabulary—on which the Indian police force was reorganized, first in Madras and then across British India, see Arnold, *Police Power and Colonial Rule, Madras 1859–1947*.

59 *Report of the Commissioners for the Investigation of Alleged Cases of Torture in the Madras Presidency*, 1:59.

60 Ibid., 1:49.

61 Ibid.

62 Ibid., 1:50–51.

63 In England, medical jurisprudence began to develop only after 1800. Initial developments in medical jurisprudence can be traced to Scotland, where the first chair of medical jurisprudence was established at the University of Edinburgh in 1807. A similar chair was established in Glasgow in 1839, although medical jurisprudence had been taught extramurally at the Portland Street Medical School since 1826. By contrast, medical testimony occupied a central place in the highly

adversarial and inquisitorial judicial system of the Continent. Generous state support and remuneration for medico-legal expertise had allowed an elaborate medical knowledge of wounds and injuries to develop. "Indeed, continental writings on forensic medicine can be considered subspecies of the legal literature on proof and procedure": Crawford, "Legalizing medicine," 99.

Photography was first used in India in 1840. Fingerprinting technology, developed in India by William Herschel, was in use by 1891, and by 1897 a system of matching fingerprints from a mass of fingerprint cards was also in place. Convinced that the capture of external traits provided a significant indication of deeper structures of vice and depravity, the pseudoscience of anthropometry extended the reach of this scopic regime even further. For an account of the hegemony of vision for colonial knowledge, see Pinney, *Camera Indica*. For the importance of techniques of identification such as tattooing, fingerprinting, and photography to the development of a colonial bureaucracy, see Singha "Settle, Mobilize, Verify."

64 The Sudder Foujdari Adalat deliberated the case on 17 January, 28 March, 4 April, 2 May, and 16 May 1855.

65 Gunnoo's aunt's testimony was important. She remembered that Gunnoo had complained of a stomachache due to piles a month earlier and noted that he had appeared weak. Deposition, wife of Baboorow, List of evidence of exhibit recorded in the Nassick Case of Culpable Homicide decided on 26 December 1854.

66 "Analyses of the proceedings in the Nassick Torture Case held before J. W. Wood, Esquire, sessions Judge of Ahmednagar," n.d., Volume 123, 1855, Maharashtra State Archives.

67 Minute, A. Remington, Puisne Judge, 16 May 1855. Remington drew on the testimony of one Ramrow Gungathur.

68 Turquand was commended by the government for his thorough investigation of the case and for alerting the Sessions Court about its importance, while Woodward was disciplined for being remiss in his duties in conducting a thorough investigation. Minute, W. H. Harrison, Puisne Judge, 16 April 1855.

69 "Analysis of the proceedings."

70 See Asad, "On Torture, or Cruel, Inhuman, and Degrading Treatment," for an argument that torture's power emanates from the secrecy surrounding

its practice. I would add that we must pay attention to the forms of publicity through which torture is made visible and address torture's power to reside in the way it functions as an open or public secret. Turquand noted that two young children, Pakhee, age 9, and Mahadeo, age 10, had taken him by the hand, to Lutek's cowshed as they had heard the story that Gunnoo was tortured. Letter No. 540, Turquand to Faujdari Adalat, n.d. See also Elizabeth Hanson, "Torture and Truth in Renaissance England."

71 Frantz Fanon describes this encounter in his transcripts of victims and perpetrators of torture during the Algerian war of independence: Fanon, *The Wretched of the Earth*.

72 Deposition of Imam Wullud Gottee, List of evidence of exhibit recorded in the Nassick Case of Culpable Homicide decided on 26 December 1854.

73 "Analyses of proceedings."

74 The court faulted Bala Bhow for waiting until 12 August to send Gunnoo to the hospital and for not responding immediately to a call to visit the cutcherry on 9 August. Minute of A. Remington, Puisne Judge, 16 May 1855. Also Letter No. 2180, 1855 Medical Board to Secretary to Government, 12 July 1855.

75 19 October 1854, letter of Acting Joint Magistrate Turquand.

76 "Analyses of the proceedings."

77 Talal Asad argues that the quantification of pain—the ability to measure incommensurable acts of suffering by addressing physical pain as a measurable quantity—brought about a significant shift in discourses of both suffering and punishment. Calibrating pain and punishment provided a control against inhuman punishment and led, in fact, to emergent conceptions of bodily integrity as a necessary condition of being human: Asad, "On Torture, or Cruel, Inhuman, and Degrading Treatment."

78 The Medical Board argued that medical jurisprudence was part of the training of Medical Officers in the company's service and that there was no reason to recommend further training. Letter No. 2180 of 1855, Medical Board office to Secretary to Government, 12 July 1855.

79 The Medical Board argued that Dr. Pelly, who had examined the victim, showed no want of knowledge. Pelly had reported that Gunnoo's rectum was extended, which could have meant that it was either open or swollen. The Sessions Judge had not questioned Pelly about the exact cause of death. Neither had

he asked Pelly to clarify his findings: Letter of 14 September 1855. Minute of M. Larken, Puisne Judge, collected by the Asst. Registrar, Sadar Adalat, 5 September 1855.

80   Minute of A. Remington, Puisne Judge, 16 May 1855.

81   Minute of W. H. Harrison, Puisne Judge, collected by Asst. Registrar, Sadar Adalat, 5 September 1855.

82   Ibid.

83   Darius Rejali has argued that torture by police and military forces is coeval with the modern exercise of power. Documents regarding torture and other human-rights abuses in Algeria, Israel, Latin America, Northern Ireland, and South Africa, to name a few obvious instances, confirm both the secrecy that accompanies the practice of torture and the extent to which police and military draw on a shared repertoire of torture instruments and methods: Rejali, *Torture and Modernity*. My point regarding the relationship between torture and conceptions of the human supports the argument about the "modernity" of torture as a technology of truth and suggests that torture becomes especially problematic when the full recognition of humanity comes to have the status of a "human right."

STEVEN PIERCE

✳

Punishment and the Political Body

Flogging and Colonialism in Northern Nigeria

In May 1914, two women were seen leaving the servants' quarters of the house of J. F. J. Fitzpatrick, the British assistant resident of Bauchi Province, Nigeria. Unfortunately for them, they were spotted by Fitzpatrick himself, who caught them and sent them to be tried by the chief *qadi* (Islamic judge) of Bauchi. The servants swore in court that they were unacquainted with the women, who were named Adama and Hassana. On the basis of the servants' testimony, the qadi convicted the women of stealing and of being prostitutes, sentencing them to six months' imprisonment and twenty-four lashes.[1]

There the matter remained until an article appeared in 1918 in the *African Telegraph*, saying that the women had been flogged in the "open market" while "stripped entirely naked." The newspaper claimed further that the lashes had been imposed at Fitzpatrick's behest and would be reapplied every month.[2] Once the story broke in the Lagos press, it quickly traveled to London, leading to questions in Parliament and thus considerable consternation in the Colonial Office. The colonial secretary explained in Parliament that women in Nigeria were flogged only in areas in which "native custom" was "unaltered" and claimed that British officials were not involved in imposing the penalty themselves.[3] The Colonial Office sent an urgent despatch to the governor of Nigeria asking that he discourage the flogging of women as much as possible. Meanwhile, with Colonial Office support, Fitzpatrick launched an ultimately successful libel action against the publisher of the *African Telegraph*.[4] The records are silent about what finally happened to Adama and Hassana.

This was one instance among many of scandals caused by flogging in Britain's colonies.[5] The dynamic press of Lagos, muckraking missionaries, and organizations like the Anti-Slavery Society regularly accused Northern Nigeria's colonial government of supporting a brutal and degrading practice. British commentators were unanimous that flogging was a traditional (and therefore, most agreed, appropriate) punishment, but for many it was also problematic. Flogging was applied to women in disregard to their modesty or inherent fragility, applied to people "too civilized" for it to be an appropriate regulatory mechanism, and too cruel to be used by a civilized government. In practice, flogging was administered differently for particular classes of people: for men, for many classes of crime; for women, usually only for adultery or slander. Adults (meaning men over sixteen) were more likely to be flogged than children; Muslims were flogged in a different manner from that applied to pagans. Government officials and the British public alike considered such distinctions both necessary and problematic. Different kinds of people were supposed to be susceptible to governance and chastisement in different ways. Even though distinctions therefore had to be drawn, they also threatened to violate the humanitarian requirements they were meant to fulfill. Flogging was simultaneously humane, necessary, and a problem. This contradiction thus demonstrates very well how Northern Nigeria's government attempted to rule its subjects, how the category of tradition was applied to assumed expediency, and how colonial notions of Nigerian society created contradictions in its modes of governance.

"A FORM OF PUNISHMENT REPUGNANT TO THE BEST IDEAS OF JUSTICE"

During the first thirty years of the colonial period, Northern Nigeria's criminal judiciary basically consisted of two parallel court systems. The larger of the two, termed the "native courts," was presided over by Nigerian judges applying "customary" law—either Islamic law administered by qadis (in Hausa, *al'kali*; pl. *al'kalai*), whose courts were mainly in the emirates of the Sokoto Caliphate and Borno, or "native custom," generally applied by chiefs in non-Muslim areas.[6] Native courts had grades assigned by the British that determined the scope of cases they could try. For the most part, legal and legitimate floggings could be imposed only by the more major, urban al'kali courts, and even they had to have their sentences confirmed by a British officer. Many of these courts had applied flogging as a penalty during the precolonial period, which is why flogging could be considered traditional.

Until the 1930s, the other system of courts, called the provincial courts, was staffed by the British political officers resident in the provinces.[7] Each province was administered by a British official termed the "resident," who was assisted by "district officers," each responsible for a part of the province. From the very beginning of the colonial period, Nigeria's government restricted the use of flogging in them; many fewer offenses were deemed worthy of the penalty.[8] In 1907, British residents reported having flogged people for theft, robbery with violence, rape, extortion, personation (impersonating government officials), assault, intimidation, slavery, drinking liquor illegally, and receiving stolen property.[9] By the time former Governor-General Lugard had published his revised instructions on the matter ten years later, that list had shrunk to personation, sexual assault, vagrancy, "endangering trains," robbery, attempted murder, slave dealing, and "casting off ships."[10] By contrast, the native courts had considerably greater latitude, as long as they claimed the penalty as traditional.

Floggings administered in Northern Nigeria had a doubly problematic quality. Although flogging was inherently "a form of punishment repugnant to the best ideas of justice,"[11] according to British officers, the peculiar demands of establishing colonial rule over primitives also required it, at least in carefully calibrated applications. Unfortunately for this paradigm of flogging as an adjunct to the civilizing mission, both native courts and provincial courts regularly exceeded their mandates, imposing floggings that were too harsh and flogging for crimes for which it was not a statutory penalty. Native courts asserted jurisdiction over southerners and Christians. Educated people subjected to the somewhat abbreviated procedures of provincial courts (often staffed by officers with little or no legal training) complained of the inadequacy of the legal process there. The provincial courts in particular were excoriated for imposing a punishment antithetical to civilized sensibilities: Without the cosmetic label "custom" that protected native courts, the provincial courts presented the spectacle of Europeans directly, unambiguously, *officially* responsible for barbarous practices.

The personnel, procedures, and legal codes of the two systems were very different, but their jurisdictions overlapped to a great extent; a case's venue was ultimately determined by the British political staff, and in practice the assignment of cases to one forum or the other could be somewhat arbitrary. Both systems regularly violated the legal canons they supposedly enforced. Al'kalai in the native courts had considerable latitude and not infrequently used their authority to extort bribes and threaten their enemies. Such incidents often were confirmed and punished by colonial authorities only when al'kalai lost favor with their emirate superiors and were accused of corruption.[12] Moreover, "native law"—the Maliki school of Islamic law—was, as anywhere, interpreted in locally specific ways, which created some diversity of the application of flogging between emirates and even between particular al'kalai. Often al'kalai justified a sentence of flogging to British officers on the basis that it was the customary punishment. Under Maliki law, flogging was stipulated as the penalty for certain crimes—brigandage, fornication, drinking alcohol, for example—which were thereby termed *hadd* offenses. Qadis also held the power to inflict floggings at their discretion. Most officers, from their writings, do not appear to have been aware of the distinction and relied on asking al'kalai what "native law" was, creating a picture that elided the texts of the Maliki school, their local interpretation, and discretionary practices. For their knowledge of Maliki law, officers had recourse to parts of one important Maliki text, Sidi Khalil's *Mukhtasar*, which a Northern Nigerian officer, F. H. Ruxton, was commissioned to translate from a partial 1878 French translation. This translation was published in 1916 and distributed to officers in Northern Nigeria.[13] Sometimes officers bothered actually to look points of law up in "Ruxton"—though rarely with any evident awareness of the complexities of interpretation and application—but more usually just asked the local al'kali for his opinion.[14]

European officers resorted to flogging in even more dubious circumstances: to punish employees for disobedience or for showing disrespect.[15] Sometimes on the latter ground, officers would send the unfortunate transgressor to an al'kali court to be flogged for his "crime." The officer responsible for the Bauchi incident, Fitzpatrick, was fond of this approach, as the case of Adama and Hassana attests. In another incident in 1914, Fitzpatrick was annoyed when a youth "grossly insulted the Resident of [Bauchi] Province and the Emir of Gombe." After ordering the boy to be struck in the face by native authority police, Fitzpatrick sent him to the al'kali's court to be flogged.[16]

Irregular and quasilegal applications of flogging by the courts were the tip of a scandalous iceberg. Flogging threatened scandal in two ways at once. Superficially less serious were the procedural problems: floggings administered when they should not have been, meted out to inappropriate people, too many lashes delivered, lashes applied improperly. Even so, officials in Nigeria and the Colonial Office were sensitive to such procedural niceties. Indeed, the second High Commissioner of Northern Nigeria instituted a special return of floggings so the penalty could be monitored more closely. Improved monitoring and record keeping promised to solve these technical problems. More threatening to the image of colonialism as a humanitarian undertaking, however, was the visceral effect of flogging as spectacle. Even if a flogging were entirely legal and carried out with scrupulous attention to approved (or, at least, justifiable) procedure, it nonetheless *appeared* brutal and degrading. This was a dicier problem, since nothing could remedy the problem of flogging's spectacular brutality. Whether seen or imagined, flogging was visibly brutal.

People subject to flogging thus had an immediate claim to the sympathy of people who considered themselves humanitarian, an appeal many victimized Africans were able to claim. A particularly eloquent example is illustrated in a letter printed in 1912 by the *African Times and Orient Review*. Its author, J. C. Taylor, was a railway clerk who had been flogged with one other clerk after having attracted the notice of the resident of Zaria:

> We were asked to prostrate on the ground before the Resident, which not being instantly done, the Resident beat us with stick, and gave orders to the Dogaris [*dogarai*; s. *dogari*: police employed by the Native Authority] to tie us with rope on our necks, and take us to the native gaol. We were at once knocked down before him and tied most brutally, and nine men on horseback with two Dogaris conveyed with inexpressible cruelty to native town Zaria, beat us along, iron chains were added to our waist and feet, and we were confined till Thursday. On Thursday he sent for us and we were brought in chains before him. I asked the Resident what I had done to bring upon myself all this punishment. He said in future when I see him passing I must prostrate as the natives of this country always do before him. Then he ordered the Dogaris to take us again to the open market and flog us twenty lashes. I am wounded all over, having nearly lost my eyesight, my hips are blistered, and I am quite unfit to appear at office.[17]

Humanitarian criticisms raised by such complaints could hardly be addressed using procedural remedies. Worse, metropolitan sentiment, once aroused, was hardly allayed by broad affirmations of colonialist realpolitik.

Perhaps because improved procedure would not address this deeper political problem, officials spent considerable attempting to demonstrate that, brutal though flogging was, it was both necessary and more humane than other alternatives. Administrative approaches to flogging scandals thus juxtaposed apologias for flogging as a practice with a minute attention to procedural detail—record keeping, methods of administration, means to apply penalties properly to the various categories of person. In this way, flogging's *political* problem, its propensity for scandal, resulted in a body of documentation as officials tried, through procedural controls, pseudoscientific speculation, and a minute attention to detail, to frame and reframe flogging as appropriate and necessary. But precisely because such techniques did not and could not alter flogging's status as a species of bodily violation, the problem remained irresolvable. To the extent that corporal punishment was conceived as a necessary adjunct to colonial governance, it also implicated the project as inherently contradictory.

SCANDAL, TRADITION, CORPOREALITY

The minimal point that flogging often touched off scandal is less revealing than the specific dynamics of the scandals emanating from Nigeria. Reformers targeting corporal punishment and other corporeal technologies had long been active elsewhere. Groups such as the Anti-Slavery Society had already diversified their activities to include a greater range of humanitarian concerns, and a network of political activists, journalists, and missionaries functioned to publicize many humanitarian outrages. In addition to these developments in an emergent humanitarian public sphere, Nigerian flogging scandals occurred at a very particular moment in colonial administrative history. Colonial regimes had long relied on the administrative apparatuses of indigenous governmental institutions, but starting in the Protectorate of Northern Nigeria, the ideology of indirect rule labeled this practice a good one in itself and placed a new emphasis on the category of political tradition as the central strategy of governing the colonized.[18] Especially as the political fortunes of Lord Lugard, the first High Commissioner of Northern Nigeria and the first governor-general of unified Nigeria, rose after his Northern Nigerian administration, indirect rule came to be associated with him and to be seen as a strategy of surpassing brilliance. Being a committed "indirect ruler" was understood as a positive good, and policy debates were increasingly carried out as debates over the exact nature of political "tradition." The ideological charms of indirect rule were most compelling within colonialist circles. Nonetheless, the valorization of political tradition arising from indirect rule had practical consequences. Not only did it fix official attention on the minimal question of whether flogging was itself "traditional," it also posed the thorny question of which traditions applied to whom. Indirect rule ultimately created a series of definitional problems concerning who could be considered a "native" for the purposes of chastisement and more generally how colonized people were susceptible to correction and governance.

An important aspect of flogging's ever present possibility for scandal was the practical difficulty of knowing—in Lagos, London, or Kaduna (the capital of the north)—what was going on in the provincial courts and native courts. Flogging returns were all very well, but scandals came from isolated (and shocking) incidents, doubly scandalous because of the possibility that they were *not* isolated. The native courts were always open to the accusation that they enforced bestial and savage law codes unequally and corruptly. The reply to this—that such savagery was "traditional" and therefore legitimate—was then buttressed by the contention that, for Nigerians native to the areas governed traditionally, these punishments were the only appropriate way of regulating their behavior. The "civilizing mission" could be accomplished only by using methods the uncivilized could understand, savage though they might be.

The provincial courts, in addition, had the potential for a second sort of corruption: indulgence by the frequently isolated British residents in atavistic orgies of flogging. This was an element in the scandal emerging from Fitzpatrick's role in the flogging of Adama and Hassana. Such anxieties had an element of justification: Colonial records are full of traces of residents who seemed to take particular pleasure in sentencing people to flogging or even demonstrated a disturbing enthusiasm for administering the floggings themselves.[19] As assistant resident of Nassarawa, Fitzpatrick had been at the center of a 1914 scandal in which he had punished a case of simple assault with flogging "in three places."[20] In fact, Fitzpatrick was dismissed from the colonial service several years after the Bauchi incident. The precipitating cause was financial irregularity, but the Colonial Office clearly perceived his propensity to cause trouble.[21]

Scandals over flogging were remarkably static across the early colonial period, in large measure because they symptomatized a continuing contradiction within colonial rule. While the colonial government could make particular cosmetic changes to flogging, the deeper difficulties remained constant. This recurrent quality is illustrated within official justifications for the practice. The first step in such accounts was to separate good instances of flogging from bad ones. Perhaps because it was the more threatening scenario for colonialism's benevolent face, heart-of-darkness floggings by colonial officers were addressed through flat denial.

Colonial Office officials almost inevitably publicly defended the British political officers who held ultimate responsibility for floggings, in both native courts and provincial courts. Truly problematic floggings were held to be exceptional. So, for example, in the 1912 flogging of the clerk J. C. Taylor, the Colonial Office vociferously defended the responsible officer in Parliament, accepting his absolute denial of responsibility.[22]

The official position in this case (and in other cases) was that such instances came about when native courts gave in to their more primitive urges and managed to escape the supervision of their British masters.[23] The problem, according to this formulation, was not with British policies so much as it was with the fact that colonial supervision could not be omnipresent. Even when prepared to admit that something was wrong, British officials tended to allude to problems very cautiously. For example, in a minute on the returns of corporal punishment for 1932, one London official wrote, "They still seem fond of using the cat at Kano." Another pointed out, his tone bemused rather than concerned, a case in which a prisoner was given twelve lashes with the cat for "wondering."[24] Officials never considered the possibility that residents might individually or structurally bear some responsibility for such cases. The other consistent concern displayed in official deliberation was the flogging of women, which aroused considerable public anxiety and disquiet in official circles. Worries about women tended to be answered with the assertion that theirs was a flogging in name only, that the main purpose of the punishment was humiliation. When most of the British (and the Western-influenced) public considered women to be too fragile for corporal punishment, Nigerian defenders of flogging replied that Nigerian floggings were a different matter and that no woman, no matter how delicate, would be harmed by the practice.

Dealing with the "bad" floggings, however, was less a problem than justifying the "good" ones. The logistical necessity imputed to flogging had somewhat different valences in the native courts and the provincial courts. In the native courts, flogging was hailed as a "traditional" method of therefore legitimate and, to Nigerians, comprehensible governance. It both was effective in achieving governmental ends and would eventually die out as Nigerian institutions evolved toward modernity—conceptualized as a state analogous to British society at the time. When investigating flogging, officers concentrated on the importance it held in indigenous systems of justice, identifying it as the only penalty likely to have a deterrent effect: "There is a certain class of ruffian to whom nothing appeals so much as causing him physical pain, in order that he should really feel this, I think the 24 lashes given is often inadequate."[25] A resident in Kano, who "believed in flogging as the most suitable punishment for the Nigerian native of the present day," considered the whips used on Nigerians "too light an article." Although they might deter "a white criminal," Nigerian whips were generally decrepit; "6 or 12 lashes with the frayed strong-ends of the present 'cat-o'-nine-tails' on a leather-skinned old gaol-bird of this country . . . is generally a farce quite appreciated by both the offender and the Warders."[26] When circularized about the possibility of abolishing flogging in 1907, officers reported that the al' kalai predicted a massive increase in crime if flogging were abolished.[27] This, too, is a recurrent theme: During a similar inquiry in 1921, the emirs of Katsina and Zaria, among others, are cited as being emphatically against abolishing flogging, "a convenient and cheap form of punishment . . . it acts as a deterrent of crime."[28]

In the provincial courts, flogging was claimed to fulfill two distinct purposes. For moderately serious criminal matters, it was the form of punishment most likely to correct the behavior of Nigerian criminals. In this way, its utility was analogous to that in the native courts. Its other arena of application, however, was the public chastisement of erring officials of the native authorities, whose crimes often would not have been "traditionally" criminal before colonization:

> The crime of extortion by a person in the Government service or by a person representing himself to be in the Government service . . . is punishable by flogging. . . . Flogging should usually be awarded for these offenses (unless the convicted person is an influential Chief), and above all it should be administered at the scene of the crime, in order that the ignorant villagers may have ocular proof that Government itself is not a participator in the exactions which have been made on them.[29]

Flogging in the native courts was one element of a system of government that would gradually transform Nigeria from semi-barbarism to civilization. In the provincial courts it also was supposed to create a more immediate kind of metamorphosis. The tutelary spectacle of the "corrupt" government official (or impostor) receiving his comeuppance was to create a new and distinctly uncustomary kind of probity in all officials of the native authority, transforming both officials' assumptions about how they could perform their offices and citizens' expectations about what appropriate official conduct might be.

The sometimes inchoate British conviction that under indirect rule "tradition" must be transformed but that it was for the time being also the only possible pattern of government (therefore necessary to enlist in its own transformation) was accentuated by the problem of flogging and criminal jurisprudence more generally. Barbarous practices and potential excesses in the native courts pointed to what seemed a thin line between primitive law and simple violence, between government officials and bandits. It was sometimes difficult to tell the difference between al'kalai and the criminals they sentenced, especially when many of the former ended up in the dock on charges of corruption. British officials interpreted native authorities' tendency to mislead them as a racial propensity for lying,[30] and this indexed a criminality in the entire race. How could criminals be chastised if they were not so different from non-criminals?

Flogging was thus supposed to be doubly instructive: appropriate to the Nigerian mind *and* demonstrating a new kind of governance. Corporal punishment ultimately would allow a wide-ranging transformation in the scope of criminality, and this, in the end, would mark a different set of behavior as criminal and at the same time inculcate "modern" forms of governance and civic socialization. Scandals in London therefore were perceived to be fueled by a public that consistently *misinterpreted* flogging as a spectacle readily understood by the non-specialist. Humanitarian critics viewed the pathos of disciplined bodies with civilized sensibilities and therefore missed its logistical necessity.

Although the spectacle of flogging was distasteful to European eyes, colonial officers claimed that it had to be considered in relation to other potential means of punishment. One official suggested that, in punishing Nigerians,

> what troubles me is not corporal punishment but the barbarity of the European punishment of imprisonment.... [I]t would be more merciful to hang [a native] at once. He pines at the loss of freedom; the unaccustomed food and sleeping arrangements cause disease—and he *dies*.[31]

Nigerians were supposed to be unable to adapt to isolation from their families and "tribes," unable to understand the reasons for their imprisonment, and likely to die from "English ventilation." Flogging, however, provided an adequate deterrent and punishment. Nigerians could understand what was happening and why, and they would survive it—at least, if the flogging was carefully regulated and monitored by British officials, and the worst excesses of "native custom" were suppressed. The claim that convicts were more likely to survive flogging than a term of imprisonment was not in itself very unreasonable, although abysmal conditions within the prisons probably had more to do with the mortality rate than a racial inability to adapt to isolation from the tribal community.

Even more significant than officials' claims for flogging's humanitarian superiority was their faith in its greater efficacy as a method of discipline. Physically punishing, rather than isolating, the body of the prisoner was held to be infinitely more appropriate to Nigeria's state of social evolution. It doubly made sense that it should be a prime ingredient in the tradition that was to be enforced, purged of its "repugnant" features. Given these assumptions about the primitivism of Nigerian individuals and the nature of Nigerian political tradition, corporal punishment was appropriate as long as it was carefully calibrated. Evidence of flogging's appropriateness to Nigeria's state of evolution was to be found in the fact that it was a feature of traditional law, and in the "scientific" fact that Nigerians were unable to benefit fully from incarceration. The rehabilitative possibilities of the prison stemmed less from its capacity to punish (if anything, colonial logic implied that imprisonment punished Nigerians more than it did the British) than from its ability to force prisoners to internalize a set of governing constraints that would eventually propel them into law-abiding lives on the outside. Colonial sociologies identified the evolutionary standing of Nigerian societies with a "tribal communism" implying that specific Nigerians were not yet individuated—or subjectified, to use the terminology of Michel Foucault[32]—in a manner that made them amenable to disciplinary practices like incarceration. The tutelary function of isolation from society and the rehabilitative possibilities of the prison were lost on Northern Nigerians.

The official position, thus, was that all Nigerians (or all male Nigerians) could be better punished by flogging than by imprisonment, reinforcing the idea that the actual mechanics of flogging were critical to its humanitarian application. Investigations of flogging found a variety of methods: differing instruments (hippo-hide whips, cat-o'-nine-tails, canes). These were discussed in terms of their potential both to cause pain and to cause injury. Pain (as chastisement) was a potential good, while injury (or, at least, permanent injury) was to be avoided. Thus, for example, during a discussion in 1933 on how to regulate corporal punishment, the lieutenant governor of Northern Nigeria produced a memo about draft regulations that would have forbidden the use of the hippo-hide whip (*bulala*) and specified the type of cane that could be used:

> It has been found that the cane in use in the Government prisons . . . does not conform to the cane described in the draft regulations. It is in fact of a diameter of 6/16 to 7/16 of an inch (in length three feet). It was this instrument that was considered by several Residents to inflict a more severe punishment than the bulala wielded in the normal manner, and the same opinion has also been expressed by some chiefs. . . . [T]he cane conforming to the regulations is at first sight . . . much more formidable a weapon than the light prison cane. It is however possible that the thicker cane, though it may bruise more, may be less liable to cut the flesh.[33]

Among officers in Nigeria, there was considerable anxiety about the distinction between Muslim courts and non-Muslim courts. The former were more trusted to administer floggings in a reasonable and controlled manner.[34] Especially because of the dangers of bestial floggings in non-Muslim areas, during the 1930s there was a successful proposal to substitute caning for whipping in all cases. This proposal was ultimately adopted across the region. It was not, however, uniformly approved. Residents claimed that the bulala was actually more merciful than a cane when used properly. Even more to the point, its use was traditional under Islamic law. For a time, therefore, regulations declared that Muslims would be whipped with the bulala, and pagans with a cane, which mirrored precolonial practices that had distinguished between Muslims and non-Muslims and therefore could be counted as traditional. Quickly, residents noted that pagans were complaining that their floggings were substantially more severe than those of their Muslim co-defendants.[35]

The instrument itself was hardly the only object of inquiry. Just as important were the methods for moderating and equalizing the severity of the lashes (often, different objects kept in the flogger's armpit), techniques for arranging the body of the flogged (clothed or naked, in prison yards or marketplaces, lying down, sitting, half-buried in the earth, drenched with water, having the prisoner covered with an antiseptic-dipped cloth before the flogging began), and treatment after flogging (having salt rubbed in the wounds, being left in the sun, being discharged to the care of family members, being returned to prison). These different methods created an opportunity for British officials to reassure one another of the ultimate logic of flogging as a means of punishing Nigerians. Different methods, they thought, reflected real and useful distinctions between categories of people. One of the most important and most widespread differences between the way in which Muslims and pagans were flogged was that when a Muslim was flogged the flogger had to keep a cowry shell in his armpit, resulting in rather less forceful blows.

The flogging of women was a considerably more delicate matter than the flogging of men. All of the spectacular problems of men victimized by the lash emerged with redoubled force when the victims were women, since any practice that brutalized men was even worse when its victims were delicate women. To add to the difficulty, with women the spectacle itself became problematic, as a flogging uncovered flesh that the demands of modesty required to remain concealed. Either a woman's back had to be uncovered for the whipping or her wrapper might be dislodged under the whip's onslaught. Interestingly, officials agreed with critics that women's inherent delicacy made the physical ordeal of flogging unsuitable for them.[36] In this instance, they were not as entranced by the notion that women's flogging was traditional as they were when men were in question. Nor did they assume that this was the only way women could be discouraged from a life of crime.[37] Instead, they tended to claim that women's flogging was not really flogging but was "flogging merely in name," a "purely formal matter and cannot physically injure anyone, man or woman."[38] The resident of Borno described the procedure in detail:

> The whip or lash is held in the hand by the three last fingers, the first finger is brought down on to the palm of the hand and the thumb on to the first finger; the right foot is brought forward. It is usual in Bornu to slightly modify the rules as to administration of the lashes by substituting the rule that three cowries are to be held in the hand of the executioner as well as the lash instead of the rules as to the arrangement of the fingers.[39]

This was more or less in consonance with Lugard's instructions that "in cases where a powerful negress becomes violent, and cannot be easily dealt with otherwise it is conceivable that she may be best dealt with by a birching on the shoulders."[40]

How precisely this directive was to fit in with the mandate to enforce native law and custom was somewhat less clear: Women had never been simply flogged for discrete incidents of unmanageability. Lugard's comment reads rather as if it were intended for metropolitan consumption and meant to be very broadly construed in Nigeria. Ultimately, any woman in trouble with the law might be considered a "powerful negress." The most frequent reasons women were flogged was for adultery (that is, married women's infidelity) and slander. Great emphasis was placed on two features: that the main part of the punishment for women was humiliation, and that the actual flogging was so light as to be almost no deterrent by itself. Again (apparently for both Muslim and pagan women), floggers kept an object in their armpits; the objects listed here (*balls* of cowries, canes) are somewhat larger than the single cowry mentioned for Muslim men and so allowed floggers somewhat less freedom of movement. Lighter whips were used. Every effort was made to protect women's modesty, and officers insisted that women always remained fully covered or, if there were a danger that their clothes might slip off during the flogging, their shoulders would be bared in such a way that the breasts would remain covered. Humiliation might be the object of women's flogging, but their modesty was allegedly always protected.

This emphasis served two purposes. More important, perhaps, in the eyes of the Colonial Office was the fact that preserving women's modesty would prevent scandals of the sort emanating from Bauchi in 1919. Part of the outraged response to the treatment accorded Adama and Hassana stemmed from the fact that they had been stripped naked in the market. Preventing a recurrence of this was entirely desirable. This is not to say that protecting women's modesty was a purely metropolitan invention. An emphasis on female purity and modesty has powerful indigenous roots. A woman's publicly being uncovered would indeed have been a substantial punishment by itself. In addition, however, women adulterers were apparently left out in the place of their flogging for considerable periods after their sentence was carried out. Officials, particularly in London, considered that this demonstrated that humiliation rather than physical chastisement was the real object of the exercise, apparently not grasping that being left out in the sun was, in Nigeria, itself a considerable and dangerous punishment.

Encoded within colonial responses to flogging scandals is a notion of colonial corporeality as a critical adjunct to government via tradition. One justification for colonialism was that colonized people were too primitive to govern themselves; their consciousnesses were not sufficiently developed for them to act as citizens in a modern state. They were not susceptible to the systems of rational incentives that governed individualized European citizen-subjects. Because the prison would not work on such primitives, corporeal techniques were the only ones that might work. This colonial logic was made more complicated by humanitarian concerns with the spectacle of violated colonial bodies. Even if corporeal techniques were necessary for disciplining aberrance, an emergent colonial public sphere also demanded that they be carefully controlled, correction rather than simple violence. British officials therefore attempted to deal with these scandals as a problem of interpretation, assuming that a proper understanding of corporeal practices would allay political problems.

TRACES OF GOVERNANCE

Northern Nigeria's British administration perceived the problems posed by flogging to be primarily ones of administrative procedure and public relations. Proper controls on the application of a necessary punishment could prevent unfortunate incidents, and any outrage about the punishment itself could be dismissed as sentimental and unrealistic. Within this paradigm, flogging was a necessary but temporary tool in a longer-term civilizing project. This, however, is at best a very partial appreciation of flogging's significance as a tactic of governance. Even if it was the official position, it is possible to discern other, contradictory official and unofficial stances, a kind of colonial doublethink. Official attempts to combat humanitarian criticism by describing (and thereby controlling) these applications of corporeal discipline implied that colonialism's critics consistently misread the significance of spectacular pain. The difficulty lay not in a sentimental public's misinterpreting a distasteful but necessary practice but, rather, in a deeper problem within the tactics of colonial power.

The scandals themselves were enabled by a particular set of conjunctures. Though no reformist society took African flogging as its primary concern, organizations like the Anti-Slavery Society and the Bars of coastal cities like Lagos and Calabar were important in bringing incidents to metropolitan attention. A lively press both in Anglophone West Africa and beyond had emerged by 1900 and provided a means to publicize certain incidents widely. With this infrastructure in place, the spectacular quality of corporal punishment proved difficult to reframe as an admirable—or, at least, a necessary—tradition. As Elaine Scarry has argued, pain is a sensory state that resists symbolization; that is indeed antithetical to a humanly signifiable world. Pain can be communicated through inchoate cries or analogies (a burning pain, a tearing pain, etc.), but its status as a sensory state without external object makes it ultimately a private experience understood by others only as a matter of faith.[41] But precisely because pain is ultimately inexpressible, it also resists explanation and excuse—that is, when a whip descends onto human flesh, the fact that the sensory state it causes cannot be communicated means, ironically, that this pain is hard to dismiss. Corporeal technologies whose details are glossed over leave room for doubt, but when their details are revealed, the pain they cause is hard to deny. In this sense, therefore, my argument diverges from Scarry's in that she emphasizes the quality of doubt emerging from the inexpressibility of pain, while I emphasize an imaginative commonality: I find it difficult to avoid having a sense of how it would feel were particular insults made to my body. To put it another way, even if the direct experience of pain is radically private, the fact that it follows predictably from specific bodily insults means that pain is, in some contexts, extraordinarily difficult to discount.

To a lesser extent, the question of female modesty worked in the same way. Female nudity was almost as difficult to deny as injury (either the women were uncovered or they were not), and, as we have seen, the colonial response was simply to deny that outrages had occurred in the first place. In this sense, then, the scandal of colonial corporeality could be contained through denial and disavowal. Pain was not pain; nudity was not nudity. And scandal recurred because this was not a credible position.[42]

For the colonial regime, flogging was necessary, however problematic. The British brought with them to Northern Nigeria at least a partial commitment to what Foucault has called a "governmental" mode of power. Ultimately they tried to rule things—people, commodities—rather than territories in the aggregate. To the extent that a government depends on governmentality as a paradigm, it operates through systems of knowledge and incentives rather than simply imposes its will through direct displays of power.[43] A commitment to governmentality conceived as a species of governmental rationality was an integral part of colonial regimes' self-conscious modernity. However, no regime is ever entirely or perfectly committed to governmentality as opposed to other modes of exercising power. The ambivalent difference at the heart of this colonial project complicated British attempts to govern Nigeria in a "modern" and "rational" way even as governmental modes of rule defined these as the ideal way to rule a modern state. Rational incentives that might govern metropolitan citizen-subjects (even if this did not always work, even in the metropole) were not so effective with Nigerian "primitives." Colonial citizenship coexisted uneasily with the ultimate civic disability of a colonialism that questioned the competence of any native to understand the British government. "Tradition," the British thought, could stand in for systems of incentives that might in a more "civilized" country govern a population of rationally calculating individuals.

Let me emphasize: I apply the label modern *not* because I claim British approaches to governance represent a distinct temporal or developmental conjuncture, but because they represent a particular approach to power and the objects of power—one that calls itself "modern" and sees itself as representing a break from the past. That is, the modern attempts to create itself *as* modern in part through identifying its other, a role filled by, among others, Nigerians. This quality of modernity concerned an attitude rather than its positive contents. It was always and necessarily incomplete. As David Scott suggests:

> Understood in this way, as a restructuring of the field, configuration and project of power, one has then to read the inscription of the modern into colonial space . . . as a governmental *reorganization* of the existing institutional and political space such that by a certain number of transforming arrangements and calculations the conduct of the colonized is constrained or urged in an *improving* direction.[44]

This colonial governmentality was inherently paradoxical.[45] The modernity of European states included their colonial projects and helped to determine the scope of their governmental ambitions. In a sense, this created a constant *agenda* for governance, a continuity between metropole and colony, even as the *tactics* of governance were altered by racialist assumptions about colonial subjects' capacity for subjectification. In such contexts, "tradition" was valorized as a transcendental reservoir of political legitimacy within the colony. It also offered a species of excuse for metropolitan critics: Colonial appropriations of tradition were a mark of cultural respect and reflected the colony's state of social evolution. Tradition was the idiom of government, but its target was the "tribe" as a collectivity. Criminals who, though still "tribal," came to state attention through individually aberrant acts posed a problem. Since they were not fully subjectified they could not be educated, reeducated, rehabilitated as potentially worthwhile citizens. A second, corporeal form of governmentality focused on their bodies, which could (without danger to their health) educate through pain. In this way, flogging was congruent with other aspects of this mode of government via "tradition." Traditional life—what we might call culture—seemed to offer the same manipulative possibilities that subjectification did for "modern" European citizens. The project, however, required not only calling "traditional" a host of innovative or, at least, disputable practices, but of assuming a brand of determinate, racialized, evolutionary difference between colonizer and colonized. Colonial corporeality, however, threatened these legitimating features of tradition even as it was deployed as an adjunct of traditional modes of discipline.

People subject to flogging may have been seen as "ruffians" and "powerful negresses," susceptible only to pain as a source of discipline, but corporeality proved highly problematic as an index of difference. Distinctions between Muslims and non-Muslims may in London have seemed a matter of evolution and nerve endings, but officers in Nigeria confronted by non-Muslims' decrying harsher whippings and greater pain were not so sanguine. Colonial corporeality proffered an avenue to governmentality that could mark and maintain categories of colonial difference, but this consistently undermined itself to the extent that it functioned through pain. In this way, the insistence that women's flogging was not *really* flogging becomes more readily explicable; pain is more believably denied than explained away. In the end, flogging demonstrates the irony and the contradictions of the strategy and marks them, quite accurately, as a scandal.

EPILOGUE

This history of early colonial Islamic law has acquired unfortunate contemporary resonances, as the reimposition of the shari'a criminal code in the northern states beginning in 2000 has contributed to a series of deadly riots. This development has resulted most notoriously in sentences of death by stoning for Safiya Hussaini of Sokoto State and Amina Lawal in Katsina State, though their convictions were ultimately overturned on appeal. As the history of flogging suggests, neither this violence of law nor the violence of identity is anything new.

The notoriety of Islamic law both now and in the early twentieth century lies in the fact that phenomenal violence (flogging, stoning, amputation) operates, however problematically, under the label of "law" but is received (in southern Nigeria, in certain circles within the north, in the West) as atrocity. The circulation of public discourse under the dichotomous rubrics of "law" and "violence" mimics and reproduces a deeper process of alienation and identification. The politics surrounding the reimposition of shari'a mirror those of flogging and were structured by an economy of reception, implication, and disavowal fundamentally similar to the one at stake in contemporary shari'a controversies.

Although the scandals over flogging died down after the criminal code was amended in 1933, as independence approached, the dominant political party of the north picked up on a long-niggling anomaly between British and Maliki law on homicide. The party forced a political compromise in which some provisions of Maliki law were incorporated into the Northern Nigerian criminal code, and the network of Islamic law courts was then stripped of its criminal jurisdiction. Nevertheless, a particular paradigm of indigeneity was by this point well established as a principle of local government, though it carried increasingly complex baggage in its connotation of autochthonous subjects as necessarily inadequate. Decolonization did not remove this, and there is still an element of it in that richer (more highly educated, more "modern") people are less likely *in practice* to be subject to the penalties of Islamic law.

The politics of indigeneity have in the years since the civil war (1967–70) become increasingly complicated, as sectional identification has simultaneously fragmented and coalesced. The tripartite Hausa–Yoruba–Igbo division that determined the course of the civil war has splintered as a more complex federal structure created incentives for more local forms of identification.[46] At the same time, a Christian-Muslim divide made salient a two-way, rather than three-way, split. In this context, the reintroduction of the courts' criminal jurisdiction must be seen as a response to the election of President Olesegun Obasanjo, a southern Christian, and as a response to some civilian governors' need to cover over the inadequacy of their regimes. Growing sectional discontent was manifested and exacerbated by riots, although they were driven in part by ambitious politicians, using bought-and-paid-for mobs of young men. It would be a mistake to view the reimposition of shari'a simply as a cynical political strategy: There certainly are ordinary people who perceive Nigeria's state of crisis and lawlessness as emerging from a breakdown in law and religious authority and who hope that shari'a can reverse what they perceive as a decline. Nevertheless, mob violence was not just a problem that shari'a might cure; it was also a driving force in its declaration and a sign of the implication of governors in illicit and illegal activity. Crimes judged harshly by Islamic courts (women's "adultery," working-class drinking, homosexuality) have long been the target of state intervention: Bars were raided, and independent women and effeminate homosexuals were arrested and imprisoned before 2000. Adultery, drinking, and homosexuality by elite men have not been penalized in the same way.

There is a telling excess to the violence of law, which in northern Nigeria has reached critical proportions. Violent technologies that appear to many as excessive and unjust serve to mark and enforce the dichotomy of the legal and the illegal. Such violence also covers over a more ideologically dangerous dichotomy between the licit and the illicit.

Proclaiming Islamic law is a sign of politicians' piety and suggests official corruption and incompetence do not exist—or are curable and (with shari'a) cured. The name of law is powerful; the name of religious law is more powerful yet. In a context in which Muslim identity has attained central political force, the name of Islamic law manages to promise both justice and a utopian future. Protest by outside observers does not alter this logic; rather, the outcry heightens it. The excessiveness of recent forms of corporal punishment and its targeting the relatively powerless suggest the need of elite men who control the judicial system to cover over their complicity in a morally dubious economy of illegal but state-sanctioned violence—the "improper" violence of the police, the ties of politicians to political terror, the widespread corruption that exists at all levels of government. Violence becomes "justice," or it becomes invisible.

Observers' not unreasonable concern is critical to the ideological functioning of this euphemizing process. Worse, this structure of participants and spectators mirrors northern Nigeria's objective location—in a peripheral, dependent economy; under a state apparatus whose governmental incentives are perverse, at best; in an ongoing, externally mandated economic crisis. Invoking law, in the name of "shari'a" or under the name "human rights," is to posit these instances of violence at discrete points of a trajectory of violent acts leading from chaos, through founding violence, to instrumental violence and the "rule of law."[47] This invocation masks complicity and effaces historical causality. Outsiders' receptions of law's violence are, in northern Nigeria, an element in its supplementary effectivity, and this is the legacy of an entire century. In this case, violence is not just law's secret supplement, though it is that. The name of law is an enabling condition for violence. The economy inherent in the violence of law, the violence before law, violence before the law depends on a set of generative principles very different from Islam's universal and egalitarian promise. The dead in the riots tend to be non-elite, as do people suffering the brutal punishments being meted out by the Islamic law courts. Colonialism's inadequate subjects have re-emerged as women, as commoners, as sodomites, as thieves.

One could read Foucault as ultimately concluding that there is a history to the intuition that the individual is autonomous, intentional, agentive, and to the intuition that the subject's self-will has political, moral, and ethical entailments. This history is not one of self-discovery or of a coming into historical self-consciousness. Rather, it reflects a shift in the strategies by which power is applied to people. One's self-understanding as autonomous and rational is precisely what makes one most permeable to power. Foucault's point was not about discrete incidents but about the trajectory of an overall set of strategies, whose effect has been to individualize and de-center the application of power. Built into the bedrock assumptions of various northern Nigerian political actors—"modern" elites, colonial officers, men—is an assumption that power is deployed in a de-centered way, that it targets rational individuals, and that some subjects are by their nature inadequate. These assumptions have a history, though obviously an elusive and ambiguous one. What is the ontological status of these discourses? Is a scandal over torture in mid-nineteenth-century India "the same" as one over flogging in twentieth-century Nigeria? Is it like disquiet over footbinding in late-nineteenth- and early-twentieth-century China? How have categories of identity—race, gender, sexuality, bourgeois respectability—traveled the globe? Part of the answer, surely, lies in the uneven consolidation of a global public, an audience and a witness to law's spectacle of violence, and the forum through which power is communicated and addresses its subjects.

I suggest that the career of Islamic criminal law in contemporary northern Nigeria is comprehensible only against the backdrop of a politics of indigeneity and the valorization of the label "custom" engendered by colonialism. Imposing criminal law not only serves to legitimate state governments as crime fighters; it also marks them as piously Muslim and emphasizes a putative alliance against the impious South and the Western world. The discursive manifestations of global, long-term shifts in regimes of power are ineluctably local, situated, contingent, ad hoc. In Nigeria, the legal recognition of cultural identity has come to mark and enforce a boundary between pious, Muslim northerners and their other—the southerner, the thief, the prostitute. This is a logic we see at play in many places. For those who suffer from it, the danger is all too close to home.

NOTES

An earlier version of this paper appeared in *Interventions: The International Journal of Postcolonial Studies* 3, no. 2 (July 2001). I gratefully acknowledge the journal's permission to print the current version. The research for this paper undertaken in Nigeria was supported by a fellowship from the Joint Committee on African Studies of the Social Science Research Council and the American Council of Learned Societies and by grants from the Wenner-Gren Foundation for Anthropological Research, Inc.; the Rackham School of Graduate Studies, University of Michigan; and the Center on Research, Tulane University. Research in the United Kingdom was supported by grants from the Rackham School of Graduate Studies, the Anthropology/History Program, and the International Institute, University of Michigan; a Jacob K. Javits Fellowship; and a Schmitt Grant from the American Historical Association. The writing was supported by fellowships from the Michigan Society of Fellows; the Advanced Study Center, University of Michigan; and the American Council of Learned Societies. Earlier portions of this paper were presented at the American Anthropological Association; at conferences at Johns Hopkins University and Columbia University; and at Rice University. Professors David Scott, David Killingray, Gyan Pandey, Anupama Rao, and Kerry Ward provided very helpful comments on those papers. I am particularly grateful to Moses Ochonu for his assistance in gathering additional archival material in Kaduna during the summer of 1999.

1 PRO CO 583/74 400.

2 Flogging of two women at Bauchi Libel Action Enclose a Statement of Claim and Defense of Defendant. 8 May 1919.

3 Northern Nigeria was proclaimed a protectorate of Great Britain in 1900, and in 1914 it was merged with the Protectorate of Southern Nigeria, creating the political entity that is today the Federal Republic of Nigeria. Northern Nigeria retained substantial integrity, however, under its own lieutenant governor, who was responsible to the governor in Lagos.

4 PRO CO 583/82. 10 November 1919. R. Barber. Fitzpatrick v. Barber + Others. Libel Action.

5 The topic has yet to receive adequate scholarly attention. Michael Crowder

has written a fascinating study of a case of an African chief who was temporarily deposed for sentencing a European to being flogged in Bechuanaland (contemporary Botswana): Crowder, *The Flogging of Phinehas Mcintosh*. See also Killingray, "Punishment to Fit the Crime," and idem, "The Rod of Empire," for studies of flogging in the army and as part of penal policy more generally.

6   There was also a third system, the Supreme Court, whose jurisdiction was limited to non-Europeans and to very limited geographical areas.

7   This paper will consider primarily the period until 1933, which is the time when flogging was a pressing political issue. At that point, the criminal code was amended to disallow whipping. Although it remained legal to cane offenders, even that was discouraged, and the regular scandals that had emerged from instances of flogging died down. Limitations of space prevent my developing a discussion of how the application of flogging changed over this thirty-three-year period, but the general tendency was for the application of flogging to be more controlled and less frequent. For the purposes of the argument here, however, note that although one could chart out shifts of this nature, the political problems posed by flogging remained more or less the same, and the ways in which it was conceptualized also were fairly constant.

8   PRO CO 446/39 189. 13 May 1904. Flogging.

9   NAK SNP 6/3 160/1907, Crimes for which Lashes were Inflicted by Residents, November 1, 1907.

10   Lord Lugard, "Memo. 3, Judicial and Legal," in Lugard, *Political Memoranda*, para. 60.

11   The comment is from a worried minute by the second High Commissioner of Northern Nigeria, Sir Percy Girouard, who nonetheless deemed it "necessary in certain cases," NAK SNP 6/3 160/1907, December 20, 1907.

12   Fika, *The Kano Civil War and British Over-Rule 1882–1940*; Pierce, *Farmers and the State*, and "Looking for the Legal"; Ubah, *Government and Administration of Kano Emirate, 1900–1930*.

13   Khalil, *Maliki Law*.

14   For a case of officers' being convinced that women's being denied their mandated inheritance shares was actually legal, see Pierce, "Farmers and 'Prostitutes.'"

15   NAK, SNP 112/1914.

16   "Aubin, A. C. Capt., Flogging of Cook by Alkali of Nafada," DO [District

Officer] to Resident, Central Province, June 25, 1914; Aubin to Resident, June 24, 1914. This was a particularly interesting case in that the young man in question, a sixteen-year-old southern Nigerian, was working for an officer in the West African Frontier Force. Several mentions of the youth's wearing a green homburg hat suggest that this is what initially attracted Fitzpatrick's unfavorable notice. In defending his actions, Fitzpatrick alleged that the young man was sleeping with his employer and that this was the real reason for the officer's outrage.

17   J. C. Taylor to Chief Engineer, 16 February 1912, printed in the *African Times and Orient Review*, October 1912, 115; paragraph break elided.

18   For general appraisals of indirect rule in Africa, see Berry, *No Condition Is Permanent*; Mamdani, *Citizen and Subject*; Ranger, "The Invention of Tradition in Colonial Africa"; idem, "The Invention of Tradition Revisited"; Spear, "Neo-Traditionalism and the Limits of Invention in British Colonial Africa."

19   E.g. PRO CO 583/126 Conf. July 18, 1924, in which a disgruntled colonial cadet accused his supervisor of improper flogging. The governor and the Colonial Office censured the officer in question but nevertheless ascribed the cadet's accusation to the officer's having reported him for bouncing a check.

20   PRO CO 583/23 7 May 1914. House of Commons, Nor. Provinces Case of *Rex v. Nichols*, 7 May 1914, PRO, CO 583/23.

21   After his dismissal from colonial service, Fitzpatrick wrote regular missives to the Colonial Office alleging widespread irregularity and impropriety in the Nigerian service.

22   *African Times and Orient Review*, August 1912.

23   Or in a later case, a southern Nigerian was tried by the *al'kali* of Bukuru for not having paid his taxes on time and sentenced to a flogging for having failed to obey the judge's order to pay. A Nigerian member of the Legislative Council asked a question about the matter, which then attracted sufficient publicity to get a question in Parliament. The governor at the time announced that he was "appalled" that the native court had so overstepped its bounds, administering a flogging for a crime not covered in the criminal code and exerting jurisdiction over a "non-native native," someone of African descent but not indigenous to the area ruled "traditionally" by the responsible Native Authority. PRO CO 583/190 1130 (1933), Flogging of a Native (Victor Eluaka) at Bukura for failure to pay tax on time.

24   PRO CO 583/183 1437 (1932), "Corporal Punishment," 1932.

25 NAK SNP 7/9 5143/1908, Flogging. Abolition of. Minute by G. Malcolm, March 30, 1909.

26 NAK SNP 7/9 5143/1908, Flogging. Abolition of. Hewby to Secretary, Zungeru, October 10, 1908.

27 NAK, SNP 6/3 160/1907.

28 NAK SNP 17/2 17415, vol. 1, Resident Zaria to Secretary, Northern Provinces, December 22, 1932.

29 Lugard, "Memo. 3," in Lugard, *Political Memoranda*, para. 41.

30 See Temple, *Native Races and Their Rulers*. Temple was an early resident in Northern Nigeria and was lieutenant governor of the Northern Provinces during the 1910s.

31 "Flogging," minute by A. J. Hastings, Conf. A., 19 May 1920, PRO, CO 583/87 29835; emphasis in the original. The same passage is cited in Killingray, "Punishment to Fit the Crime?"

32 According to Foucault, subjectification is a process by which people become enmeshed in systems of incentives and of identification that make them amendable to manipulation by greater webs of power. Even the intuition that one is an individual is a way in which one can be manipulated.

33 Secretary, Northern Provinces, to Chief Secretary, Lagos, 12 August 1933, NAK SNP 17415.

34 The distinction was drawn quite polemically in 1920 by Governor Clifford, who contrasted floggings in the "non–Muhammadan Provinces," which he claimed were supervised by an "illiterate fetish-worshipper, belonging to an African people of by no means a high type" who could not therefore "wisely or safely be invested with such extensive powers." The result of doing this, Clifford claimed, was perfectly illustrated by a scene from eastern Nigeria. "I saw two prisoners with intractable ulcers on their buttocks, the unhealed effects of floggings administered by the Native court some three weeks previously." PRO CO 583/87 29835, Conf. A, Flogging. Clifford to CO, May 19, 1920.

35 NAK, SNP 17/2 17415.

36 In the very different setting of emancipation-era South Africa, Scully notes that it was held that flogging women made it particularly difficult for their husbands to be free men, since they were obliged to overcome their "natural" instincts to protect their women: Scully, *Liberating the Family?*

37   An exception to this, however, was reported by the acting resident of Nassarawa Province, who said he was told that the prostitutes surrounding mining camps "are more afraid of corporal punishment than of imprisonment." NAK 6224/1914, Women, Not to be Flogged by Order of Native courts, Sciortino to Secretary, Northern Provinces, March 10, 1915.

38   NAK 6224/1914, Arnett to Secretary, Northern Provinces, March 29, 1914.

39   NAK SNP 8/1 329/194, Women Flogged by Order of Native courts, Ruxton to Secretary Northern Provinces, February 24, 1915.

40   NAK 6224/1914, Secretary, Northern Provinces, to Residents, All Provinces, January 20, 1915.

41   Scarry, *The Body in Pain*.

42   One is reminded today of this strategy in right-wing commentators' responses to the scandals of Abu Ghraib. Rush Limbaugh, for example, insisted, "This is no different than what happens at the Skull and Bones initiation." The transcript is no longer available at www.rushlimbaugh.com but can be viewed at http://mediamatters.org/items/200405050003 (accessed 5 January 2005).

43   Michel Foucault, "Governmentality."

44   Scott, *Refashioning Futures*, 152–53, emphasis in the original.

45   Idem, "Colonial Governmentality."

46   See Joseph, *Democracy and Prebendal Politics in Nigeria*; Laitin, *Hegemony and Culture*.

47   See Benjamin, "Critique of Violence."

DOROTHY KO

※

Footbinding and Anti-footbinding in China

The Subject of Pain in the Nineteenth and Early Twentieth Centuries

Wiping off the sweat on his face one suffocating summer day in 1902, the reformer Jin Yi wrote in his stuffy study in a small town in southern China: "In my dreams I see a white-skinned European son. On a day like today, he would set off with a rolled cigarette in his mouth and a walking cane in his hand. With his wife leaning by his shoulders and an infant son trailing along, he strolls the wide boulevards of London, Paris, and Washington with his head held up high and his arms swinging briskly by his side. What happiness! How care-free!" Jin, who styled himself "Jin-Yi-the-Lover-of-Liberty," added wistfully, "I wish I could go there."[1] Everything about the white man, from his bodily posture and companionate marriage to the openness of the metropolitan cityscape in which he moved, announced his virility and superiority.

In contrast, Jin complained about his predicament in a "freedom-less continental kingdom in eastern Asia" where he "crouched in a tiny freedom-less room, breathing the air of listless thoughts."[2] His novel perspective of defining one's place from a location *outside* China signaled the end of the self-centered certainty of the Middle Kingdom and announced a new global perspective born of a colonial condition. But the nascent nation called "China" remained the elusive subject of his desires. Jin's malaise was emblematic of a political and intellectual crisis that rocked the foundation of the old imperium in the second half of the nineteenth century, culminating in its collapse in 1911. The ruling Manchu, or Qing, dynasty (1644–1911) suffered a series of humiliating military defeats at the hands of the British in the Opium War of 1840; of the French in 1860; and worst of all, of the Japanese in 1895. Interpolated into a new global consciousness, the educated elite became obsessed with the colonization of India and the partition of Poland. The male scholars in particular feared that they, too, would perish as "slaves of a lost state."[3]

Jin Yi's fantastic image of the white man's freedom is likely to have resulted from reading the Chinese "new fiction" that flourished around 1895–1910, a genre that embodies the multivocality and contradictions of the key transitional era. Jin's envy of the white man's virility in turn propelled him to political action in the form of journalistic writing, another new cultural field. The words that spilled from Jin Yi's writing brush were published in 1903 as a pamphlet, "The Women's Tocsin (Nüjie zhong)," which was hailed as the first systematic manifesto of women's liberation in China. Naming footbinding as the first of four cardinal harms being inflicted on the women of old China (the others being ornamentation, superstition, and cloistering), Jin warned: "If we want to avoid the perils of extinction, we must begin with liberating feet."[4]

Effeminized in the face of white superiority, male reformers thus came to recognize the liberation of their women as a necessary condition for their own freedom. In this entanglement between emergent male and female subjectivities lies the colonial logic of women's liberation in general, and the liberation of feet in particular. As a corollary of this logic, the humiliation that "China" suffered on the global stage was being imputed on the bodies of its "women," now being construed as a monolith unified by pain, enslavement, and victimization. In this way, footbinding figured as "national shame," and its eradication became a matter of national urgency in the anti-footbinding campaigns that raged from the 1890s to the 1900s.

ANTI-FOOTBINDING AS NATIONALISM

The beginning of anti-footbinding as an organized social movement was rooted in the colonial conditions that China faced in the second half of the nineteenth century: Although China escaped formal colonization, its cultural authority and discursive power were eroded by the penetration of Christian missionaries, foreign military advisers, and naval engineers into its interior provinces. Indeed, the very first anti-footbinding society was founded by a Reverend MacGowan in 1875 in the southern treaty port of Amoy (Xiamen). Chinese activists followed suit in neighboring Guangdong Province by forming local pacts of reformed-minded patriarchs who pledged that their sons would not marry tiny-footed brides. These scattered efforts gained momentum in 1895–98, when China's unexpected defeat at the hands of Japan precipitated a crisis. Campaigns against footbinding became an integral part of the nascent nationalist movement among the educated male elite, as evinced by Jin Yi's manifesto.

As a result, anti-footbinding societies proliferated in the coastal areas in the 1900s, often under state or official sponsorship. So identified was footbinding with the shame of the old order that among the first legislative measures of the new republic established in 1912 was to outlaw the practice. Under international and national assault, footbinding began to disappear in the coastal regions in the first two decades of the twentieth century, but in the interior regions it remained popular into the 1930s and even the 1950s.[5] The figure of the woman with bound feet was thus a synecdoche of the new nation but only in negation: She was everything that new China was not. Embodying this logic of bifurcation, she marked the indelible boundaries between tradition and modernity, the liberated man and enslaved woman, as well as China and the other nations.

Writing of the British colonial government's attempt to outlaw female circumcision in Kenya in 1926, Susan Pedersen observed that "the ritual unmaking and reworking of women's bodies became . . . central to the construction of national identity."[6] In China as in Kenya, the female body became the interlocutor between the colonizer and the colonized, but the terms of this interlocution could not have been more different. Whereas Jomo Kenyatta and his proto-nationalist colleagues in the Kikuyu Central Association defended clitoridectomy as the linchpin of age-old communal and social orders, Chinese nationalists agitated to dispose of the old regime of corporeal subjugation altogether. That no nationalist—or any intellectual, for that matter—would dream of defending footbinding was in large part due to the colonial conditions of shame that accompanied footbinding's global visibility.

That the anti-footbinding movement achieved only limited success in eradicating the practice was also due largely to its rhetorical strategy. Using the tactics of exposé that prevailed in a national and transnational culture of shame and shaming, the polemic of the anti-footbinding reformers made a previously tabooed body part textually and visually available to a global reformist public. This exposure, however, was humiliating to the very women the movement purportedly was trying to liberate or save. This contradictory logic engendered a bifurcated womanhood. The handful of educated women who organized anti-footbinding efforts and those girls who made speeches in school assemblies became political actors in public arenas. Their political agency, however, was gained at the expense of the silenced majority who did not attend schools and whose speech was out of sync with the modern language of national liberation. It was the latter, as it turned out, who adopted a stance similar to Kenyatta's plea of "leave us alone."

The contradictory logic of negation and bifurcation that undergirded the formation of modern national and gendered subjects in China at the end of the nineteenth century and beginning of the twentieth century is most evident in the discourse of pain popularized by the anti-footbinding campaigns. Focusing on the rhetoric of anti-footbinding, and especially its narration of women's pain, this chapter examines the terms in which the anti-footbinding discourse produced the female body as a political entity as well as its implications for the fractured formation of women's subjectivity and national sovereignty in the nineteenth century and early twentieth century.

HEAVENLY FEET: THE MISOGYNIST RHETORIC
OF ANTI-FOOTBINDING

Male scholars in China have frequently denounced the violence of footbinding since its inception as a social practice in the eleventh century. But these efforts, aided by imperial prohibition edicts in the seventeenth and eighteenth centuries, failed to diminish the cultural aura of the practice, which derived from the Confucian value of *wen* (culture, civility, clothed bodies). Only in the nineteenth century, when it was exposed to the far more potent forces of colonial reason and the missionary's scrutiny, did footbinding begin to appear vulgar, dated, and barbaric. Only then did anti-footbinding as an organized political and social movement become thinkable.

Anti-footbinding—the absence of footbinding, to be exact—also acquired the new name of "heavenly feet" (*tianzu*, later also rendered natural feet; *tianzu* is a linguistic category that did not exist in classical Chinese). The English term was coined by Reverend MacGowan in 1875 when he established the Heavenly Foot Society in Amoy. MacGowan, of the London Missionary Society, first arrived in Amoy on the heels of the Second Opium War, which opened up five treaty ports to foreign commerce and the interior to missionary penetration in 1860. As he cast his eyes ashore from the steamer, he saw the China that he was predisposed to see: "It is sadly wanting in cheerful colours, and what seems most needed are a few paint brushes to give it a more modern look, and a very large number of stiff brooms to sweep away the dust and grime which have slowly fallen upon them during the past centuries and dyed everything grey."[7]

Anti-footbinding turned out to be at once the broom that swept away millennial dust and the paintbrush with which modern (read, Christian) female and national subjectivities were to be inscribed. In 1875, MacGowan called a meeting of all the women who attended Christian churches in Amoy. Amid warnings of a riot in the city—so threatening was the idea of a female assembly—sixty to seventy showed up, all uneducated women of the working class, according to MacGowan. Later, in writing, he denounced the practice by appealing to a concept of the body absent in Chinese thinking: "It had completely destroyed the grace and symmetry with which Nature had endowed the women. We are apt to forget that within the feet lies the secret of the exquisite poise and beautiful carriage that embody within them the very poetry of motion, and that add so much to the charm that women by a divine right seem naturally to possess."[8] The doctrine of anti-footbinding is thus predicated on the alien construct of a God-given natural body that realizes its beauty in motion. It is not surprising that this figure resembles that of the "white-skinned European son" in journalist Jin Yi's imagination.

In 1878, a participant at one of the biannual meetings of the Heavenly Foot Society transcribed a long essay by a Reverend Ye titled, "Discourse on Quitting Footbinding (Jie chanzu lun)." Eschewing the imported lingo of "heavenly foot," the Chinese pastor preferred a more indigenous term—"quitting footbinding"—borrowed from the quitting opium-smoking campaigns. He also displayed a malaise about being scrutinized by the world that was absent in MacGowan: "Looking around the world today, no women other than those in China bind their feet. This shows that when God made men, there was no divergence in the shape of male and female feet," implying China was uniquely barbaric in world time and geography.[9]

MacGowan was sympathetic to mothers, whereas Reverend Ye viewed them as the culprit: "The [Christian] principle of loving others begins with loving one's own children. How can you inflict pain onto your daughter's feet at age five or six, binding them as tightly as a branding iron, blocking the vital energy (*qi*) from circulating like putting a cangue on the ankle? . . . I see that during binding, the daughter often cries in pain, but the mother would strike her and make the pain even more unbearable." Reverend Ye had even less sympathy for the daughter, a "seductress (*yaoji*)" who "beautifie[d] her looks to promote licentiousness." She sinned in "drawing others' gaze to her." Mother and daughter were thus locked in the perpetuation of an atrocity that was synonymous with the female condition. There is no mention of men's responsibility or complicity.[10]

The construction of a unified womanhood bound in suffering and shame became more pronounced when Chinese reformers took up the cause of anti-footbinding as the cornerstone of their nationalist agenda. In a seminal essay written in 1896–97, "On Women's Education," the leading intellectual and journalist Liang Qichao (1873–1929) denigrated the female half of the population as "those with round heads but pointy feet." Referring to a saying by Mencius that "those who dwell in leisure without an education are close to beasts," Liang stated that, since women "from the ancient times to the present day" have been unschooled, they have fared no better than beasts. Although the majority of men were also uneducated, he conceded, these men were at least ashamed of themselves, but the women were so ignorant that they did not even feel the shame. This was the root of China's weakness. "All two hundred million of our women are consumers (*fenli*; partakers of profit); not a single one has produced anything of profit. . . . No wonder men keep them as dogs, horses and slaves."[11]

The misogynist tone of the Christian and nationalist rhetoric is striking: Before they could be liberated and saved, the majority of Chinese women had to be denigrated as temptresses and slaves, a subhumanity that was wasted and wasteful—in sum, a burden and a threat for the paterfamilias. How ironic that debasement and a priori denial of full humanity served as the necessary condition of women's eventual freedom. This misogyny was rooted in the male elite's own feelings of inadequacy. The destruction wrought by imperialist gunboats was so traumatic that educated men experienced it as their imminent personal effeminization; the crisis of the nation took the intimate form of a crisis in masculinity that undermined their collective, corporeal, and sexualized selves. Perhaps it is no accident that they dwelled on the destructive powers of pain in denouncing footbinding.

It is important to remember that reform-minded men like Jin Yi and Liang Qichao also harbored an unspoken longing, a desire to stroll on the wide boulevards of Europe with liberated, companionate wives in tow. In spite of, and because of, its misogyny, anti-footbinding was the foundation of imaginations of a new womanhood. Discourses of anti-footbinding constructed new subjectivities on several grounds. In figuring the female body as the subject of political intervention, these discourses wrote the body as a political entity into being; they gave concrete form to the abstraction of womanhood by envisioning bonds of pain between mother and daughter; they delineated the difference between

China and the West on the basis of a "cultural contrivance." Furthermore, as will be mentioned later, when the anti-footbinding movement grew in the 1920s–30s, female agents were recruited to lend voices of authenticity—public speaker, organizer, and author—enabling new public agencies and subjectivities.

The contradictions between the destructive and constructive aspects of anti-footbinding are most evident in the discourses of pain produced by the new political agents—educated women writers—themselves.

BIFURCATED WOMANHOOD: THE PROBLEM OF "AUTHENTIC VOICE"

Inherent in the denouncement of the pain of binding feet is the conditions of bifurcated womanhood—the writing subject on the one side and the suffering subject on the other. To a certain extent, this bifurcation is rooted in the very dynamics of sympathetic identification. When the body in pain belongs to a weaker, illiterate woman, there is great temptation for the educated reformer not only to feel her pain but also to speak up on her behalf. When the sufferer occupies an inferior position to that of the reader on the social, ethnic, or gender hierarchy, the latter's sympathy often serves to reinforce such hierarchies.

This dynamic of bifurcation is shown in the recollections of the female educator Zhang Mojun (1884–1965): "In my childhood, I used to sleep in the same bed with my older sister. One night I was awakened by the sound of chirping sobs; I saw her sitting up with the quilt over her shoulders, holding her feet in her hands and weeping, her face streaked with tears. She looked miserable. I asked her what was wrong. She replied in a low voice, 'My feet have been bound by Nanny Ho. Although during the day it makes walking difficult, I can still bear the pain. But at night, my feet get hot under the quilt, and I can't sleep with the cutting pain. What am I to do?'" Incensed, Zhang leaped to tear off her sister's binders, but her sister resisted, fearing that this would provoke their mother. At daybreak, Zhang beseeched their mother to let her sister off the hook. She also made her own wish clear: "I would rather no man showed any interest in me all my life than trying to curry favor injuring the body my parents gave me." Zhang later joined the Revolutionary Alliance (Tongmeng Hui) and took part in the 1911 revolution.[12]

As Zhang chose to remember it, her sister's pain and helplessness awakened her to the lingering power of traditional customs and were instrumental to her resolution to become a revolutionary. Male and female activists recounted many similar stories in the revolutionary era of the early twentieth century. Like Zhang's, these memories' power and limitations are embedded in their teleological structure. The vividness with which Zhang recalled her sister's pain fifty years after the fact was impressive indeed: the chirping sobs, the cradling to alleviate the burning sensation, her descriptions of pain as "cutting." Although the experience was her sister's, Zhang's words enjoy an empirical if not moral authority that derives from her authentic knowledge: I was there in bed with my sister; I know. The vividness of Zhang's memory attests to the rhetorical power of pain but also calls its reliability into question. Did she remember correctly? Are the words "cutting pain" hers or her sister's?

Often overjoyed to discover a lively female voice, historians and feminist scholars are all too ready to grant that voice unquestioned authority. Testimonials, firsthand accounts, and autobiographies, especially those of the often silent "Third World woman" or "traditional woman," acquire an aura of authority, promising truthful revelations of the women's inner feelings and motives. In the case of Zhang Mojun and her sister, this celebration leads one to overlook that there is a gap between voice and experience: The revolutionary who told of the suffering did not have bound feet herself; the sister who experienced the pain was the one being spoken for. There should in fact be two distinct female voices telling the story of footbinding and the modern nation, but the sister's name and voice were erased because they were being contained—indeed, colonized—by Mojun, the more educated and "liberated" of the two.

My interest in complicating the transparency of "voice" stems from my dissatisfaction with the exclamation often heard in human-rights discourse: "Pain is pain is pain." Neither Zhang Mojun's voice nor her sister's experience is a "natural" occurrence. It was produced by language in specific cultural and historical contexts—in this case, China's search for modernity in a global colonial context in the nineteenth century.[13] The appearance of a new category of female public figures, from the celebrated poet martyr Qiu Jin to Zhang Mojun, is an important milestone in this process. But the emergence of the modern female subject came with a corollary—or, to be exact, a price: The submergence of the majority of women whose inability to write and read rendered them not only speechless but also worthless. Their inferior status of being the "recently dated" was etched on their very bodies; their voices were rendered inaudible at the same time they were being mobilized as political agents and economic citizens. Their emergence as political entities is thus doomed from the start.

The Chinese Woman Writer: She seizes our attention because writing commended supreme cultural prestige in the bygone world of the Confucian literati just as it did among such modern men of letters as Jin Yi and Liang Qichao. Contemporary scholars have been quick to celebrate the entrance of women into this male vocation whenever it happened—be it in the late Ming or late Qing period—and analyze the difficulties involved in the formation of the female writing subject.[14] As illuminating as this analysis has been, this fixation has led to a negligence of other forms of corporeal expression: embroidery and shoemaking for example. The relationship between women's handiwork, market value, and self-worth underwent momentous changes during China's march to modernity, but its impact on female subjectivity remains dimly understood. This enormous undertaking lies outside the scope of this chapter; suffice it to say that reading the anti-footbinding rhetoric has made me painfully aware of the limitations of the "female writer's voice" that spoke of suffering in a monotone that echoed the male reformist voice.

Whatever happened to Zhang's sister? What bodily traces did she leave? What complicated calculations transpired in the mind of their "old-fashioned" mother? The disappearance of these women from the nationalist script suggests that the subject of pain and the writing subject could not inhabit the same time zone; only one could be modern. So powerful is the grip of the modernist anti-footbinding polemic over the imagination of the contemporary scholar and reader in China as in the Anglophone world that many have come to mimic its conceptualization of the female condition in bifurcated terms: the once liberated writing agent on one hand and the twice-victimized woman with bound feet on the other.

VISIBILITY AND THE PUBLIC

The persuasive power of Zhang's authority as female narrator is absent in accounts of footbinding before the nineteenth century. Although we do not have the space in this chapter to substantiate this statement, the predominant *theme* of the premodern Chinese literary discourse on footbinding is suffering, but its rhetorical *effect* is diffuse and remote. The immediacy of female pain, manifested in its power to incite the reader or viewer to action, constitutes a radical mode of social critique that is a modern phenomenon. The prehistory of narratives like Zhang's has to be sought in a host of technological and sociocultural forces that changed the image and meaning of pain in the nineteenth century. These changes culminated in a rupture in the late-nineteenth-century anti-footbinding discourse, enabling a synergy between visual and literary disclosures that created a spectacle of female pain unmatched in its shocking realism.

A constellation of technological and cultural forces in the nineteenth century created a new environment for the experience and expression of bodily pain. First and foremost is the advent of visuality and its powerful hold on the imagination of modern viewers, a change brought about by the invention of photography and the x-ray. As early as the 1850s, the first commercial photographic operation appeared in Shanghai. By the 1870s, a handful of professional studios were in business in the city.[15] The enduring popularity of photography, coupled with the medical and artistic use of x-ray radiographs in the early decades of the twentieth century, publicized images of women and female body parts with growing explicitness. Traditional paintings depicted the erotics of footbinding for male pleasure, a stark contrast to the fixation on female suffering in premodern prose. These two mediums of narration were conjoined and their messages synchronized for the first time in the late Qing, imparting immediacy to the representation of pain in another body.

Also relevant is the reconfiguration of the inner and outer realms, and the place of woman in them, in the late Qing urban landscape. The shifting boundary between the inner and outer realms was in large part expressed—or felt—visually, a function of what people could see, what they saw, and how they saw it. Nowhere were the connections between a modern life and changing ways of seeing more evident than in Shanghai. In 1873, city lights were installed in the Chinese neighborhood of Southern Market. Public space was associated with illumination and brightness, the ability to see and to be seen. In the year before, night-soil porters were ordered to put lids on their buckets as they worked the streets.[16] The private, like the unsavory emissions from the inner body, had to be concealed.

The previously hidden female body came into increasing public view in the last decades of the nineteenth century not only in photographic images, but also in theaters and gardens. A handful of highly educated women capitalized on their status as the subject of public gaze to become political figures and speakers. In the years 1901–05, educated women such as Chen Xiefan and Xue Qinjin gave speeches in anti-imperialist rallies in Zhang Garden, the garden of merchant and newspaper promoter Zhang Shuhe (1850–1919), in Shanghai. The presence of a female body standing on a public podium—and acting as a speaking subject, no less—subverted the traditional ideals of a hidden domestic woman, known as "the inner person." The importance of this subversion can hardly be exaggerated. Women's speech-making changed the voice of the female writer and facilitated the emergence of the female reader and audience as political subjects, as Amy Dooling and Kristina Torgeson have argued.[17]

The changing urban visual culture and its heightened visibility of women afforded the anti-footbinding activists new tools and venues of social critique. By the time the movement spread to provincial cities throughout the country in the first two decades of the twentieth century, reformers made good use of photographic images and women's speech-making to expose the ills of the antiquated practice. As early as 1905, the Natural Foot Society in Suzhou enlisted an unnamed woman to lecture on ways to minimize pain in letting feet out.[18] Later, the active recruitment of female middle school students to denounce the practice in school auditoriums and to work as "feet inspectors" in rural areas was by and large a positive "coming out" experience for the female students. But these attacks on footbinding contributed to an environment in which the female body—bound or unbound—became part of a national spectacle, a condition that has ambivalent implications for the production of new female subjectivities.

THE PENETRATIVE MODE: A NEW SPECTACLE OF FEMALE PAIN

The new technique of making a spectacle out of private female suffering first appeared as a literary device. This new technique of spectatorship—what I call a "penetrative mode"—was heralded in a popular novel, *Flowers in the Mirror* (*Jinghua yuan*), by a maverick philologist, Li Ruzhen (circa 1763–1830). First published in 1821 and reissued in updated editions in 1828 and 1832, this long and complex novel became legendary for one small episode as the pivotal text in the literary disclosure of women's pain. The famous episode in chapter 33 in which the cosmetics merchant Lin Zhiyang is captured in the Country of Women and forced to undergo the binding ordeal became the most often cited depiction of footbinding as torture not only in the anti-footbinding polemic but also in scholarly literature today. Before analyzing the rhetorical power and narrative strategy of chapter 33, I will highlight its radical inventiveness by surveying a more conventional passage in chapter 12 of the same novel.

In this earlier episode, Lin and his traveling companions Tang Ao and Duo Jiugong are visiting the Country of Gentlemen, a Confucian utopia. Tang and Duo are engaged in an amicable conversation with gentleman Wu Zhihe when Wu broaches the subject: "I heard that in your country girls have their feet bound. In the beginning of binding, your daughters, suffering a hundred kinds of pain (*tongku*), cradle their feet and wail. Then their skin would slough off and the flesh becomes rotten, their feet dripping in blood. During binding, they can't sleep at night and can't swallow a bite. Many become stricken by diseases as a result. At first I thought that these daughters are unfilial, and their mothers, not having the heart of killing them, use this method to punish them. Little did I know that it is all for beauty!"[19]

These words from the mouth of the idealized Confucian gentleman were couched in such a way as to shame Li's contemporary readers in the dystopia of Qing China. As such the spectacle of pain, part of a broader sociopolitical critique, was useful to Li's activist agenda of reforming current customs. It is important to note that although Wu's description of the girls' pain is vivid, he is twice removed from the scene of binding and the body in pain. In this episode, the writer or speaker does not attempt to annihilate the distance between himself and the sufferer. Pain in another body is conveyed by a superficial description of open wounds. Similar to the revolutionary Zhang's memoir, the body in pain is known through observable action (rubbing feet, sleeplessness) and voice (sobs or wailing).

This mode of expressing pain may be termed the "literati" mode, recalling as it does elements of the literati discourse of footbinding. The Song scholar Che Ruoshui (fl. 1274), for example, heralded the criticism of footbinding as undeserved corporeal punishment: "A little girl not yet four or five is innocent and guiltless, but infinite suffering was being inflicted upon her."[20] Yuan Mei (1716–98), another famous critic who was also an anti-Buddhist, likened the "flaying of a daughter's limbs" to cremating one's parent's remains. The literati mode, a secondhand narration characterized by a constant maintenance of distance between narrator and sufferer, simply *asserts* that footbinding is torture.

The episode about the merchant Lin's humiliation in the hands of the Amazonian queen employs a different strategy: It not only asserts but also illustrates just how torturous footbinding was. This third-person description of Lin's binding process is matter of fact, if not clinical, in tone, and the vocabulary of pain is unremarkable. But the reader is taken to a new proximity to the body in pain, if not inside the sufferer's psyche:

> The dark-bearded palace lady sits on a stool and splits the length of white silk into two long halves. First she places Lin Zhiyang's right foot on her knee, sprinkles alum powder in between the toes, squeezes the five digits tightly against one another, and then she bends the foot with such force that it arches into the shape of a full bow. Immediately she swaddles the foot with the silk cloth. As soon as she wraps the binder twice, another palace lady steps up with needle and thread to seal it tightly. One swaddles ferociously, the other stitches without slack. Lin Zhiyang is bound by four palace ladies on his sides; another two hold his foot so tight that he can't even move a fragment of an inch. When binding is done, he only feels waves of throbbing pain (*tengtong*) on his feet, like being scorched by burning charcoal. Unwittingly his heart sinks and he bursts into tears, crying: "You're killing me (*kengshi an le*)!"[21]

Couched in the third person, this narrative begins with a detached survey of Lin Zhiyang's condition as the immobilized victim, then gradually leads the reader closer to the point of feeling his bodily sensation. We hear his scream in the first person, a figure of speech absent in premodern discourses. This narrative strategy of moving from the outside in culminates in a brush with Lin's mind: "Having cried for a long time, Lin Zhiyang thinks long and hard but can't come up with a way out. All he can do is to beg the ladies: 'Please, please my dear elder brothers, can you intercede on my behalf in front of your king? I already have a wife, how can I be his concubine?'"[22] The reader's sympathy for Lin, so exposed in his vulnerability and gender confusion, enhances the comical effect of the scene.

This mode of penetrating narration, aiming at the interior psyche of the subject in pain, cuts a contrast with the old literati mode. The vantage point of the narrator in the former mode is moving like a laser beam that closes in on the sufferer, whereas the distance is maintained between narrator and sufferer in the penetrating mode. It is this presence of immediacy, not the gender inversion in itself or the implicit equation of footbinding with corporeal punishment (*darou*, flesh beating), that distinguishes this episode of Lin Zhiyang's ordeal as a modern text.

This new mode of narrating pain was used most effectively in conjunction with another device: The exaggeration of the asymmetry between male (a subject position assumed by the palace women) and female (Lin) power in the production of pain. Lin suffered at least three physical ordeals, being first pierced and bound and then caned for insubordination. The middle-aged palace ladies who pierced his ears were all "tall in stature and strong in body; their mouths were covered with beards," august embodiments of *yang* forces. Lin was overpowered by four women, and his feet were held by another two: Even before his feet were crippled, he was immobilized. Lin's physical suffering is thus used to dramatize the myth of male dominance.

This exposure of the structural inequality between the male and female subject positions renders *Flowers in the Mirror* an extremely effective and influential political polemic. Liberal critics in China and elsewhere have lauded it as China's first feminist novel for its radical attack on footbinding and support for women's education.[23] Surely, Lin Zhiyang's footbinding scene made a dramatic propaganda script for the anti-footbinding campaign, and as such it was reenacted on stages far and near. It exposes male privilege as much as female pain and in so doing rouses readers to excitement and action. We should note, however, the profound one-sidedness in the manner and terms in which this disclosure was conducted: Lin Zhiyang's experiencing pain and screaming as a woman. As carnivalesque as this gender inversion may be, it reinscribes the identification of woman with body and the privilege of man as the speaking subject. This ventriloquism bespeaks the difficulty of narrating pain as the experience of a female *speaking* subject.

Both the literati narrative mode in chapter 12 and the penetration mode in chapter 33 attest to the contradictions involved in the formation of the female subject in and of pain. This is because the spectatorship of pain is inherently paradoxical: The effectiveness of social critique hinges on making an exposé of female pain, which accentuates the association of femaleness with passivity and victimhood. The more publicized the violence against the female, the more immobilized she becomes and less likely is she to act—not unlike Lin Zhiyang being held down by the dark-bearded palace ladies. The narrator, either with his panoptic eyes in the literati mode or with his shooting laser-beam eyes, is superior to the sufferer. He sees, he knows, and he writes.

Narratives of women's pain thus confer power on those who publicize them, be they male reformers or urban educated women. Their ability to speak, write, or act is all the more impressive when exercised on behalf of others. Denunciations of footbinding thus simultaneously bring two subject positions into being: the agentic reformer and his victimized, always feminized, other. From this perspective, the rhetorical power and political limitations of the polemics against footbinding in *Flowers in the Mirror* were wrought of the same contradictory logic that was to plague the anti-footbinding campaigns organized half a century after the novel's publication.

A NEW WAY TO SEE THROUGH BONES

The penetrating narrative mode heralded by *Flowers in the Mirror* is a visualizing technique that anticipates the photographic lens. The step-by-step reduction of distance between the narrator and the female subject was literally reenacted by John Thomson, photographer of things Chinese who sojourned in China for almost five years. His famous book *Illustrations of China and Its People*, first published in 1874, included a photograph showing the right foot of a tiny-footed woman displayed next to a left male foot.

Thomson described his own doggedness in getting at the truth of this inscrutable female ordeal: "This picture, NO. 39, shows us the compressed foot of a Chinese lady; and I regard it as one of the most interesting in my collection. Who the lady is, or where she came from, I cannot say. I had been assured by Chinamen that it would be impossible for me, by the offer of any sum of money, to get a Chinese woman to unbandage her foot, and yet gold and silver are arguments in favour of concessions which operate in the Celestial Empire with more than usual force. Accordingly, all my efforts failed until I reached Amoy, and there, with the aid of a liberal-minded Chinaman, I at last got this lady privately conveyed to me, in order that her foot might be photographed. She came escorted by an old woman, whom also I had to bribe handsomely before she would agree to countenance an act of such gross indecency as the unbandaging the foot of her charge."[24]

Once ridded of its ornate façade, the literary splendor of footbinding was also destroyed: "And yet, had I been able, I would rather have avoided the spectacle, for the compressed foot, which is figuratively supposed to represent a lily, has a very different appearance and odour from the most beautiful and sacred of flowers." The photographic lens—indeed, the photographer himself—stripped off the cloth binders and gave the viewer a picture of the body beneath the skin. This exposure of interiority is a poignant mode of social critique, offering in one image the full rhetorical force of Lin Zhiyang's footbinding episode.

The photographic lens, in this sense, represents a new imaging technique that operates on the same distance-reduction principle of the literary mode of penetration. The coexistence of these two media, using a similar "realistic" mode of narration, in the last decades of the nineteenth century made women's pain "real" to myriad readers. The concurrence of the organized anti-binding campaign, which gained national prominence in the 1880s and 1890s as part of the reformers Kang Youwei's and Liang Qichao's modernizing efforts, provided institutional channels of dissemination for this new reality.

Thomson's photograph of the bare skin was a sensational revelation in the 1870s; in another three decades, even the opacity of skin and flesh was melted away by the ultimate machine of penetration: x-ray. A critical moment in the anti-footbinding movement—and, indeed, in China's transition to a modern way of knowing—occurred in the early years of the 1900s. In a flurry of publicity sponsored by the Manchu state after the Boxer fiasco, edicts prohibiting footbinding were posted in and out of the walled capital of Beijing. Government notices were also posted on street corners in towns from Beijing to Zhangjiakou.[25] Spurred by encouragement from the Manchu court and, occasionally, from provincial authorities, Chinese-initiated anti-footbinding societies proliferated on the local level at the end of the nineteenth century and beginning of the twentieth century.[26] Official support gave the anti-footbinding efforts an unprecedented visibility. The spectatorship of feet became dispersed geographically and socially, as it moved out of covered venues of schools, assembly halls, or churches to the open air. By 1904, the Natural Foot Society (Tianzu hui) reported that it had distributed over 100,000 tracts in Shanghai and two interior cities, Chengtu and Xian. Propaganda materials were also distributed along the well-traveled railway lines from Tianjin to Shanhaiguan.

One picture popularized by the Natural Foot Society, titled "A New Way to See through Bones" (*tougu xinfa*; also "a new way to penetrate the bones"), became the iconic representation of women's corporeal pain. I know nothing about the history of the production of this picture. I can only surmise that it resembled a black-and-white drawing showing the deformed bones inside the skin. Titled "The Results of Footbinding: An x-Ray Photograph of a Chinese Woman's Foot," the photograph was published in the *Illustrated London News* on 15 February 1908. The caption explained that it was "a sketch made from a photo by the Rev. W. A. Cornaby." The upper-left-hand corner of the image was dominated by a Chinese slogan denouncing the binding of feet as unnatural—hence, un-Christian: "The contrivance of man-made culture mutilates the natural harmony of heaven." This frequently reproduced image represents the culmination of the penetrating mode of literary narration. In offering a new vista into the monochrome interior of self, the imaging technique of x-ray transformed the viewer's understanding of self and body.

The x-ray beam was discovered by Wilhelm Roentgen (1845–1923), a German physicist at the University of Würzburg, in 1895. It is remarkable that in barely one decade this way of seeing—and, perhaps, x-ray machines themselves—found its way to China.[27] Indeed, the dissemination of the technology was swift within Europe and globally, aided in no small way by the portability and low cost of the equipment as well as ignorance about the lethal side effects of radioactivity. But even more important to its instant popularity is the sensational public response to the novel sight of the interior of one's own body.

It is not an exaggeration to say that x-ray radiographs transformed visual culture in Europe and America. The science writer Bettyann Holtzmann Kevles has argued that the late nineteenth century witnessed a contest of two senses: visual against audio. With the invention of the phonograph by Thomas Edison in 1877, many observers expected hearing to be the sense of the future. But "the discovery of x-rays marked the beginning of a new epoch in science and medicine.... They shifted the scales of the sense, making visual images, which they helped redefine, the dominating venue for exchanging information in the new century."[28] x-rays redefined the aesthetics of "looking at" as "looking through" and in so doing led people to question the judgment of the naked eye and the ability of photography to record the whole truth.

In Europe, the new episteme of x-ray was connected to knowledge and perception of sexuality from the start. Not only did it transform the boundary between public and private, relaxing the boundary of privacy as a result; it also facilitated a craze for the hidden and the subconscious that Freud so famously explored. The gender implications of new images of the female body are mixed: "The rays simultaneously de-eroticized the body—breast bones without breasts are essentially asexual—while they accentuated the differences in the pelvic girdle and exposed uterus and ovaries."[29]

In short, the social and cultural history of x-ray in Europe and America suggests that a simple radiograph could revolutionize the viewer's understanding of self, sexuality, privacy, and veracity. The impact of x-rays on visual cultures in modern China requires further research. It is clear, however, that without considering the impact of medical imaging we cannot have a full understanding of interiority and its relations to modernity in China. In analyzing novels and short stories, literary critics have often considered depiction of the protagonist's interiority, or psychological state, a modern and positive development. Our survey of the literary and visual representations of pain, however, has suggested that the penetrating gaze into the interior female body has far less salutary implications.

In the case of the anti-footbinding campaign, the reformers' zeal in eradicating a national shame created, ironically, a sensationalist spectatorship that exposed female anatomy. The narrative modes and machines of penetration not only stripped the coverings off the female body but also turned it inside out. The male reformers were propelled by a sense of embarrassment and shame in front of the advanced nations; the suffering of Chinese women made them lose face. Ironically, in championing the end of footbinding they exposed the women to the same humiliation. The fixation on national shame in the nationalist discourse blinded them to the private shame experienced by the women with bound feet.

This culture of shame and shaming was part and parcel of the colonial conditions of global unevenness in political and discursive powers that restructured desires on the transnational, national, and personal levels. As Jin Yi's white-man envy shows, the male reformer was imperiled by China's military defeats and the futility of his own thoughts and action—the conjoining of national and personal emasculation. When a male reformer agitated over the traditional bondage of women, he was seeking to rescue himself from his own imminent enslavement. The liberation of Chinese men, in fact, *required* the liberation of their women. Yet in the process of liberating feet, the male reformers (and such educated females as Zhang Mojun, who assumed a male subject position) resorted to tactics of shaming and exposé that conferred power on themselves but made it even more difficult, if not impossible, to recognize the *other* woman as a political and moral agent.

MADAME AXIU'S PAINFUL HISTORY

This self-contradictory logic of the tactics of exposé and shame explains both the rhetorical appeal and political limitations of women's testimonies. I thus conclude this chapter by reiterating my reluctance to romanticize a form of agency based on revelations of an essentialized core of "interiority." A typical women's testimony that appeared in the 1930s was titled "Painful History of Bending Lotus (*Aolian tongshi*)." The author, one Madame Axiu, began her story by highlighting the power inequalities between men, who controlled the word, and women, bound by the bodily experience of pain. Following a line of critique heralded by *Flowers in the Mirror* but irrelevant in the 1930s, thirty years after the Civil Service Examination was abolished, Madame Axiu registered her complaints with the literati, who so loved the bound foot that "they took to embellish it with flowery words."[30]

She continued: "But for us, generations of women whose bodies are being subjected to this [*shenshou*, the same words for the passive voice], it is no different from a criminal being subjected to the cangue, or worse. As the proverb says of the cruelty of this act, 'a pair of small feet, a tub full of tears.' As someone who had a personal experience of this, I'm willing to express in words [lit., to give shape to] the pain of broken tendons and crushed bones I went through then, so as to awaken all lotus-loving gentlemen of the world."

Madame Axiu's "Painful History" was written in the first person and anthologized under her name; other women's testimonies were often presented as transcriptions by a male scribe. The importance of Madame Axiu's testimony was the novelty of the category of "footbound woman author," who presumably knew best about the bodily sensations of pain. As voices of interiority, women's testimonies switched the narrative point of view away from the literati "flowery words" that used to constitute footbinding's aura. The realism of the female voice of suffering served as an antidote to the male voice of privilege. But as the inside of the body lost its mystique to the x-ray, these voices from the inside also seemed to lose their authority and appeal.

It is hardly surprising that the female voice tells us nothing new about pain. Madame Axiu's vocabulary is uneventful, consisting as it does of an overuse of the word pain (*tong* or *teng*) as a noun and an adjective. Once she used a tired simile—"as painful as being sliced by a knife"—but in the end resorted to the incommensurability of pain. "In the humidity and dampness after rain, no words can give shape to the pain felt by a footbound person." Other women's voices that circulated in the 1930s, often billed as "self narrations (*zishu*)" but transmitted by scribes, can be more colloquial and expressive, but they fare no better in linguistic inventiveness. The same is true of ethnographic interviews. After the shock of Lin Zhiyang's ordeal and x-ray radiographs, any narrative of pain is anticlimatic. By 1940, the Chinese heartland was occupied by Japan; a civil war was brewing between the nationalists and the communists; and the anti-footbinding movement was forgotten in the face of more urgent threats to the nation.

CODA: ANTI-FOOTBINDING IN COMPARATIVE CONTEXTS

Elaine Scarry has suggested that pain generates new meanings in a process called "bodily translation," which has two faces: as war and as ritual sacrifice in peaceful times. By way of this cultural mechanism, an open wound on an individual body lends value and concreteness to an abstract entity that is otherwise difficult to imagine. Scarry also called this a process of "substantiation" or "fiction generation," involving as it does the "translation of the material fact of the body into a disembodied cultural fiction."[31] I would argue that the cultural fiction being written in discourses of female pain in the nineteenth century was none other than the nascent Chinese nation.

This focus on the productiveness of pain may shed light on the comparability between footbinding and other practices of bodily mutilation. In her 1974 book *Gyn/Ecology*, Mary Daly used the conflation of "Chinese footbinding" with "African female genital mutilation" and "Indian satee," alongside Nazi experiments and plastic surgery, to transubstantiate the myth of a universal ("planetary") patriarchy. Daly's Eurocentrism, lack of historical specificity, and insensitivity to cultural differences has been thoroughly critiqued, but the rhetorical power of her poetics and analysis remains strangely fresh and relevant, as is her anger and bitterness over her marginalization. Daly's premise—that there is a common power dynamic behind atrocities committed on the bodies of women at disparate times and in various spaces—cannot be dismissed outright. Wherein lie the conditions of this commonality, and how was it engendered?

Part of the answer, at least as far as footbinding, female genital cutting, and sati are concerned, lies in the global colonial conditions—not colonial governance per se—in which "China," "Africa," and "India" found themselves during the time these atrocities entered into EuroAmerican (and indigenous) discourses. In this chapter, I have emphasized four aspects of the "colonial condition" that rendered "the woman with bound feet" such a contradictory and necessary figure to the emergent metropolitan reformist public: global unevenness in political and discursive powers; the conjoining of "national" and personal emasculation; the entanglement of male and female liberations; and the fracturing of the female subject.

Focusing on the career of bodily violence in colonial governance, other essays in this volume have shown how the bodies of the flogged sailor or the tortured prisoner were caught in between the simultaneity of the disciplinary impulse of colonial corporeal techniques and the liberationist impulse of humanitarian efforts to save them. The predicament of the body of the footbound woman—and perhaps that of the *excisée* and sati, as well—was radically different. As a remnant of "tradition," she was caught in between temporalities, entering into modernity already as a failure and an embarrassment. The very conditions of her coming into recognition and public visibility are none other than those of her enslavement. In this chapter, I have emphasized how these contradictions produced a cultural fiction of the "modern nation" and new female subjectivities, both resting on an idealization of the white man and his sovereignty.

These conditions produced a power dynamic that perpetuated the practices of bodily violence in modern times—witness rising incidences of sati after the British prohibited it; the determination of Chinese immigrant mothers to bind their daughters' feet in the Kingdom of Hawaii; and the Ngaitana ("I circumcise myself") movement among teenage girls in defiance of a 1952 ban in Meru, Kenya. The incentives behind these perpetuations are vastly different, constituting a subject that awaits elaboration in a separate volume. Suffice it to conclude here that the figure of the female body in pain, far from being immobilized, has had quite a productive career. Rajeswari Sunder Rajan has known this all along. Hence, as early as 1990 she suggested that we need to "see pain as a stage rather than a state and to regard the subject in pain as a dynamic being rather than a passive 'space.' "[32]

NOTES

A slightly different version of this chapter is published in David Wang and Shang Wei, eds., *From the Late Ming to the Late Qing: Dynastic Decline and Cultural Innovation* (Cambridge, Mass.: Council for East Asian Studies, Harvard University, forthcoming). Steven Pierce and Anupama Rao pushed me to recast this essay for a nonspecialist audience. I am grateful for their critical acumen and timely interventions. I also thank the students in my "Gendered Controversies" seminar at Barnard College who have taught me a great deal about the politics and ethics of the body.

1 Jin, *Nüjie zhong*, 1.
2 Ibid.
3 On the trope "slave of a lost country," see Karl, *Staging the World*, 33–38.
4 Jin, *Nüjie zhong*, 15.
5 Earlier scholarship emphasized missionaries' initiatives in the founding of the anti-footbinding movement. The revisionist works of Chia-lin Pao-Tao and Li You-ning stress that Chinese nationalist input was just as important. Most recently, the works of Lin Weihong and Julie Broadwin attempt to highlight the importance of women's interests to the outcome of the campaigns. See Lin, "Qingji de funü buchanzu yundong, 1894–1911." See also Broadwin, "Walking Contradictions."
6 Susan Pedersen, "National Bodies, Unspeakable Acts," 648. On Jomo Kenyatta's defense of clitoridectomy as "the *conditio sine qua non* of the whole teaching of tribal law, religion, and morality," like "Jewish circumcision," see Kenyatta, *Facing Mount Kenya*, 128.
7 MacGowan, *Beside the Bamboo*, 42.
8 Idem, *How England Saved China*, 21.
9 Bao zhuozi, "Xiamen jie chanzu hui," in Li and Zhang, *Jindai Zhongguo nuquan yundong shiliao*, 839–40. As Lin Weihong has shown, in the early 1870s

Christian communities in China debated whether footbinding was a categorical sin and whether women had to let their feet out before they could become Christian. An 1878 meeting resolved that footbinding was not a doctrinal matter, and that the family of believers had the right to choose the best course of action: Lin, "Qingji de buchanzu yundong," 152–53. For summaries of these debates in the *Chinese Recorder* between 1869 and 1870 (by Dr. Dudgeon, H.G., J.C. Kerr), see Lin Qiumin, "Jindai Zhongguo de buchanzu yundong," 30–32.

10   Baozhuo zi, "Xiamen jie chanzu hui," in Li and Zhang, *Jindai Zhongguo nuquan yundong shiliao*, 839–40.

11   Liang Qichao, "Lun nüxue," in Li and Zhang, *Jindai Zhongguo nuquan yundong shiliao*, 549–50; although often cited independently, it is a section of a longer essay, "Bianfa tongyi." Joan Judge has pointed out that the arguments and tropes of this essay served as a blueprint for subsequent reformist writings on women's education: Judge, "Reforming the Feminine," 170. Rebecca Karl has analyzed Liang's trope of "women as slaves," which was part and parcel of the trope of all citizens as slaves (*wangguo nu*, colonized subjects): Karl, " 'Slavery,' Citizenship, and Gender in Late Qing China's Global Context."

12   Chang, "Opposition to Footbinding," 125–28.

13   Simply put, the experience of pain of, say, a Song woman can never be retrieved. As such, it challenges a fundamental understanding about a historian's métier: to recover, in as truthful a manner as possible, historical reality as the people experienced it in their times. Joan Scott has critiqued such a project in her "Experience." Veena Das, in turn, first raised the question of how to feel the pain in another body in terms of linguistic and reading strategy in her "Language and Body."

14   The groundbreaking work in this important project is Meng and Dai, *Fuchu lishi dibiao*. Recently, Wendy Larson reframed the question of a female writing subject in a larger context of the traditional discourse of female talent and virtue: See Larson, *Women and Writing in Modern China*.

15   For photography and other changes in the visual culture of late Qing Shanghai, see Xiong, "Zhang yuan." For the contributions of the foreign concessions to changing visual and political culture, see idem, "Shanghai zujie yu Shanghai shehui sixiang bianqian." For the history of early photography in China, see Thiriez, *Barbarian Lens*.

16 Xiong, "Shanghai zujie yu Shanghai shehui sixiang bianqian," 128–31.

17 For the relationship between the female speaking and writing subject, see Dooling and Torgeson, *Writing Women in Modern China*, esp. 4–9. On Chen Xiefen and anti-imperialist rallies in Zhang Garden, see ibid., 83–86. On female assemblies and speeches in Zhang Yuan, see Xiong, "Zhang yuan," 35–42. Xiong argues that Zhang Garden, which opened in the spring of 1885, was the first public space in Shanghai. From 1886 to 1893, admission fees were charged as the garden grew in popularity, becoming Hyde Park and Coney Island rolled into one. The rise of other public gardens and entertainment venues in the 1910s brought the demise of Zhang Garden, which closed its doors in 1918: Xiong, "Zhang yuan," 32–33.

18 The impact of these lectures multiplied as transcripts appeared in newspapers. In this case, the text of the Suzhou lecture was published in *Anhui suhua bao*, the Anhui newspaper edited by Chen Duxiu, and *Yubao* in Henan: Zheng and Lu, *Jindai Zhongguo funü shenghuo*, 43–45.

19 Li, *Jinghua yuan*, 78. A similar description of rotten toes and dripping blood appears later in the novel, at the beginning of chapter 34: ibid., 240.

20 Age "four or five" is according to Chinese count, which assumes a person to be one year old when born: Che, *Jiaoqi ji*, 20a.

21 Li, *Jinghua yuan*, 237.

22 Ibid.

23 Liberal critics from Hu Shih to Lin Yutang, spokesmen of the Chinese enlightenment, have lauded *Flowers in the Mirror* as China's first feminist novel. Recent scholars have raised doubts from different vantage points. Stephen Roddy, for example, has provided an alternative reading to the elevation of women in the novel. Situating the gender inversion that structured the story in a crisis of epistemology and self-identity of the literati in the early nineteenth century, Roddy suggests that the elevation of women's learning can be understood as an expression of Li Ruzhen's sympathy with Han evidential scholarship (*Hanxue*). Women's learning, marked by women's intellectual curiosity and philological interest in playing with language in the novel, is a stand in for Han evidential scholarship. Conversely, men's learning, so stifled by the careerism bred by the civil-service examination, represented the state orthodoxy of Song learning. In other words, the criticism of gender inequality in the novel could be merely "figural," motivated as it was by philological concerns prevalent in intellectual

circles at the time, and may not refer to gender inequality in society: Roddy, *Literati Identity and Its Fictional Representations in Late Imperial*, 171–229. Maram Epstein, in turn, has interpreted gender inversion in terms of yin-yang structuring, hence situating it in a framework larger than socially constructed male-female relations. According to Epstein, the representation of yin in the novel is complicated and contradictory. Although women's knowledge and talent were elevated, the female emperor Wu Zetian's rule was cast as source of cosmic disorder. She, too, cautioned against "politically engaged readings" that construe the novel as a feminist manifesto: Epstein, "Engendering Order."

24 Thomson, *Illustrations of China and Its People*, n.p.

25 Li and Zhang, *Jindai Zhongguo nüquan yundong shiliao*, 872. See also Lü and Zheng, *Zhongguo funü yundong, 1840–1921*, 163–64.

26 The historian Lin Weihong has argued that these local Tianzu huis were ineffective in ending footbinding, populated as they were by a minority of local leaders who rallied to curry favor with their superiors. These local official and semi-official organizations lacked broad-based support among the local elites, who were overwhelmingly conservative: Lin, "Qingji de funü buchanzu yundong," 177–78.

27 I am still researching the history of the transmission of radiography to China. The Peking Union Medical College (PUMC), established in 1921, included a Department of Radiography. Built on the Johns Hopkins model and funded by the Rockefeller Foundation, the PUMC was the key institution for introducing foreign medical technology to China. But at the time of its establishment, medical uses of x-ray had already become routine in China: See Bullock, *An American Transplant*.

28 Kevles, *Naked to the Bone*, 24.

29 Ibid., 134. On changing boundaries of privacy, see ibid., 123.

30 Yao, *Caifei lu*, 255–58. One of the earliest first-person testimonies of women with bound feet is that of Gao Xixiang of Huating county, titled, "Chanzu fu zhi xianshen shoufa" (A footbound woman stands up and speaks up). Her words of complaint were dictated to a literate neighbor, Madamee Yinmei, and published in *Tianzu huibao*, no. 1, 1907, 161–63.

31 Scarry, *The Body in Pain*, 125–26ff.

32 Sunder Rajan, "The Subject of Sati," 10.

LAURA BEAR

※

An Economy of Suffering

Addressing the Violence of Discipline in Railway Workers' Petitions to the Agent of the East Indian Railway, 1930–47

Research in the Agent's Record Room of the Eastern Railway risks turning history into a ledger. Endless accounting of indents, wages, leave rules, allowances, and provident funds suggests a railway bureaucracy concerned with the disenchantment of the world. Most accounts of railway history have followed the lead of this kind of documentation. Historians have long argued that the massive railway bureaucracy drew the laborers who worked for it into new habits of work discipline. From the 1840s, the government leased the building and running of railways to private companies. These companies were kept under close scrutiny in the most minute operations by the railway department in the civil service. Toward the end of the nineteenth century, some companies came under state control. Railway workers, so the argument goes, were members of a new kind of civil society governed by regular procedure and regulations.[1] Yet also filed away in the archive of the railway, which was called the East Indian Railway under the Raj, are petitions sent by employees and their relatives in the period from 1930 to 1947 that seem not to belong to an atmosphere of regularized discipline at all. Instead, they contain a supernatural, royal, and moral language of violence, tyranny, suffering, and despair. They tell of secret conspiracies, physical disfigurement, and brutal beatings and predict riots and impending disasters. For example, a

Mrs. Packwood, the widow of a driver on the East Indian Railway whose sons also worked on the railway, complained to the agent in 1930:

> Regret to address you again, but I find that the cursed low who are aiding and abetting in mischief and crafty black denominations have been cruelly detaining my sons and myself in my welfare and instead of doing my fatherless sons and myself the good that is necessary we are fighting and praying and making known our request and yet we are out of our calculations. . . . My sons and myself have been deliberately persecuted and amazed and riled and vexed and tortured and at every turn. . . . We have been incessantly disfigured and discoloured.[2]

Petitions like this one seem to be fragments from a world quite different from that of the railway bureaucracy. Yet as I will show in this chapter, these petitions were active engagements with the strange experience of working under the command of this institution. They came not from outside the procedures of the railway but from the paradoxes of inhabiting the space of the other body in its disciplinary regime. The bureaucracy promised rule-governed fair procedure and economic necessity as its guiding principles, but it also continually insisted on the difference necessary in the treatment of Indian labor and on the multiple taxonomies of bodies marked with signs of race, community, and respectability. Workers and their families lived in the hiatus between the promise of the universal, objective operation of procedural and economic laws and the everyday practice of discipline that insisted on difference. In their petitions they described this hiatus as a kind of violence. In particular, petitioners insisted on the space of discipline as a place of bodily suffering and despotic tyranny. Each petition is a small scandal that insists on the humanity of colonial subjects. More important, their historical effects, as we will see, could not be contained by the attempts of colonial bureaucrats to read them as examples of native irrationality.

The analysis of the railway petitions in this chapter begins with an account of their emergence from the discussions of how to deal with the discontent of Indian workers in the period from 1928 to 1930. It then turns to the recurrent modes of address in the petitions and explores them as a response to the paradoxes of the railway bureaucracy. Linking the accounts of an economy of suffering in these petitions to their wider, unexpected impact, I describe how they helped to forge a public critique of the legitimacy of the railway bureaucracy. Finally, using ethnographic material I explore contemporary tales of an economy of suffering among clerks in the Eastern Railway headquarters.

DESPOTISM AND THE "INDIAN WORKER": THE ORIGIN OF PETITIONS AND THE ROYAL COMMISSION ON LABOUR, 1929–30

Petitioning originated in the attempts of British railway officials to reestablish the legitimacy of their administration of the economy in the wake of widespread strikes during the 1920s that had paralyzed the railway network and other sectors. These disputes had threatened the specter of recurrent civil disobedience, if not revolution. In response to this, a Royal Commission on Labour was set up in 1929 to inquire into the measures that needed to be introduced to improve the welfare and contentment of workers. This commission set out to replace older colonial racial inequalities in the workplace with practices that emphasized principles of Taylorist welfare. There was much that needed to be altered on the railways. The contractual and social space occupied by the railway worker was one in which he was racialized and criminalized. His labor was marked as distinct in an intricate classification of hierarchies of command, salary, and leave rules, in which he was "European, Eurasian, West Indian or Negro descent pure of mixed, non-Indian Asiatic or Indian."[3] The successive Railway Acts of 1854, 1869, and 1890 made him into an individual with criminal responsibility for his insobriety of habits, breaches of discipline, and failure to prevent accidents. He was not a subject of legal rights. Instead, he occupied a space in which once he signed a contract with a railway company he had to give up even his private status as a plaintiff. Personal differences and disputes between the railway police and company employees were settled departmentally, and the prosecution of employees under the Railway Act was at the discretion of the agent. The status of workers as members of civil society was restrained, as well. Workers could not communicate or publish information about the affairs of the company, under threat of dismissal.[4] Not surprisingly, when the Railway Board inquired into the sources of discontent among workers for the Royal Commission, it found that the sources were punitive fining, racial employment hierarchies, instability of service, and arbitrary practices of dismissal. Therefore, the members of the board set out to discuss the means for a complete reform of the management of Indian workers with the companies. Yet the fundamentally hierarchical and anachronistic practice of petitioning emerged out of this liberal impulse. So why and how did the practice of petitioning eventually develop as a solution for capturing back the discontent of railway workers from union activities?

The Railway Board may have been initially in favor of reform, but the individual companies gradually persuaded it that current practices should be retained. They also ensured that any new measures that were introduced did not undermine the hierarchical and arbitrary power of superior officers. Their reasoning was that special arrangements were necessary to deal with inefficient, undisciplined, and insubordinate Indian labor. They also suggested that unions should not be given any status to represent the individual cases of workers because these organizations were politically immature and workers were too irrational to resist the rabble-rousing of political organizations of "outsiders."[5] As a result, the Railway Board finally decided that existing practices would be left in place with a promise to gradually end racial distinctions. But alongside these practices, to recapture what they called the interests and affections of workers, local works committees—or Faidamand Panchayats—should be set up. These councils were modeled on Indian "traditional" village councils, composed of equal members of the staff selected by vote among various classes of employees and of railway officers. They would discuss issues to do with the welfare of the staff such as quarters, sanitation, recreation, and conditions of work, and their recommendations would be considered by the agent.[6] It was hoped that these procedures would capture discontent back into a regularized system of decision making.

But these councils would not be allowed to consider individual cases, as this would enable subordinates to question the authority of higher officials. Instead, the Railway Board suggested that individual workers be allowed to question their dismissal, fining, and general treatment by sending petitions to Area Welfare Councils and to the agent of the railway. The practice of petitioning emerged in an attempt by British railway officials to retain their authority to guide the economic governance of India without fundamentally reforming the unequal disciplinary practices of the bureaucracy. The practice was therefore born in a space of colonial governmentality which translated Taylorist discourses into idioms seen as appropriate to Indian realities. Workers could live in the hope of receiving justice and of democratic rights, but these would not be guaranteed by political representation, legal rights, or negotiation with union officials. Instead, rights would be guaranteed by "traditional" works councils and the act of petitioning a figure of authority. In spite of the original intentions of the Royal Commission to remove racial inequalities and hierarchical work arrangements, the managers of the railways found a new way to materialize unequal colonial relationships and the difference of Indian employees. This was justified as necessary for the management of other bodies whose labor could not be guaranteed solely by practices of worker welfare.

What, then, were the rules of exchange between the agent and a worker seeking redress through petitioning? This was intended as a purely individual transaction. No pleaders, union officials, or anyone other than the worker involved could make representations on a case. The agent preserved the sublime authority of the bureaucracy by promising to consider whether facts had been established by his subordinates, whether the facts provided sufficient grounds for taking action, and whether the penalty was excessive or reasonable. In return, the employee agreed to couch his appeal without disrespectful or improper language. The figure of the agent maintained a fiction of the possibility of justice in a bureaucratic system that removed most possibilities of this. Theoretically, the agent could decide to pass on the petition, if it was necessary, to the governor-general. Ultimately, the highest authority in this chain of decision making was His Majesty, the King Emperor of India.[7] The petitioner had become more akin to a subject addressing a sovereign than a worker who had rights and was part of an industrial enterprise.

The railway worker was thus given the seductive possibility of directly demanding justice and of confronting figures of power with their suffering. It is not surprising that railway officials despaired at the quantity of petitions that crossed their desks. Sweepers, workshop laborers, guards, drivers, assistant stationmasters, ticket collectors, clerks, and their relatives seized the opportunity for an intimate encounter through writing that might change their fate. The bureaucracy seemed to have succeeded more than it could have hoped in capturing the interest of railway workers. But to call this a success is premature. The content of the petitions very often did not match the expectations of railway officials. The scribbled comments on them chart their shocked surprise at the apparent madness of the language of the petitions. Railway officers often wrote on them "irrelevant, please file" or "this woman is completely crackbrained." For them these petitions were, as one retired railway official put it in his memoirs, "congestion on the circuits" generated by the misunderstandings of railway employees.[8] The strangeness of the language of the petitions was interpreted by British railway officials as further evidence of Indians' profound difference from themselves. It was another example of what the Royal Commission on Labour claimed was the deficiency of reason among Indian workers, which could be improved by their further incorporation into the habits and procedures of the bureaucracy.[9] The content of the petitions did not match the rules laid down by the Railway Board, either. Half of the petitions preserved in the record room were requests for a redress of injustice or reinstatement, but another quarter were complaints, often anonymous, about the corruption and immorality of superiors. Therefore, the introduction of the practice of petitioning did not take the shape officials intended.

In the next section, I analyze some of the recurrent content and form of these petitions that so perplexed railway officials. I argue that, far from not sharing a language of authority with the railway bureaucracy, petitioners confronted that bureaucracy with its own paradoxical practices.

The contents of the petitions reveal the lineaments of a contradictory and despotic colonial civil society in which there was a disturbing simultaneous presence of taxonomies of economic efficiency, respectability, race, and community. The language of the petitions also reflects the strains of writing of mental and physical suffering in the lines of civility. Yet it also reveals a redeployment of languages of caste, bureaucratic honor, kingship, justice, economic efficiency, and respectability in ways that demanded accountability from the bureaucracy.

VIOLENT JUSTICE: ROYAL AGENTS AND ACCOUNTING FOR BRIBERY

In the petitions workers sent to the agent, it is striking how the railway bureaucracy appears as a place of despotism and potential violence. It is not that petitioners complained of actual acts of violence—in fact, as I will discuss later, they rarely did this. Instead, the letters are full of violent metaphors used to describe what officials would have considered regular procedure and of images of the agent as a ruler. The petitions often opened by making it explicit that they did not consider the bureaucracy to be a place of routinized discipline by endowing the agent with the power of a sovereign. Workers began their petitions with phrases such as, "We pray to God that you may adorn the high chair of Agent and may God grant you long life so that we the staffs may get pure consolation and peace and justice from your noble soul."[10] They suggested that the agent's power was not neutral and regularized, but that "it is only your hand that can feed the hungry and destroy the convicted."[11] The workers wrote in idioms of repentance, pledging, "I faithfully promise never again to commit myself, as it this time means destruction for all eternity."[12] Appearing before the agent in writing was a matter of his releasing you from "shots of trouble unable for bearing" by his "act of kindness."[13] Seeking reemployment was not a matter of ability or efficiency but of "forgiveness, I sincerely assure you Sir, that my repentance is greater than my sin."[14] The agent was addressed as an omnipotent sovereign in phrases such as, "With your unquestioned authority and immense power at your disposal you can very easily season that justice with mercy, a divine virtue!"[15]

Often petitions used monarchical language to flatter figures of authority, but they equally used it in an attempt to shame the agent by attempting to confront him with the violent justice of the bureaucracy. Many petitions complained that the agent and his officers behaved like a tyrannical king surrounded by corrupt courtiers. One worker described his dismissal as a "murder of justice,"[16] adding the complaint, "Kind Sir! A murderer even is given a fair chance of defence and demonstration, but myself on the contrary have been disposed of."[17] Another petitioner wrote that he could not understand the excessive enactments of punishment against him, since he had "neither beaten with hands, bamboos, sticks, bomb nor shells, nor hanged nor killed, looted or plotted or attacked any king or employers nor have my family done so."[18] These petitions, which aimed to flatter or shame the agent into action, confronted the bureaucracy with its own despotic procedures. The everyday practice of colonial discipline on the railways was indicted as a form of violent justice.

Other railway workers tried to draw attention to their cases by issuing threats or by predicting a violent end to the agent's rule over them. Cutting through the pretence that an exchange of evidence presented in good order would help their case, they sought instead to intimidate the agent using the same violence against him that the bureaucracy had enacted on them. A former guard threatened physical violence against the agent if he did not respond, writing, "To see justice done I am ditermined [sic] if not by EIR then by the Viceroy and perhaps by myself which you know by this what I mean there being no need to make it plain. . . . I am not a man who will tolerate interference and that I am a man that should be well left alone."[19] A group of sweepers warned that, if their case was not listened to, "there will be a day of retribution. The children of Adam are limbs of one another and are all produced from the same substance, when the world gives pain to one member the others also suffer uneasiness. 'Death' is the foe."[20] Other petitioners amplified their threats with supernatural insights. A former ticket collector predicted, "Today I have seen dream that your throne will be shifted from Delhi to Calcutta nearly on 13 April 1932 and will not be good and no one will hear your case."[21] In these threats, petitioners suggested that the true currency of interaction in the railway was intimidation, but they also warned that the agent's power over them was reversible.

There are echoes here of older idioms of monarchical and bureaucratic power that have been infused with a new salience by the introduction of the practice of petitioning on the railways. In the images of the agent as a king responsible for the well-being of his subjects at times of crisis, there are obvious references to idioms of *sakti, dharmic* action, and honor used by peasants in their relationships to zamindars.[22] The reversibility of the agent's power can also be linked to an earlier fragility of personal honor and authority that is based on the devotion of followers and the relative status of other people. Ideas common among the bureaucrats of Mughal successor states in northern and eastern India seem to be given new life in these documents, as well. In particular, the image of the employees of the railway as part of the same "body" suffering the same pain reanimates the sense that *nawabi* bureaucrats had of states as human bodies that required all their elements from officials to subjects to continue to exist.[23] Yet we must remember that the image of the agent as a despot or king, of the railway as a place of violence, and of the reversibility of the agent's power were recurrent in petitions whether they were written by Anglo-Indian, British, or Indian railway workers.

In each of the petitions, we have not a simple recurrence of older forms but a palimpsest of experiments in how to address the agent. There is an attempt to forge a language, and its features need to be related to the form itself and to the experiences workers had of railway justice. The sense of the reversibility of the agent's power and of its dependence on the cooperation of subjects is evoked by the intimacy of the petition form itself, which offered the promise of a potentially close relationship with a figure of authority. The hope of railway workers was that the agent was really somehow equally dependent on their maintaining this relationship. But the choice of monarchical and violent images reflects the fact that the railway bureaucracy left its workers seeking justice from an agent who, with a single autocratic act, could change their fortune. And most of them had been subjected to a bureaucracy that was not in fact accountable, even though it promised it was. Under the contracts signed by railway workers, the employee had no recourse to external legal devices through which to achieve recompense. Instead, all offenses and dismissals were dealt with departmentally. First, the employee was presented with a charge sheet listing the offenses for which he was required to submit a written explanation. He was then brought before the officer competent to dismiss him, and if that officer thought a case existed, a departmental inquiry was ordered.[24] The inquiry partook of all the language of guilt, innocence, and proof that one would expect in a legal proceeding. But workers and unions complained that the hearings were far from objective, since British officers always supported the decisions of other officers and never believed the workers' side of the story. In addition to this, the machinery of the Watch and Ward Department, introduced for the purposes of guarding railway property, and of the Government Railway Police, introduced to enforce the Railway Acts, was used to spy on the behavior of employees in anticipation of their committing offenses. Even in cases in which these agencies failed to gain proof of misdemeanors or crimes, if they were "convinced" that a man, through slackness or connivance, was responsible for illegitimate acts, they could inform the divisional superintendent, who could discharge the employee.[25] The category of discharge did not require the process of departmental inquiry unless the employee had completed ten years of service. If the employee could not be found guilty, he could be discharged at the discretion of the divisional superintendent on general grounds.[26] It is hardly surprising that despotic ghosts and violent metaphors were brought to life in the petitions by this autocratic colonial economy, which ultimately rested on the figure of the Indian worker as someone who did not have the same dexterity of reason as the hereditary working classes in Britain.[27]

Petitions were filled with another kind of metaphor of violence. Workers sent petitions that told scandals of corruption to the agent, which were described as the cause of tyranny and "butchering" of the employees.[28] Petitioners sometimes offered themselves as spies and rigorously followed the accounting procedures of proof that were practiced by the railway itself. But they turned these against British or Anglo-Indian officers. For example, a former train examiner wrote to the agent to inform him that he had been on "secret service" and had gone out for the benefit of king and country on a "real pilgrimage" to discover the misdemeanors of his British officers.[29] In these petitions on corruption, the language of economics and accounting hovered around the acts of bribery themselves, which were described as having been "enumerated," "recommended," and "accounted" by those who took them.[30] The slipping of this language of bureaucratic procedure into the realm of illicit acts blurred the distinction between legitimate acts of deduction and those driven by the selfish, individual economic interests of superiors. Petitions often suggested that in fact "terrorism is the stock in trade of the railway," which possessed a "secret code of conduct" that did not match the conduct rules supplied to employees that forbade bribery.[31] Petitioners addressed the agent, showing him that the unequal power given to superiors to frame rules and change them "at their own sweet will," and their greater credibility in the bureaucracy, enabled them to practice "tyranny" and to "torture, degrade and humiliate the men . . . to kill their soul."[32] Many of these petitions in fact suggested that bribery was the symptom of the rapacious desires that colonial economics itself produced by its racial hierarchies of command, which meant that the word of superior British officers was always believed over that of Indian workers.

Some petitioners argued that economy and efficiency were irrelevant in the context of the enterprise of the colonial railways. For example, a group of ticket examiners in Howrah division sent a petition arguing that the forecasts of rumors and networks of bribery undermined the economic forecasts of the bureaucracy itself. Hearing that if they paid they could be promoted to head train examiners, they did not believe the rumor because they thought the railway was having financial difficulties and could not afford to make new appointments. But they bitterly realized that the railway "does not require competent hands at present" when a junior train examiner was appointed after paying the requisite bribe and the other vacant positions were filled by Anglo-Indians.[33] By protesting against the bureaucracy, they demonstrated that it created superiors with rapacious economic self-interest and a belief in racial taxonomies that undermined their wise governance of the prosperity of the railway and its workers. In more theoretical terms, both the violent metaphors used to describe the effects of bribery and the assertion that corruption was caused by the rules and racial hierarchies of the bureaucracy insisted that a kind of foundational violence suffused the disciplinary practices and rules of the railway.

When railway workers sent requests for personal reinstatement or the removal of unjust fines to the agent they were following the rules for the submission of petitions. Those rules were intended to deal with individual cases of dismissal or punishment. But the accusations of bribery had not been solicited by the organization. Why, then, did railway workers send them? The carefully itemized lists of railway materials misappropriated and of circuits of corruption represent a palimpsest of diverse strategies and understandings of the bureaucracy. Some petitions may have been inspired by simple vindictiveness that sought to disguise personal dislike in acts of public duty. Sometimes the genuine hope of petitioners was that the agent, as a sublime figure of British justice, would make superior officers accountable. They were usually disappointed. If he found the accusations credible, the agent would refer them to the officer accused, who would reply that they were untrue. But what is interesting is that railway workers, even if they were just pursuing a personal vendetta, thought that the agent would be interested in their information. This assumption rests in part on the ways in which the excuse of potential corruption was used by the Watch and Ward Department and Railway Police as a reason to spy on employees. Some petitions explicitly mimicked the reports of the department. It also rests on a long experience of precolonial and colonial bureaucracies as institutions that recruited spies and, later, news writers. Suggestively, as well, most of these petitions on bribery hover between simple reports and personal indictments of the agent himself. Hindi and Bengali pamphleteering had a long history of insisting that the selection of unworthy officials represented an absence of merit on the part of a ruler. A good government had long been seen as a bureaucracy whose subjects would be assured swift justice and would be protected from oppression by public officials. These theories of the polity had been used to criticize British rule since the first days of the East India Company.[34] It was, I think, the elective affinity between these versions of just governance and the measures used by the bureaucracy to stamp out corruption among lower railway officials that made sending a petition on bribery an irresistible opportunity to bring the agent himself to account. This combination produced a profoundly new way to critique the foundational violence of the railway bureaucracy, which workers experienced in the daily, unequal practice of disciplinary procedures. Both the petitions about bribery and those which addressed the agent as a sovereign held him and the bureaucracy fully accountable for the corporeal well-being of workers and refused to accept the ways in which bureaucratic rules measured legitimate and illegitimate acts of discipline. These rules and railway justice were nothing but violence.

SUFFERING BODIES: MARKS OF PAIN, BUREAUCRATIC DISHONOR, RACE, AND COMMUNITY

The petitions sent to the agent are full of descriptions of bodies as expressive surfaces. The bodies of petitioners appear as irrefutable evidence of suffering, often with a kind of forensic detail of sickness and the marks of labor. The bodies of other people have a different role. They display surface evidence of deeper dishonor or of race or community origins. Overall, the tales told about the physical body reflect the experience employees had of a workplace in which there was a contradictory simultaneous presence of Taylorist notions of welfare and colonial racial and community hierarchies.

Railway workers repeatedly wrote confidential tales of the marks of pain on their bodies to the agent. Believing in the intimacy of their relationship with the agent, they sent him long and detailed descriptions of the histories of their family's sicknesses, begging for intervention.

These petitions sought to demonstrate how workers had become "sufferers in life, due to life and labour on the railway."[35] They cited examples of how their work had left them "pale and dried up" and "drifting in the vast ocean of woes and miseries in a watery cemetery."[36] A former railway guard, after carefully listing unfair fines and, finally, his dismissal from service, sent a photograph of his face demonstrating an injury he received during his work on the railway. He wrote, "I have an ever-lasting scar on my face. . . . [W]ith this disfigured countenance and the inner injury as the annexed photo shall indicate, I am getting discharged . . . and shall have to countenance the severest kind of hardship that one can expect in the world."[37] For the petitioner, the photograph provided the ultimate proof that labor on the railways was all about "punishments coming in torrent losing all proportion and ends of justice."[38] Others directly related their work on the railways and its punitive systems to their declining health. One widow claimed that the paying of fines by her husband, a stationmaster, led to his death, and that the health of her husband declined in direct proportion to the deductions from his salary. She wrote, "The shock was too great for him as would be evident from his attendance record to show that with payment of each of the instalments of payment he fell ill. So keen was his feeling of injured innocence over this fine."[39] These petitioners reject the distinction between discipline and violence and argue that labor on the railways is a form of corporeal "wanton punishment" that disfigures the body of the laborer.[40] They insist that the railway has a duty to care for their well-being and challenge it to live up to its promised Taylorist intentions.

However, petitions that expose superior officers for unfairness or corruption present a different aspect of the body as evidence that has more to do with the older, more established colonial hierarchies of respectability and race. They provide a litany of moral faults visible in the physical behavior and appearance of their senior workers and fellow officers. These workers of "great temptation" take "bribes for fornication," or to provide money for abortions.[41] Many of them offer physical signs of this immorality and betrayal of what they call bureaucratic honor. For example, a group of clerks from Howrah wrote, "What to say of the character of Mr. Jones? It can be proved from the syphilitic eruption of Mr. Jones who always enjoys the sweet company of low sweeper women of Inward and makes amorous gestures with them."[42] They add that the officer unfairly promoted one of his friends because the friend helped him get secret treatment for syphilis at the Calcutta Hospital of Tropical Medicine. Similarly, some laborers from the Lucknow locomotive works reported, "Here are two bribe eaters one of them is the chief man i.e. Mr. Hemming Production engineer . . . who remember who has got 3 lady typists, one was pregnant and Mr. Hemming took her to Simla and tried through the Doctors and organised an abortion and brought her back."[43] Even though it is implicit in most of the documents, some petitioners explicitly convey the series of condensed associations between race, caste, morality, and correct economic behavior that lie behind these accusations. For example, one petitioner complaining of the actions of a sanitary inspector, states: "Please arrange an European Sanitary Inspector instead of the one who by appearance will himself exhibit his face like Negro or 3rd class Anglo Indian of dome breedy."[44]

What this concern with physical signs of bureaucratic honor reveals is something that remained unacknowledged in the debates about procedures for dismissal and fining in the Royal Commission on Labour. In its memorandum, the Railway Board claimed that, in the interests of economic efficiency, it needed to retain the power to summarily dismiss workers. It stated that decisions in departmental inquiries into employees were made purely on the basis of the individual's profitability. But in practice, these procedures of discipline rested on a moral schema that clothed British officers with a greater aura of respectability and justified their command of what was called "the railway family."[45] In their daily activities, the Watch and Ward staff and government Railway Police scrutinized the moral habits of railway staff. Employees were dismissed due to their inability to maintain discipline because they had acquired "very immoral habits," showed "moral turpitude," or had "seduced the wife of another."[46] The concern of petitioners with bureaucratic honour and secrets of immorality was an attempt to turn this kind of procedure against fellow workers and superior officers. There were two grounds on which railway workers seem to have based such a reversal: first, by taking seriously the opportunity to whisper secrets into the ear of the agent through the private medium of the petition; and second, on an elective affinity between notions of caste, bureaucratic and kingly honor, and the moral hierarchy of the railway. Ideologies of bureaucratic and royal command had long rested on notions of a virtuous honor shown externally in physical appearance and behavior. The link to substantialized notions of caste in the petitions I have described is clear. However, in the context of petitions to the railway, these notions of caste were deployed to question the legitimacy of British and Anglo-Indian railway officials. What the petitions ultimately reveal is that within the workplace there was a troubling simultaneous presence of economic, moral, and racial logic in operation. Many of the petitions attempted to attract the attention of the agent by offering bodily evidence of the railway bureaucracy's own racial, visual, essentialist disciplinary practices that linked race to respectability and efficiency. But these petitions also revealed the fantastic and impossible monsters that these practices engendered.

Another mode of address in the petitions attempted to gain the agent's attention by using the other bureaucratic typology of the bodies of workers—that of community. From the 1890s on, the railways had attempted to balance the numbers of different communities in departments under the assumption that this would prevent corruption and make the bureaucracy impartial. In the 1930s, they began to implement policies in the name of social justice that would balance the percentage of different communities employed in the railways according to the size of their population. Petitioners were supposed to write to the agent as individuals seeking economic justice for themselves, but they often used their community identity to make their individual cases. For example, a discharged punching clerk first listed his family's service to the government during the 1857 rebellion, dispelling any ideas that he came from a disloyal population. He then suggested that his status as a Muslim had meant that he had not received equal treatment from the railway bureaucracy: "Being a Mohamedan and without any patron I was helpless to ventilate my grievances for redress." He made his final argument for his reinstatement on the grounds that "I humbly pray that I may kindly be given a chance in any capacity and anywhere that you may be pleased to put me according to the Government of India orders that the 19% Muslims should be provided in the railway department."[47] Thus, he seeks to exchange his community affiliation for its value in the calculations of governance. Other discharged workers took another tactic and traded in the paranoia about community conspiracies that guided the Railway Board's calculations of the percentages of castes and creeds employed in the railway. They accused their Hindu or Muslim superiors of favoring their own communities. However, other petitions argued that the railway bureaucracy's trading in communal conspiracies, threats, and calculations only led to injustice and the production of illusory paranoia. These petitions suggested that Hindu or Muslim officers used their high position to circulate communal rumors to cover up their own attempts to extract bribes. All of these appeals circle around the problematic eruption of the calculations of community in the economic governance of the railways. A typical example comes in an anonymous letter describing the oppressions of the Patna Junction Goods Shed staff by a Hindu officer who used his high position to circulate communal rumors to cover up his own attempts to extract bribes. When the workers refused to follow his instructions to take bribes from merchants, he informed the Watch and Ward staff and the government Railway Police that

> the irregularity [of] whatever took place in this good shed is entirely due to communal faction and I thank to the enquiring officers that without thinking on this point and enquiring into the truthfulness of his statement they report the fact to the office and the result of which the innocent Mohammedan staff of Patna junction good shed are swept without any blame. Out of four Mohammedan, two are already transferred and two are in consideration. . . . He oppresses the innocent staff.[48]

This letter circles around the eruption of the communal into the economic and the problematic relationship set up between them by colonial political economy. Here, instead of community operating as a sign of economic efficiency, the trading in signs of community covers up illegitimate economic acts. The radical instability of the bureaucracy's typological systems of populations and their procedures of proof are simultaneously critiqued and deployed. This instability is the space occupied by the railway worker's body, which was enumerated, individualized, and simultaneously placed in community spaces.

The disciplinary measures and workplace practices of the railway bureaucracy in the period up to independence were contradictory in their production of expressive surfaces on the bodies of employees. Taylorist practices of welfare and notions of economic efficiency individualized the bodies of workers and made them the responsibility of the bureaucracy. The bureaucracy also encouraged workers to see themselves and others as possessing a group essence in their body that related them to a community or caste. Alongside these newer measures, older colonial hierarchies of morality and race continued. Petitions to the agent express the paradoxes of trying to reconcile these different logics of the body and of working under these contradictory practices. Workers suggest that the coexistence of these various forms produced an economy of suffering that made their bodies vulnerable to many kinds of violence: illness from labor, oppression from immoral superiors, and communal attack. They speak in the petitions of the hybrid and divided selves that the bureaucracy dealt in as a result of its adaptation of Taylorist welfare to a colonial context.

ACTS OF VIOLENCE AND VIOLENT WRITING

So far I have described how the petitions reflect the contradictions between the bureaucracy's unequal disciplinary practices and its universalist claims that it existed to protect the economic efficiency of the railways and the welfare of its employees. The gap is rendered as a form of violence that leads to tyranny, corporeal suffering, and communal violence. To end this section, I will discuss, first, the kinds of violence that can be hinted at only in the lines of these documents, and second, the kinds of writing they contain. I will then turn to the material impact of the practice of petitioning.

One kind of evidence of suffering appears rarely in the petitions: accounts of physical attacks. From oral histories I have collected, it seems that such attacks were fairly common in the environs of railway colonies, if not in the workplace. The absence of such evidence is somewhat surprising, as the content of documents is far from restrained in its indictment of superior officials and in its trading of scurrilous information about them. When accounts of attacks do appear, they are hidden in long lists of other kinds of misdemeanors. Petitioners began by attempting to attract the interest of the agent by listing exactly how much money could be reclaimed by the administration if it instituted an inquiry. In the middle of descriptions of furniture, ghee, and misappropriated uniforms, they place secrets that are disparate in their brutality. Item number twenty-two of one of these lists is a description of "Laloo Cooly shot in the chest while pig shooting" by a superior, for example, and item fifteen of another tells how a case of "Dilchand's wife beaten by a driver" was hushed up.[49] Petitioners seem to have clothed their outrage in the language of economics, claiming that they had nothing in view but to "save revenue pocketted by so called tin god of the railway."[50] Given the expansive descriptions of other kinds of suffering, the violent threats issued by petitioners to the agent, and the metaphors of violence that suffuse the petitions, this deserves analysis. Petition writing was based on a notion of civil procedure and the free exchange of words between people who occupied very distinct positions in the railway hierarchy. Explicit descriptions of violence would have ruptured the founding fiction of this form—that such an exchange was even possible—by highlighting the extreme inequalities of position between sender and recipient. Such descriptions would finally have ended an exchange and shown that railway justice and paternalism was founded on a lie. This, I think, is why petitioners were so hesitant to report such things to the agent, and it explains why, when they did, they hid violent acts among lists of economic waste as just another instance of a loss of resources.

The form of the petition, like all of the bureaucratic writing on the railways, lived in the illusion that language was a neutral, administrative tool, authored by individual agents through which truths could be established. The form of the petition relied on this assumption, as well. But railway workers experienced this neutrality in a very different way, and the modes of address of petitions reflect the strains of maintaining the fictions of bureaucratic writing. The only kind of legitimate agency left to railway workers was to write a petition. As a result, some petitioners struggled to give their letters as much authority as possible by borrowing the forms of bureaucratic documents and legal memoranda, and even sometimes by using East Indian Railway notepaper. Attempting to give their words as much force as possible, they also wrote tales of high drama and vivid literary style. Some workers completely abandoned bureaucratic forms of language altogether and, instead—after months of petitioning—sent the agent poems. A former assistant stationmaster wrote:

> Oh God, Oh Lord! I pray to thee
> Be pleased enough to excuse me
> Please save my kind masters
> D. S. Howrah and the Agent E.I.R.
> I am a poor man got some thing to state
> Before their honour regarding my fate
> After 29 years service in E.I.R.
> Have to beg door to door as a street beggar
> This is not desirable at the End of Life
> as my sorrows always looked by my children and my wife
> Their honour therefore should be pleased
> By which my troubles may be ceased.[51]

The petitions' content also stretched the neutrality of bureaucratic writing by describing an institution in which words issued from above had a murdering force. The petitioners wrote of "your hope-killing letter," divisional managers' acting "at the stroke of" their "mighty pen," and "the maiden whiteness" of their "service sheets" as having been "ruthlessly defiled" by black marks.[52] The violent hierarchy of bureaucratic language is explicitly criticized in some petitions, such as that sent to the agent on behalf of sweepers employed at Moghalserai. Accused by the local head sweepers of irregularities, the sweepers complain that there is no one to speak on their behalf to the local sanitary inspector; the rest of the petition becomes a meditation on the "filthy languages" of those in charge over them.[53] This language turns the sweepers into beasts of burden under the control of their superiors with no hope of redress because the bureaucracy has already named them as those who deserve demerit marks. They wrote:

> We think the story of the fox suits exactly, who on being seen running away and limping someone asked what calamities occasioned him so much tripidation [sic]. He replied, I hear that they are going to press a camel into service (like above quoted supervisors) your honour may observe and like our impudence as to what relationship is there between us the camel and what resemblance have we to that animal, our reply is to be silent, for if the malignant out of evil design should say this is a camel and we should be seized, who would be so solicitous for our relief as to order an enquiry into our grievances?[54]

It is the hierarchy of bureaucratic naming and its fictitious neutrality that these sweepers suggest turned them from a fox into a camel, a free animal into a beast of burden, and innocent into guilty, and that reduced them to silence in the face of the "false judgement of things."[55]

Overall, the documents I have described struggle with the inequalities of the agency provided to workers by the fact that their only right in a situation of injustice was to write letters to the agent. Their theatrical, evocative language is provoked by the very inequalities of the agency left to them. They all attempt to show suffering in the lines of civility. Ultimately, it is this civility that appears as a kind of violence, because it is so difficult to insert their experiences and outrage into its notion of good form and the neutrality of bureaucratic writing. Most petitions began as an attempt to flatter power or to call it to account, but with the strain of writing, the petitions became scandalous literary tales. In their attempts to cross the boundary between the bureaucracy and their everyday experience in the material form of petitions, railway workers were forging a quite distinct language of critique. Some of this language was based on their understanding of the practices of the railways. Other elements were derived from older understandings of power and institutions. But these experiments to address the agent on his own terms have one important element in common: They seized the opportunity of petition writing and used its fictions of reciprocity and fair procedure to a very different end from that intended by officials. They used this practice to hold the agent and his officers accountable for the violence of colonial discipline.

This language of critique escaped its confinement to the files of failed claims in the East Indian Railway headquarters. If we look at the union newspapers, memoranda, and strikes on the railway in the same period, from 1930–40, we find that their mobilization was built on similar attacks on the legitimacy of railway discipline as violent, immoral, rapacious, and despotic. Union pamphlets and newspapers are filled with stories of cases of adultery by British railway officers, petty embezzlement as a sign of moral turpitude, and the measurement of the suffering of laboring bodies. The crossover of the modes of address is more than coincidental. Oral histories I have collected from people who were union activists in the 1940s show that one of their main activities was to help workers compose petitions to headquarters. As they sat together discussing the worker's case, they forged a common public language of the violence of discipline. Flash points for union action were the acts of humiliation carried out by upper subordinate British and Anglo-Indian foremen and officers. This all suggests that the petitions were a practice that made the gap between the claims of the bureaucracy to be a neutral guarantor of economic governance and its reality as a punitive system of command all too explicit. In their efforts to cross the boundary between the state and society in the form of the petition, workers were forced to confront the hollowness of the claims to legitimacy of the bureaucracy. Paradoxically, railway officials had created the space for such an experience of dissonant hiatus by adapting European practices of Taylorist worker welfare into the "Indian" idiom of the petition. The Railway Board aimed to capture the interests and affections of workers, but it succeeded only in turning the witnessing of the scandals of discipline into a public discourse.

DESPOTISM AND WELFARE: LATE COLONIAL AND POSTCOLONIAL CIVIL SOCIETY

The contradictory mixture of Taylorist welfare and colonial hierarchy seen in the railway bureaucracy in 1930–47 did not disappear with independence. There is a strong family resemblance between late colonial practices and developments aimed to rebuild the railways into a national enterprise. Racial distinctions were removed, but workplace hierarchies and disciplinary procedures continued to have a colonial stamp. In 1947, the report of the Indian Railway Inquiry Committee looked for ways to reform the railway bureaucracy in an effort to remove all traces of its colonial past. The railway officers who were consulted complained of recent legislation that had made it more difficult to summarily dismiss and fine subordinate workers. They argued that the railways should not be subject to the recent Payment of Wages Act, which protected workers from reductions to lower posts, fines, and dismissal, and that "supervisors should be vested with a power to inflict prompt punishment for minor offences."[56] These recommendations were put into effect. From 1953 to 1955, the Ministry of Railways carried out an investigation into corruption on the railways. As a result of this, Vigilance Departments and secret networks of spies were set up to report on the personal wealth, habits, and suspect practices of all railway staff and their families. The investigative committee also argued that, in the service of stamping out corruption, the power to impose swift punishments on employees should be delegated as widely as possible within the organization.[57] In this inquiry and in the Vigilance Departments, the state railways reappropriated the moral critique of the petitions and unions in the service of sacrifice for the greater national good. Yet they simultaneously re-created colonial hierarchies in the workplace. In fact, they institutionalised them and made them more dispersed throughout the bureaucracy. Vigilance Departments would officially take over the unofficial role of the old, colonial railway police in scrutinizing the private and public behavior of employees. In addition, every railway officer would also have the power of the old agent to summarily dismiss and judge the fitness of employees under him. In this context, the growth of political and democratic rights was shadowed by the institutionalization and dispersal of colonial hierarchies. It is perhaps not surprising, then, that in my ethnographic work at the Eastern Railway headquarters, the moral language of critique forged through the process of petition writing also lives on. In the final, short ethnographic section of my chapter, I will address the fate of this witnessing of bureaucratic violence as part of contemporary accounts of national economics.

Inside the offices of Eastern Railway headquarters in Calcutta, regular procedure is enacted in a medium of transparent, mundane orders guided by standardized rules and regulations. Yet anyone who enters the offices also encounters an overwhelming atmosphere of despotic authority. As one waits to be instructed to sit; listens to barked conversations on the phone in Hindi, punctuated by English swear words; and watches clerks enter, eyes downcast, and then wait often for an hour for attention, the atmosphere is tense. In spite of their absence from regular procedure, petitions continue to be written informally in the guise of letters to superior officers. Outside the offices, in back corridors and stairs gathered around paan and cha stalls, clerks tell tales of ruthless authority. To give you a sense of the tales, I will recount some of the stories of violent discipline told to me by Mr. Basu, a personnel librarian.

When I met Mr. Basu, he was in his thirties and had been demoted to his job as a librarian after having worked as a clerk in the Vigilance Department at Eastern Railway headquarters. His father and grandfather had both worked on the railways. His present job, he claimed, had not been one that he had sought. One of his fellow workers in the Vigilance Department had accused him of taking bribes; nothing was proved, so he was let off lightly and given the less important job of librarian. Mr. Basu was bitter about this experience, insisting that the Vigilance Department existed merely to persecute the poor who could not pay them off. The railway headquarters were filled for Mr. Basu with many examples of this injustice. One day he pointed to the man who served tea under one of the staircases and insisted that this man had been a high-level officer, who falsely accused of bribery, had begged the authorities for at least the position of serving tea. As we walked back to his office through one of the back corridors, he added conspiratorially that in the evening no one wanted to work near here, because a man falsely accused of corruption had shot himself in this place, and at night you could still hear the shot ringing out.

Satish was in love with one of the clerks from an adjoining office, Lolita, but lived in fear that other, jealous workers would find out. He would only meet and talk with her outside of the offices. He feared that other workers would spread rumors that he was immoral, that he took bribes and spent them on prostitutes, to sabotage their relationship and to bring him to the attention of the Vigilance Department again. In his position as personnel librarian, Satish had a constant stream of visitors to his office, railway workers from all over Bengal and Bihar. They had been dismissed and came to consult the books in his library and to ask him for help in writing "petitions." Satish presented himself as an expert in drawing up these letters and in "fixing" new posts for people. As I got to know Satish better over a couple of years, problems in his relationship with Lolita developed (her parents disapproved), and people started to spread rumors about him in the offices. One day I showed him an old petition—a particularly "mad" one whose author, driven to his wits' end from years of writing to the agent, presented himself as Prince Albert and had enclosed poems that he said Queen Victoria had written to him. Satish laughed and said that soon, he, too, would be writing petitions like that to the divisional manager. He then told me a ghost story, which I had heard from many other clerks: At night, the railway protection force guarding the building heard the sound of *ghazals* (Urdu couplets about loss and love set to music) and the laughter of women coming from the British replica of a Mughal dome that covered the divisional manager's office at the top of the building. This, he said, was the ghost of the Mughal *darbars* (gathering of people in the presence of authority) that used to take place on the site on which the railway headquarters were built. In this story, the colonial image of the despotism of previous rulers collapsed into the Raj past and into the present of national economics in one condensed image. Satish's tales of violent discipline, of the suffusion into his working and private life of rumors and paranoia, revive all the language of the colonial railway petitions.

Satish's ghost story, which suggests continuity between his personal dilemmas and a past of colonial governance, is more than an evocative end piece for my account of the practice of petitioning in the colonial railway bureaucracy. It suggests that the everyday state as he experiences it in the railway headquarters is far too close to the violence and inequalities of colonial rule. In one of the largest bureaucracies in India, the postcolonial growth of workers' rights and democratic institutions has left little mark on personal interactions. Similarly, these rights are not the point of origin of the Vigilance Departments or of the powers of railway officers. Quite clearly, forms of colonial governmentality and responses to it continue to develop within contemporary Indian institutions as eerie, disturbing presences. This suggests more broadly that postcolonial civil society in Indian and other contexts needs to be understood as a hybrid descendant of Taylorist welfare and colonial hierarchy.

CONCLUSION: PETITIONING AND "OTHERS"

This analysis of a colonial archive of petitions has wider implications for theoretical models of disciplinary forms of governance and understandings of the modern state. Since the 1980s, historians of Europe have singled out petitions as a peculiarly rich kind of documentary source.[58] They have argued that petitions do not just reflect social relationships; they materially constitute ties between government and its subjects. They suggest that, in the exchange of petitions, a certain kind of hierarchical bond is established between ruler and ruled that helps to consolidate the existence, seductive attraction, and reach of centralized state forms.[59] Yet it has also been noted that the tie of petitioning eventually breaks, in part because of the contradictory dialectic of deference and defiance present in the act of writing such documents. Petitions have often become the locus for demands for other kinds of political rights.[60] The restrictions of their form frequently sow a seed of discontent that contributes to the emergence of new relationships between state and society mediated by a public sphere. Other arguments suggest that petitions are superseded by the growth of administrative institutions that regulate the subjectivity and family life of the populace.[61] The consensus is that petitioning is eventually displaced by the increase in other kinds of political rights and institutions.[62] Historians suggest that petitioning is a peripheral, anachronistic right that is an exception to the norm. Yet from the perspective of the colonial situation of the Indian railways, the continuance of the right to petition looks much more significant. As petitioning is a fundamentally hierarchical form, we need to ask in all contexts who—what categories of people—come under its purview and why these categories of people are not defined as under normal rules of redress. These are important questions, because, as in the Indian railways, those who petition are in some way defined as essentially distinct from citizens with generalized rights. Those who are made to petition fall into a different category that, through contrast, helps to constitute the citizen with wider access to and a less supplicant relationship with justice. An analytical focus on petitioning has the potential to reveal the continuing violent and despotic face of states with democratic and disciplinary institutions when they deal with those who are marked as other. It is highly significant that in the United States, the right to petition Congress for the redress of grievances is most widely used for immigration cases.[63] Individuals who do not fit the normalized notion of citizens, often because of political affiliation, race, or unconventional family arrangements, are brought into a supplicant relation with democratic institutions. In more general terms, we need to recognize that petitioning as a form contributes to the ghostly continuance of despotic, personalized, and omnipotent power within the institutions of the modern state.

NOTES

1 For examples of economic analyses of the railways that emphasize the arrival of capitalism in an alien social landscape, see Hurd, "Railways." For de-

bates about railway economy in a Marxist frame, see Das Gupta, "Capital Investment and Transport Modernisation in Colonial India." On technology transfer, see Headrick, *The Tentacles of Progress*. On managerial issues and capitalism, see Hurd, *Building the Railways of the Raj, 1850–1900*.

2 Agent's Record Room, Eastern Railway, Kolkata (hereafter, ARR), Petition Files (AE) (1930–1947), AE763/4, 40.

3 *Proceedings of the Railway Conference*, 20.

4 *Handbook of Rules and Regulations for All Departments of the East Indian Railway*, 175, 179.

5 "Staff Councils and Welfare Committees," *Railway Department: Labour A Proceedings: Case 3-L/1–15*, October 1929, India Office Library, London, 9.

6 Ibid., 15.

7 "Rules Regulating the Discharge and Dismissal of State Non-Gazetted Railway Servants," in *East Indian Railway Rules for Employees*, 31.

8 Mitchell, *The Wheels of Ind*, 63, 67.

9 *Memorandum by the Railway Board to the Royal Commission on Labour*, 189.

10 ARR, 12 April 1934, AE763/5, 124.

11 Ibid., 4 January 1935, AE518/1, 53.

12 Ibid., 16 September 1930, AE578, 15.

13 Ibid., 1 July 1930, AE763/3, 67.

14 Ibid., 29 August 1935, AE578, 105.

15 Ibid., 1 July 1930, AE763/3.

16 Ibid., 6 April 1928, AE1205, 43.

17 Ibid.

18 Ibid., 23 November 1933, AE1386/6, 102.

19 Against Discharge by Subordinate Staff, ibid., 2/9/31, AE1386/4, Appeals, 89.

20 Miscellaneous Correspondence, ibid., 11/6/34, AE763/6,164.

21 Appeals against Discharge by Subordinate Staff, ibid., 1/3/32, AE386/5, 100.

22 See Price, *Kingship and Political Practice in Colonial India*. *Shakti* is the Sanskrit-derived term used for power in both religious and political contexts. *Dharma* is the Sanskrit-derived term used for a notion of correct cosmological order that is guaranteed in part by correct behavior, in particular the conduct of rulers.

23 Chatterjee, "History as Self-Representation." *Nawabi* is the term for bureaucrats who worked for the wide range of Mughal-influenced states that ruled India in the eighteenth century.

24 "Rules Regulating the Discharge and Dismissal of State Non-Gazetted Railway Servants," in *East Indian Railway Rules for Employees*, 31.

25 Letter from Chief Operating Superintendent to Agent East Indian Railway, ARR, 18/9/25, AE 230.

26 Ibid., 15.

27 *Memorandum by the Railway Board to the Royal Commission on Labour*, 151.

28 ARR, 12/5/34, AE763/5, 124.

29 Ibid., 28/11/33, AE1386/6, 91.

30 Ibid., AE763/3, 98.

31 Ibid., 8/9/30, AE763/3, 103.

32 Ibid.

33 Ibid., 24 June 1931, AE763/5, 78.

34 Chatterjee, "History as Self-Representation."

35 ARR, 26 February 1934, AE763/5, 85.

36 Ibid., AE763/5, 213.

37 Ibid., AE763/5, 34.

38 Ibid.

39 Ibid., 18 July 1933, AE763/5, 67.

40 Ibid., AE763/5, 34.

41 Ibid., AE763/3, 41; ibid., AE763/4, 25.

42 Ibid., 12 May 1934, AE763/5, 124.

43 Ibid., AE763/4, 25.

44 Ibid., 26 April 1934, AE763/6, 115.

45 *Indian State Railways Magazine*, vol. 1, no. 1, October 1927.

46 From (in order of quotation) ARR, December 1927, AE761/1, 87; ibid., 11 March 1933, AE1386/6, 68; ibid., AE763/423.

47 Ibid., 8 November 1935, AE1386/6.

48 Ibid., AE763/3, n.d. (probably September 1930).

49 Ibid., 27 June 1930, AE763/3, 67.

50 Ibid., 5 May 1930, AE763/3, 89.

51 Ibid., 8 September 1931, AE578, 192.

52 Ibid., AE763/3, 101; ibid., 15 July 1931, AE1478/3, 200.

53 Ibid., 11 June 1934, AE763/6, 164.

54 Ibid.

55 Ibid.

56 *Report of the Indian Railway Inquiry Committee*, 161–62.

57 *Report of the Railway Corruption Enquiry Committee, 1953–55*.

58 See Davis, *Fiction in the Archives*; Foucault, "The Life of Infamous Men."

59 See Forge and Foucault, *Le désordre des familles*; Nubola, "Supplications between Politics and Justice"; Te Brake, *Shaping History*; Zaret, *Origins of Democratic Culture*.

60 See Tilly, *Popular Contention in Great Britain 1758–1834*; Zaret, *Origins of Democratic Culture*.

61 See Forge and Foucault, *Le désordre des familles*.

62 See Lunn and Day, "Deference and Defiance"; Nedostup and Liang, "Begging the Sages of the Party-State"; Ota, "Private Matters."

63 See Ota, "Private Matters."

SUSAN O'BRIEN

※

Spirit Discipline

Gender, Islam, and Hierarchies of Treatment

in Postcolonial Northern Nigeria

In December 1995, as a group of adolescent girls at a secondary school in Kano, Nigeria, celebrated the completion of their exams with late-night singing and dancing on the grounds of their Goron Dutse campus, an old woman appeared from the bush and asked them to stop their revelry and quiet down so that she and her family could get some rest. According to the popular story that circulated throughout the city in the months that followed, the girls responded to the old woman's admonition with disrespect and mockery, dancing with even greater abandon and jeering at her with the nonsense words, "Sumbuka! Sumbuka!"[1] as she slowly retreated back into the bush from which she had come. That night, and in the days and weeks to follow, a majority of these young women fell sick in an episode of mass possession that pitched them into bouts of "madness" (*hauka*) that were at once comic and frightening. With mixed bemusement and horror, witnesses recounted scenes in which the affected women burst into lewd dances, alternately laughing and crying uncontrollably, or collapsed into states of paralysis or mute apathy. The Sumbuka "disease," as it became known popularly, proved to be contagious, and soon it became apparent that the mere fact of being female made one susceptible to Sumbuka's spread. Outbreaks at two other secondary schools in the Kano area were reported, and Sumbuka began "catching" girls and women as they visited their afflicted sisters and friends at homes and hospitals throughout the city.

The behavior exhibited by Sumbuka's young victims was not unknown to Kano residents. It was easily recognized as spirit possession, a condition popularized by the public performances of *'yan bori* (members of the *bori* spirit-possession sect) and made familiar by popular knowledge of the major spirit personalities in bori's pantheon. Yet mass schoolgirl possession of this kind was, by all accounts, new to Kano, and it precipitated a minor crisis among government health officials and school administrators, who sought both to contain the untoward publicity of the outbreak and to find an effective treatment for the girls' ongoing illnesses without endorsing a non-Islamic therapeutic response. The expertise of 'yan bori and, to a lesser extent, *bokaye* (Hausa herbalists) in dealing with spirit-caused illnesses has been a contentious matter for several centuries, since the 1804–10 jihad of Shehu Usman 'dan Fodio consolidated an Islamic state encompassing most of present-day northern Nigeria. Not only are the healing methods of 'yan bori condemned as *shirk* (associating others with God), one of the most serious religious infractions in Islam, but in contemporary Kano the bori lifestyle is associated with poverty, illiteracy, and moral transgression, making initiation into the sect an unlikely solution for the affected girls, who came primarily from privileged and respected families. While most Muslim Hausa are quick to acknowledge the existence of spirits as creations of Allah on the basis of well-known Quranic passages and the traditions of the Prophet (*hadith*), forms of involvement with the spirit world index distinctions of class, education, and gender in Kano society. Sufi religious figures are known to interact with and even marry *aljannu* (spirits), and these relationships are viewed as both symbols and sources of their *baraka* (charisma).[2] Yet public possession by and sacrifice to aljannu is both socially and religiously suspect and closely identified with the activities of 'yan bori.

Hausa *malamai* (Islamic scholars/teachers) in Kano, some of whom were directly affected by the Sumbuka affair through their own daughters' illnesses, were forced to respond to the public distress as expressed in a popular rhyming song:

Sumbuka ya shigo gari	Sumbuka entered the town
Asibiti babu magani	The hospital has no medicine [for it]
Boka ya gaji	The *boka* [Hausa herbalist] grows tired
Malam sai ka taimaka!	Malam you must help us!

In a short time, various Sufi malamai began experimenting with methods of Islamic exorcism, based on instructive texts from Saudi Arabia and Egypt. In addition, they launched an educational campaign stressing a Muslim's obligations to convert aljannu to Islam, expel them when they interfere in human lives, and avoid the heretical healing practices of bori practitioners. These methods of exorcism involve the recitation of specific Quranic verses and an aggressive, even violent, approach to the possessing spirits and their human hosts, in sharp contrast to bori adepts who establish lifelong relationships with the afflicting spirits to prevent recurring illness. Yet the newly adopted Islamic methods mirror bori therapeutics and depart from the most common Islamic approaches to spirit afflictions in northern Nigeria in that they induce possession and negotiate with spirits as part of the healing process.

Kano malamai report that this form of Islamic treatment, called *rukiyya*, was as old as Islam itself[3] and that the term was derived from *rakani*, the Arabic word for treatment, which means using prayer from the Qur'an and other hadith in the treatment of illness and in particular to expel evil spirits from the body. (In Hausa, the process is referred to as *cire iskoki*, to pull out the spirits.) Some malamai I interviewed reported that they had been employing these methods quietly in their own homes for as long as twelve years and used them to address spirit-caused problems experienced by their wives, female relatives, and neighborhood women.[4] But all noted the dramatic increase in rukiyya healing and of spirit-induced problems in Kano in the wake of the Sumbuka episode. Indeed, these methods rapidly gained broader popularity among a predominantly female clientele, including a large number of married housewives in the old city, who began flocking to malamai with newly established practices. Significantly, these new practitioners initiated the institutionalization of rukiyya practice into a clinical format, with standardized fees and intake forms that documented the symptoms, treatment, and outcome of each patient's illness.[5]

Both the possession episode and the Islamic therapeutic response captured the public imagination in Kano, particularly after malamai began to circulate cassette recordings of their healing sessions and lectures on spirit exorcism in markets throughout the city. Unlike the widespread skepticism about the veracity of bori adepts' possession, no one seemed to question the authenticity of the spirit voices recorded by Hausa malamai, the potential harm those spirits threatened, or the importance and legitimacy of the malamai's work of exorcism. In radically expanding this ritual arena for dealing with spirit afflictions, one with all of the trappings of Islamic piety and learning, these malamai began to reconfigure established belief and practice concerning human relationships to the spirit world. Indeed, their stated goals were even more ambitious, as they touted their capacity to regulate both public health and the moral or ethical underpinnings of social behavior through their control of the spirits.

In this chapter, I suggest how, through possession illness and rukiyya healing, a group of Sufi malamai and their patients generate a narrative of community that articulates and responds to a sense of communal crisis, brought about by both state-driven modernization and the virulence of anti-Sufi reformers. The rhetoric and practice of rukiyya produce and reinforce categories and boundaries of difference that are central to their sense of community.[6] In the ritual of rukiyya, efforts to convert and expel non-Muslim spirits and to admonish and correct the misbehavior of Muslim spirits produce a social dramaturgy in which the difference between men and women, believer and non-believer (Christian, pagan), is explicitly articulated and performed. The therapeutic process targets Hausa women as the symbolic markers of difference between the second two groups, "as symbols and agents of change, that must be brought into line with new orthodoxies."[7] Rukiyya thus focuses attention on the permeable bodies of women as the boundaries of community that must be vigilantly defended against foreign (spirit) penetration and attempts to control women's behavior to minimize the risk of this threat. In the process of "disciplining" the offending spirits and their human hosts with physical violence, malamai assert their own authority in this critical healing realm, attempt to reinterpret the experience of illness for the affected women, and potentially reformulate categories of difference like gender, religion, and class. Rukiyya targets female bodies as particularly vulnerable to spirit intrusion and thus in need of corporeal discipline, perpetuating a normalizing process with deep historical roots in this area. But the physical violence of rukiyya is channeled into a completely new idiom of biomedical treatment that publicly marks girls and women as a different category of person, as the "inadequate subjects" (see the introduction and Steven Pierce's essay in this volume) of modern Islamic society that require the use of new governing technologies focused on the individual.

The specific contours of rukiyya practice reflect the divisive ground of contemporary northern Islamic identity politics. In professing a textual approach and a familiarity with transnational Islamic linkages, young rukiyya scholars distance themselves from an older generation of Sufi malamai and demonstrate the influence of Wahhabi reformers on mainstream Muslim identification and self-presentation in northern Nigeria. Yet, as a ritual practice, rukiyya bucks the trend toward a more individual mode of religiosity propounded by anti-Sufi reformers and reemphasizes the embeddedness of Muslim faith and practice in social relations and local cultural contexts. And because rukiyya focuses on the discipline of female bodies and behavior, it points to the centrality of questions about women's autonomy and mobility in the emergence of Islamic modernity.

ISLAM, MODERNIZATION, AND HAUSA CULTURAL ANXIETY

Religious conflict over therapeutic practice like that generated by Sumbuka has important historical precedents in Hausaland. When Fulani jihadists overthrew the Habe rulers of the Hausa city-states in the early nineteenth century, an important feature of their program of Islamic reform involved the transformation of local healing practices. The jihadists thus sought to destroy the spirit-based therapeutics of bori and supplant them with healing based on Islamic *materia medica* and Prophetic medicine.[8] Bori practice in the Hausa city-states was associated with female political leadership and provided a ritual healing arena of particular importance to women, and the jihadists' interest in Hausa healing can be viewed in part as an attempt to control female bodies and offset female political power in the Sokoto Caliphate.[9] The jihadists failed to transform Hausa therapeutic practices completely, however, and bori has survived to the present day, retaining special ritual importance for women. Moreover, the problem of spirit intervention in human lives continues to compromise male Islamic hegemony in northern Nigeria, sanctioning as it does alternative and independent life courses for afflicted women and sustaining indigenous healing practices based on the religious authority of spirit mediums. Yet the jihad did succeed in inserting an ideological emphasis on proper Muslim practice into definitions of the state and the individual's relation to it.

Since the oil-boom years of the 1970s, Sufi sociopolitical domination of northern Nigeria has been challenged by both anti-Sufi Islamic reformers and rapid modernization, which have made Western education and employment outside the home widely available to women for the first time. Scholars have pointed to the traumatic changes of the oil-boom years, and the gross inequities in the distribution of wealth to which it gave rise, in explaining the proliferation of Islamic movements and organizations since the 1970s.[10] Most significantly, the Wahhabi-inspired reformist group Izala[11] has challenged Muslim Hausa identity from within and provoked an intense public debate about the meaning of Islamic "orthodoxy"[12] that has often resulted in public violence.[13] In attacking the alleged aberrations of local Islamic practice, groups like Izala hope to bring Hausa Islam into conformity with a new, international basis of Islamic identity focused on Arab centers of power.[14] For many West African Muslims, Saudi Arabia in particular provides an appealing model of Islamic modernity, in which economic and technological development is achieved without the perceived moral decline of Western industrialized societies.[15]

One of the major changes accompanying the oil-boom years in Kano was the implementation of the Universal Primary Education (UPE) program in 1976, through which Western education became widely available in northern Nigeria for the first time. In the north, Western secular education was layered on top of an Islamic base, and efforts to combine the two educational traditions in single institutions produced secondary schools for boys like the School for Arabic Studies in Kano, established in 1976. The Women's Arabic Teachers' College, the school at which the Sumbuka incident originally occurred, was the first institution of this type for girls, established in 1978. While many Hausa fathers, particularly those who are themselves well educated, have supported their daughters in obtaining an education beyond the primary level, it is also clear that many are anxious and ambivalent about the results. Barkindo suggests that Western education for women was, for many Hausa men, one of the more troubling aspects of the Western course of modernization:

> More disturbing for some, however, have been the increasing number of western-educated girls who have remained unmarried. In one of his Ramadan sermons of 1989, Shaikh Isa Waziri, one of the leading *'ulama* of Kano, called attention to this development and called on well-to-do men to take extra wives as a partial solution to this "calamity," as he referred to it.[16]

The major gains in education for Hausa girls and women in the past twenty-five years have produced conflicts and anxiety for Muslim Hausa women, as well. Many women express ambivalence and guilt about the adult education classes they attend, which they see as interfering with their more important obligations as wives, mothers, and good Muslim women. While government radio and television campaigns urge women to attend adult education programs, the social atmosphere of heightened religiosity and conservatism created by the reformists places a particularly heavy burden on women, whose behavior, physical appearance, and public visibility are scrutinized and critiqued most closely. Fatima Lawson's interviews with women at one such adult education program in Kano suggests some of the misgivings they have about their own education:

—It is quite difficult as Muslims who want to follow the rules of Islam to be in a school where religion is not properly emphasized and that could make you lose face with Allah and not realize it.... [I]f you want to be a good Muslim, it will be hard to be in an establishment like this.... I mean, an institution that is created by Christians.

—The rules that govern these schools are foreign to us. I don't know why men are allowed to intermingle with women that are not related to them in any way.

—I think seclusion is the most trying aspect of our situation here, because if you want to practice seclusion in the right sense of the word, you should not come out of your house.[17]

As these reflections by married women indicate, the life expectations of Muslim Hausa women and their lived realities are changing at a much slower pace than are their educational opportunities. As Barbara Callaway and Lucy Creevey suggest, despite changing patterns of female education, "a girl is still expected to marry, to marry young, and to marry a husband chosen for her; to be submissive to him; and to have co-wives whether or not that is her wish. She will have between five and fifteen children and probably will be divorced more than once."[18] A Hausa woman will most likely also live her married, childbearing years in some form of seclusion (*kulle*). The student body of the Women's Arabic Teachers' College at Goron Dutse is composed primarily of the daughters of Kano's elite families, most of whom are destined, despite their education, to be married off to a husband of their father's choosing, in many cases to a much older man of status, and to spend their lives as respectable wives and co-wives in conditions of material comfort but limited personal freedom. As a group, these young women are perfectly positioned to experience the social contradictions that face women who have greater opportunities for mobility and education yet must still conform to conservative social expectations of a woman's life course.

A secondary school for girls in Kano is thus a site of considerable social tension, one in which the "contradictions of modernity" are experienced with full force. Several recent studies of outbreaks of female possession in the "developing" world persuasively link these episodes to periods of rapid modernizing change and the new gender inequalities they produce.[19] Some of these cases have occurred in factories and have been described as "rituals of rebellion" by exploited Third World women thrown into alien and highly repressive capitalist relations of production.[20] The vast majority of documented cases of "mass hysteria," however, have occurred in school settings in "an atmosphere of long-term pre-existing tension."[21] In all of these cases, it is clear that the school emerges as the principal site for mass female possession, or "hysteria," precisely because it typifies or serves as the vehicle for disruptive modernizing change. As modernist institutions focused on rationality and learning, these schools are engaged in the project of "disenchanting the world" and encouraging the emergence of individual rational autonomy. The ironic outbreak of dissociative histrionics among girls in these settings could be viewed as an embodied expression of stress and conflict,[22] or, alternatively, as a symbolic rejection of the schools' efforts to disenchant the world. Certainly, the spirit-possession idiom has been widely acknowledged as an outlet for dissent and resistance to social and political power, albeit one which does not ultimately undermine dominant structures or authority.[23] The fact that these pressures and reactions occur within a process understood as modernization demonstrates how modernizing and state institutions serve to create women as inadequate modernist subjects.

The contradictions between the expectations of and opportunities for Hausa women in Kano, heightened by the unique pressures of the Western educational setting, go a long way toward explaining the immediate cause of possession outbreaks at secondary schools for girls and adult education classes for women. But the broader female response to rukiyya healing reflects a much older division between male and female religious worlds and their different understandings of social reality and their own lives as being mediated by spirits. Indeed, as in many parts of the developing world,[24] the symbolic identity of women in Hausa culture is in part expressed through susceptibility to spirit possession. Both the Sumbuka possession and the Islamic response can be seen as revealing contributions to ongoing debates about the proper place of women in Muslim Hausa society. As such, they are less straightforward than arguments made, for example, by female activists who explicitly debate Muslim women's appropriate social and religious roles in magazine publications or political communiques. The perspectives of the women who flock to the Islamic rukiyya healers are more difficult to decipher, framed as they are in the language of physical distress. Possession illness tends to mystify agency and obscure intent, but it also demands a response, and it is here that the affected women are forcing change in religious practice and extending the terms of existing debates about women's roles and obligations in Muslim Hausa society. And they are doing so through a form of popular consciousness, possession illness, which is far more accessible to the majority of Kano women than the Federation of Muslim Women's Associations of Nigeria (FOMWAN) feminist interpretation of Islamic doctrine, a scholarly exercise that requires literacy in Arabic, Hausa, or English.[25]

GENDERED CONFLICTS, ISLAMIC COMMUNITY: RUKIYYA HEALING AND THE DISCIPLINING OF "OTHER" BODIES

Rukiyya practitioners have capitalized on the Sumbuka crisis to call attention to spirit possession as a problem of much greater magnitude and concern than the unprecedented cases of schoolgirl possession might suggest[26] and to legitimize a practice that has been subject to debate and controversy among Muslim scholars in Kano.[27] In an audiotaped lecture titled "Healing Human Beings (*Garkuwar 'dan Adam*),"[28] Malam Chedi, a scholarly advocate of rukiyya, explains:

> There is a cure for every illness in the Holy Quran. What cannot be cured by the Quran cannot be cured. The Quran provides cures to illnesses of the heart—disbelief, cruelty, selfishness—as well as illnesses of the body. Most of the illnesses of the human body, up to 90 percent are caused by the spirits, and are meant to prevent you from worshipping God fully. Let a man not forget that he has a great rival in Satan, who never tires of sending these spirits to block his path to God.

He goes on to assert the efficacy of rukiyya treatment in dealing with both emotional and physical illnesses that remain beyond the reach of the Western biomedicine provided at government hospitals. With bold claims like these, and with their nearly exclusive focus on spirit affliction as the cause of both religious indiscipline and physical illness, the contemporary champions of rukiyya in Kano are staking out distinctive ideological ground that bears contextualization within the complex religious politics of contemporary Kano.

In theory and practice, they explicitly distinguish themselves from the practitioners of both Western biomedicine and bori healing. And implicitly, their conflation of medical and spiritual discourses puts them at odds with the approach of Wahhabi reformers in Nigeria who embrace the benefits of modern biomedical treatment and have even established clinics in Kano to make these services available to their followers.[29] Yet rukiyya practice also clearly draws on the methods and resources of all three of these groups. Hence, it incorporates both the clinical format of Western biomedicine and the induced possession and dialogue with spirits characteristic of bori while also proclaiming reliance on foreign texts made available in Kano by Wahhabi reformers in the past decade or so.[30] In their familiarity with both Wahhabi classics and a whole corpus of more "modern" texts being published in Saudi and Egypt, this younger cohort of Kano ʿulama distance themselves from an older generation of Sufi scholars who remain skeptical about the knowledge and authority derived from books available to all in the market place.[31] Some prominent older Sufi scholars like Sheik Isa Waziri have publicly criticized the practice of rukiyya, while its younger practitioners reply that it is ignorance of the texts in use that makes the older generation wary of their methods.[32] Indeed, many local Sufi scholars still view the secrecy of prescriptions found in *kundi* (a malam's bundle of loose papers containing his secret prayers and charms) to be critical to their efficacy. Moreover, these same scholars view the close relationship between scholar and student as the only proper context for transmitting Islamic knowledge. For them, the impersonal nature of marketplace transactions render Islamic texts that are acquired in that way impotent; the secret knowledge transmitted from teacher to student is only effective if one has been granted permission (*izne*) to use it.

Rukiyya practitioners are thus implicated in local debates about Islamic authority. Like the conflicts between Izala and Sufi defenders of local Islamic practices, their rhetoric and practice can be viewed as part of the struggle over who defines Islamic "orthodoxy" in contemporary Kano. Unlike the doctrinal debates that have characterized much of Sufi-Izala conflict, however, and in which positions are clearly delineated and oppositional, the embrace and expansion of rukiyya healing in Kano cannot be read in such stark confrontational terms. The position of the scholars in these debates and the implications of the healing regime they create is decidedly ambivalent and inchoate, reflecting the increasingly sensitive political ground of Islamic identity politics in Kano and the wariness of many well-educated scholars to identify their sectarian affiliations and denounce other groups. Clearly, rukiyya practitioners are influenced by the visions of Islamic modernity propagated by anti-Sufi reforms. They thus make their sources of knowledge and authority transparent and provide their services within a modern clinical context that they claim is more efficient than existing Islamic healing methods. And they are eager to emphasize the importance of transnational intellectual linkages to their work.

Yet, if the "shift from Sufism to anti-Sufism entails a reorientation from a communal to an individualistic mode of religiosity, and seems to be more in tune with the rugged individualism of capitalist social relations,"[33] then contemporary rukiyya practice must be seen as a bulwark against this transition. As a healing and disciplinary regime, rukiyya is aimed at creating a narrative of belonging in which Islamic orthodoxy is defined in terms of Sufism and the clearest, least controversial shorthand for heterodoxy is bori. For nearly two centuries, bori practice has constituted the lowest-hanging fruit in local debates over proper Islamic practice. The crisis of schoolgirl possession has provided a fortuitous opportunity for the Muslim mainstream (Sufi malamai) to deflect attention away from the Wahhabi critique of Sufism by renewing their assault on bori miscreance.[34]

The development of Islamic exorcism can thus be viewed as the latest installment in the ongoing competition between Islamic and indigenous Hausa healers that has its roots in the nineteenth century and that originally served to marginalize female political and ritual authority. With the rapid development of an orthodox Islamic approach to possession, Hausa malamai have attempted to contain the subversive possibilities of bori practice in which spirit demands displace those of Islamic male authority. They are in fact explicit in defining their own healing practice in opposition to that of bori practitioners. As Sheikh Faruq Chedi, a well-respected Muslim scholar located in the old city, remarked:

> I want to draw your attention to the fact that what we are doing is in total contrast to bori, and it is set to destroy bori completely. Bori is not accepted in Islam.... Today people are suffering from many illnesses and the only way some people have thought to solve their problems is to visit 'yan bori. In our own view, we agree that whoever goes to a 'dan bori, he will lose three things. Number one he will lose his faith. He will lose his faith and he will then lose his money. You could lose all that you have without getting well ... and thirdly you will complicate your condition of health.[35]

Although malamai primarily condemn bori practitioners for their attention to the spirit world, they also condemn the lifestyle of bori adepts as contrary to Islamic norms of marriage, seclusion, and public separation of the sexes.[36] When a woman is initiated into bori, the spirits that are troubling her are identified, and a relationship of mutual aid is established with them in a seven- to fourteen-day celebratory ritual in which other women play key roles and in which the patient is surrounded by the network of bori adepts with whom she will come to share supportive social and economic ties. Often spirits prevent women from staying in their marital homes, from bearing children, or otherwise from conforming to gendered social expectations. Initiation into bori can be seen as an acknowledgment and acceptance of spirit intervention that also provides women with an independent economic base as healers. Well-established and popular female bori healers often remain unmarried and head households, receiving from their live-in initiates payment in both respect and a percentage of their earnings as bori performers and spirit mediums.

Although the methods of rukiyya stand in stark contrast to those of bori, as a healing practice rukiyya addresses most of the problems, social and physiological, that continue to make bori so popular among Muslim Hausa women. In systematizing and institutionalizing this form of treatment in Islamic health centers across Kano, Hausa malamai collapse the spatial and discursive divide between public and private that has marked the difference between male and female observance of Islam in Hausaland. Through the private, individualized treatment of rukiyya, malamai attempt to pattern female behavior and control female bodily comportment. The ritual produces its own strange paradoxes and contradictions. Hence, it provides transgressive spirits and their female hosts a rare voice in a public, Islamically pious setting, and furnishes the uncommon spectacle of unrelated adult Muslim men and women in close physical proximity, engaging in often vulgar verbal exchanges, albeit by spirit proxy. The profanity of the spirits' actions and language are in fact showcased in the healing ritual and their commodified audio recordings. These spirit trespasses serve both to obscure and naturalize the violence of this new disciplinary regime, for who could object to the punishment of such arrogant and intrusive spirits? The impropriety of the spirits' actions and words thus veil the violence of the malamai's therapeutic response.

In contrast to bori's strategy of ritually establishing lifelong relationships with spirits to effect a cure, Islamic exorcists attempt to expel spirits from their human hosts through intimidation and dialogue. By shouting powerful Quranic verses into the right ear of the afflicted woman, malamai call the spirits and then engage in an angry dialogue with them, attempting to convert them to Islam and persuade them to leave the woman in peace. Powerful *suras* (chapters from the Qur'an, of which there are 114) are used to "burn" intransigent spirits until they scream in pain and agree to the malamai's demands. The spirits' insolent or evasive responses often provoke malamai to physical violence in this dialogue, which includes slapping and punching the spirit hosts on the face, head, feet, and back. These sessions can thus be disturbing scenes as two or three malamai circle around the sick woman and smack, scream at, and insult her.

In one sense, the malamai's violence can be read as a ritual inscription of prevailing gender hierarchies, in which women's negative association with tradition is reinforced. Malamai explain women's susceptibility to spirits, for example, in terms of moral laxity and their inattention to Islamic prescriptions, in marked contrast to bori healers, who explain spirit attention in terms of inheritance or a spirit's love for an individual. When asked why he thought the majority of his patients—in his estimate, 95 percent—were women and children, Sheikh Faruq Chedi responded: "Women are very careless. They don't want to pray. They dress the way they want. They are only interested in ornamenting their bodies. They are careless about their religion. That is why the spirits enter easily into their bodies."[37] Rukiyya treatment certainly focuses attention on problematic female bodily comportment and behavior. The diagnostic form from the Dan Fodio Islamic Health Center in Dorayi, for example, lists nine behavioral recommendations for the afflicted women, which include the recitation of certain Quranic verses at morning and evening prayers, wearing the *hijab*[38] at all times, and refraining from watching television and videos or putting photos on the walls of their rooms. The injunction to wear the hijab at all times is particularly striking, given that this very conservative form of dress remains fairly uncommon in Kano.

Nevertheless, malamai's techniques go beyond counseling women simply to change their behavior, to be more pious and devout to avoid spirit attack. In fact, Islamic exorcism departs from earlier Islamic approaches to spirit attack in Hausaland and mirrors bori therapeutics in that malamai induce possession and negotiate with spirits as part of the healing process. Rukiyya therapeutics thus create an unusual new ritual healing arena in which the moral language and intent of Islamic reform converge with a realm of moral discourse animated by the action of spirits and the language of possession. The focus on negotiation with spirits suggests the malamai's perception of the futility of education or even confinement to the home in controlling unruly and disturbingly permeable female bodies. In fact, other common explanations that malamai cite for spirit attraction to women—their physical attractiveness or the fact that they stay at home more—serve to naturalize female susceptibility to the devious influence of spirits.

In expanding this healing arena, malamai are potentially opening a Pandora's box by allowing unpredictable spirits to perform and accepting that spirits prevent women from fulfilling their marital obligations, and even entice them into adulterous affairs. While malamai claim that "the devil and the spirits have no power over a person who is constantly reading the Holy Quran," their experiences in treating patients often reveal situations in which women are attacked by the spirits for reasons beyond their control. Observation of a number of Malam Chedi's healing sessions revealed that one woman was punished by a spirit because her father had inadvertently stepped on the spirit's baby and killed it; others were "charmed" by enemies or rivals who sent spirits to attack them through 'yan bori intermediaries. In these situations, the malamai clearly hold the spirits, not their afflicted patients, accountable for the harm done. And although malamai assert human authority over the spirit world, it is not at all clear that they have established that control in practice. They are in fact quick to point out that because spirits, like their human intermediaries, the *'yan bori*, tend to lie, cheat, and break their promises, they cannot be trusted and are difficult to outwit. Indeed, malamai reported cases in which spirits returned again and again to plague a woman after they had already agreed to depart. Scholars thus agree that only constant vigilance, prayer, and research can successfully counter the seemingly boundless "defensive mechanisms" of the spirits. Thus, Islamic methods of expulsion appear to be as contingent on the cooperation of the spirits as on a patient's piety and faith.

Rukiyya practitioners appeal to a shared Hausa historical experience and common cultural ground that distinguishes them from Muslims in Saudi Arabia or Iran. Hence, they direct attention to the persistence of spirit power and create a forum in which well-known historical personalities from the bori pantheon have a chance to perform.[39] One is tempted to view these performances, in which "untrained" women are ridden by "untamed" spirits, as potentially anarchic and subversive forums for spirits to challenge Islamic authority. Yet I suggest that the real significance of the malamai's employment or cooptation of the possession idiom in their treatment is that it makes their claims to control and authority over both women and the spirit world far more popularly compelling and hence more effective than, for example, Izala's rigid condemnations of Sufism.

In fact, the dialogues between spirits and malamai produced in rukiyya sessions can be read as narratives of inclusion that reinforce, through their emphasis on defense and protection against intrusive spirits, a sense of common identity and unity among their participants. This point can be more fully understood through a close examination of a single healing session recorded by Malam Chedi and his assistants in October 1996.[40] In this case, the patient was a young woman named Fatima whose first marriage had ended in divorce and who was having trouble marrying again. She also suffered from headaches, stomachaches, and frequent bad dreams. The session began, as always, with readings from the Holy Qur'an intended to elicit the response of any spirits inhabiting the body of the patient. After establishing that the first spirit to appear on Fatima was named Sarkin Duna—a royal leader among the spirits, as indicated by his title of Sarki (king)—the malamai proceeded, as they always did, to try to determine whether the offending spirit was Muslim or not. From there, they sought to convince him to convert.

M: Are you a Muslim?
DUNA: No.
M: So you are an unbeliever.
DUNA: Yes, of course.
M: I want you to accept Islam.
DUNA: In Islam there is no *girma* [status, prestige].
M: You can retain your girma if you become a Muslim; nobody will stop your leadership.
DUNA: I want to become a Muslim but in Islam there is no wine and no women, and these are my favorite things. I cannot do without them.
M: Of course there's no wine or women in Islam, but if you accept Islam, God will provide you with something more sweet than alcohol and women.

Islam is a simple religion. God created Adam and the spirits so that they would worship him, and that is why we want you to accept Islam. Accept Islam and you will become our brother, and God will forgive you all of your sins.

The malamai quickly convinced Duna to accept Islam, to recite the profession of faith, and to choose a new Muslim name. He chose the name Umar, and they continued:

> M: Your presence in the body of this woman is not good because you are causing her to suffer and prevent her from getting married. We want you to leave the body of this woman.
> UMAR: It is a difficult thing.
> M: It is simpler than accepting Islam and you accepted Islam. If you leave her body, God will provide you with something better than her body.
> UMAR: I swear it is difficult.
> M: Why did you enter into her?
> U: I saw her and fell in love with her.
> M: Umar, please, how many are you in her body?
> UMAR: We are seven.
> M: Are they all Muslims?
> UMAR: There are Muslims among them.
> M: So there are some unbelievers in her body. Umar, what we want you to do is to totally submit to the way of God. So you will refrain from drinking alcohol and chasing women. If you do this, God will put you in his paradise where there is alchohol sweeter than that on earth and women more beautiful than those of this world. God doesn't want to put you in his hellfire, that is why he decided to put you on the right path.

The malamai then tried to convince Umar to use his leadership status among the other spirits to convert them to Islam and to send them out of Fatima. They then secured Umar's oath to leave Fatima, never return, and never enter the body of another Muslim. Once Umar departed, the malamai briefly checked in with Fatima, who complained of a pain in her leg, and began moaning in a deep guttural voice. The malamai asked "Who are you? Who are you?" in an angry tone until the spirit Sunusi identified himself. When asked if he was a Muslim, Sunusi replied that he worshipped the sun, like his parents before him. The malamai tried to convince Sunusi to convert to Islam like his leader, Sarkin Duna. But Sunusi replied that he did not understand Islam as Sarki seemed to, and he thus could not embrace it as his own religion. A very long dialogue ensued between the malamai and Sunusi about the tenets and verifiability of Islamic truth. The malamai talked themselves into a logical quagmire by suggesting that because Sunusi had never been near the sun and because the sun disappears from view at night and behind clouds during the day, it is not worthy of worship and cannot in fact protect its devotees. Sunusi was quick to point out the obvious shortcoming of their argument:

s: But you didn't see your Prophet, and you don't even see the God you are worshipping. But I can see the sun. And the Quran you read, how can you prove to me that it is truly revealed by God, because I know there are many books of its kind, like the one used by the Christians. How can I know that this is the true book revealed by God? I want to be convinced of who is right between you, me, and the Christians—who is on the right path?

m: Sunusi, thank you for your question. Now, you said that you can see the sun but we cannot see God. Now, I believe that you have sense.

s: Yes, I can say that I have.

m: But Sunusi, have you ever seen your sense?

s: No.

m: Does that prove its absence?

s: No, it doesn't.

m: Your sense is less powerful than God, but it cannot be seen. I think now you will agree that God exists. Now about the books you asked me to differentiate between. God did reveal a book to the Christians, but they changed it, and that is why it does not have power over everything the way that the Quran does. And if you read the Holy Quran you will know that it is more important and more powerful than any book, and you will be convinced that it is from God. It is the same book everywhere you go in the world, whereas the Bible differs from place to place. And second, if I read the Bible to you, you will not feel anything, but if I read to you from the Holy Quran you will feel something, you will burn. If it were not from God, you would not feel as if you were melting when we read.

During the next half hour of the session Sunusi was alternately confrontational and evasive about his commitment to convert, and the malamai responded with anger and violence to his reticence. In the course of the interrogation, however, they discovered that Fatima was "given" to Sunusi as a gift that he claimed that he "could not refuse" and that he had given Fatima food and drink that contained charms commissioned by other humans through the work of 'yan bori. After eliciting Sunusi's promise to leave Fatima for good, the malamai continued their search for the origins of Fatima's problems. One of the next spirits who arrived was thirty-year-old Saudatu, who identified herself as a Muslim and reported that she had first entered into Fatima when the girl was taken to her first matrimonial home. She said that she had entered Fatima through her vagina and had been staying in her back since then. When asked what problems she had been causing Fatima, Saudatu replied that she was in the habit of "inviting our men to her." Although the malamai were initially alarmed and indignant that a fellow Muslim would invite male spirits to have sex with a married woman, in the end they were conciliatory and simply secured her promise to leave, explaining that, "since you are a Muslim like us, we don't want you to be punished."

Among the last two spirits the malamai encountered in this session was John the preacher. The malamai immediately sought to convert John, insisting that the Christian religion he followed was "not true, because God has no son, nor does he have a father and mother." When their efforts to convert him met with resistance ("I have practiced this faith for many years; I cannot leave it overnight"), the malamai then demanded to know why and how he entered Fatima. He replied that he had been invited to come and stay in Fatima's body, but that he was also angry with her and her father for insulting his faith. John further explained how the sister of Fatima's father was ultimately responsible for the young woman's predicament, for she had arranged for the girl to be charmed even before her birth. He described how the spirit originally sent to kill Fatima in the womb had instead rendered her permanently vulnerable to spirit intrusion: "They put a room in her heart through which every spirit who comes across her can enter. A spirit was sent to destroy her when she was still in the womb, but he loved her and he built that room. As long as this room exists, she will never be free from the spirits."

This particularly successful, but in many ways quite typical, rukiyya session illustrates the four principal arguments I have made in this article. The dialogue dramatizes, first of all, the extent to which rukiyya healing mirrors bori therapeutics by (1) locating both the source and the cure for physical and emotional ailments within the conduct of social relations; and (2) relying on control of the spirit world to diagnose and cure or manage these problems. Hence, the malamai discovered, in the end, that Fatima's lifelong problems with the spirits had been caused, for reasons yet unknown, by her aunt, and they implored the parade of spirit personalities to aid them in understanding the layers of symptoms she manifested. While rukiyya practitioners emphasize that their goal is to expel spirits, not appease them as bori adepts do, in practice they negotiate with spirits in very similar ways and assume the necessity of long-term management of recurring spirit problems. In many ways, the tactics and outcomes of rukiyya are similar to those of Protestant exorcists in Madagascar who make conversion to their faith a prerequisite of treatment and who, much like local spirit mediums, rely on communication with the spirits to chase them away.[41] As Lesley Sharp explains: "Thus, on one hand, exorcists successfully integrate two seemingly divergent or conflicting epistemologies. On the other, through conversionary tactics, they undermine indigenous cultural logic."[42] The shared logic of bori and rukiyya therapeutics is significant for what it tells us not only about the continuing importance of bori in Hausa society, but for the insight it provides into the context of contemporary Islamic identity politics in Kano. In this sense, rukiyya practice demonstrates how the majority of Kano Muslims resist Wahhabi visions of Islamic modernity, in which an individual's relationship with God is mediated only by one's knowledge of and adherence to the Qur'an and the hadith. In contrast, by focusing attention on the tireless scheming of malevolent spirits and their human accomplices, rukiyya discourse and practice suggests that the maintenance of health and of appropriate Muslim behavior requires more than individual knowledge of Islamic texts, but also ritual interventions and everyday mediation by powerful malamai.

Second, the dialogue with Fatima's spirits vividly demonstrates how rukiyya sessions produce a narrative of belonging in religious terms. As we saw in the malamai's interactions with Sarkin Duna, Sunusi, and the preacher John, rukiyya practitioners are preoccupied with identifying the religious identity of the spirits and attempting to convert the non-Muslims among them. This focus provides the malamai ample opportunities to expound on the distinctiveness, simplicity, and ultimate truth of Islam vis-à-vis other faiths, and didactic monologues by individual malamai draw stark boundaries between believer and non-believer. Yet, as the nimble rhetorical skills of the spirit Sunusi in the dialogue demonstrate, rukiyya sessions also showcase the more whimsical, satirical side of Hausa expressive culture in which spirit possession figures so prominently. These appearances ground the narrative of Islamic community in a very specific Hausa history and context. They also reinforce the message of religious unity and brotherhood by dramatizing the external threat posed by outsiders who stubbornly refuse to conform to "Islamically" defined norms of moral conduct and who scheme secretly with each other to fulfill their own desires at the expense of their human victims.

Third, in reading the spirit dialogue one sees how rukiyya serves to naturalize female susceptibility to spirit possession and the human misbehavior that spirits cause. The very fact that women disproportionately enact possession in the rukiyya context serves to powerfully dramatize the permeability of female bodies, as spirits testify to entering through and lodging in different anatomical regions of their hapless hosts. Moreover, the spirit dialogues emphasize women's vulnerability as objects of male (spirit) desire, as spirits like Sarkin Duna admit to the great difficulty of leaving Fatima's body and renouncing his appetite for women more generally in becoming a Muslim. Even the Muslim spirit Saudatu admits to pimping Fatima's body to her male friends and family. Thus, although rukiyya provides women with a legitimate Islamic forum in which to give voice to and potentially resolve their problems, it also reinscribes notions of sexual difference in which women's ability to be good Muslims is compromised by their sexual allure and porous bodies. Women (and spirits) are thus identified as inadequate members of the community of believers.

Finally, I have suggested that ruqiyya marks a new and important trajectory to shifting strategies of power and discipline in northern Nigeria. Novel forces labeled modernization have intensified pressures on Muslim Hausa women and girls, sparked new forms of spirit possession, and inspired healing techniques that move individualizing technologies of the self outside of state bounds (as Western medicine did in Europe) and cast debates about inadequate subjects into a religious idiom.

CONCLUSION

In the years since Sumbuka dramatically arrived in Kano, most of its initial victims have found relief from their bizarre symptoms and moved on with their lives, settling into their first marriages at the relatively late age of seventeen or eighteen. Outbreaks at other secondary schools for girls continue to erupt periodically, however, and the Islamic response that Sumbuka inspired has established itself as a more permanent innovation on Kano's therapeutic and religious landscape. By October 1996, Malam Chedi had begun to systematize his practice and transform it into a clinic with patient intake and outtake forms, a room where intransigent cases can be treated over a longer term, an expanded training program for the assistants who carry out the bulk of his work, and a fee of 200 naira (roughly $2.40) charged to all clients prior to assessment.[43] The enormous popularity of his practice suggests that it has become more than an emergency measure against the urgent cases of mass possession at secondary schools in the Kano area. Visits to Kano in 1998 and 2000 confirmed that Malam Chedi's practice continues to thrive, and new Islamic health centers on the same model have sprouted up in different parts of Kano's sprawling metropolis. Between 1998 and 2002, the ruqiyya practice of Malam Abdullahi, founder of the Dan Fodio Islamic Health Center in Dorayi, expanded dramatically, enabling him to build a much larger health center with accommodations for long-term patients and a permanent staff of four ruqiyya specialists. While these centers continue to remain beyond the interest or control of the state, Malam Chedi observed that it would be a good idea if the government would contribute monetarily to their efforts and coordinate them with the biomedical services provided by the public health services; yet he is most concerned with asserting the superiority of rukiyya methods to Western biomedicine. He thus claimed that 85 percent of the patients at a local hospital were suffering from spirit-caused illnesses that modern medicine could not cure, and he even boasted that he had successfully treated a case of AIDS. Malam Chedi's attitude, and the success of the rukiyya clinics of which he is a part, suggest that in practical matters of health, it is religious leaders and community, not the postcolonial state, that produce the medical discourses and healing techniques through which governing power in northern Nigeria is "absorbed" by the population in the course of everyday life.[44]

In their efforts to build an authoritative discourse of Islamic orthodoxy, a generation of young Sufi malamai have created a new disciplinary regime for women that differs markedly from existing channels of social control and institutionalizes a new "technology of power" that works directly on and through the bodies of afflicted women. While the ambiguity of the ritual arena and the tenuous control malamai exert over the spirits suggest the ultimate impracticality of their project of control, rukiyya nevertheless provides a new mechanism through which women regularly enact—and malamai routinely punish—female difference and deviance on the corporeal plane. Rukiyya also perpetuates a discourse of difference between believer and non-believer that affirms a northern "narrative of community" that is at odds with Nigerian national unity based on a secular state and with individualizing versions of Islamic modernity propagated by Wahhabi reformers. Ultimately, rukiyya practice demonstrates the significance of gender and local religious practice in mediating these projects of Islamic reform. Rukiyya thus serves to place women's problems and bori possession discourse at the center, not the margins, of this contentious process of reform.

NOTES

An earlier version of this essay appeared in *Interventions: The International Journal of Postcolonial Studies* 3, no. 2 (July 2001). I am grateful for permission to reprint the current version. I would also like to thank John H. Hanson and Rig K. van Dijk for their comments on an earlier version of this article, and the anonymous reviewers of Duke University Press and Steven Pierce for their help in shaping this final version.

1 Sumbuka is neither a word nor a proper name in Hausa, and most people I spoke with about the Sumbuka episode (including girls who attended the secondary school, bori practitioners, and malamai who treated the girls) suggested that it was simply a nonsense word coined by the girls to chide the old lady who appeared to them. Conerly Casey suggests that Sumbuka was the name by which the spirit identified herself to the girls and was also the name that Kano residents attributed to a similar elderly female spirit who was rumored to be appearing at the doors of Kano residences demanding water and frightening their occupants: Casey, "Medicines for Madness," 71–74.

2 Sufism (*tasawwuf* in Arabic) is a spiritual or mystical aspect of Islam that developed alongside, and in reaction to, the formalistic tenets of scripturalist Islam. Sufi religious "brotherhoods" or "paths" (*tariqa*; pl. *turuq*)—in particular, the Qadriyya and the Tijaniyya—have been powerful political players in northern Nigeria since the early nineteenth century. Indeed, until the recent challenges of Islamist groups like Izala, Sufism has undeniably constituted the "mainstream" or "orthodox" in Hausa Islamic practice.

3 When asked about the origins of rukiyya, Malam Salisu Adamu pointed to its pre-Islamic roots in the miraculous healing works of Jesus: "The person who first started doing this is the prophet Isa or Jesus, who used to cure lepers and the blind. But in Islam the Prophet Muhammad (PBUH ["peace be upon him," a phrase uttered normally by Muslims after each reference to the Prophet Muham-

mad]) is the first person to do it": interview with the author, Kano, Nigeria, 29 July 1998.

4   Malam Lawan Adamu, a thirty-nine-year-old malam in the old city, reported that he had begun practicing rukiyya twelve years before, when his wife was affected by the spirits: interview with the author, Kano, Nigeria, 29 July 1998.

5   Strikingly, the adult women who quickly filled the rukiyya clinics showed symptoms that were remarkably akin to those of the schoolgirls, in contrast to cases like that described by Lesley Sharp, in which a particularly violent and dangerous class of spirits, the *njarinintsy*, attacked only adolescent schoolgirls in Madagascar, while the more sedate and helpful *tromba* spirits affected only adult, married women: See Sharp, *The Possessed and the Dispossessed*, 224.

6   Aihwa Ong has noted that in many postcolonial states, social groups dislocated by modernizing change undergo crises in cultural identity and respond by creating "counterideologies that are obsessively concerned with controlling resources, group boundaries, and articulating belonging in transcendental terms": See Ong, "State versus Islam," 187.

7   Ibid.

8   Abdalla, *Islam, Medicine, and Practitioners in Northern Nigeria*; idem, "Medicine in Nineteenth Century Arabic Literature in Northern Nigeria"; idem, "The Ulama of Sokoto in the Nineteenth Century." Based on the actions and statements of the Prophet Muhammad, Prophetic medicine emphasizes the role of revelation in attaining knowledge and certainty in medicine and the healing powers of prayer and Quranic texts.

9   Boyd, *The Caliph's Sister*; Boyd and Mack, *Collected Works of Nana Asma'u, Daughter of Usman 'Dan Fodio*.

10   Barkindo, "Growing Islamism in Kano City since 1970"; Lubeck, "Islamic Political Movements in Northern Nigeria"; idem, "Islamic Protest and Oil-Based Capitalism"; Watts, "The Shock of Modernity."

11   The full name of this group is Jama'atu Izalat al-Bidah wa Iqamat al-Sunnah (roughly, Removal of False Innovations and the Establishment of Orthodox Tradition).

12   Hunwick, "Sub-Saharan Africa and the Wider World of Islam"; Umar, "Changing Islamic Identity in Nigeria from the 1960s to the 1980s."

13 Ibrahim, "The Politics of Religion in Nigeria"; idem, "Religion and Political Turbulence in Nigeria."

14 For insight into challenges from Izala in Niger, see Masquelier, "Debating Muslims, Disputed Practices," and "Identity, Alterity, and Ambiguity in a Nigerien Community."

15 Ferme, "What 'Alhaji Airplane' Saw in Mecca, and What Happened When He Came Home."

16 Barkindo, "Growing Islamism in Kano City since 1970," 96.

17 Lawson, "Islamic Fundamentalism and Continuing Education for Hausa Women in Northern Nigeria," 93–114.

18 Callaway and Creevey, *The Heritage of Islam*, 64.

19 Hodgson, *Gendered Modernities*.

20 Ong, "The Production of Possession"; idem, *Spirits of Resistance and Capitalist Discipline*.

21 Bartholomew, *Exotic Deviance*, 167. For a historical overview of these cases as they appear in scientific journals, see ibid., chap. 6. In Europe, this pattern of mass female "hysteria" was common in the second half of the nineteenth century and early part of the twentieth century, "in response to rigid rationalist educational discipline in many schools in such countries as France, Switzerland, and especially Germany": ibid., 168. During the twentieth century, such cases have been most evident in schools within Malaysia and central and eastern Africa, the latter occurring primarily in Christian missionary schools that introduced new foreign ideas and enforced strict discipline, including the rigid separation of boys and girls: Dhadphale and Shaikh, "Epidemic Hysteria in a Zambian School"; Harris, "'Possession Hysteria' in a Kenya Tribe." In some cases, such as Madagascar, scholars have linked epidemic schoolgirl possession with a very particular set of gendered circumstances: unwanted pregnancies among adolescent girls who have migrated alone from rural areas to attend school in the city: Sharp, *The Possessed and the Dispossessed*. In Malaysia, cases of mass female possession have become commonplace in Muslim boarding schools since the early 1960s, when Islamic revivalism took root and these new religious educational institutions, notorious for their strict discipline and lack of privacy, were created: Ackerman and Lee, "Mass Hysteria and Spirit Possession in Urban Malaysia."

22   In describing the violent possession of schoolgirls by njarinintsy spirits in Madagascar, for example, Sharp suggests that a "message of chaos and dysfunction is conveyed through the actions of the victim's body" and that the spirits symbolically communicate the "disorder and fragmentation" experienced in the girls' lives: Sharp, *The Possessed and the Dispossessed*, 241.

23   Boddy, *Wombs and Alien Spirits*; Ong, *Spirits of Resistance and Capitalist Discipline*. As Dorothy Hodgson describes the prevalence of possession among Masai women in Tanzania, "Through spirit possession, women voice their complaints about their economic, political, and social disenfranchisement, at once internalizing their despair and expressing their predicament": Hodgson, *Once Intrepid Warriors*, 116.

24   Kapferer, *A Celebration of Demons*.

25   Despite recent gains in women's education in northern Nigeria, Callaway and Creevey report that only about 6 percent of girls go beyond lower-level primary school: Callaway and Creevey, *The Heritage of Islam*, 64. This is not, of course, to discount the critical importance of organizations like FOMWAN in promoting social and political agendas of benefit to women. For this emphasis, see Yusuf, "Hausa-Fulani Women."

26   Casey notes about her interview with two malamai who practice rukiyya that, "while government officials considered Sumbuka to be unusual and communally disabling, these *malamai* believed the possessions to be of less significance than the multitudes who suffer possession on a daily basis but who go unnoticed by the government": Casey, "Medicines for Madness," 90.

27   Casey reports that the two scholars she interviewed practiced rukiyya somewhat clandestinely, since some in the Islamic community viewed the practice as committing shirk.

28   This tape was recorded and sold by Malam Chedi to educate the populace about the efficacy of rukiyya and to advertise his practice. It was recorded on 7 October 1996.

29   In the Suleyman Crescent neighborhood of Kano, for example, Sheikh Aminu din Abubakr established both a school for married women and a clinic to which eye doctors from Saudi Arabia come once a year and provide free treatment.

30   Among the books cited by or shown to me by rukiyya practitioners in

Kano were an English translation of Ibn Taymeeyah, *Essay on the Jinn (Demons)*, trans. Abu Ameenah Bilal Philips (Riyadh: Tawheed Publications, 1989); Abdul Fidda Muhammad Arif, *How Can We Cure and Prevent?* (Saudi Arabia, Riyadh: Mahmud Printing Press, 1990); *The Rules of Ruqiyya According to the Shari'a* (Riyadh: Dar al-Asima, 1994); Majdi Muhammad Shahawi, *Godly Cures for Magic, Jinns, and Satan* (Cairo, 1992); Abdulhamed Kishik, *Cures from the Qur'an for Magic, Jealousy, Madness, or Spirit Possession* (Cairo, 1993).

31 This younger generation of Sufi scholars distinguishes itself from older scholars through its education in Western-style schools. Many of the rukiyya scholars I interviewed, for example, graduated from the School for Arabic Studies in Kano.

32 Interview by the author with Malam Abdulsalam Ibrahim Adam, Kano, Nigeria, 31 July 1998.

33 Umar, "Changing Islamic Identity in Nigeria from the 1960s to the 1980s," 178.

34 Imam, "Working within Nigeria's Shari'a Courts"; Sanusi, "Shariah and the Woman Question."

35 Interview by the author with Malam Faruq Chedi, Kano, 2 November 1996.

36 For a discussion of how bori provides both the material and imaginative resources that enable Hausa men and women to build lives that diverge from normative social expectations, see O'Brien, "Power and Paradox."

37 Chedi interview.

38 Literally "curtain" in Arabic; in contemporary Kano the hijab refers to the more conservative form of women's veiling adapted from Middle Eastern practice, which takes the form of a single piece of black cloth that encircles the face and falls below the woman's waist.

39 Many of these spirits appear in descriptions of the bori pantheon in accounts published 1913–14 to the 1970s: Besmer, *Horses, Musicians, and Gods*; Greenberg, *The Influence of Islam on a Sudanese Religion*; Tremearne, *The Ban of the Bori*; idem, *Hausa Superstitions and Customs*. These spirit personalities are often stock characters familiar to Kano residents not only through bori performance but also through a range of Hausa tales, drama, and prose that have defined the parameters of Hausa identity for decades: Furniss, *Poetry, Prose, and Popular Culture in Hausa*, 92–95.

40   Although I attended many rukiyya sessions at Malam Chedi's clinic, I was not present at this one and choose to discuss it here in detail because of the coherence of the dialogue between the three malamai conducting the exorcism and the seven different spirits that presented themselves during the nearly two-hour session. Not all sessions that I attended or listened to on tape provide such comprehensible exchanges between spirits and humans, since spirits often refuse to identify themselves or to converse in an intelligible way They simply moan, howl, and weep as the malamai assault them with the verses from the Qur'an. In all cases in which possession is successfully induced, a certain level of chaos and confusion results from the agitation of both human and spirit participants.

41   "The act of communication is central to the act of exorcism, especially when exorcists engage the spirits themselves. . . . Their style of interaction with these spirits parallels that of *tromba* mediums, or other indigenous healers, who seek to placate or cajole a spirit into staying (in the case of *tromba*) or departing peacefully (as with a *njarinintsy*). Exorcists, however, take this one step further: they taunt, scold, and lecture spirits and then they drive them, with force, from their victims": Sharp, *The Possessed and the Dispossessed*, 271.

42   Ibid.

43   The matter of payment for fulfilling what the malamai themselves describe as their religious obligation has become a controversial point. Bori adepts seize on this fact to level charges of extortion at malamai, and inevitably these new healing practices have given rise to opportunists and charlatans, as Malam Chedi himself concedes. Yet his own reputation appears to be above suspicion. Malam Chedi is currently a lecturer at Bayero University in Kano; he is pursuing a Ph.D. in Arabic studies and regularly lectures at various forums throughout Kano to receptive youthful audiences.

44   Michel Foucault has suggested that modern state power is not so much imposed on populations as absorbed into society through the capillary "actions" of the human sciences and social techniques that permeate the conduct of everyday life: Foucault, *The History of Sexuality, Volume 1*, 139–46.

YVETTE CHRISTIANSE

※

Selections from *Castaway*

Castaway began with what is by now a familiar gesture for writers and theorists of anti- and postcoloniality—namely, an argument with history.[1] This argument was staged in personal terms in that I had wanted to bring to the fore a voice for which there is no discursive place in any formal history. It was, in short, my grandmother's voice. Over the years since the double loss of her disappearance into Alzheimer's and then her death, mourning for her had become entwined with her stories of her girlhood on the island of St. Helena in the South Atlantic, an island known most famously in history as the place on which Napoleon Bonaparte died.

The choice to shape this project as a poetic sequence had a number of significant results. The first of these was the realization that, as with any good haunting, not only one voice will want to push through the membrane of language. The lost, or what Toni Morrison has called the "unspeakable things unspoken," are legion.[2] Thus, where I had been pushing toward one voice, many pushed back in turn. A fiction of fragmentation emerged as the form in which that multiplicity (still only partial) expressed itself. *Castaway* is therefore composed of poems that operate as fragments of "lost" books whose narrators include historical figures such as Napoleon, a sixteenth-century Portuguese exile named Ferñao Lopez, and an exiled and unnamed Xhosa prophet. Other narrators are fictional characters, some of whom may have existed in some margin, somewhere. This fictional fragmentary "evidence" was an overt attempt to find a poetic form for discussions about fragmentary discourses staged in trauma studies and subaltern studies. .[3]

One receives instruction from writing. In this case, my lesson was to listen to something very specific—namely, a warning against writerly violence, which takes its energy from private longings that may override the autonomy of a subject of interest. This is, for me, an important task for a writer of any genre: to listen to the very language that one is working with, to listen to the sedimentation through which it passes, to listen for traces of what had been shed or even longed for by a word, and what such a word might open to in a phrase or set of phrases. From this, one learns how to relinquish any rigidity that an initial project, particularly an overtly political project, might push one toward. In my own case, the personal began to recede as history, in its grand and militarist march, began to repeat itself from the outset. Napoleon could not be shaken free of his perch on St. Helena. His insistent presence had to be acknowledged, though not exorcised, at the beginning of the book. Strangely, my struggle against this presence enabled the emergence of those things which had been cast into the shadow of the very idea of "Napoleon St. Helena." The conceit of this writing became one of a violent "forcing" of *my* imagined Napoleon into a deeper prison. Nothing but bad days and bad dreams emerged for history's famous leader, he became stuck on the conjured island of my longing's imagination. But this alone would have been deeply dissatisfying and damaging. The "castaways" of history deserved something more. And *Castaway*, the book, was to be a work of mourning and discovery, not incarceration within a rather childish and too easy vengeance.

One presence that did throw Napoleon's largely privileged incarceration on St. Helena into relief was that of the Portuguese nobleman, Fernão Lopez, who had been mutilated by his own leader for resisting Portugal's attempts to colonize Goa in the early 1500s. Lopez, who had jumped ship at St. Helena during a return voyage to Portugal, has come to stand for colonialism's violence against its own, as well as the insatiability of the theatrics of power.

In all of this, a voice still escaped my pen, and in this, some liberation was permitted. My grandmother never speaks. She never materialized despite my listening, and what I hear is utterly untranslatable: qualities of sound, a sweet biting way that came down on a consonant, a barely audible shaping of a vowel—so beautiful it breaks the heart as it retreats, as if to say, "This is not right, this prying, no matter how much your longing pays me respect." And so, obedient, I learned to listen to this absence and now consider it a resistance. And this is why: There remains a demand for the personal among writers who continue to observe the many effects of colonialism and neocolonialism, with their race and gender biases, in this long late twentieth century and early twenty-first century. In these contexts, the personal is made to operate as the culminating register of authenticity or guarantee of rhetorical efficacy. Yet what kind of service might this be pressed into when one is not watching? Everything cannot be on display for the curiosity of readership or a writer's own longing for resolution. Certain silences are necessary. One must concede to the dead a necessary privacy. And perhaps this will afford the living time to consider how the personal may be co-opted into an enticing self-violence—this last is the seduction: the sense of being able to sing one's own narrative into the teeth of a grand history.

My recognition of this seduction was shaped by the poems themselves, but also by the years of research that produced them, research that included rereading the many essays about figures like Saartje Baartman, the so-called Hottentot Venus, and the Tasmanian Truganini—women subjected to a dissecting violence of nineteenth-century colonial "science" that severed the subject, particularly the female subject, from self-knowledge. For such reasons, among others, it does not disturb me that the single voice I had hoped to make room for eludes me. Not even the "pervasive sadness"[4] of a voice "conquered" by the narrative triumph of history exists. And yet, this is as it should be. I can only orient myself toward *this* lost voice. I can only set my ear in some direction that may catch it as it recedes into privacy. Beyond that, silence has to suffice. In this, silence is the wall against melancholia, on one hand, and sentimentality, on the other. And perhaps it is also the case that melancholia is not entirely held at bay. That too is livable, but self-delusion is not. Writing that creates a "vicinity," rather than a fixed place, a crypt toward which one directs one's newly implicated ekphrastic gaze has to suffice.

FROM *THE LOST DIARIES OF FERNÃO LOPEZ, THE ISLAND'S FIRST EXILE*

Letter to General D'Albuquerque—On the Pleasures of Taste

J'avais, j'avais ce gout de vivre loin des hommes, et voici que les Pluies...
—SAINT-JOHN PERSE[5]

Last night when the rains came like tongues
on the lances of a devil god—the one I saw
that night your mast pricked the horizon,
made a hole big enough for you to enter
with your pincers and tongs, your burning
coals and mission of The Book—I sat up
like a lost man, the lost man I have become—
for the man who looses his tongue and at least
one hand, not to mention a nose and ears is,
you would agree, lost even in the eyes of
those who may have known him. Last night

when the rains came like tongues on the
lances of a devil god, I reached for water.
Such thirst. And do you know, General,
how hard it is to quench a thirst when you
have no tongue? A tongue, I have discovered—
O great conqueror and true believer—is
necessary for many things. Ask the man who
savours an evening meal as he rides the last
miles home, or the woman who trembles as she

holds her lover's tongue in her mouth, or the
child who holds its ground with one rude gesture.

I would taste the salt on the air as it blows
from that graveyard, the ocean I once loved. I
would taste the rain and learn to tell where
it has risen from and what year, like a
connoisseur of wines, and I would be drunk
too soon for refusing to spit an atom away.
I would learn every story and song from every
leaf, even those that blow in like tired birds
on their migrations around the world. I would
break open lemon after lemon in my lemon groves
and douse my missing sense, oh what is my stolen

sense, and dance to the agony of that delight,
General. I would be able to tell you chapter
and verse of every book in The Book you held up
to my face in your anger. Do you know, great
hero and measure of the world, I have learnt
that words must be like fruit—each a taste,
each an ingredient for a palate in need of
refreshment: "ocean," an orange from Tangier
as its peel breaks away from the pale soft
pap it wears—and I have always loved the
pith of citrus, for its temperament; "mouth,"

an apple from any orchid, but one that's lain
long in a storeroom and gathered its sweetness
like a bride and groom in the weeks before
they are allowed to touch—ah, their smiles
at the banquet. I could offer you more, like
morsels for a guest at my table, this table of
rock and a mountain that grows other mountains

like a strange tree dropping strange fruit. I
would find a way to tell their vintage, their
good years and poor and always wash my mouth
clean with the simple taste of water, dear General.[6]

Letter to General D'Albuquerque—On the Pleasures of Touch

"Vieil homme aux main nues."
—SAINT-JOHN PERSE[7]

Now it is especially wicked, now it is grandly
cruel—the goats bring their muzzles to me
each morning, as if to have them tested.
And perhaps there are things I know nothing of,
things that go on in the island's sharp dark,
things that threaten their downy chins
while I sleep with my arms around myself.
Perhaps it is those things I must reassure
them against. So they come, nuzzling like
children, sweet children. And, oh my General—
you man amongst men—I am like a woman
who mourns the loss of her breasts.

It is the memory, sire, the memory that is
cruel, crueler than the coal-singed axe,
the cauterising blade, crueler than pain
that hammers itself into bronze bracelets
around a man's wrist, or into the heart
of the wife he will never see again.
I tell you, the roughest surface,
the coarse pink of a tiger's tongue—
I would calibrate each ridge, each edge
and take the marks they leave as

their signals of love and affection for
what is now my missing joy, General oh

voyager of the spicy world, soldier
of steel, maker punishments our God
would admire. Memory is the worst thing
in the morning and in the fluid night—
those times of waking and entering sleep.
In some places, those places you know
nothing of—except as places that
fill your scales and our King's hands—
oh hands, hands that end in the flurry
of fingers rifling through the wind, the
hair of a favourite child, a laughing woman's
skirts, fingers that search for knots in a beard,

pluck melodies from halls in a different heaven
like fruit from the leaves of the generous tree—
in those places—and there are sounds
you will never dream of—those places
where a man can forget the body of Christ
to savour instead the delight of dancing
on the back of a blue boy-god who licks
butter from his fingers—in those places
there are rituals to mark the arrival of night,
its retreat. They secure the heart's many gates,
ease all passages, and memories are sweetened
around their saddest edges, General.

But. Here. Surviving the inquisition of
nights in the island's heretical winds.
Without the simplest protection for
the palm of my hand, or against the flea
that can only be pinched loose by quick fingers—

oh, what is missing is the intimacy
between forefinger and the soft ball
of the thumb. My General, defender of the
Faith, great man and angel of the seas,
the morning visit of my goats breaks my heart.
And there are days I long to invite you to
breakfast, here amongst the muzzles of innocence.

Letter to General D'Albuquerque—On Desire

Grain. The yellow scent a cool quiet mat
under her bare feet. I kissed everything
that day. And I curse you, General. Hell
and more hell to you. Nails under your feet.
Heat in the most delicate tissue of your bowel.
I kissed the leaves of trees too dumb
in their drunken green to know. I kissed
the leavened bread. I kissed the holy shadow
of the gate over a celibate's path.

And it was never enough. Not if
there were twice as many blades
of grass. And I kissed the moon glazed
water gathering on the tiles where
rain fell—that air of heaven itself
breaking to its knees. And there was
no god but her, no paradise or judgment
but her. And what do you kiss when you are
on your own, Caesar of the East? What hands
remind your skin? Is there a woman who comes
and does she sing over your body, raise it
to where the waters will not even hold a bird?

And do you forget borders and destinations,
duties and the long reining lies of countries
and their citizens? Do you kiss her for the
sounds in her throat? Do you kiss her for
the length of her fingers and the tips of her
hair? Do you kiss her for the lance of desire
that lays you low at the gates of your body?
Do you pray with the art of a bird singing
as you are transformed and take off into
those avenues of the wind that carry you
in her smooth wake above crazy storms
and tortured trees? I ask you this, General
as one whom you have taught about distance and desire.

Letter to General D'Albuquerque—On Solitude

On other days the island breaks its anchorage,
begins a strange migration from gravity's wide domain,
begins to separate as if dust from dust itself,
as if all this rock has been the illusion
which we, and I in particular, have served
for some steady purpose that travels
with us wherever we go, in full health or
in every range and degree of sickness.

On such days, Oh Great Reader of the Winds
and Hand at the Helm, the light that accompanies
the disintegration is the light of tiny insects
disturbed by memory and forgetfulness
as the island separates and lifts in silence
and there is no-one to turn to, to ask,
"Is this real?" On such days, I press the

palm of my hand to my mouth, find in the
palm of my hand all anchorage, all gravity

and the measure of distance—say, the sun from
this unstable place, the tip of a leaf to its stem,
the interval between the print of my left foot
and the print of my right—all distances in
the palm of my hand, even this sacrilege itself,
General. And who is here to chastise my false
astronomy, my diabolical upheaval of God's
universe? My goats shift together on these days,
not a satanic hair between them, careful of their throats.

And I range the full length of where, on other days,
most days, the island keeps its normal hours,
holds its normal shape. Look to the east and
that is me, to the west and I am the same while
the island rests still and golden in the space of
angels. I write of this to you, my General, protector
of my faith. Write back soon, send word
if you are eager to join me. I will show you
how to close your ears to the noise of angels
as they walk about the island before they send it back.

Letter to General D'Albuquerque—On Forgiveness

> Ha! qu'on m'evente tout ce leurre!
> —SAINT-JOHN PERSE[8]

When I was a boy and even, yes, as a man,
I took pleasure in pollens that made soldiers sneeze.
I knew the arrival of girls who had walked through
flower beds by the notes that swirled around them—

those portions of air which have been dusted by stamens
and sing of these quick touching interludes, General,
the private pleasures and excitements hidden from all
but for the sun glinting on their eyelashes, the quick
delicate dip and flare of their nostrils. And I have
loved the air around horses fresh from a morning canter,
the flanks of the rider who strides up newly washed stairs
past vases of day-old roses bred from the Malagasy strain.

But oh, I must tell you, General, most measurable man,
I must tell how those soft messages of air that charm
and delight in other places—those places I have lost
and those you have conquered—those delights are
a different matter here. They cut and sting, and
some days I burn as if in hell. And I long for the
silence of pollen free days. The pallor of empty
air. And some days I lower myself to remorse
like a man who has lost his head for arrogance
before God. Some days I ask if there are
things that cannot be forgiven, and what
the worst punishment would be. Some days

I believe it is to be lost entirely, to
slip through the cracks that appear after
the island has shaken itself in rage
against its anchorage, out here, between
the whalers and cargo ships, the man-o-wars
and sailors who cough and spit in the
acrid mornings. Ah, but then . . . that talc
stirs, the spores of rebellion rise, and
I welcome the buckshot that blows from the
smallest blossom, so small a spider may crush it.
On these days, my General of Generals,
Governor of our King's good fortune, I approach

something that is close to forgiveness.
I forgive the yellow flower whose name
I do not know. I forgive it for the innocence
of its face. I forgive the sweet bearded goats
for the exhalation of their coarse hides
which shed stiff gray hairs into the milk
I claim from them. And have you drunk
their milk, oh Caesar of the spicy seas?
Have you tasted its earth, and has your
head turned, grown tight around the temples,
and are you reminded as I am of the grave
in which we will lie, waiting for the trumpet's call?

NOTES

1   Christianse, *Castaway*.

2   Toni Morrison, "Unspeakable Things Unspoken: The Afro-American Presence in American Literature," in Angelyn Mitchell, *Within the Circle: An Anthology of African American Literary Criticism from the Harlem Renaissance to the Present* (Durham, N.C.: Duke University Press, 1994), 368–98, esp. 377.

3   See, for example, Gyanendra Pandy's argument that "unofficial" subaltern experience can be discerned through discursive fragments. See "In Defense of the Fragment: Writing about Hindu-Muslim Riots in India Today," *Representations*, no. 37, specical issue: Imperial Fantasies and Postcolonial Histories (winter 1992): 27–55.

4   Ranajit Guha, "A Conquest Foretold," *Social Text*, no. 54 (spring 1998): 85–99, ESP. 97.

5   "Once, once I had a taste for living far from men, but now the rains . . .": Saint-John Perse, *Pluies* (*Rains*, 1943).

6   Fernão Lopez traveled to Goa in the early 1500s with Afonso D'Albuquerque, Portuguese general and colonizer of the region, who left him in charge of a group of Portuguese to settle and "rule" the local population. On his return, D'Albuquerque found that Lopez and others had converted to Islam and sided

with Muslim resistance to the Portuguese. Upon capture, Lopez and other "renegades" were punished by having their right hands and the thumb of their left hands severed. Their tongues, ears, and noses were also cut off as a reminder of their treachery. Lopez's hair and beard were scraped off with clamshells in a process known as "scaling the fish." He remained in India for some years until he was to be returned to Portugal. He left his ship at the then uninhabited island of St. Helena, becoming its first exile and a figure of curiosity and myth. He planted lemon groves and tended a flock of goats. There are claims that Defoe based Robinson Crusoe on Lopez.

7 "Old man with naked hands": Saint-John Perse, *Image a Crusoe* (*Pictures for Crusoe*).

8 "Ha! Let all this delusion be aired out": Saint-John Perse, *Vents* (*Winds*, 1946).

Bibliography

Abdalla, Ismail. "Medicine in Nineteenth Century Arabic Literature in Northern Nigeria: A Report." *Kano Studies* 1, no. 4 (1979): 91–99.

———. "The Ulama of Sokoto in the Nineteenth Century: A Medical Review." Pp. 61–83 in *African Healing Strategies*, ed. Brian du Toit and Ismail Abdalla. New York: Trado-Medic Books, 1985.

———. *Islam, Medicine, and Practitioners in Northern Nigeria*. Lewiston, N.Y.: Edwin Mellen Press, 1997.

Abrams, Philip. "Notes on the Difficulty of Studying the State (1977)." *Journal of Historical Sociology* 1, no. 1 (1988): 58–89.

Ackerman, S. E., and R. L. Lee. "Mass Hysteria and Spirit Possession in Urban Malaysia: A Case Study." *Journal of Sociology and Psychology* 1 (1978): 24–35.

Agamben, Giorgio. *Homo Sacer: Sovereign Power and Bare Life*. Trans. Daniel Heller-Roazen. Stanford, Calif.: Stanford University Press, 1998.

Alavi, Seema. *The Sepoys and the Company: Tradition and Transition in Northern India, 1770–1830*. Delhi: Oxford University Press, 1995.

Aly, Götz. *Architects of Annihilation: Auschwitz and the Logic of Destruction*. Trans. A. G. Blunden. London: Weidenfeld and Nicolson, 2002.

Amin, Shahid. *Event, Metaphor, Memory: Chauri Chaura, 1922–1992*. Berkeley: University of California Press, 1995.

Anagol, Padma, "The Emergence of the Female Criminal in India: Infanticide and Survival under the Raj." *History Workshop Journal*, no. 53 (2002): 73–93.

Anderson, Benedict. *Imagined Communities: Reflections on the Origin and Spread of Nationalism*. Rev. ed. London: Verso, 1991.

Anderson, Clare. "Race, Caste, and Hierarchy: The Creation of Inter-convict Conflict in the Penal Settlements of South East Asia and the Indian Ocean, c. 1790–1880." *Tasmanian Historical Studies* 6, no. 2 (1999): 81–95.

Appiah, K. Anthony. *In My Father's House: Africa and the Philosophy of Culture*. New York: Oxford University Press, 1992.

Apter, Andrew. "On Imperial Spectacle: The Dialectics of Seeing in Colonial Nigeria." *Comparative Studies in Society and History* 44, no. 3 (2002): 564–96.

Arens, William. *The Man-Eating Myth: Anthropology and Anthropophagy*. New York: Oxford University Press, 1979.

Arnold, David. *Colonizing the Body; State Medicine and Epidemic Disease in Nineteenth-Century India*. Berkeley: University of California Press, 1993.

———. *Police Power and Colonial Rule, Madras 1859–1947*. Delhi: Oxford University Press, 1986.

———. "European Orphans and Vagrants in India in the Nineteenth Century." *Journal of Imperial and Commonwealth History* 7 (1979): 104–27.

Asad, Talal. "On Torture, or Cruel, Inhuman, and Degrading Treatment." Pp. 285–308 in *Social Suffering*, ed. Arthur Kleinman, Veena Das, and Margaret Lock. Delhi: Oxford University Press, 1998.

Atieno Odhiambo, E. S. "Woza Lugard? Rhetoric and Antiquarian Knowledge." *Canadian Journal of African Studies* 34, no. 2 (2000).

Baepler, Paul, ed. *White Slaves, African Masters: An Anthology of American Barbary Captivity Narratives*. Chicago: University of Chicago Press, 1999.

Baker, Ernest A. *Cassell's French–English, English–French Dictionary*, ed. J. L. Manchon. New York: Funk and Wagnalls, 1951.

Bala, Poonam. "State and Indigenous Medicine in Nineteenth and Twentieth Century Bengal, 1800–1947." Ph.D. thesis, University of Edinburgh, 1987.

Balfour, Ian, and Eduwardo Cadava. "And Justice for All? The Claims of Human Rights." *South Atlantic Quarterly* 103, nos. 2–3 (2004).

Ballhatchet, Kenneth. *Caste, Class and Catholicism in India, 1789–1914*. Richmond, Surrey: Curzon, 1998.

———. *Race, Sex, and Class under the Raj: Imperial Attitudes and Policies and Their Critics, 1793–1905*. New York: St. Martin's Press, 1980.

———. *Social Policy and Social Change in Western India: 1817–1830*. London: Oxford University Press, 1957.

Barkindo, B. M. "Growing Islamism in Kano City since 1970: Causes, Forms, and Implications." Pp. 91–105 in *Muslim Identity and Social Change in Sub-Saharan Africa*, ed. Louis Brenner. Bloomington: Indiana University Press, 1993.

Barrow, John. *An Account of Travels into the Interior of Southern Africa in the Years 1797 and 1798* (1801). Repr. ed. London: Johnson Reprint Corporation, 1968.

Bartholomew, Robert E. *Exotic Deviance: Medicalizing Cultural Idioms—From Strangeness to Illness*. Boulder: University Press of Colorado, 2000.

Baynes, C. R. *Hints on Medical Jurisprudence*. Madras, 1853.

Bear, Laura Gbah. "Miscegenations of Modernity: Constructing European Respectability and Race in the Indian Railway Colony, 1857–1931." *Women's History Review* 3 (1994): 531–48.

Beccaria, Cesare. *Of Crimes and Punishment* (1764). Trans. Jane Grigson. New York: Marsilio Publishers, 1996.

Bechervaise, John. *A Farewell to My Old Shipmates and Messmates; with Some Examples, and a Few Hints of Advice*. Portsea: W. Woodward, 1847.

Beidelman, T. O. *Colonial Evangelism: A Socio-Historical Study of an East African Mission at the Grassroots*. Bloomington: Indiana University Press, 1982.

Benjamin, Walter. "Critique of Violence." Pp. 277–300 in *Reflections: Essays, Aphorisms, Autobiographical Writings*. Trans. Edmund Jephcott. New York: Schocken Books, 1978.

Bennett, Herman L. *Africans in Colonial Mexico: Absolutism, Christianity, and Afro-Creole Consciousness, 1570–1640*. Bloomington: Indiana University Press, 2003.

Berger, Mark. "Imperialism and Sexual Exploitation: A Response to Ronald Hyam's 'Empire and Sexual Opportunity.'" *Journal of Imperial and Commonwealth History* 17 (1988): 83–89.

Berry, Sara. *No Condition Is Permanent: The Social Dynamics of Agrarian Change in Sub-Saharan Africa*. Madison: University of Wisconsin Press, 1993.

Besmer, Fremont E. *Horses, Musicians, and Gods: The Hausa Cult of Possession-Trance*. South Hadley: Bergin and Garvey, 1983.

Bhabha, Homi. *The Location of Culture*. New York: Routledge, 1994.

Biewenga, Ad. *De Kaap de Goede Hoop: Een Nederlandse vestigingskolonie, 1680–1730*. Amsterdam: Uitgeverij Promestheus/Bert Bakker, 1999.

Blackburn, Robin. *The Overthrow of Colonial Slavery, 1776–1848*. London: Verso, 1988.

Blussé, Leonard. *Strange Company: Chinese Settlers, Mestizo Women and the Dutch in VOC Batavia*. Dordrecht: Foris Publications, 1986.

Boddy, Janice. *Wombs and Alien Spirits: Women, Men, and the Zar Cult in Northern Sudan*. Madison: University of Wisconsin Press, 1989.

Bolster, W. Jeffrey. *Black Jacks: African-American Seamen in the Age of Sail*. Cambridge, Mass.: Harvard University Press, 1997.

Botha, C. Graham. *General History and Social Life of the Cape of Good Hope*. Cape Town: C. Struik, 1962.

Boyd, Jean. *The Caliph's Sister: Nana Asmau, 1793–1865: Teacher, Poet, and Islamic Leader*. London: Frank Cass, 1989.

Boyd, Jean, and Beverley Mack, eds. *Collected Works of Nana Asma'u, Daughter of Usman 'Dan Fodio*. East Lansing: Michigan State University Press, 1997.

Bradlow, Edna. "Mental Illness or a Form of Resistance? The Case of Soera Brotto." *Klieo* 23 (1991): 4–16.

Brasseaux, Carl A. "Slave Regulations in French Louisiana." Pp. 209–25 in *The French Experience in Louisiana*, ed. Glenn R. Conrad. Lafayette: University of Southwestern Louisiana Press, 1995.

Broadwin, Julie. "Walking Contradictions: Chinese Women Unbound at the Turn of the Century." *Journal of Historical Sociology* 10, no. 4 (1997): 418–43.

Brown, Samuel. *Report on the Bengal Military Orphan Society and Valuation*. London: Charles and Edwin Layton, 1873.

Brown, Wendy. *States of Injury: Power and Freedom in Late Modernity*. Princeton, N.J.: Princeton University Press, 1995.

Buck-Morss, Susan. "Hegel and Haiti." *Critical Inquiry* 26, no. 4 (2000): 821–65.

Buettner, Elizabeth. "Problematic Spaces, Problematic Races: Defining Europeans in Late Colonial India." *Women's History Review* 9, no. 2 (2000): 277–97.

Bullock, Mary Brown. *An American Transplant: The Rockefeller Foundation and Peking Union Medical College*. Berkeley: University of California Press, 1980.

Burchell, Graham, Colin Gordon, and Peter Miller, eds. *The Foucault Effect: Studies in Governmentality*. Chicago: University of Chicago Press, 1991.

Burg, B. R. *Sodomy and the Perception of Evil: English Sea Rovers in the Seventeenth-Century Caribbean*. New York: New York University Press, 1983.

Burke, Timothy. *Lifebuoy Men, Lux Women: Commodification, Consumption, and Cleanliness in Modern Zimbabwe*. Durham and London: Duke University Press, 1996.

Burton, Antoinette M. *At the Heart of the Empire: Indians and the Colonial Encounter in Late-Victorian Britain*. Berkeley: University of California Press, 1998.

——. *Burdens of History: British Feminists, Indian Women, and Imperial Culture, 1865–1915*. Chapel Hill: University of North Carolina Press, 1994.

——. *Dwelling in the Archive: Women Writing House, Home, and History in Late Colonial India*. New York: Oxford University Press, 2003.

Burton, Richard F. *Goa, and the Blue Mountains; or, Six Months of Sick Leave*. Berkeley: University of California Press, 1991.

Butler, Judith. *Bodies That Matter: On the Discursive Limits of "Sex."* London: Routledge, 1993.

——. *Gender Trouble*. New York: Routledge, 1990.

———. *Precarious Life: The Powers of Mourning and Violence*. London: Verso, 2004.

Byrn Jr., John D. *Crime and Punishment in the Royal Navy: Discipline on the Leeward Islands Station, 1784–1812*. Aldershot: Scolar, 1989.

Cain, P. J., and A. G. Hopkins. *British Imperialism: Crisis and Deconstruction, 1914–1990*. London: Longman, 1993.

———. *British Imperialism: Innovation and Expansion, 1688–1914*. London: Longman, 1993.

Callaway, Barbara, and Lucy Creevey. *The Heritage of Islam: Women, Religion, and Politics in West Africa*. Boulder, Colo.: Lynne Rienner Publishers, 1994.

Canny, Nicholas P., and Anthony Pagden, eds. *Colonial Identity in the Atlantic World, 1500–1800*. Princeton, N.J.: Princeton University Press, 1987.

Caplan, Lionel. "Iconographies of Anglo-Indian Women: Gender Constructs and Contrasts in a Changing Society." *Modern Asian Studies* 34 (2000): 863–92.

Casey, Conorly. "Medicines for Madness: Suffering, Disability and the Identification of Enemies in Northern Nigeria." Ph.D. thesis, University of California, Los Angeles, 1997.

Chakrabarty, Dipesh. "Domestic Cruelty and the Birth of the Subject." Pp. 117–48 in *Provincializing Europe: Postcolonial Thought and Historical Difference*. Princeton, N.J.: Princeton University Press, 2000.

———. *Provincializing Europe: Postcolonial Thought and Historical Difference*. Princeton, N.J.: Princeton University Press, 2000.

Chang Mo-chün. "Opposition to Footbinding." Pp. 125–28 in *Chinese Women through Chinese Eyes*, ed. Li Yu-ning. Armonk, N.Y.: M. E. Sharpe, 1992.

Chatterjee, B. "Cornwallis and the Emergence of Colonial Police." *Bengal Past and Present* 102, no. 2 (July–December 1983): 1–11.

Chatterjee, Indrani. "Colouring Subalternity: Slaves, Concubines and Social Orphans in Early Colonial India." Pp. 49–97 in *Subaltern Studies X*, ed. Gautam Bhadra, Gyan Prakash, and Susie Tharu. Delhi: Oxford University Press, 1999.

———. *Gender, Slavery and Law in Colonial India*. New Delhi: Oxford University Press, 1999.

Chatterjee, K. "History as Self-Representation: The Recasting of a Political Tradition in Late Eighteenth-Century Eastern India." *Modern Asian Studies*, 32, no. 4 (1988).

Chatterjee, Partha. *The Nation and Its Fragments: Colonial and Post-Colonial Histories*. Princeton, N.J.: Princeton University Press, 1993.

Chatterjee, Partha, ed. *Wages of Freedom: Fifty Years of the Indian Nation-State*. Delhi: Oxford University Press, 1998.

Che Ruoshui. "Jiaoqi ji." *Qinding Siku quanshu, zibu* 10, *zajia lui* 3.

Chevers, Norman. *A Manual of Medical Jurisprudence in India: Including the Outline of a History of Crime against the Person in India*. Calcutta: Thacker, Spink, 1870.

Choksey, R. D. *The Aftermath 1818–1826*. Bombay, 1950.

———. *Montstuart Elphinstone, The Indian Years 1796–1827*. Bombay, 1971.

Christianse, Yvette. *Castaway*. Durham and London: Duke University Press, 1999.

Clark, Anna. *The Struggle for the Breeches: Gender and the Making of the British Working Class*. Berkeley: University of California Press, 1995.

Cmiel, Kenneth. "The Recent History of Human Rights." *American Historical Review* 109, no. 1 (2004): 117–35.

Cockerill, A. W. "The Royal Military Asylum (1803–1815)." *Journal of the Society for Army Historical Research* 79 (2001): 25–44.

Cohn, Bernard. *An Anthropologist among the Historians and Other Essays*. Delhi: Oxford University Press, 1990.

Colley, Linda. *Britons: Forging the Nation, 1707–1837*. New Haven, Conn.: Yale University Press, 1992.

———. *Captives*. New York: Pantheon, 2002.

Collingham, E. M. *Imperial Bodies; the Physical Experience of the Raj, c. 1800–1947*. Cambridge: Polity Press, 2001.

"The Colonization Mania." *Colburn's United Service Magazine*, vol. 3, 1858, 340–48.

Comaroff, Jean. *Body of Power, Spirit of Resistance: The Culture and History of a South African People*. Chicago: University of Chicago Press, 1985.

Comaroff, Jean, and John L. Comaroff. "Occult Economies and the Violence of Abstraction: Notes from the South African Postcolony." *American Ethnologist* 26, no. 3 (1999): 279–301.

———. *Of Revelation and Revolution: Christianity, Colonialism, and Consciousness in South Africa*, vol. 1. Chicago: University of Chicago Press, 1991.

Comaroff, John L., and Jean Comaroff. *Of Revelation and Revolution: The Dialectics of Modernity on an African Frontier*, vol. 2. Chicago: University of Chicago Press, 1997.

Comaroff, John L., and Jean Comaroff, eds. *Civil Society and the Political Imagination in Africa: Critical Perspectives*. Chicago: University of Chicago Press, 1999.

Cooper, Frederick. *Colonialism in Question: Theory, Knowledge, History*. Berkeley: University of California Press, 2005.

———. "Conflict and Connection: Rethinking African History." *American Historical Review* 99 (1994): 1516–43.

———. "Review: Mahmood Mamdani, Citizen and Subject: Contemporary Africa and the Legacy of Late Colonialism." *International Labor and Working Class History* 52 (1997).

Cooper, Frederick, and Randall Packard, eds. *International Development and the Social Sciences: Essays on the History and Politics of Knowledge*. Berkeley: University of California Press, 1997.

Cooper, Frederick, and Ann Laura Stoler. "Between Metropole and Colony: Rethinking a Research Agenda." Pp. 1–58 in *Tensions of Empire: Colonial Cultures in a Bourgeois World*, ed. Frederick Cooper and Ann Laura Stoler. Berkeley: University of California Press, 1997.

Cooper, James Fenimore. *The Red Rover*, ed. Warren S. Walker. Lincoln: University of Nebraska Press, 1963.

Coronil, Fernando. *The Magical State: Nature, Money, and Modernity in Venezuela*. Chicago: University of Chicago Press, 1997.

Corrigan, Philip, and Derek Sayer. *The Great Arch: English State Formation as Cultural Revolution*. Oxford: Basil Blackwell, 1985.

Cox, Edmund. *Police and Crime in India* (1910). Reprint. ed. New Delhi: Manu Publications, 1976.

Crain, Caleb. "Lovers of Human Flesh: Homosexuality and Cannibalism in Melville's Novels." *American Literature* 66, no. 1 (March 1994): 25–53.

Crawford, Catherine. "Legalizing Medicine: Early Modern Legal Systems and the Growth of Medico-Legal Knowledge." Pp. 89–116 in *Legal Medicine in History*, ed. Michael Clark and Catherine Crawford. Cambridge: Cambridge University Press, 1994.

Crenshaw, Kimberlé, ed. *Critical Race Theory: The Key Writings That Formed the Movement*. New York: New Press, 1995.

Crowder, Michael. *The Flogging of Phinehas Mcintosh: A Tale of Colonial Folly and Injustice: Bechuanaland, 1933*. New Haven, Conn.: Yale University Press, 1988.

Crowquill, Sylvanus. "Barrack Sketches—No.1; the Man That Wants a Wife." *East India United Service Journal*, vol. 23, May 1836, 334.

Dalrymple, William. *White Mughals: Love and Betrayal in Eighteenth-Century India*. London: HarperCollins, 2002.

Dana [Jr.], Richard Henry. *Two Years before the Mast*. New York: Bantam, 1959.

Daniel, E. Valentine. *Charred Lullabies*. Princeton, N.J.: Princeton University Press, 1996.

Danner, Mark. *Torture and Truth: America, Abu Ghraib, and the War on Terror*. New York: New York Review Books, 2004.

Das Gupta, Ranajit. "Capital Investment and Transport Modernisation in Colonial India." Pp. 67–92 in *Essays in Honour of Professor S. C. Sarkar*. Delhi: Prakashan, 1976.

Das, Veena. "Language and Body: Transactions in the Construction of Pain." Pp. 67–92 in *Social Suffering*, ed. Arthur Kleinman, Veena Das, and Margaret Lock. Berkeley: University of California Press, 1997.

Das, Veena, ed. *Mirrors of Violence: Communities, Riots, and Survivors in South Asia*. Delhi: Oxford University Press, 1990.

———. *Violence and Subjectivity*. Berkeley: University of California Press, 2000.

Das, Veena, and Deborah Poole, eds. *Anthropology at the Margins of the State*. Santa Fe, N.M.: School of American Research, 2004.

Davidoff, Leonore, and Catherine Hall. *Family Fortunes: Men and Women of the English Middle Class, 1780–1850*. Chicago: University of Chicago Press, 1987.

Davin, Anna. "Imperialism and Motherhood." *History Workshop* 5 (1978): 9–65.

Davis, David Brion. *The Problem of Slavery in the Age of Revolution, 1770–1823*. Ithaca, N.Y.: Cornell University Press, 1975.

———. *The Problem of Slavery in Western Culture*. Ithaca, N.Y.: Cornell University Press, 1966.

Davis, Natalie Zemon. *Fiction in the Archives: Pardon Tales and their Tellers in Sixteenth-Century France*. Stanford, Calif.: Stanford University Press, 1987.

Dawdy, Shannon Lee. "La Ville Sauvage: 'Enlightened' Colonialism and Creole Improvisation, 1699–1769." Ph.D. thesis, University of Michigan, Ann Arbor, 2003.

De Kock, Victor. *Those in Bondage*. Pretoria: Union Booksellers, 1963.

Derrida, Jacques. "Force of Law." Pp. 3–67 in *Deconstruction and the Possibility of Justice*, ed. Drucilla Cornell, Michael Rosenfeld, and David Gray Carlson. New York: Routledge, 1992.

Dhadphale, M., and S. P. Shaikh. "Epidemic Hysteria in a Zambian School: The Mysterious Madness of Mwinilunga." *British Journal of Psychiatry* 142 (1983): 85–88.

Dirks, Nicholas. *Castes of Mind: Colonialism and the Making of Modern India*. Princeton, N.J.: Princeton University Press, 2001.

———. "The Policing of Tradition: Colonialism and Anthropology in Southern India." *Comparative Studies in Society and History* 39, no. 1 (1997): 182–212.

———. *The Scandal of Empire*. Cambridge, Mass.: Harvard University Press, forthcoming.

Dooling, Amy D., and Kristina M. Torgeson. *Writing Women in Modern China*. New York: Columbia University Press, 1998.

Drescher, Seymour. *Capitalism and Antislavery: British Mobilization in Comparative Perspective*. Houndmills: Macmillan, 1986.

Duara, Prasenjit. *Rescuing History from the Nation: Questioning Narratives of Modern China*. Chicago: University of Chicago Press, 1995.

Dube, Saurabh. *Untouchable Pasts: Religion, Identity, and Power among a Central Indian Community, 1780–1950*. Albany: State University of New York Press, 1998.

Dubois, Laurent. *A Colony of Citizens: Revolution and Slave Emancipation in the French Caribbean, 1787–1804*. Chapel Hill: University of North Carolina Press, 2004.

———. *Les esclaves de la République: L'histoire oubliée de la première émancipation, 1789–1794*. Paris: Calmann-Lévy, 1998.

Duboys, J. *Recueils de Reglements, Edits, Declarations et Arrêts, Concernant le Commerce, l'Administration de la Justice, et la Police des Colonies Françaises de l'Amerique et les Engagés, avec le Code Noir et l'Addition Audit Code*. Paris: Les Libraires Associez, 1744–45.

Durkheim, Emile. *Suicide: A Study in Sociology*. Trans. J. A. Spaulding and G. Simpson. Glencoe, Md.: Free Press, 1951.

East Indian Railway Rules for Employees. Calcutta: East Indian Railway Press, 1930.

Ellms, Charles. *The Pirates Own Book: Authentic Narratives of the Most Celebrated Sea Robbers*. Salem, Mass.: Marine Research Society, 1924.

Elphick, Richard, and Hermann Giliomee, eds. *The Shaping of South African Society, 1652–1840*. Cape Town: Maskew Miller Longman, 1989.

Eltis, David. *Economic Growth and the Ending of the Transatlantic Slave Trade*. New York: Oxford University Press, 1987.

"English Women in Hindustan." *Calcutta Review* 4 (1845): 96–127.

Epstein, Maram. "Engendering Order: Structure, Gender, and Meaning in the Qing Novel *Jinghua yuan*." *Chinese Literature: Essays, Articles, and Reviews* 18 (1996): 101–27.

Ernst, Waltraud. "Colonial Lunacy Policies and the Madras Lunatic Asylum in the Early Nineteenth Century." Pp. 137–65 in *Health, Medicine and Empire:*

Perspectives on Colonial India, New Perspectives in South Asian History, ed. Biswamoy Pati and Mark Harrison. Hyderabad: Orient Longman, 2001.

Ernst, Waltraud. "Colonial Policies, Racial Politics and the Development of Psychiatric Institutions in Early Nineteenth-Century India." Pp. 80–100 in *Race, Science and Medicine, 1700–1960*, ed. Waltraud Ernst and Bernard Harris. London: Routledge, 1999.

Escobar, Arturo. *Encountering Development: The Making and Unmaking of the Third World*. Princeton, N.J.: Princeton University Press, 1995.

Fanon, Frantz. *Black Skin, White Masks*. Trans. Charles Lam Markmann. New York: Grove Press, 1967.

———. *The Wretched of the Earth*. Trans. Constance Farrington. New York: Grove Press, 1986.

Feldman, Allen. *Formations of Violence: The Narrative of the Body and Political Terror in Northern Ireland*. Chicago: University of Chicago Press, 1991.

Ferguson, James. *The Anti-Politics Machine: "Development," Depoliticization, and Bureaucratic Power in Lesotho*. Cambridge: Cambridge University Press, 1990.

Ferguson, Niall. *Colossus: The Price of America's Empire*. New York: Penguin, 2004.

———. *Empire: How Britain Made the Modern World*. London: Allen Lane, 2003.

Ferme, Mariane C. "What 'Alhaji Airplane' Saw in Mecca, and What Happened When He Came Home: Ritual Transformation in a Mende Community." Pp. 27–44 in *Syncretism/Anti-Syncretism: The Politics of Religious Change*, ed. Charles Stewart and Rosalind Shaw. London: Routledge, 1994.

Fika, Adamu Mohammed. *The Kano Civil War and British Over-Rule 1882–1940*. Oxford: Oxford University Press, 1978.

Firebrace (Colonel). "On the Errors and Faults in our Military System." *Colburn's United Service Magazine*, vol. 2, 1843, 537–47.

Fisch, Jorg. *Cheap Lives and Dear Limbs: The British Transformation of the Bengal Criminal Law, 1769–1817*. Wiesbaden: Franz Steiner Verlag, 1983.

Fisher, Michael H. *Counterflows to Colonialism: Indian Travellers and Settlers in Britain, 1600–1857*. Delhi: Permanent Black, 2004.

Forge, Arlette, and Michel Foucault. *Le désordre des familles: Lettres de cachet des Archives de la Bastilles au XVIIIe Siecle*. Paris: Editions Julliard/Gallimard, 1982.

Foucault, Michel. *Discipline and Punish: The Birth of the Prison*. Trans. Alan Sheridan. New York: Vintage Books, 1979.

———. "Governmentality." Pp. 87–104 in *The Foucault Effect: Studies in Govern-*

mentality, ed. Graham Burchell, Colin Gordon, and Peter Miller. Chicago: University of Chicago Press, 1991.

———. *The History of Sexuality*, Volume. 1: *An Introduction*. Trans. Robert Hurley. New York: Vintage, 1980.

———. *The History of Sexuality*, Volume 2: *The Use of Pleasure*. Trans. Robert Hurley. New York: Vintage, 1990.

———. *The History of Sexuality*, Volume 3: *The Care of the Self*. Trans. Robert Hurley. New York: Vintage, 1988.

———. "The Life of Infamous Men." In *Michel Foucault: Power, Truth, Strategy*. Sydney: Feral Publications, 1979.

Freehling, William W. *Prelude to Civil War: The Nullification Controversy in South Carolina, 1816–1836*. New York: Harper and Row, 1966.

"From Camp to Quarters; or Life in an Indian Cantonment after Field Service." *Colburn's United Service Magazine*, vol. 2, no. 3, 1859.

Fukazawa, H. K. *The Medieval Deccan: Peasants, Social Systems and States, Sixteenth to Eighteenth Centuries*. Delhi: Oxford University Press, 1991.

Fuller, C. J., and John Harriss. "Introduction." Pp. 1–30 in *The Everyday State and Society in Modern India*, ed. C. J. Fuller and Veronique Benei. London: Hurst, 2001.

Furniss, Graham. *Poetry, Prose, and Popular Culture in Hausa*. Washington, D.C.: Smithsonian Institution Press, 1996.

Gardener, Lloyd C., and Marilyn B. Young, eds. *The New American Empire: A 21st Century Teach-in on U.S. Foreign Policy*. New York: New Press, 2005.

Ghosh, Durba. "Making and Un-making Loyal Subjects: Pensioning Widows and Educating Orphans in Early Colonial India." *Journal of Imperial and Commonwealth History* 31 (2003): 1–28.

Gilbert, Arthur N. "The *Africaine* Courts-Martial: A Study of Buggery and the Royal Navy." *Journal of Homosexuality* 1, no. 1 (1974): 111–22.

———. "Buggery and the British Navy, 1700–1861." *Journal of Social History* 10 (1976): 72–98.

Gilchrist, J. B. *The General East India Guide and Vade Mecum*. London: Kingsbury, Parbury and Allen, 1825.

Goldberg, David Theo, ed. *Anatomy of Racism*. Minneapolis: University of Minnesota Press, 1990.

———. *The Racial State*. Malden: Blackwell Publishers, 2002.

Goldberg, Jonathan. *Sodometries: Renaissance Texts, Modern Sexualities*. Stanford, Calif.: Stanford University Press, 1992.

Gould, Robert F. *Military Lodges*. London: Gale and Polden, 1899.

Gould, Stephen Jay. *The Mismeasure of Man*. 2d ed. New York: W. W. Norton, 1996.

Greenberg, Joseph. *The Influence of Islam on a Sudanese Religion*. New York: J. J. Augustin, 1947.

Greenblatt, Stephen. *Marvelous Possessions: The Wonder of the New World*. Chicago: University of Chicago Press, 1991.

Grosz, E. A. *Space, Time, and Perversion: Essays on the Politics of Bodies*. New York: Routledge, 1995.

———. *Volatile Bodies: Toward a Corporeal Feminism*. Bloomington: Indiana University Press, 1994.

Guha, Ranajit. "Chandra's Death." *Subaltern Studies* 5 (1987): 135–65.

———. *Elementary Aspects of Peasant Insurgency in Colonial India*. Delhi: Oxford, 1983.

———. *A Rule of Property for Bengal: An Essay on the Idea of Permanent Settlement*. Paris: Moulton, 1963.

Guha, Sumit. "An Indian Penal Regime: Maharashtra in the Eighteenth Century." *Past and Present* 147 (1995): 101–26.

Gune, V. T. *The Judicial System of the Marathas*. Yeravada, Poona: Deccan College, 1953.

Gupta, Akhil. "Blurred Boundaries: The Discourse of Corruption, the Culture of Politics, and the Imagined State." *American Ethnologist* 22, no. 2 (1995): 375–402.

———. *Postcolonial Developments: Agriculture in the Making of Modern India*. Durham and London: Duke University Press, 1998.

Gupta, Anandswarup. *Crime and Police in India up to 1861*. Agra: Sahitya Bhavan, 1974.

Hall, Catherine. *White, Male and Middle Class: Explorations in Feminism and History*. Cambridge: Polity Press, 1992.

Hall, Catherine, Keith McClelland, and Jane Rendall. *Defining the Victorian Nation: Class, Race, Gender and the Reform Act of 1867*. Cambridge: Cambridge University Press, 2000.

Hall, Gwendolyn Midlo. *Africans in Colonial Louisiana: The Development of Afro-Creole Culture in the Eighteenth Century*. Baton Rouge: Louisiana State University Press, 1992.

Hamer, Philip M. "British Consuls and the Negro Seamen Acts, 1850–1860." *Journal of Southern History* 1, no. 2 (May 1935): 138–168.

———. "Great Britain, the United States, and the Negro Seamen Acts, 1822–1848." *Journal of Southern History* 1, no. 1 (February 1935): 3–28.

Handbook of Rules and Regulations for all Departments of the East Indian Railway. Calcutta: East Indian Railway Press, 1916.

Hanger, Kimberly S. *Bounded Lives, Bounded Places: Free Black Society in Colonial New Orleans, 1769–1803.* Durham and London: Duke University Press, 1997.

Hansen, Thomas Blom, and Finn Stepputat, eds. *States of Imagination: Ethnographic Explorations of the Postcolonial State.* Durham and London: Duke University Press, 2001.

Hanson, Elizabeth. "Torture and Truth in Renaissance England." *Representations* 34 (1991): 53–84.

Hardt, Michael, and Antonio Negri. *Empire.* Cambridge, Mass.: Harvard University Press, 2000.

Harootunian, Harry. *Overcome by Modernity: History, Culture and Community in Interwar Japan.* Princeton, N.J.: Princeton University Press, 2000.

Harris, Grace. "'Possession Hysteria' in a Kenya Tribe." *American Anthropologist* 59, no. 6 (1957): 1046–66.

Harrison, Mark. *Climates and Constitutions: Health, Race, Environment and British Imperialism in India.* Delhi: Oxford University Press, 1999.

Harrold, Frederick S. "Jim Crow in the Navy, 1798–1941." *United States Naval Institute Proceedings* 105 (September 1979): 46–53.

Hawes, C. J. *Poor Relations: The Making of the Eurasian Community in British India, 1773–1833.* London: Curzon, 1996.

Headrick, Daniel. *The Tentacles of Progress: Technology Transfer in the Age of Imperialism, 1850–1940.* New York: Oxford University Press, 1988.

Heese, H. F. *Reg en Onreg: Kaapse Regspraak in die Agtiende Eeu.* Belville: Instituut vir Historiese Navorsing, Universiteit van Wes-Kaapland, 1994.

Hegel, Georg Wilhelm Friedrich. *Phenomenology of Spirit.* Trans. Arnold Vincent Miller. Oxford: Clarendon Press, 1977.

Hendrickson, Hildi, ed. *Clothing and Difference: Embodied Identities in Colonial and Post-Colonial Africa.* Durham and London: Duke University Press, 1996.

Hendrickson, Kenneth E. *Making Saints: Religion and the Public Image of the British Army, 1809–1885.* Madison, N.J.: Fairleigh-Dickinson University Press, 1998.

Hersh, Seymour M. *Chain of Command: The Road from 9/11 to Abu Ghraib.* New York: HarperCollins, 2004.

Hichberger, J. M. *Images of the Army: The Military in British Art, 1815–1914.* Manchester: Manchester University Press, 1988.

Hitchcock, Tim. *English Sexualities, 1700–1800*. New York: St. Martin's Press, 1997.

Hobbes, Robert George. "Calcutta." *Bentley's Miscellany*, vol. 30, 1851, 361–68.

Hodgson, Dorothy L. *Once Intrepid Warriors: Gender, Ethnicity, and the Cultural Politics of Maasai Development*. Bloomington: Indiana University Press, 2001.

Hodgson, Dorothy L., ed. *Gendered Modernities: Ethnographic Perspectives*. New York: Palgrave, 2001.

Holt, Thomas C. *The Problem of Freedom: Race, Labor, and Politics in Jamaica and Britain, 1832–1938*. Baltimore: Johns Hopkins University Press, 1992.

———. *The Problem of Race in the Twenty-First Century*. Cambridge, Mass.: Harvard University Press, 2000.

Horsman, Reginald. *Race and Manifest Destiny: The Origins of American Anglo-Saxonism*. Cambridge, Mass.: Harvard University Press, 1981.

Hough, William. *Military Law Authorities*. Calcutta: W. Thacker, 1839.

Hunt, Nancy Rose. *A Colonial Lexicon: Of Birth Ritual, Medicalization, and Mobility in the Congo*. Durham and London: Duke University Press, 1999.

Hunwick, John. "Sub-Saharan Africa and the Wider World of Islam: Historical and Contemporary Perspectives." Pp. 28–54 in *Encounters between Sufis and Islamists*, ed. Eva Evers Rosander and David Westerlund. Athens: Ohio University Press, 1997.

Hurd, Ian. *Building the Railways of the Raj, 1850–1900*. New Delhi: Oxford University Press, 1995.

Hurd, John. "Railways: The Beginnings of the Modern Economy." Pp. 737–62 in *The Cambridge Economic History of India*, Volume 2 *(c. 1757–c. 1970)*, ed. D. Kumar and Meghnad Desai. Cambridge: Cambridge University Press, 1983.

Hyam, Ronald. *Empire and Sexuality: The British Experience*. Manchester: Manchester University Press, 1990.

Ibrahim, Jibrin. "The Politics of Religion in Nigeria: The Parameters of the 1987 Crisis in Kaduna State." *Review of African Political Economy* 45–46 (1989): 65–82.

———. "Religion and Political Turbulence in Nigeria." *Journal of Modern African Studies* 29, no. 1 (1991): 115–36.

Imam, Ayesha. "Working within Nigeria's Sharia Courts." *Human Rights Dialogue* 2, no. 10 (2003).

Ingersoll, Thomas N. *Mammon and Manon in Early New Orleans: The First Slave Society in the Deep South, 1718–1819*. Knoxville: University of Tennessee Press, 1999.

Jacquemont, Victor. *Letters from India; Describing a Journey in the British Do-*

minions of India, Tibet, Lahore and Cashmere, during the Years 1828, 1829, 1830, 1831. London: Edward Churlton, 1834.

Jin Yi. *Nüjie zhong.* Shanghai: Datong shuju, 1903.

Joseph, Richard A. *Democracy and Prebendal Politics in Nigeria: The Rise and Fall of the Second Republic.* Cambridge: Cambridge University Press, 1987.

Judge, Joan. "Reforming the Feminine: Female Literacy and the Legacy of 1898." In *Rethinking the 1898 Reform Period: Political and Cultural Change in Late Qing China,* ed. Rebecca E. Karl and Peter Zarrow. Pp. 158–79. Cambridge, Mass.: Harvard University Asia Center, 2002.

Kadam, V. S. "The Institution of Marriage and the Position of Women in Eighteenth Century Maharashtra." *Indian Economic and Social History Review* 25, no. 3 (1988): 341–70.

Kapferer, Bruce. *A Celebration of Demons: Exorcism and the Aesthetics of Healing in Sri Lanka.* Bloomington: Indiana University Press, 1983.

Kaplan, Martha. "Panopticon in Poona: An Essay on Foucault and Colonialism." *Cultural Anthropology* 10, no. 1 (1995): 85–98.

Karl, Rebecca. "'Slavery,' Citizenship, and Gender in Late Qing China's Global Context." Pp. 212–44 in *Rethinking the 1898 Reform Period,* ed. Rebecca Karl and Peter Zarrow. Cambridge, Mass.: Harvard University Council on East Asian Publications, 2002.

———. *Staging the World: Chinese Nationalism at the Turn of the Twentieth Century.* Durham and London: Duke University Press, 2002.

Kaye, John William. *Doveton; or, the Man of Many Impulses. By the Author of "Jerningham."* 3 vols. London: Smith, Elder, 1837.

———. *Peregrine Pultuney: or, Life in India.* 3 vols. London: John Mortimer, 1844.

———. *The Story of Basil Bouverie. By the Author of "Peregrine Pultuney."* 3 vols. Calcutta: privately printed, 1842.

Keegan, Timothy. *Colonial South Africa and the Origins of the Racial Order.* Cape Town: David Philip, 1996.

Kennedy, Dane. *The Magic Mountains: Hill Stations and the British Raj.* Berkeley: University of California Press, 1996.

Kennedy, Paul M. *The Rise and Fall of British Naval Mastery.* New York: Scribner's, 1976.

Kenyatta, Jomo. *Facing Mount Kenya.* New York: Vintage, n.d. [1965].

Kerber, Linda K. "The Meanings of Citizenship." *Journal of American History* 84, no. 3 (December 1997): 833–54.

Kerr, Derek N. *Petty Felony, Slave Defiance, and Frontier Villainy: Crime and Criminal Justice in Spanish Louisiana, 1770–1803.* New York: Garland, 1993.

Kevles, Bettyann Holtzmann. *Naked to the Bone: Medical Imaging in the Twentieth Century*. New Brunswick, N.J.: Rutgers University Press, 1997.

Khalidi, Rashid. *Resurrecting Empire: Western Footprints and America's Perilous Path in the Middle East*. Boston: Beacon Press, 2004.

Khalil, Sidi. *Maliki Law: Being a Summary from French Translations of the Mukhtasar of Sidi Khalil* (1916). Trans. F. H. Ruxton. London: Luzac, 1978.

Killingray, David. "Punishment to Fit the Crime? Penal Policy and Practice in British Colonial Africa." In *Pour une histoire de l'enfermement et de l'incarceration en Afrique XIXe–XXe siècles*, ed. Florence Bernault. Paris: Karthala, 2000.

———. "The Rod of Empire: The Debate over Corporal Punishment in the British African Colonial Forces, 1888–1946." *Journal of African History* 35 (1994): 201–35.

Kochanski, Halik. *Sir Garnet Wolseley: Victorian Hero*. London: Hambledon, 2000.

Kooiman, Dick. *Conversion and Social Equality in India: The London Missionary Society in South Travancore in the 19th Century*. New Delhi: Manohar Publications, 1989.

Kumar, Ravinder. *Western India in the Nineteenth Century: A Study in the Social History of Maharashtra*. London: Routledge and Kegan Paul, 1968.

Labaree, Benjamin W., et al. *America and the Sea: A Maritime History*. Mystic, Conn.: Mystic Seaport Museum, 1998.

Lahiri, Shompa. "Patterns of Resistance: Indian Seamen in Imperial Britain." Pp. 155–78 in *Language, Labour and Migration*, ed. Anne J. Kershen. Aldershot: Ashgate, 2000.

Laitin, David D. *Hegemony and Culture: Politics and Religious Change among the Yoruba*. Chicago: University of Chicago Press, 1986.

Landau, Paul. *The Realm of the Word: Language, Gender, and Christianity in a Southern African Kingdom*. Portsmouth: Heinemann, 1995.

Langley, Harold D. *Social Reform in the United States Navy, 1798–1862*. Chicago: University of Illinois Press, 1967.

Laqueur, Thomas. *Making Sex: Body and Gender from the Greeks to Freud*. Cambridge, Mass.: Harvard University Press, 1990.

Larson, Wendy. *Women and Writing in Modern China*. Stanford, Calif.: Stanford University Press, 1998.

Lavery, Brian. *Nelson's Navy: The Ships, Men, and Organization, 1793–1815*. Annapolis: Naval Institute Press, 1994.

Lawrence, Henry. *Adventures of an Officer in the Service of Runjeet Singh* (1845). Karachi: Oxford University Press, 1975.

Lawson, Charles. *At Home on Furlough*. 2d ed. Madras: Madras Mail Press, 1875.

Lawson, Fatima. "Islamic Fundamentalism and Continuing Education for Hausa Women in Northern Nigeria." Ph.D. thesis, University of Minnesota, Minneapolis, 1995.

Leenaars, Antoon, ed. *Suicidology*. London: Jason Araonson, 1993.

Levine, Philippa. *Prostitution, Race and Politics: Policing Venereal Disease in the British Empire*. London: Routledge, 2003.

———. "Rereading the 1890s: Venereal Disease as 'Constitutional Crisis' in Britain and British India." *Journal of Asian Studies* 55 (1996): 585–612.

Li Ruzhen. *Jinghua yuan*. Beijing: Renmin wenxue chubanshe, 1990.

Li Yuning and Zhang Yufa, eds. *Jindai Zhongguo nüquan yundong shiliao*. Taipei: Zhuanji wenxue chubanshe, 1975.

Lin Qiumin. "Jindai Zhongguo de buchanzu yundong (1895–1937)." M.A. thesis, Guoli Zhengzhi daxue, Taipei, 1990.

Lin Weihong. "Qingji de funü buchanzu yundong, 1894–1911." *Guoli Taiwan daxue lishi xuexi xuebao* 16 (1991): 139–80.

Linebaugh, Peter, and Marcus Rediker. *The Many-Headed Hydra: Sailors, Slaves, Commoners, and the Hidden History of the Revolutionary Atlantic*. Boston: Beacon Press, 2000.

Lü Meiyi and Zheng Yongfu. *Zhongguo funü yundong, 1840–1921*. Zhengzhou: Henan renmin chubanshe, 1990.

Lubeck, Paul. "Islamic Political Movements in Northern Nigeria: The Problem of Class Analysis." Pp. 244–60 in *Islam, Politics, and Social Movements*, ed. Edmund Burke and Ira Lapidus. Berkeley: University of California Press, 1988.

———. "Islamic Protest and Oil-Based Capitalism: Agriculture, Rural Linkages, and Urban Popular Movements in Northern Nigeria." Pp. 268–90 in *State, Oil, and Agriculture in Nigeria*, ed. Michael Watts. Berkeley: University of California Press, 1987.

Lugard, Frederick. *Political Memoranda: Revision of Instructions to Political Officers on Subjects Chiefly Political and Administrative 1913–1918*. 3d ed. London: Frank Cass, 1970.

Lunn, Ken, and Ann Day. "Deference and Defiance: The Changing Nature of Petitioning in British Naval Dockyards." Pp. 131–50 in *Petitions in Social History*, International Review of Social History Supp. 9, ed. L. Heerma van Voss. Cambridge: Cambridge University Press, 2002.

MacDonald, Michael, and Terence Murphy. *Sleepless Souls: Suicide in Early Modern England*. Oxford: Clarendon Press, 1990.

MacGowan, John. *Beside the Bamboo*. London: London Missionary Society, 1914.

———. *How England Saved China*. London: T. Fisher Unwin, 1913.

MacKinnon, Kenneth. *A Treatise on the Public Health, Climate, Hygiene, and Prevailing Diseases of Bengal and the North-West Provinces*. Cawnpore: Cawnpore Press, 1848.

MacMullen, John M. *Camp and Barrack Room; or, the British Army as it is, by a late Staff Sergeant of the 13th Light Infantry*. London: Chapman and Hall, 1846.

"The Madras Native Army." *Calcutta Review* 33 (1859): 148.

Maduell Jr., Charles R. *The Census Tables for the French Colony of Louisiana from 1699 through 1732*. Baltimore: Genealogical Publishing, 1972.

Malchow, H. L. *Gothic Images of Race in Nineteenth-Century Britain*. Stanford, Calif.: Stanford University Press, 1996.

Malkki, Liisa H. *Purity and Exile: Violence, Memory, and National Cosmology among Hutu Refugees in Tanzania*. Chicago: University of Chicago Press, 1995.

Mamdani, Mahmood. *Citizen and Subject: Contemporary Africa and the Legacy of Late Colonialism*. Princeton, N.J.: Princeton University Press, 1996.

———. *Good Muslim, Bad Muslim: America, the Cold War, and the Roots of Terror*. New York: Pantheon Books, 2004.

———. *When Victims Become Killers: Colonialism, Nativism, and the Genocide in Rwanda*. Princeton, N.J.: Princeton University Press, 2001.

Mani, Lata. *Contentious Traditions: The Debate on Sati in Colonial India*. Berkeley: University of California Press, 1998.

Marshall, P. J. "The White Town of Calcutta under the Rule of the East India Company." *Modern Asian Studies* 43 (2000): 307–32.

Martin, Emily. *The Woman in the Body: A Cultural Analysis of Reproduction*. Boston: Beacon Press, 1987.

Martin, J. Ranald. *The Sanitary History of the British Army in India, Past and Present*. London: Savill, Edwards, 1868.

Masquelier, Adeline. "Debating Muslims, Disputed Practices: Struggles for the Realization of an Alternative Moral Order in Niger." Pp. 219–50 in *Civil Society and the Political Imagination in Africa: Critical Perspectives*, ed. John L. Comaroff and Jean Comaroff. Chicago: University of Chicago Press, 1999.

———. "Identity, Alterity, and Ambiguity in a Nigerien Community: Competing Definitions of 'True' Islam." Pp. 222–44 in *Postcolonial Identities in Africa*, ed. Richard Werbner. London: Zed Books, 1996.

Mazower, Mark. "Violence and the State in the Twentieth Century." *American Historical Review* 1158–78 (2002): xv, 242.

McClintock, Anne. *Imperial Leather: Race, Gender, and Sexuality in the Early Colonial Context*. New York: Routledge, 1995.

McCosh, John. *Advice to Officers in India*. London: W. H. Allen, 1856.

McCurry, Stephanie. *Masters of Small Worlds: Yeoman Households, Gender Relations, and the Political Culture of the Antebellum South Carolina Low Country*. New York: Oxford University Press, 1995.

McVay, Pamela. "'I Am the Devil's Own': Crime, Class and Identity in the Seventeenth Century Dutch East Indies." Unpublished Ph.D. dissertation, University of Illinois, Urbana-Champaign, 1995.

Memorandum by the Railway Board to the Royal Commission on Labour. Simla: Government of India Press, 1930.

Meng Yue and Dai Jinhua. *Fuchu lishi dibiao*. Zhengzhou: Henan renmin chubanshe, 1989.

Meriwether, Robert L., ed. *Papers of John C. Calhoun*. Columbia: University of South Carolina Press, 1959.

Metcalf, Thomas R. *The Aftermath of Revolt: India, 1857–1870*. Princeton, N.J.: Princeton University Press, 1964.

Micelle, Jerry A. "From Law Court to Local Government: Metamorphosis of the Superior Council of French Louisiana." Pp. 408–24 in *The French Experience in Louisiana*, ed. Glenn R. Conrad. Lafayette: University of Southwestern Louisiana Press, 1995.

"Military Colonization in India." *Colburn's United Service Magazine*, vol. 2, 1858, 534–45.

Military Orphan Society. *Rules and Regulations of the Lower Branch of the Military Orphan Society*. Calcutta: Military Orphan Press, 1850.

Millett, Allan R. *Semper Fidelis: The History of the United States Marine Corps*. New York: Macmillan, 1980.

Minois, George. *History of Suicide: Voluntary Death in Western Culture*. Baltimore: Johns Hopkins University Press, 1999.

Mintz, Sidney W. *Sweetness and Power: The Place of Sugar in Modern History*. New York: Viking, 1985.

Mitchell, J. W. *The Wheels of Ind*. London: Thornton and Butterworth, 1934.

Mitchell, Timothy. *Rule of Experts: Egypt, Techno-Politics, Modernity*. Berkeley: University of California Press, 2002.

Moogk, Peter N. "'Thieving Buggers' and 'Stupid Sluts': Insults and Popular

Culture in New France." *William and Mary Quarterly*, 3d series, vol. 44, no. 4 (October 1979): 524–47.

Morley, Henry, and W. H. Wills. "The Soldier's Wife." *Household Words* 11, no. 265 (21 April 1855): 278–80.

Morris, Thomas D. *Southern Slavery and the Law, 1619–1860*. Chapel Hill: University of North Carolina Press, 1996.

Morrison, Michael A., and James Brewer Stewart, eds. *Race and the Early Republic: Racial Consciousness and Nation-Building in the Early Republic*. Lanham, Md.: Rowman and Littlefield, 2002.

Moses, Wilson Jeremiah. *Afrotopia: The Roots of African American Popular History*. Cambridge: Cambridge University Press, 1998.

Mouat, Frederic John. *The British Soldier in India*. London: R. C. Lepage, 1859.

Mudimbe, V. Y. *The Invention of Africa: Gnosis, Philosophy, and the Order of Knowledge*. Bloomington: Indiana University Press, 1988.

Murray, Martin. "Configuring the Trajectory of African Political History." *Canadian Journal of African Studies* 34, no. 2 (2000).

Murrell, William Meacham. *Cruise of the Frigate Columbia*. Boston: Benjamin B. Mussey, 1840.

Nedostup, Rebecca, and Liang Hong-ming. "Begging the Sages of the Party-State: Citizenship and Government in Transition in Nationalist China, 1927–1937." Pp. 185–207 in *Petitions in Social History*, International Review of Social History Supplement 9, ed. L. Heerma van Voss. Cambridge: Cambridge University Press, 2002.

Newton-King, Susan. *Masters and Servants on the Cape Eastern Frontier*. Cambridge: Cambridge University Press, 1999.

Nigam, Sanjay. "Disciplining and Policing the 'Criminals by Birth,' Part 1: The Making of the Colonial Stereotype—The Criminal Tribes and Castes of North India." *Indian Economic and Social History Review* 37, no. 2 (1990): 131–64.

———. "Disciplining and Policing the 'Criminals by Birth,' Part 2: The Development of a Disciplinary System, 1871–1900." *Indian Economic and Social History Review* 37, no. 3 (1990): 257–88.

Nubola, Cecilia. "Supplications between Politics and Justice: The Northern and Central Italian States in the Early Modern Age." In *Petitions in Social History*, International Review of Social History Supplement 9, ed. L. Heerma van Voss. Cambridge: Cambridge University Press, 2002.

Obeyesekere, Gananath. "Cannibal Feasts in Nineteenth-Century Fiji: Seamen's Yarns and the Ethnographic Imagination." Pp. 63–86 in *Cannibalism and the Colonial World*, ed. Francis Barker, Peter Hulme, and Margaret Iversen. Cambridge: Cambridge University Press, 1998.

O'Brien, Susan M. "Power and Paradox: Discourses of Gender, Healing, and Islamic Tradition in Northern Nigeria." Ph.D. thesis, University of Wisconsin, Madison, 2000.

Oddie, Geoffrey A. *Social Protest in India: British Protestant Missionaries and Social Reforms, 1850–1900*. New Delhi: Manohar, 1979.

O'Hanlon, Rosalind. *Caste, Conflict, and Ideology: Mahatma Jotirao Phule and Low Caste Protest in Nineteenth-Century India*. Cambridge: Cambridge University Press, 1985.

Oldenburg, Veena Talwar. *The Making of Colonial Lucknow, 1856–1877*. Princeton, N.J.: Princeton University Press, 1984.

Omissi, David. *The Sepoy and the Raj; the Indian Army, 1860–1940*. London: Macmillan, 1994.

Ong, Aihwa. "The Production of Possession: Spirits and Multinational Corporations in Malaysia." *American Anthropologist* 15, no. 1 (1988): 28–42.

———. *Spirits of Resistance and Capitalist Discipline: Factory Women in Malaysia*. Albany: State University of New York Press, 1987.

———. "State versus Islam: Malay Families, Women's Bodies, and the Body Politic in Malaysia." Pp. 159–94 in *Bewitching Women, Pious Men: Gender and Body Politics in Southeast Asia*, ed. Aihwa Ong and Richard Peletz. Berkeley: University of California Press, 1995.

Ortner, Sherry B. "Resistance and the Problem of Ethnographic Refusal." *Comparative Studies in Society and History* 37, no. 1 (1995): 173–93.

Ota, Nancy K. "Private Matters: Family and Race and the Post–World-War-II Translation of 'American.'" Pp. 209–34 in *Petitions in Social History*, International Review of Social History Supplement 9, ed. L. Heerma van Voss. Cambridge: Cambridge University Press, 2002.

Pagden, Anthony. *Lords of All the World: Ideologies of Empire in Spain, Britain and France, c.1500-c.1800*. New Haven: Yale University Press, 1995.

Paget, Georgina Theodosia Fitzmoor-Halsey. *Camp and Cantonment: A Journal of Life in India in 1857–185*. London: Longman, Green, Longman, Roberts and Green, 1865.

Pandey, Gyanendra. *Remembering Partition: Violence, Nationalism, and History in India*. Cambridge: Cambridge University Press, 2001.

Peabody, Sue. *"There Are No Slaves in France": The Political Culture of Race and Slavery in the Ancien Régime*. New York: Oxford University Press, 1996.

Pedersen, Susan. "National Bodies, Unspeakable Acts: The Sexual Politics of

Colonial Policy-making." *Journal of Modern History* 63 (December 1991): 647–80.

Peers, Douglas M. *Between Mars and Mammon: Colonial Armies and the Garrison State in Early-Nineteenth Century India*. London: Tauris, 1995.

———. " 'The Habitual Nobility of Being': British Officers and the Social Construction of the Bengal Army in the Early Nineteenth Century." *Modern Asian Studies* 25 (1991): 545–70.

———. "Imperial Vice: Sex, Drink and the Health of British Troops in North Indian Cantonments, 1800–1858." Pp. 25–52 in *Guardians of Empire: The Armed Forces of the Colonial Powers, c.1700–1964*, ed. David Killingray and David Omissi. Manchester: Manchester University Press, 1999.

———. "Privates Off Parade: Regimenting Sexuality in the Nineteenth Century Indian Empire." *International History Review* 20, no. 4 (1998): 823–54.

———. "Sepoys, Soldiers and the Lash: Race, Caste and Army Discipline in India, 1820–1850." *Journal of Imperial and Commonwealth History* 23 (1995): 211–47.

———. "Torture, the Police and the Colonial State in Madras Presidency, 1816–1855." *Criminal Justice History* 12 (1991): 29–56.

Pemberton, Charles Reece. *The Autobiography of Pel. Verjuice*, ed. Eric Partridge. London: Scholartis, 1929.

Pemberton, John. *On the Subject of "Java."* Ithaca, N.Y.: Cornell University Press, 1995.

Penn, Nigel, "The Northern Cape Frontier Zone, 1700–1815." Unpublished Ph.D. thesis, University of Cape Town, 1995.

Philbrick, Nathaniel. *In the Heart of the Sea: The Tragedy of the Whaleship Essex*. New York: Viking, 2000.

Pickering, W. S. F., and Geoffrey Walford, eds. *Durkheim's Suicide: A Century of Research and Debate*. London: Routledge, 2000.

Pierce, Steven. "Farmers and 'Prostitutes': Twentieth-Century Problems of Female Inheritance in Kano Emirate, Nigeria." *Journal of African History* 44, no. 3 (2003): 463–86.

———. *Farmers and the State in Colonial Kano: Land Tenure and the Legal Imagination*. Bloomington: Indiana University Press, 2005.

———. "Looking for the Legal: Land, Law, and Colonialism in Kano Emirate, Nigeria." Ph.D. thesis, University of Michigan, Ann Arbor, 2000.

Pinney, Christopher. *Camera Indica: The Social Life of Indian Photographs*. Chicago: University of Chicago Press, 1997.

Police Torture and Murder in Bengal. Reports of Two Trials of the Police of the District of Burwan in August and September 1860, Confirmed by the Sudder Nizamut. Calcutta: Bengal Printing, 1861.

Poovey, Mary. *Uneven Developments: The Ideological Work of Gender in Mid-Victorian England.* Chicago: University of Chicago Press, 1988.

"The Portuguese in North India." *Calcutta Review* 5 (1846): 243–93.

Povinelli, Elizabeth. *The Cunning of Recognition: Indigenous Alterities and the Making of Australian Multiculturalism.* Durham and London: Duke University Press, 2002.

Prentice, Rina. *A Celebration of the Sea: The Decorative Art Collection of the National Maritime Museum.* Greenwich, Conn.: National Maritime Museum, 1994.

Price, Pamela G. *Kingship and Political Practice in Colonial India.* Cambridge: Cambridge University Press, 1996.

Proceedings of the Railway Conference. Simla: Government of India Press, 1900.

Raben, Remco. "Batavia and Colombo: The Ethnic and Spatial Order of Two Colonial Cities." Unpublished Ph.D. thesis, Leiden University, 1996.

Ranger, T. O. *The African Voice in Southern Rhodesia, 1898–1930.* London: Heinemann, 1970.

———. "The Invention of Tradition in Colonial Africa." In *The Invention of Tradition*, ed. E. J. Hobsbawn and T. O. Ranger. Cambridge: Cambridge University Press, 1983.

———. "The Invention of Tradition Revisited." In *Legitimacy and the State in Twentieth-Century Africa: Essays in Honor of A. H. M. Kirk-Greene*, ed. T. O. Ranger and Olufemi Vaughan. Houndmills: Macmillan, 1993.

———. *Revolt in Southern Rhodesia, 1896–7: A Study in African Resistance.* Evanston: Northwestern University Press, 1967.

Rao, Anupama. "The Caste Question: Untouchable Struggles for Rights and Recognition." Unpublished ms.

Rao, Anupama, and Steven Pierce. "Discipline and the Other Body: Correction, Corporeality, and Colonial Rule." *Interventions* 3, no. 2 (2001): 159–68.

Rao, V. D. "A Note on the Police of the City of Poona." *Journal of Indian History* 36 (1958): 223–28.

Rasor, Eugene. *Reform in the Royal Navy: A Social History of the Lower Deck, 1850 to 1880.* Hamden, Conn.: Archon, 1976.

Rediker, Marcus. *Between the Devil and the Deep Blue Sea: Merchant Seamen, Pirates, and the Anglo-American Maritime World, 1700–1750.* Cambridge: Cambridge University Press, 1987.

Rejali, Darius M. *Torture and Modernity: Self, Society, and State in Modern Iran*. Boulder, Colo.: Westview Press, 1994.

———. "Torture as a Civic Marker: Solving a Global Anxiety with a New Political Technology." *Journal of Human Rights* 2, no. 2 (2003): 153–71.

Renford, Raymond K. *The Non-Official British in India to 1920*. New Delhi: Oxford University Press, 1987.

Report of the Commissioners for the Investigation of Alleged Cases of Torture in the Madras Presidency Submitted to the Right Honourable Governor-in-Council of Fort Saint-George on the 16th April 1855. 2 vols. Madras: Fort St. George Gazette Press, 1855.

Report of the Indian Railway Inquiry Committee. New Delhi: Railway Board, 1948.

Report of the Railway Corruption Enquiry Committee, 1953–55. New Delhi: Government of India Press, 1955.

Riley, Denise. *"Am I That Name?" Feminism and the Category of "Women" in History*. Minneapolis: University of Minnesota Press, 1988.

Roberts, Emma. *Scenes and Characteristics of Hindos*. 3 vols. London: W. H. Allen, 1835.

Roberts, Randy, and James S. Olson. *A Line in the Sand: The Alamo in Blood and Memory*. New York: Free Press, 2001.

Roddy, Stephen J. *Literati Identity and Its Fictional Representations in Late Imperial China*. Stanford, Calif.: Stanford University Press, 1998.

Roediger, David R. *The Wages of Whiteness: Race and the Making of the American Working Class*. New York: Verso, 1991.

Rosberg, Carl, and John Nottingham. *The Myth of "Mau Mau": Nationalism in Kenya*. New York: Praeger, 1966.

Roseberry, William, Lowell Gudmundson, and Mario Samper K. *Coffee, Society, and Power in Latin America*. Baltimore: Johns Hopkins University Press, 1995.

Ross, Robert. *Cape of Torments: Slavery and Resistance in South Africa*. London: Routledge and Kegan Paul, 1983.

Rubin, Alfred P. *The Law of Piracy*. Newport, R.I.: Naval War College Press, 1988.

Ruskin, John. *Complete Works*. New York: Thomas Y. Crowell, 1905.

Sala-Molins, Louis. *Le Code noir, ou Le calvaire de Canaan*. Paris: Presses universitaires de France, 1987.

Sánchez-Eppler, Karen. *Touching Liberty: Abolition, Feminism, and the Politics of the Body*. Berkeley: University of California Press, 1993.

Sanders, Mark. *Complicities: The Intellectual and Apartheid*. Durham and London: Duke University Press, 2002.

Sanneh, Lamin O. *West African Christianity: The Religious Impact*. Maryknoll, N.Y.: Orbis Books, 1983.

Sanusi, Lamido Sanusi. "Shariah and the Woman Question." *Weekly Trust*, September 18, 2000.

Scarry, Elaine. *The Body in Pain: The Making and Unmaking of the World*. New York: Oxford University Press, 1985.

Scheper-Hughes, Nancy. *Death without Weeping: The Violence of Everyday Life in Brazil*. Berkeley: University of California Press, 1992.

Schwarz, Philip J. *Slave Laws in Virginia*, Athens: University of Georgia Press, 1996.

Scott, David. "Colonial Governmentality." *Social Text* 43 (1995): 191–220.

——. *Refashioning Futures: Criticism after Postcoloniality*. Princeton, N.J.: Princeton University Press, 1999.

Scott, James C. *Weapons of the Weak: Everyday Forms of Peasant Resistance*. New Haven, Conn.: Yale University Press, 1985.

Scott, Joan Wallach. *Gender and the Politics of History*. New York: Columbia University Press, 1988.

——. "Experience." In *Feminists Theorize the Political*, ed. Judith Butler and Joan W. Scott. New York: Routledge, 1992.

——. *Only Paradoxes to Offer: French Feminists and the Rights of Man*. Cambridge, Mass.: Harvard University Press, 1996.

Scully, Pamela. *Liberating the Family? Gender and British Slave Emancipation in the Rural Western Cape, South Africa, 1823–1853*. Portsmouth, N.H.: Heinemann, 1997.

Sedgwick, Eve Kosofsky. *Between Men: English Literature and Male Homosocial Desire*. New York: Columbia University Press, 1985.

Seed, Patricia. *Ceremonies of Possession in Europe's Conquest of the New World, 1492–1640*. New York: Cambridge University Press, 1995.

Senior, Elinor Kyte. *British Regulars in Montreal: An Imperial Garrison, 1832–1854*. Montreal: McGill–Queen's, 1981.

Sharp, Lesley. *The Possessed and the Dispossessed: Spirits, Identity, and Power in a Madagascar Migrant Town*. Berkeley: University of California Press, 1993.

Shell, Robert. *Children of Bondage: A Social History of the Slave Society at the Cape of Good Hope*. Johannesburg: Witwatersrand University Press, 1994.

Sherwood, Sophia Kelly, and Henry Sherwood. *The Life of Mrs. Sherwood, (Chiefly Autobiographical) with Extracts from Mr. Sherwood's Journal during His Imprisonment in France and Residence in India*. London: Darton, 1854.

Singha, Radhika. *A Despotism of Law*. Delhi: Oxford University Press, 1998.

——. "Settle, Mobilize, Verify: Identification Practices in Colonial India." *Studies in History* 16, no. 2 (2000): 151–98.

Smith, Gaddis. "Black Seamen and the Federal Courts, 1789–1860." Pp. 321–38 in *Ships, Seafaring, and Society: Essays in Maritime History*, ed. Timothy J. Runyan. Detroit: Wayne State University Press, 1987.

Solow, Barbara L., and Stanley L. Engerman, eds. *British Capitalism and Caribbean Slavery: The Legacy of Eric Williams*. Cambridge: Cambridge University Press, 1987.

Spear, Jennifer M. "Colonial Intimacies: Legislating Sex in French Louisiana." *William and Mary Quarterly* [3rd Ser.] 60, no. 1 (2003): 75–98

——. " 'They Need Wives': Métissage and the Regulation of Sexuality in French Louisiana, 1699–1730." Pp. 35–59 in *Sex, Love, Race: Crossing Boundaries in North American History*, ed. Martha Hodes. New York: New York University Press, 1999.

Spear, Thomas. "Neo-Traditionalism and the Limits of Invention in British Colonial Africa." *Journal of African History* 44, no. 1 (2003): 3–27.

Spierenburg, Pieter. *The Spectacle of Suffering: Executions and the Evolution of Repression: From a Preindustrial Metropolis to the European Experience*. Cambridge: Cambridge University Press, 1984.

Spiers, Edward. *The Army and Society, 1815–1914*. London: Longman, 1980.

Spindel, Donna. *Crime and Society in North Carolina, 1663–1776*. Baton Rouge: Louisiana State University Press, 1989.

Spivak, Gayatri Chakravorty. *A Critique of Postcolonial Reason: Toward a History of the Vanishing Present*. Cambridge, Mass.: Harvard University Press, 1999.

Stanley, Peter. *White Mutiny: British Military Culture in India*. London: Hurst, 1998.

Steele, Arthur. *The Hindu Castes: Their Law, Religion and Customs* (1826). Repr. ed. Delhi: Mittal Publications, 1986.

Stokes, Eric. *The English Utilitarians and India*. Oxford: Clarendon Press, 1959.

Stoler, Ann Laura. *Carnal Knowledge and Imperial Power: Race and the Intimate in Colonial Rule*. Berkeley: University of California Press, 2001.

——. "Making Empire Respectable: Race and Sexuality in Twentieth-Century Cultures." *American Ethnologist* 16, no. 2 (1989).

——. *Race and the Education of Desire: Foucault's History of Sexuality and the Colonial Order of Things*. Durham and London: Duke University Press, 1995.

———. "Rethinking Colonial Categories: European Communities and the Boundaries of Rule." *Comparative Studies in Society and History* 31 (1989): 134–61.

———. "Tense and Tender Ties: The Politics of Comparison in North American History and (Post)Colonial Studies." *Journal of American History* 88, no. 3 (2001): 829–65.

Stoler, Ann Laura, and Frederick Cooper. "Between Metropole and Colony: Rethinking a Research Agenda." Pp. 1–56 in *Tensions of Empire: Colonial Cultures in a Bourgeois World*, ed. Frederick Cooper and Ann Laura Stoler. Berkeley: University of California Press, 1997:.

Strachan, Hew. *Wellington's Legacy: the Reform of the British Army, 1830–1854*. Manchester: Manchester University Press, 1984.

Suleri, Sara. *The Rhetoric of English India*. Chicago: University of Chicago Press, 1992.

———. "The Subject of Sati: Pain and Death in the Contemporary Discourse on Sati." *Yale Journal of Criticism* 3, no. 2 (1990): 1–23.

Tabili, Laura. "*We Ask for British Justice*": Workers and Racial Difference in Late Imperial Britain. Ithaca, N.Y.: Cornell University Press, 1994.

Tait, P. M. "On the Mortality of Eurasians." *Journal of the Statistical Society of London* 27 (1864): 324–56.

Taussig, Michael T. *Shamanism, Colonialism, and the Wild Man: A Study in Terror and Healing*. Chicago: University of Chicago Press, 1986.

Taylor, Jean Gelman. *The Social World of Batavia: European and Eurasian in Dutch Asia*. Madison: University of Wisconsin Press, 1983.

Te Brake, Wayne. *Shaping History: Ordinary People in European Politics, 1500–1700*. Berkeley: California University Press, 1998.

Temple, Charles. *Native Races and Their Rulers; Sketches and Studies of Official Life and Administrative Problems in Nigeria*. Cape Town: Argus, 1918.

Thiriez, Régine. *Barbarian Lens: Western Photographers of the Qianlong Emperor's European Palaces*. Amsterdam: Overseas Publishers Association, 1998.

Thomas, Lynn M. *Politics of the Womb: Women, Reproduction, and the State in Kenya*. Berkeley: University of California Press, 2003.

Thomson, John. *Illustrations of China and Its People*. London: Sampson Law, Marston, Low and Searle, 1874.

Tilly, Charles. *Popular Contention in Great Britain 1758–1834*. Cambridge, Mass.: Harvard University Press, 1995.

Tremearne, Arthur. *The Ban of the Bori: Demons and Demon-Dancing in West and North Africa*. London: Heath Cranton and Ouseley, 1914.

Tremearne, Arthur. *Hausa Superstitions and Customs: An Introduction to the Folk-Lore and the Folk*. London: J. Bale Sons and Danielsson, 1913.

Trumbach, Randolph. *Sex and the Gender Revolution, Volume 1: Heterosexuality and the Third Gender in Enlightenment London*. Chicago: University of Chicago Press, 1998.

Trustram, Myna. *Women of the Regiment: Marriage and the Victorian Army*. Cambridge: Cambridge University Press, 1984.

Turley, Hans. *Rum, Sodomy, and the Lash: Piracy, Sexuality, and Masculine Identity*. New York: New York University Press, 1999.

Ubah, C. N. *Government and Administration of Kano Emirate, 1900–1930*. Nsukka: University of Nigeria Press, 1985.

Umar, Muhammad Sani. "Changing Islamic Identity in Nigeria from the 1960s to the 1980s: From Sufism to Anti-Sufism." Pp. 154–78 in *Muslim Identity and Social Change in Sub-Saharan Africa*, ed. Louis Brenner. Bloomington: Indiana University Press, 1993.

Usner, Daniel H. *Indians, Settlers, and Slaves in a Frontier Exchange Economy: The Lower Mississippi Valley before 1783*. Chapel Hill: University of North Carolina Press, 1992.

Valle, James E. *Rocks and Shoals: Order and Discipline in the Old Navy, 1800–1861*. Annapolis: Naval Institute Press, 1980.

Van der Chijs, J. A., ed. *Nederlandsch–Indisch Plakaatboek, 1602–1811. Zeventiende Deel*. Batavia: Landsdrukkerij; 'sHage: M Nijhoff, 1900.

Van Deursen, A. T. *Plain Lives in a Golden Age: Popular culture, religion and society in seventeenth century Holland*. Cambridge: Cambridge University Press, 1991.

Van Onselen, Charles. *Chibaro: African Mine Labour in Southern Rhodesia, 1900–1933*. London: Pluto Press, 1976.

Vaughan, Megan. *Curing Their Ills: Colonial Power and African Illness*. London: Polity Press, 1991.

Villiers du Terrage, Marc de. *The Last Years of French Louisiana*. Trans. Hosea Phillips. Lafayette: Center for Louisiana Studies, University of Southwestern Louisiana, 1982.

Visram, Rozina. *Asians in Britain: Four Hundred Years of History*. London: Pluto, 2002.

Walkowitz, Judith R. *City of Dreadful Delight: Narratives of Sexual Danger in Late-Victorian London*. Chicago: University of Chicago Press, 1992.

Walley, Christine. "Searching for 'Voices': Feminism, Anthropology, and the

Global Debates over Female Genital Operations." *Cultural Anthropology* 12, no. 3 (1997): 405–38.

Walvin, James. *Black and White: The Negro and English Society.* London: Penguin, 1973.

Ward, Kerry. "The Bounds of Bondage: Forced Migration from Batavia to the Cape of Good Hope during the Dutch East India Company Era, c. 1652–1795." Ph.D. thesis, University of Michigan, Ann Arbor, 2002.

——. "Imperial Discipline: Criminality at the Cape of Good Hope in the Context of Dutch East India Company Rule, c. 1652–1795." Unpublished paper presented at the Annual Meeting of the African Studies Association, Nashville, Tenn., 16–19 November 2000.

Washbrook, David, "Law, State and Agrarian Society in Colonial India," *Modern Asian Studies* 15, no. 3 (1981): 649–721.

Waters, Anne, "Family Disputes, Family Violence: Reconstructing Women's Experience from Eighteenth-Century Records." Pp. 3–14 in *Images of Women in Maharashtrian Society*, ed. Anne Feldhaus. Albany: State University of New York Press, 1998.

Watson, Alan D. "North Carolina Slave Courts, 1715–1785." *North Carolina Historical Review* 60, no. 1 (1983): 24–36.

——. *Slave Law in the Americas*. Athens: University of Georgia Press, 1989.

Watts, Michael. "The Shock of Modernity: Petroleum, Protest, and Fast Capitalism in an Industrializing Society." In *Reworking Modernity: Capitalisms and Symbolic Discontent*, ed. Allan Pred and Michael Watts. New Brunswick, N.J.: Rutgers University Press, 1992.

Weber, Max. *The Protestant Ethic and the Spirit of Capitalism*. London: Routledge, 1992.

White, Brenda. "Training Medical Policemen: Forensic Medicine and Public Health in Nineteenth-Century Scotland." Pp. 145–66 in *Legal Medicine in History*, ed. Michael Clark and Catherine Crawford. Cambridge: Cambridge University Press, 1994.

White, Owen. *Children of the French Empire: Miscegenation and Colonial Society in French West Africa, 1895–1960*. Oxford: Clarendon, 1999.

Whitehead, Judy. "Bodies Clean and Unclean: Prostitution, Sanitary Legislation, and Respectable Femininity in Colonial North India." *Gender and History* 7 (1995): 41–63.

Whiting-Spilhaus, M. *The First South Africans and the Laws Which Governed Them*. Cape Town: Juta and Company, 1949.

Williams, Eric Eustace. *Capitalism and Slavery*. New York: Russell and Russell, 1961.

Williamson, Captain Thomas. *The East India Vade-Mecum; or, Complete Guide to Gentleman Intended for the Civil, Military or Naval Service*. London: Black, Parry and Kingsbury, 1810.

Wilson, Kathleen. *The Island Race: Englishness, Empire, and Gender in the Eighteenth Century*. London: Routledge, 2003.

Worden, Nigel. *Slavery in Dutch South Africa*. Cambridge: Cambridge University Press, 1984.

Worger, William H. *South Africa's City of Diamonds: Mine Workers and Monopoly Capitalism in Kimberley, 1867–1895*. New Haven, Conn.: Yale University Press, 1987.

Xiong Yuezhi. "Shanghai zujie yu Shanghai shehui shixiang bianqian," Pp. 124–45 in *Shanghai yanjie luncong*, vol. 2. Shanghai: Shanghai shekeyuan chubanshe, 1989.

——. "Zhang yuan: Wan-Qing Shanghai yige gonggong kongjian yanjiu," *Dang'an yu shixue* 6 (1996): 34–35.

Yang, Anand, ed. *Crime and Criminality in British India*. Tucson: University of Arizona Press, 1995.

——. "Disciplining 'Natives': Prisons and Prisoners in the Early Nineteenth Century." *South Asia* 10, no. 2 (1987): 29–45.

Yao Lingxi, comp., *Caifei lu*. Tianjin: Shidai gongsi, 1934.

Youe, Chris. "Mamdani's History." *Canadian Journal of African Studies* 34, no. 2 (2000).

Young, Robert. *Colonial Desire: Hybridity in Theory, Culture and Race*. London: Routledge, 1995.

——. *White Mythologies: Writing History and the West*. London: Routledge, 1990.

Yusuf, Bilkisu. "Hausa-Fulani Women: The State of the Struggle." Pp. 90–108 in *Hausa Women in the Twentieth Century*, ed. Catherine Coles and Beverley Mack. Madison: University of Wisconsin Press, 1991.

Zaret, David. *Origins of Democratic Culture: Printing, Petitions and the Public Sphere in Early-Modern England*. Princeton, N.J.: Princeton University Press, 2000.

Zheng Yongfu and Lu Meiyi. *Jindai Zhongguo funü shenghuo*. Zhengzhou: Henan renmin chubanshe, 1993.

Contributors

LAURA BEAR is a lecturer in the Department of Anthropology at the London School of Economics. She is author of *The Jadu House: Intimate Histories of Anglo India* (Doubleday, 2000). Her monograph *An Economy of Morals: A Genealogy of National, Public and Domestic Sentiments on the Indian Railways* is currently under review.

YVETTE CHRISTIANSE is associate professor of English at Fordham University, where she teaches African American literature, poetics, and postcolonial studies. She is the author of *Castaway* (Duke University Press, 1999), a collection of poetry.

SHANNON LEE DAWDY is assistant professor of anthropology and social sciences at the University of Chicago. She is completing a manuscript titled, *"The Devil's Empire": French New Orleans and the Shadows of Colonialism*.

DOROTHY KO is professor of Chinese history at Barnard College, Columbia University. She has recently completed a monograph on the discourse of footbinding in China (University of California Press, forthcoming). She is the author of *Every Step a Lotus: Shoes for Bound Feet* (University of California Press, 2001) and *Teachers of the Inner Chambers: Women and Culture in Seventeenth-Century China* (Stanford University Press, 1994).

ISAAC LAND is assistant professor of history at Indiana State University. He is currently completing a manuscript titled, *The Sailor's Pleasure: Atlantic Masculinities in an Age of Revolution, 1750–1850*.

SUSAN O'BRIEN is assistant professor of history at the University of Florida. She is currently completing a manuscript on the social history of the *bori* spirit-possession movement in northern Nigeria.

DOUGLAS M. PEERS is associate professor of history and associate dean of the Faculty of Social Sciences at the University of Calgary. He is the author of

Between Mars and Mammon: Colonial Armies and the Garrison State in Early-Nineteenth Century India (Tauris, 1995); the co-editor (with David Finkelstein) of *Negotiating India in the Nineteenth Century Media* (Macmillan, 2000); and the co-editor (with Lynn Zastoupil and Martin Moir) of *J. S. Mill's Encounter with India* (University of Toronto Press, 1999).

STEVEN PIERCE is lecturer in history at the University of Manchester. He is the author of *Farmers and the State in Colonial Kano: Land Tenure and the Legal Imagination* (Indiana University Press, 2005).

ANUPAMA RAO is assistant professor of South Asian history at Barnard College, Columbia University. She is currently completing a manuscript titled, *The Caste Question: Untouchable Struggles for Rights and Recognition*. She is the editor of *Caste and Gender: Debates in Indian Feminism* (Kali for Women Press, 2003).

KERRY WARD is assistant professor of history at Rice University. She is currently completing a manuscript on slavery and forced migration within the Dutch East India Company.

Index

Abu-Ghraib, 2, 29
Adams, John, 43, 95–96, 99
Afghanistan, 2
Africa, 1–3, 8, 10, 19, 26; Pan Africanism, 19
Al'kali court, 187–90
Amok, 54–56
Anderson, Benedict, 8–9
Anglo-Indian, 115, 117–21

Barbarism, 1–2
Beccaria, Cesare, 36
Bechervaise, John, 100, 102
Benjamin, Walter, 7, 16
Bentinck, William, 134–35
Bio-power, 15; bio-political state and, 7, 12, 15–16, 28–29. *See also* Foucault, Michel
Body: colonial, 4, 12, 19, 30, 80; female, 221, 238; as material evidence, 174; native, 21–22; political technologies of the, 20; violation of, 5, 19, 21, 27, 191. *See also* Colonialism; Evidence; Gender; Violence
Boisseau, Wentworth, 103
Bori, 274–76, 278, 284–87, 293
Botha, Graham 52
Bradlow, Edna, 54
British East India Company, 8. *See also* English East India Company
Butler, Judith, 5

Calcutta, 27
Campbell, Alexander, 159
Cannibalism, 96
Cape of Good Hope, 23, 37–57
Carter, Jimmy, 2
Chatterjee, Indrani, 13, 131
Chatterjee, Partha, 17, 135, 137, 142
China: foot binding in; 215–39; masculinity in, 26; nationalism in, 215–25. *See also* Foot binding
Churchill, Winston, 93
Civilization: flogging and, 202; government and, 4, 21; mission and, 1, 128, 193. *See also* Flogging; Government
Code Noir, 24, 61, 63–66, 69, 74, 76, 78–79
Cold War, 2, 6, 18
Colonialism, 19, 26; body and, 4, 12, 19, 30, 80; citizenship and, 26, 204; civil society and, 249, 268; corporeality and, 4–6, 8, 15, 19–22, 30, 205; decolonization and, 18, 19; difference and, 21; discipline and, 2, 4, 12, 16, 17, 21; governmentality and, 4–5, 11, 17–19, 26, 203–5, 247, 268; law and, 155; regimes of, 20; subjects and, 21; violence and, 23. *See also* Body; Corporeality; Discipline; Government; Law; Violence
Congo, Louis, 24, 61–62, 67–71, 80

Cooper, Fred, 17
Cooper, James Fenimore, 100
Corporeality, 19, 21; colonialism and, 4–6, 8, 15, 19–22, 30, 205; discipline and, 92, 94, 110; flogging and, 196–98; punishment and, 2, 21, 26, 38, 56, 62, 65, 68, 80, 256; technology and, 5, 19, 21, 24, 27–28, 201, 203; violence and, 5, 22, 160–61, 167. *See also* Colonialism; Discipline; Flogging; Punishment; Violence
Counterinsurgency, 21
Creole personnel: conspirators, 77; slave owners, 61, 77–79. *See also* Slaves, slavery
Creole regime, 24, 74
Crime, criminals: classification of, 155; criminality and, 37, 196; administration of justice and, 80; native, 25; secularization of, 37. *See also* Justice

Daly, Mary, 238
Dante's *Inferno*, 37
Discipline: colonial, 2, 4, 12, 16–17, 19, 21; corporal, 92, 94, 110; judicial, 25; public discourse and, 264; regimes of, 7, 38, 56, 244, 268; techniques of, 1, 4, 25; *Rukiyya* healing of women and, 27, 277, 286–88, 294. *See also* Colonialism; Corporeality; Justice; *Rukiyya* healing
Docker, Hilton, 105
Donne, John, 43
Dutch East India Company, 8, 23, 38–40, 44–48, 53, 56–57

English East India Company, 8, 93, 104–5, 120, 124–26, 128
Enlightenment, 15, 44; reason, 14; thought, 9

Ethnicity, 21
Eurasian, 118, 121–22, 126, 130–31, 133
Evidence: body and, 174; of torture 13, 165, 170, 173–74. *See also* Body; Torture

Family, 14
Fanon, Franz, 6, 11–12
Flogging, 21, 26, 91–95, 102, 111, 187–88; for adultery, 200; as civilizing project, 202; as corporal punishment, 196–98; criminal jurisprudence and, 196; as deterrent, 195, 197; by European officers, 190; under Islamic law, 189; in native courts, 196; Charles Pemberton on, 98–99, 102; in provincial courts, 195; as spectacle, 190, 196; of women 194, 199, 200–201, 205; scandals and, 191, 192, 201; as traditional punishment, 187, 192, 200. *See also* Civilization; Corporeality
Foot binding, 26; comments on, 215–16, 217, 220–21, 222–25, 224, 227, 228, 229, 232, 235–36; construction of femininity and, 221; discourses of pain and, 222; erotics of, 218, 225; movement against, 26, 216–17, 219–20, 226, 230; nationalism and, 223; as national shame, 216; new technologies of, 232–34. *See also* Gender
Foucault, Michel, 5, 7, 12–13, 15–17, 56–57, 198, 203, 208–9. *See also* Bio-power
France, 63–64, 66–67; colonial rule of, 61; French Revolution and, 14, 94

Gender, 12–13, 15, 21, 27, 39; Chinese subjects and, 218; construction of femininity and, 221; female body and, 221, 230, 238; feminists and,

14; flogging of women and, 194, 199, 200–201, 205; third world women and, 281. *See also* Body; Flogging; Foot binding
Global capitalism, 7, 8
Government: civilized, 4, 21; colonial administrators and, 156–57, 163; disciplinary regimes of, 7, 38, 56, 244, 268; governmental mode of power and, 203; governmental rationality and, 204; governmentality and, 2–5, 10–11, 17–19, 22, 26, 203–5, 247, 268; postcolonial forms of governance and, 18; technologies of governance, 18. *See also* Civilization; Colonialism; Discipline; Postcoloniality
Guantánamo Bay, 2, 29

Haitian Revolution, 78–79
Hausa *malamai*, 274, 276–77, 285–86
Henry Dana Jr., Richard, 101–2
Human rights, 2–3, 5–6, 10, 22, 30, 208; humanitarian public sphere and, 192; humanitarian reform and, 2, 3, 6, 7
Hume, David, 43

Iberian empire, 8
India 3, 13, 18, 115–44, 151–75, 243–69; Indian army and, 25
Indonesia, 13
Iraq, 2, 22, 28, 175
Islam, 27, 28
Islamic exorcism, 285. See also *Rukiyya* healing

Johnson, William, 107–8
Justice, 21; administration of, 25, 163; criminal, 80; judicial discipline and, 25; judicial practices and, 25; judicial torture, 56, 67; medical jurisprudence and, 172; native courts and judicial institutions of, 25, 26, 188–89, 193, 196; provincial courts, 188–89, 193; state, 63. *See also* Crime; Discipline; Law; Native institutions; Torture

Kant, Immanuel, 43
Kenya, 1
Kipling, Rudyard, 115, 119

Labor: bonded, 39; community and, 258–59; corporal punishment and, 256; Royal Commission on, 245–47, 257
Lascar, 104–9
Law, 17, 21, 23; civil, 46; colonialism and, 155; confession and, 162, 169; company, 46; customary, 187, 189; Islamic, 189, 198, 199, 206–7; legal regime and, 7; native courts and, 26, 188–89, 193, 196; parallel court system and, 290–300; penal, 153; precolonial India and, 156; rule of, 160, 168, 208; Sharia, 207–8; violence as, 175. *See also* Colonialism; Justice; Native institutions; Punishment
Lawrence, Henry, 129
Liberalism 3, 8, 10, 14, 20–22, 26
Lopez, Fernao, 28, 303–4
Louisiana, 22–24, 61–69, 78–80
Lugard, Governor General, 188, 200. *See also* Nigeria

Madras Presidency, 161
Malamai, 275–77, 286–88, 289, 290–93, 294; gender hierarchy and, 287
Malays, 53, 54, 55, 90, 100–101; law and legal code of, 53, 55
Mamdani, Mahmood, 18
Masculinity, 24, 26; Chinese, 26; crisis in, 221
Matrimony, 25
Mau Mau rebellion, 1
Merchant Shipping Acts, 106, 109

Mina conspiracy (1790), 78
Minois, George, 36, 42, 45
Modernity, 15, 16, 204; colonial and, 16. *See also* Colonialism
Monstuart, Elphinston, 151, 159
More, Thomas, 42
Munro, Thomas, 163
Murrell, William Miacham, 90–91, 99, 101–2

Napoleon, 303–4
Nasik, 151, 155
Nationalism, 26; identity and, 26; state and, 18
Native institutions: courts, 26, 188–89, 193, 196; judicial institutions, 25; police, 159–60, 164, 168. *See also* Justice; Law
Navigation Act (1660), 105
Negro Seaman Acts, 93, 103, 107–8
Newspapers: *African Telegraph*, 186; *African Times and Orient Review*, 190
Newton-King, Susan, 47
New Orleans, 24, 62, 65–66, 75–76, 78
Nigeria, 26–27, 186–209, 273–97; indirect rule in, 192; J. F. J. Fitzpatrick in, 190, 193

Orientalism: oriental despots and, 161; oriental societies and, 154
Orphans: education of, 136; Lower Orphan Asylum and, 138, 141; of soldiers, 136, 137; school for, in Bengal, 140; treatment of, 137–38; Upper Orphan School and, 39

Pedersen, Susan, 217
Pemberton, Charles, 98–99, 102
Petitions: bureaucracy and, 257, 261–62; on corruption, 253, 256; metaphors of violence and, 252, 261; monarchical language and, 250–51; moral language of violence and, 243; moral critique of, 265; petitioners' bodies and, 255; on physical attacks, 261
Peshwai, 153
Piracy, pirates, 24, 96, 97, 100, 104
Pointe Coupee, 24
Politics of indigeneity, 207
Portuguese in India, 122
Postcoloniality: civil society and, 268; governance and, 18. *See also* Government
Public sphere, 7, 15; colonial public and, 22; humanitarianism and, 192; metropolitan public, 22, 168. *See also* Human rights
Punishment: corporal, 21, 26, 38, 56, 62, 65–66, 80, 256; *Dandaniti*, 153; penal code/law and, 153, 156; penal practices and, 22, 38; penal regime and, 154, 156; punishment of suicide, 41; tradition and, 156. *See also* Corporeality; Law; Suicide

Queen Victoria, 155

Race, 4, 10, 13, 15, 20–21, 24, 39, 64, 70, 80; as barrier to employment, 133; contemporary constructions of, 120; interracial sexual relations and, 25, 117, 120; marriage and, 25; negritude and, 19. *See also* Racial boundaries; Sexuality
Racial boundaries, 13; racial categories and, 10–11, 19, 20, 23–25, 63, 72; racial difference and, 12, 19; racial prejudices and, 116; racial rule and, 80; racial violence and, 28; in Victorian writings, 115; sexual identity and, 118. *See also* Sexuality; Violence
Railways: bureaucracy of, 27, 243–44, 249, 252–55, 258; Faidamand

Panchayats and, 246; Indian Railway Inquiry Committee and, 265; Railway Acts and, 245; Railway Board and, 246–47, 257; workers, 27, 243–69

Rebellion, 20–21

Recognition, 11, 28

Reformers in China: Jin Li, 215–16; Liang Qichao, 220; Zhang Mojun, 222–25

Religion 21; religious orthodoxy and, 27

Report of the Commission for the Investigation of the Alleged Cases of Torture in the Madras Presidency, 161

Roberts, Emma, 115

Royal Navy, 91–93, 95, 97–99

Rukiyya healing, 275–77, 281–84, 286–88, 293; *bori* and, 293; female bodies and, 277, 286–88, 294; Islamic modernity and, 284; Malam Chedi and, 282, 288, 295; negotiation with spirits and, 287–89, 293–95; Sheikh Faruq Chedi and, 285, 287. *See also* Discipline

Ruskin, John, 109

Ryotwari, 162

Sailors, 90–111 *passim*

Saint-Dominigue, 64–65

Savagery, 1–2, 24, 78, 80, 193

Scarry, Elaine, 202–3, 237

Select Committee on East India Affairs, 159

Seneca, 42

Sepoy, 125–26, 128–29, 131, 135

Sepoy mutiny, 155

Sexuality, 21, 22–23 25; contemporary constructions of, 120; homosexuality, 95, 123,124; interracial sexual relations and, 25, 117, 120; racial and sexual identity and, 118; of soldiers, 123; sexual violence and, 166. *See also* Race

Shakespeare's *Hamlet*, 42

Sharp, Lesley, 293

Slaves, slavery, 9–10, 22, 24, 28, 38, 40–41, 48–49, 52, 56–57, 61–62, 64–66, 68, 69–70, 71, 74, 77–78, 79; Atlantic system of, 9; Creole slave owners and, 61, 78, 79; labor and, 9, 37; movements against, 10, 187, 192, 202; slave owners and, 48, 62–66, 71–75, 76–78, 80; slave rebellion and, 49, 62, 65; society and, 39, 48, 66, 78; status and, 22; suicide and, 48, 49–50, 56–57; trade and, 10, 56; white slavery and, 97. *See also* Creole personnel

Sodomy, 24, 93–94, 97, 104, 123

South Asia, 18

South Carolina, 103, 107–8

South East Asia, 8

Spain: administration of, 79; colonialism and, 62, 77; colonial law of, 77

Spirit possession, 27, 274

St. Helena, 304

Sufi malamai, 275–77

Suicide, 22–23, 36–41, 45–46, 53, 56; Christianity on, 43; criminalization of, 37, 55; David Hume, on, 43; in detention, 52; family and, 41; Georges Minois on, 43; Immanuel Kant on, 43; insanity and, 44; John Adams on, 43; John Donne on, 43; Richard Gilpin on, 42; Seneca on, 42; of slaves, 48, 49, 50, 56–57; Thomas More on, 42. *See also* Slaves, slavery

Sunder Rajan, Rajeshwari, 239

Torture, 3, 21–22, 25, 28, 156–58, 161, 164–66, 168, 174, 258, 261; commissions on, 157, 161, 163–64, 167;

Torture (*continued*)
conventions against, 29; flogging and, 21, 26; John Barrow on, 56; judicial examinations and, 56, 67; medical evidence of, 165, 169, 170, 173–74; medical testimony on, 165, 169, 173; Thomas Munro on, 163; police and, 160, 173; regime of, 152; report on prevalence of (1826), 250; revenue and, 167; testimony and dying declaration and, 151, 172. *See also* Evidence; Flogging; Justice

United States, 2, 6, 28
U.S. Navy, 90–91, 92–93, 95–97, 109

Victoria, Queen, 155
Violence, 2–12, 16–19, 20, 26, 168; counter violence and, 169; as civility, 263; colonialism and, 23; corporal, 5, 22, 160–61, 167; intimate, 152; as law, 175; moral language of, 27, 168; racial, 28; sexual, 166; violated body and, 5, 19, 21, 27, 191. *See also* Body; Colonialism; Corporeality; Race; Sexuality

Wahabbi reformers: biomedical treatment and, 283; challenge to Sufism and, 278; critique of Sufism and, 284; influence of, on *Rukiyya*, 277; *Izala*, 278. See also *Rukiyya* healing; Sufi malamai
Widows, 134
Worden, Nigel, 49

Yan Bori, 27, 274, 288, 292

Library of Congress Cataloging-in-Publication Data
Discipline and the other body : correction, corporeality,
colonialism / edited by Steven Pierce and Anupama Rao.
p. cm.
Includes bibliographical references and index.
ISBN 0-8223-3731-2 (cloth : alk. paper)—
ISBN 0-8223-3743-6 (pbk. : alk. paper)
1. Colonies—Administration. 2. Postcolonialism. 3. Violence.
4. Punishment. 5. Human rights. I. Pierce, Steven, 1968–
II. Rao, Anupama.
JV412.D46 2006
325′.3—dc22   2005030740